FOOD CHEMISTRY

some other AVI books

Dairy Science and Technology

BYPRODUCTS FROM MILK, 2ND EDITION *Webb and Whittier*
DAIRY LIPIDS AND LIPID METABOLISM *Brink and Kritchevsky*
FUNDAMENTALS OF DAIRY CHEMISTRY *Webb and Johnson*

Food Science and Technology

ATTACK ON STARVATION *Desrosier*
FISH OILS *Stansby*
FOOD ANALYSIS: THEORY AND PRACTICE *Pomeranz and Meloan*
FOOD OILS AND THEIR USES *Weiss*
FOOD PROCESSING OPERATIONS, VOLS. 1, 2, AND 3 *Joslyn and Heid*
FOOD SCIENCE, 2ND EDITION *Potter*
FREEZING PRESERVATION OF FOODS, 4TH EDITION, VOLS. 1, 2, 3, AND 4
   Tressler, Van Arsdel, and Copley
FRUIT AND VEGETABLE JUICE PROCESSING TECHNOLOGY, 2ND EDITION
   Tressler and Joslyn
FUNDAMENTALS OF FOOD PROCESSING OPERATIONS *Heid and Joslyn*
HANDBOOK OF SUGARS *Junk and Pancoast*
LABORATORY MANUAL FOR FOOD CANNERS AND PROCESSORS, 3RD EDI-
   TION, VOLS. 1 AND 2 *National Canners Association*
MICROBIOLOGY OF FOOD FERMENTATIONS *Pederson*
PHOSPHATES IN FOOD PROCESSING *DeMan and Melnychyn*
PRACTICAL FOOD MICROBIOLOGY AND TECHNOLOGY, 2ND EDITION
   Weiser, Mountney, and Gould
QUALITY CONTROL FOR THE FOOD INDUSTRY, 3RD EDITION, VOLS. 1 AND 2
   Kramer and Twigg
SAFETY OF FOODS *Graham*
SEED PROTEINS: SYMPOSIUM *Inglett*
SOYBEANS: CHEMISTRY AND TECHNOLOGY, VOL. 1 *Smith and Circle*
TECHNOLOGY OF FOOD PRESERVATION, 3RD EDITION *Desrosier*
TECHNOLOGY OF WINE MAKING, 3RD EDITION *Amerine, Berg, and Cruess*
WATER IN FOODS *Matz*

Nutrition and Biochemistry

CARBOHYDRATES AND THEIR ROLES *Schultz, Cain, and Wrolstad*
CHEMISTRY AND PHYSIOLOGY OF FLAVORS *Schultz, Day, and Libbey*
FOOD ENZYMES *Schultz*
LIPIDS AND THEIR OXIDATION *Schultz, Day, and Sinnhuber*
MILESTONES IN HUMAN NUTRITION *Goldblith and Joslyn*
NUTRITIONAL EVALUATION OF FOOD PROCESSING *Harris and Von Loesecke*
PROBIOTICS *Sperti*
PROGRESS IN HUMAN NUTRITION, VOL. 1 *Margen*
PROTEINS AND THEIR REACTIONS *Schultz and Anglemier*
PROTEINS AS HUMAN FOOD *Lawrie*
SELENIUM IN BIOMEDICINE *Muth, Oldfield, and Weswig*
SULFUR IN NUTRITION *Muth and Oldfield*
YEAST TECHNOLOGY *Reed and Peppler*

FOOD CHEMISTRY

By L. W. AURAND, Ph.D.
Professor of Food Science and Biochemistry,
North Carolina State University,
Raleigh, North Carolina

and A. E. WOODS, Ph.D.
Professor of Chemistry,
Middle Tennessee State University,
Murfreesboro, Tennessee

WESTPORT, CONNECTICUT
THE AVI PUBLISHING COMPANY, INC.
1973

© *Copyright 1973 by*
THE AVI PUBLISHING COMPANY, INC.
Westport, Connecticut

Library of Congress Catalog Card Number: 73–85051
ISBN-0-87055-142-6

Printed in the United States of America

Preface

It was the intent of the authors to present various principles of biochemistry together with such other facts that were deemed most important to an effective grasp of the subject of food chemistry. The primary emphasis is on the composition of foods for the maintenance of life together with the aesthetic quality of food. An attempt was made to outline the chemical and physical nature of the various types of nutrients, the biological function of these nutrients in living cells, and their intermediary metabolism. A brief consideration was given to the kinds of chemical compounds that are the constituents of living cells and the precursor materials that can be used for their biosynthesis. In addition to the above materials which include proteins, carbohydrates, lipids and inorganic materials, foods also supply a number of organic compounds which are essential for life. The latter include the vitamins, essential amino acids, and polyunsaturated fatty acids, etc. It is hoped the reader will learn to appreciate the various molecular mechanisms whereby living cells transform the potential energy of foods into a form of energy that can be used to meet the requirements for their various activities and for their growth and reproduction. In addition to discussing the various segments of intermediary metabolism and metabolic regulation, an effort was made at the end of the text to show the close relationship of biochemistry to flavor, color, and acceptability of foods.

The present work is intended primarily for college undergraduates. However, the authors have tried to make the text rigorous enough in its fundamentals to be useful, at least as a review, for those individuals engaged in the various segments of the food industry.

In the preparation of the text, the authors have made use of texts, reviews and other works of reference. At the end of each chapter are bibliographical references to aid the reader who wishes to investigate further the respective areas of subject matter.

The authors wish to acknowledge their indebtedness to their associates who have given them advice and assistance in the preparation of the book. The authors gratefully acknowledge the scientific guidance and collaboration of Doctors M. Bender, M. Wells, R. Horton, S. B. Tove, G. H. Wise and Professor T. Bell. Our thanks also go to Mr. F. Wiles who prepared most of the figures for publication and Mrs. M. Emory and Miss J. Manasco for their able secretarial assistance. Special thanks go to Dr. J. E. Wiser for his support in all aspects of the preparation of this manuscript. We are especially indebted to the reviewers of the various chapters: Doctors P.

K. Bates, F. J. Francis, N. F. Haard, G. E. Inglett, G. MacKinney, S. A. Matz, N. Potter, and G. Reed. Also we are appreciative of the guidance of Dr. D. K. Tressler, and Mr. J. J. O'Neil of Avi Publishing Company.

Finally, the authors wish to express their deep appreciation to their wives, Eleanor and Saundra, for their words of encouragement and their support during the writing of this book.

L. W. AURAND
A. E. WOODS

March 1973

Contents

CHAPTER 1

Water

Introduction

The role of water in food presents itself first in the basic beginnings of carbohydrate synthesis via the photosynthetic process. Hydrations, dehydrations, and hydrolysis reactions as well as the solvent properties of water also occupy important parts in both the breakdown and the reassimilation processes necessary to convert the rudimentary foodstuffs to more specific metabolites in plants and animals. The unique characteristics of water are best understood by examining the water molecule in the ice, liquid water, and the vapor state.

Molecular Water

Natural water consists primarily of $H_2^{16}O$ with minor quantities of $H_2^{18}O$, $H_2^{17}O$, and HDO; thus, almost all experimental data relative to water have been gathered on the naturally occurring isotopes. However, throughout this discussion natural water will be designated H_2O.

The water molecule is a nonlinear, polar covalently bonded compound containing two hydrogen atoms bonded to oxygen by single covalent bonds. The three dimensional structure of water is the result of hybridization of the s and p levels of the second energy level of oxygen. The first energy level of oxygen is completed with two electrons. The $2s$ level of oxygen also is filled with 2 electrons. The 3 dumbbell shaped $2p$ clouds are set at right angles to one another. Each can hold two electrons. Three electrons enter separate $2p_x$, $2p_y$, and $2p_z$ levels, the last electron pairs up to fill the the $2p_x$ level. This leaves $2p_y$ and $2p_z$ levels still incomplete and therefore available for bonding with 2 hydrogen atoms. When sufficient activation energy is available, the $2s$ and $2p$ electrons hybridize and distort into 4 pear-shaped clouds. Two of these electron clouds still have vacancies and are available for bonding with hydrogen. The bond angle of the water molecule is near 104.52Å, while the bond length is 0.9572Å (Fig. 1.1).

The polarity of the individual molecules as well as their orientations are considered to be the origin of the large dielectric constant (78.5 @ 25°C) of liquid water. The dielectric constant measures the relative effect of the medium on the force with which two oppositely charged plates attract each other. Numerically, the dielectric

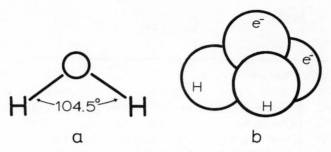

FIG. 1.1 MODELS OF THE WATER MOLECULE

a. Geometry. b. Hybrid electron orbitals.

constant is equal to the ratio of charges of electricity, $D = \dfrac{C_{\text{liquid}}}{C_{\text{air}}}$, where C_{liquid} and C_{air} are the electrical capacity of the condenser filled with liquid and with air.

The permanent electric dipole moment of water is considered to be near 1.84×10^{-18} esu cm. The term dipole moment is a measure of the tendency of a molecule to orient itself in an electrical field. The water molecule has an asymmetric distribution of electrons which results in one side being positively charged with respect to others. Such a molecule has no net charge, but will tend to orient itself in an electrical field with the negative sides toward the positive pole and vice versa.

Water is a good solvent for dissolving salts because it has a very high dielectric constant; i.e., the tendency of water to oppose the electrostatic forces of attraction between charged ions is high. This relationship to the dielectric constant can be expressed mathematically as:

$$F = \frac{e_1\, e_2}{D r^2}$$

where F is the attractive force between two ions of opposite charge, e_1 and e_2 are the charges on the ions, and r is the distance between them.

When salts dissolve in water, the substances dissociate into positive and negative ions, the charges attract mantles of water around themselves to form stable hydrated shells and it is the presence of these shields that separate the charged ions from one another in aqueous solution. The degree of hydration will depend on the charge density of a particular ion and therefore will be greater for small ions than for larger ions carrying the same quantity of charge. Such moderating effects are important in biological systems. For example, the potassium ion has a larger diameter than the sodium ion, but the hydrated potassium ion is smaller than the hydrated sodium ion.

Hydrogen bonding is one of the most outstanding features of the water molecule. Although it is difficult to give a precise definition of a hydrogen bond, certain characteristics are evident. Since the water molecule is a nonlinear polar covalent molecule, it would be expected to have a δ^- end (the oxygen) and a δ^+ end (the hydrogens). The oxygen is more electronegative than hydrogen (3.5 vs 2.1 on the Pauling electronegativity scale). These differences in the electron attracting ability of the two ends of the water molecule lead to a strong interaction between water molecules more commonly referred to as hydrogen bonding.

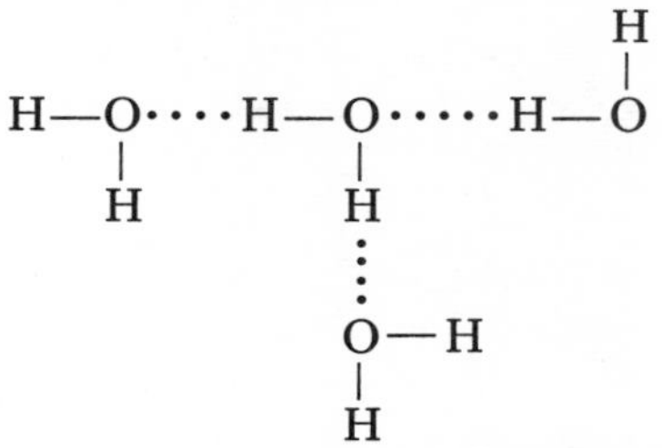

$$
\begin{array}{c}
\hspace{12em} \text{H} \\[-0.3em]
\hspace{12em} | \\[-0.3em]
\text{H—O}\cdots\text{H—O}\cdots\cdots\text{H—O} \\[-0.3em]
\hspace{1em} | \hspace{4em} | \\[-0.3em]
\hspace{1em}\text{H} \hspace{4em}\text{H} \\[-0.3em]
\hspace{6em} \vdots \\[-0.3em]
\hspace{5.5em}\text{O—H} \\[-0.3em]
\hspace{6em} | \\[-0.3em]
\hspace{6em}\text{H}
\end{array}
$$

The above structure shows only the two dimensional associations of water molecules; however, the associations permeate the entire body of the liquid, forming three-dimensional arrangements that can coexist. Liquid water has been regarded as an essentially crystalline system closely resembling ice structure in which groups of molecules are tetrahedrally coordinated with openings sufficiently large to hold free, noncoordinated water molecules, while still retaining the three dimensional structure. The main difference between ice structure and water structure is the higher bulk density of the liquid due to the presence of nonassociated molecules in the structure openings.

Another model of liquid water proposes that clusters of water molecules, which are highly hydrogen-bonded, are mixed with non-hydrogen-bonded molecules which make up approximately two layers between the clusters. The whole system is held together by strong van der Waals-London forces. This model conveniently explains the supercooling of water prior to crystallization.

Still another liquid water structural model considers water molecules to form structures which retain the bond angles and intermolecular distances of ice but have larger cavities. The structures are stable due to hydrogen bonding. Finally, liquid water may possibly be considered to be a flexible extension of the ice structure wherein the flexibility of the hydrogen bonds is greatly increased when compared to ice.

Changes in temperature can cause changes in the ratio of the various three-dimensional structures. This is evidenced by the uncertainty as to whether or not hydrogen bonding exists in water vapor. Infrared spectroscopic studies of water vapor indicate the virtual absence of hydrogen bonds in contrast to ice and liquid water. Approximations of the strength of the hydrogen bond in liquid water can be deduced from estimates of the percent of hydrogen bonds broken at various temperatures. It is estimated that 35 to 47% of the hydrogen bonds remain intact at 37°C (human body temperature). This would indicate that hydrogen bonding plays a major role in water-solute interactions in physiological processes, since water not only could hydrogen bond to itself but to other polar molecules such as carboxylic acids, alcohols, carbohydrates, etc. as shown below.

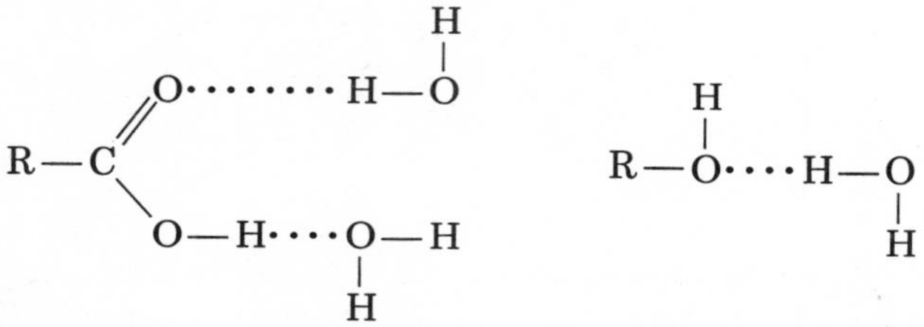

$$
\begin{array}{ccc}
 & H & \\
 & | & \\
O\cdots\cdots H-O & & H \\
\diagup & & | \\
R-C & & R-O\cdots H-O \\
\diagdown & & | \\
O-H\cdots O-H & & H \\
 & | & \\
 & H & \\
\end{array}
$$

Additionally, hydration of cations and anions by water would be expected since the negative end of the water molecule would tend to orient around positive ions while the positive end of the water molecule would be attracted to the negative ions.

Hydrogen bonds are not solely confined to water. Molecules, such as protein containing large numbers of hydrogen, nitrogen, and oxygen atoms are linked by hydrogen bonds.

The simplest view of solution in water can be visualized using sucrose (a polar covalent compound) and sodium chloride (an ionic-bonded compound). When the sugar dissolves, hydrogen bonds form between the molecules of water and the polar groups of the sugar molecule to hold the sugar in solution. The salt dissolves in a somewhat different manner. The electrical attraction of the polar water molecule to the positive sodium ions is greater than the attraction holding the ions together. The positive ends of the water molecule pull on the negative ions of the salt while the negative ends of the water molecule pull on the positive ions of the salt. The crystal structure disintegrates, the bonding forces between the ions are destroyed, and the ions go into solution.

Physical Properties of Water

The properties of water can be divided into two classes; namely, chemical changes and physical changes. In the former, the changes involve the breaking of bonds between the H and O atoms, while in the latter the water molecule remains intact. Life is dependent upon both classes. The hydrolysis of sucrose in the stomach and hydrolysis of triglycerides in the intestine are examples of chemical changes.

Water is such a common substance that its physical properties are taken for granted. However, in comparison with other liquids, water is a unique compound. For example, water has a higher melting point and boiling point when compared with other substances of similar molecular weight (Table 1.1). Water has a much

TABLE 1.1

PHYSICAL PROPERTIES OF WATER AND OTHER
SUBSTANCES OF LOW MOLECULAR WEIGHT

Substance	Formula	Molecular Weight	Melting Point ($^\circ$C)	Boiling Point ($^\circ$C)
Methane	CH_4	16	-184	-161
Ammonia	NH_3	17	-78	-33
Water	H_2O	18	0	$+100$
Hydrogen fluoride	HF	20	-83	$+20$
Hydrogen sulfide	H_2S	34	-86	-61
Hydrogen chloride	HCl	36	-115	-85
Oxygen	O_2	36		-183
Nitrogen	N_2	28		-196

higher melting point and boiling point than might be expected. This difference is due chiefly to the hydrogen bonds between the individual water molecules; as a consequence water is present as a liquid at most environmental temperatures.

Another unusual property of water is its high specific heat, which means that large amounts of heat can be absorbed or released with a relatively small change in temperature. This property is of considerable importance in absorbing or storing heat in tissues.

Similarly, the latent heat of fusion and heat of vaporization are high for water. These properties are a direct result of the strength of hydrogen bonding between water molecules. When the temperature of water is low, the bonds become strong enough to hold the molecules together in ice form. The latent heat of fusion may be expressed as the number of calories (80 cal/gm) required to convert 1 gm of ice at 0°C into liquid at the same temperature.

Let us now consider some of the peculiarities of water. When

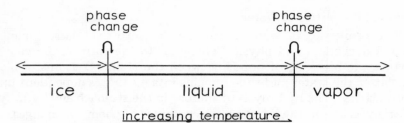

FIG. 1.2. EFFECT OF TEMPERATURE ON PHYSICAL STATES OF WATER

water freezes it expands; conversely, when it melts it contracts. Water is one of the few substances that has this property. At the melting point there is no change in temperature but rather a change from the solid state to the liquid state (Fig. 1.2). The 80 cal/gm is absorbed by the solid phase and is utilized to break the hydrogen bonds that hold the water molecules in the crystalline lattice. The water molecules are more irregularly arranged but a substantial number of hydrogen bonds still remain. As energy is added the number of bonds decrease but the liquid phase remains until 100°C is reached. At this temperature still more bonds must be broken for water to go to the vapor state without a change in temperature. This conversion of liquid to vapor requires a large amount of heat of vaporization. The latent heat of vaporization ($\Delta Hv = 540$ cal/gm, for water is defined as the number of calories required to change 1 gm of liquid to vapor at the boiling point.

Although no one theory completely explains the anomalous properties of water, the expansion on freezing is apparently due to water molecules going from the less ordered liquid state to the more ordered solid crystalline state. A given number of molecules would occupy a larger volume. On melting of ordinary ice (Ice I) the structure collapses to form a structure of greater density (Ice III) and a small number of free water molecules. As the temperature increases from 0° to 4°C, the water becomes denser or the properties of Ice III-like structure increases to a maximum. Above 4°C the number of free water molecules increases and the density decreases in a normal fashion.

Solubility of Biological Compounds

Nonionic polar compounds such as sugars, alcohols, aldehydes, ketones, organic acids, and many other compounds are solublized in water by hydrogen bonding. In biological systems the highly polar water molecule lowers the hydrogen bonding between solutes rendering them quite susceptible to association (solubility) in water. Un-ionized groups on side chains of proteins, lipid-ester groups, RNA and DNA are among a host of polar substances found in biological fluids, tissues, and membranes. Water being a relatively small molecule can fit into the recesses, grooves, or crevices in the protein molecules. Globular proteins and DNA chains appear not to allow water into their interior structure since the interior of both the helix of DNA and protein is apolar. The secondary and tertiary structure of globular protein favor an apolar environment, and intramolecular hydrogen bonding predominates over the interaction of these molecules with water. However, both globular proteins and DNA are highly hydrated on their surfaces.

In unfolded globular proteins, or in proteins such as collagen, there is a strong interaction of the protein molecules with water.

It has been suggested that the Watson-Crick double helix might be incorporated into the three-dimensional structure of water with the DNA molecule filling some of the cavities in the water structure. Water also will fit into the lipid-protein interface of biological membranes and serves to help mediate the transport of nutrients and metabolites into and out of an aqueous environment.

The interrelationship between the properties of macromolecules and water structure has a profound effect on the physical properties of the macromolecule. If the hydrogen-bonding capacity of the macromolecule to water is high the macromolecules will show a high solubility; e.g., DNA has highly polar phosphodiester groups extending outward from the axis of the helix. Additionally, DNA solutions are highly viscous. If there is sufficient water-solute interaction by hydrogen bonding, causing immobilization of the water molecules, gelation can occur. Conversely, if the solute has a high degree of hydrogen bonding, either between molecules or within molecules, then its association with water would be very low and the macromolecule would likely be insoluble.

Chemical Reactions Mediated by Water

Water is an active participant in reactions of biochemical importance. Some of the chemical reactions mediated by water are listed in Table 1.2 along with the approximate values of $\Delta G^{\circ\prime}$ (pH 7 and 25°C).

The energy of biological reactions which do not involve oxidation-reduction is dependent upon the magnitude of the equilibrium constant. Since water often is a reactant or a product in these reactions, its concentration and its role in ionizing reactants and products must

TABLE 1.2

SOME REACTIONS MEDIATED BY WATER

Reaction	$-\Delta G^{\circ\prime}$ $(pH\ 7)$[1] Kcal/Mole
H_2O + dipeptide $\longrightarrow$ amino acids	3
H_2O + triglyceride $\longrightarrow$ fatty acids + glycerol	3
H_2O + acetyl-SCoA $\longrightarrow$ acetic acid + CoASH	7
H_2O + glucose-6-PO_4 $\longrightarrow$ glucose + phosphoric acid	3
H_2O + acetyl phosphate $\longrightarrow$ acetic acid + phosphoric acid	10
H_2O + ATP $\longrightarrow$ ADP + phosphoric acid	7
H_2O + sucrose $\longrightarrow$ glucose + fructose	7

[1] $\Delta G^{\circ\prime}$ = standard free energy where all constituents are $1M$ except hydrogen ion. Water is considered to have an activity of 1.0.

be taken into consideration. From the equilibrium expression for the hydrolysis of ethyl acetate

$$K_{eq} = \frac{[CH_3COOH]\ [CH_3CH_2OH]}{[Ethylacetate]\ [HOH]}$$

it is obvious that any change in the concentration of reactants of products would change the numerical value of K_{eq}. This in turn would be reflected in a change in the chemical energy of the system ($\Delta G^{\circ\prime}$).

Water is the only medium of biological significance in which dissociation can occur. Acids and bases interact with the water molecule or its ion (H_3O^+) where water acts either as a H^+ donor or acceptor.

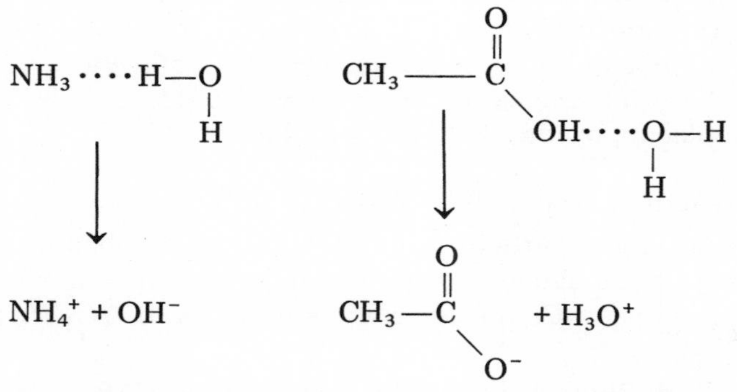

When a hydrogen bond forms between water and the carboxyl hydrogen of an acid such as acetic acid, there is competition between the oxygen of water and the hydroxyl oxygen of the acid for this hydrogen. Whether the hydrogen goes with the water as

H_3O^+ or remains attached to the acetate is determined in part by the stability of the acetate ion. It is known that acetate is stabilized by resonance which allows 1.3% of the acetic acid molecules to undergo dissociation to give

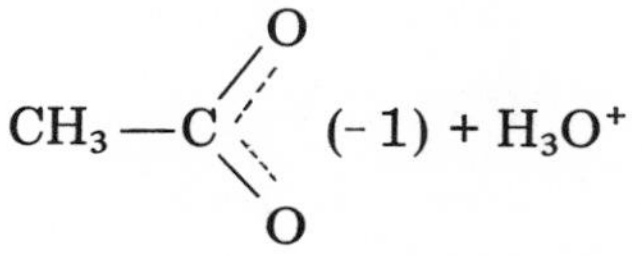

$$CH_3—C\underset{O}{\overset{O}{<}}\ (-1) + H_3O^+$$

Water as a Nutrient

Water is essential for the normal functioning of the cell. It enters the body as a greater part of the liquids imbibed and as a part of the foods ingested. Some water is formed within the body as the end-product of metabolic processes. The daily water balance for an average individual is shown in Table 1.3. Water balance may be

TABLE 1.3

WATER BALANCE

Water	Volume (ml)
Intake	
Liquid foods (soups, coffee, milk, H_2O)	1100
Solid foods (moisture)	500–900
Water of metabolism	400
Output	
Vaporization: (400 ml expired as moist air-lung),	
(600 ml skin-sweat)	920–1000
Feces	80–100
Urine	1000–1300

defined as the equilibrium between water intake and water output. With respect to water intake, it is observed that solid foods contribute a significant portion of daily water requirements. Most foods rarely contain less than 70% water and frequently more. For example, corn is 70% water, apples contain approximately 80% water, and tomatoes 95% water. With respect to the water of metabolism, the amount produced from the metabolism of the various food nutrients is as follows: 0.6 gm water per gram of carbohydrate, 1.1 gm of water per gram of lipid, and 0.4 gm water per gram of protein. With respect to water output, it is observed that the output through the lungs and skin is about the same as that voided in the urine.

Excessive loss or gain in water is reflected in alterations in the distribution of the water in the body compartments. In these cases, nutritional therapy is mandatory.

BIBLIOGRAPHY

CLAPP, L. B. 1967. The Chemistry of the OH Group. Prentice-Hall, Englewood Cliffs, N.J.

EISENBERG, D., and KAUZMAN, W. 1969. The Structure and Properties of Water. Oxford University Press, Fair Lawn, N.J.

KAVANAU, J. L. 1964. Water and Solute-Water Interactions. Holden-Day, San Francisco.

MAHLER, H. R., and CORDES, E. H. 1971. Biological Chemistry, 2nd Edition, Harper and Row Publishers, New York.

MATZ, S. A. 1965. Water in Foods. Avi Publishing Co., Westport, Conn.

PAULING, L. 1967. The Chemical Bond, Cornell University Press, Ithaca, N.Y.

SOBER, H. A. (Editor). 1968. Handbook of Biochemistry. Chemical Rubber Co., Cleveland, Ohio.

SUTCLIFFE, J. 1968. Plants and water. The Institute of Biology's Stuides in Biology, No. 14. Edward Arnold, London.

U.S. DEPT. OF AGR. 1955. Water, Yearbook of Agriculture. U.S. Govt. Printing Office, Washington, D.C.

WHIPPLE, H. E. (Editor). 1965. Forms of water in biological systems. Ann. N.Y. Acad. Sci. *125*, 249–772.

CHAPTER 2

Solutions

Biological materials contain from 70 to 90% water. As a consequence, we are dealing almost exclusively with aqueous solutions or with substances in which the aqueous phase determines the physical properties of the material. A knowledge of some of the properties of solutions should be of value to understand what is happening in the material. For the sake of brevity and simplicity in presentation, the ensuing discussion will be in terms of aqueous solutions; however, the same facts and principles are applicable to biological materials in general.

Methods of Expressing Concentrations

A discussion of the methods of denoting the concentration of solutions is as follows:

(1) The molar system of concentration gives the gram-molecular weights of solute in a liter of solution. It has been established that a formula weight of any substance contains 6.02×10^{23} (Avogadro's number) particles. Thus, the molecular weight in grams of a substance per liter of solution represents a one molar concentration, and at the same time 6.02×10^{23} particles (assuming no dissociation has taken place). Molar concentrations are indicated as $1M$, $0.1M$, $0.01M$, etc., according to the number of gram-molecular weights present per liter solution.

The terms millimole and milliequivalent are frequently used. The term millimolar denotes one-thousandth molar; $0.001M$. Consequently, the expressions $1.0M$, $0.1M$, and $0.01M$ are equivalent to 1000, 100, and 10 millimoles, respectively. A milliequivalent is equivalent to a millimole if the valence of the ion is 1, but for ions of other valency the milliequivalent is determined by dividing the molecular weight of the compound by the factor 1,000n where n is the valency of the ion.

(2) Molal solutions contain a gram-molecular weight of solute dissolved in 1000 gm solvent. The volume is not a liter and varies with the volume of the formula weight of dissolved solute. Molal solutions provide a definite ratio of solute to solvent molecules. The symbol m is used to denote molalities.

(3) Percent by weight represents the grams of dissolved material (solute) present in 100 gm of solution.

(4) Percent by volume indicates the grams of dissolved material in 100 ml of solution.

(5) The normal system of concentration is usually applied to acids, bases, and oxidizing solutions. A normal solution (N) contains one gram equivalent weight of a material dissolved in one liter of solution. A normal solution (N) of an acid contains 1.008 gm of available hydrogen ion per liter of solution. A normal solution (N) of a base contains in one liter 17.008 gm available hydroxyl ion. Bronsted defined bases as proton acceptors. This definition is appropriate for nonhydroxyl containing bases. A normal solution of an oxidizing agent has an oxidizing value per liter of 8.000 gm of oxygen, or will accept 6.02×10^{23} electrons per liter. A normal solution of a reducing agent has a reducing value per liter of 1.008 gm of hydrogen, or will donate 6.02×10^{23} electrons per liter.

Characteristics of Solutions

A solution may be defined as a physically and chemically homogenous mixture of two or more substances in which the solute is in an ionic or molecular state of subdivision. This is in contrast to the colloidal state which will be discussed in Chap. 3. A typical example of some commonly encountered solutions are:

Solution	Solute	Solvent
gas in liquid	air	water
liquid in liquid	acetic acid	water
solid in liquid	sugar	water
gas in solid	bubbles	mineral
solid in solid	gold	glass

A solution is made up of two components, the solvent and the solute. The solvent may be defined as a substance (usually a liquid) capable of dissolving another substance. The solvent is usually present in the larger quantity, while the solute is present in smaller amounts. In certain cases, however, the quantities may be reversed without change in terminology. For example, we may have a 5% or a 50% solution of sugar in water, and in both cases the water is considered the solvent and the sugar, the solute.

The solubility of a substance depends upon the tendency of the molecules to leave their associates and enter the solution. This tendency of the solute to enter the solvent is termed solution pressure. As the molecules (or ions) go into solution, they diffuse in all directions, and some of them return to the surface of the solute; as the number of molecules in solution increase, the number returning to the solute will increase. This process is called diffusion pressure, and is proportional to the concentration of the dissolved molecules. All substances dissolve more or less in solvents. If the amount of solute dissolved is very high relative to the amount of the solute (high solution pressure) the substance is said to be soluble. Conversely, when the solution pressure is low, the solubility will be low. The solubility of substances increases with an increase in temperature, although the reverse may occur in a few instances, as a result of increasing the kinetic energy of the molecules. Solubility curves provide information regarding the relative solubility of different solutes, as well as the effect of temperature on their solubility. A steep curve indicates that change in temperature has a marked effect (e.g., KNO_3); a flat curve indicates the opposite (e.g., NaCl). A sudden break in a curve indicates a change in state of matter, such as loss of water of hydration (e.g., $Na_2SO_4 \cdot 10\ H_2O$).

When a state of equilibrium exists between the rate of solution and the rate of return to the solid condition, the solution is said to be saturated. Two things are required in order that such an equilibrium may exist: first, the solute concentration in the solution must have reached the saturation value, and second, solid solute must be present with which an exchange of dissolved solute may take place. In some cases a solution (e.g., sodium acetate) may be prepared which contains more than the saturation amount of dissolved solute. A solution of this type may be prepared by the addition of a saturating amount of solute to a solvent held at an elevated temperature. The solution is then cooled slowly and carefully (to prevent precipitation) creating a condition in which the dissolved solute is not in equilibrium with the undissolved solute. Such a solution is said to be supersaturated. It is an unstable condition and, if a particle of the given solute is dropped into this solution, it will instantly start the exchange of molecules. This process is called seeding or inoculation. The same effect can generally be accomplished by sudden cooling or vigorous shaking.

In the case of slightly soluble substances, such as $CaSO_4$ and $BaSO_4$, the size of the particles is important. It is a well-known fact that if a solution is in contact with both fine and coarse particles the fine particles will go into solution, making the solution saturated with respect to the larger particles. Material will then be deposited on the larger particles and they will grow larger. The net result will be a disappearance of the smallest particles and an increase in the size of the largest ones. This process is called digesting a precipitate.

Physical Properties of Solutions

Colligative Properties.—In the discussion below, it is proposed to consider the so-called colligative properties of a liquid solution; that is, those properties which depend on the number and not the nature of the molecules present.

Osmotic Pressure.—If a solution containing 1 gm mol wt (mole) of a substance dissolved in 1000 gm of water is separated from water by a membrane permeable to the solvent as shown in Fig. 2.1, the water will pass through the membrane into the solution, but the solute does not pass through the semipermeable membrane into the solvent; pressure (P) is evident by movement of the solution up the capillary. This would continue until such a pressure (22.4 atm) had been reached, then further diffusion of water into the solution would cease. To prevent the change in concentration of the original solution, one may apply pressure (π) which will just suffice to prevent the entrance of water (solvent) through the membrane into the solution. The hydrostatic pressure which brings the solution into equilibrium with the pure solvent is a measure of the osmotic pressure of the solution. The passage of water through a semi-

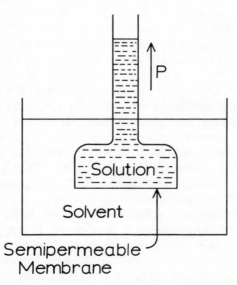

FIG. 2.1. DIAGRAM OF A SIMPLE OSMOTIC PRESSURE APPARATUS

permeable membrane is called osmosis. It will be recalled that a common method for determining the molecular weight of a substance, which can be converted into a gas, is to measure the volume occupied by a given weight of the substance when converted into a gas. From this one can calculate the weight of a substance necessary to give a volume of gas 22.4 liters at 0°C and 760 mm pressure, and the result is the molecular weight of the substance calculated according to the equation $PV = nRT$. In a similar manner, one may use an osmotic pressure method for determining the molecular weight of a substance which is soluble in water using an analogous equation $\pi = mRT$, where π = osmotic pressure, m = molality, R = gas constant, and T = °K. For example, if 10 gm of a substance, which does not ionize, is dissolved in 1000 gm of water at 0°C, it will give an osmotic pressure of 1 atm; 224 gm in 1000 gm of water will give an osmotic pressure of 22.4 atm. Hence, 224 would be the molecular weight of the substance.

A corollary to the above discussion is that osmotic pressure is independent of the "kind" of molecules, but is dependent upon the number of molecules. Solutions that contain the same numbers of molecules in equal volumes and at like temperatures exert the same osmotic pressure.

Vapor Pressure.—A volatile liquid exerts its own characteristic vapor pressure. The latter pressure increases with temperature until the vapor pressure of the solution equals the pressure of the atmosphere above it, at which time the solution will boil. The temperature at which this phenomenon will occur depends first on the liquid, and second on the external pressure. If we lower the pressure of the atmosphere above the solution, as by applying a vacuum, the boiling point occurs at a lower temperature. For example, water would boil at 25°C if the pressure of the atmosphere were 23.8 mm. Conversely, if we raise the pressure of the atmosphere, as in pressure cooking, the boiling point is raised to a higher temperature. What we understand, however, as the true boiling point of a liquid is the temperature at which its vapor pressure equals the standard atmosphere (760 mm). According to this, the true boiling point of water is 100°C.

In foods, one is interested in the effect of nonvolatile substances in water. The vapor pressure of such an aqueous solution is due solely to the water. However, it is reduced to a fraction of its vapor pressure in pure form as given in the equation below:

$$\text{Mole fraction} = \frac{\text{moles (solvent)}}{\text{moles (solute)} + \text{moles (solvent)}}$$

Thus, nonvolatile solutes depress the vapor pressure of a solution.

Boiling Point Elevation.—It is a fact of common experience that the boiling point of a solution is invariably higher than that of the pure solvent, provided only that the solute is not volatile.

The elevation in boiling point of solutions is best accounted for by an application of the kinetic theory. In a solution, the solute molecules, by their attraction, hold back the solvent molecules and thereby interfere with the passing of solute molecules into the vapor state. Therefore, a temperature higher than is required for the pure solvent will be required to bring the vapor pressure of the solution up to the atmospheric pressure. The increase in the boiling point is dependent upon the number of molecules in a given volume of solvent. Thus, the presence of 1 mole of solute in 1000 gm of water raises the boiling point 0.52°C. This value is commonly referred to as the molal boiling point elevation constant (k_b). The specific value for k_b is characteristic for a particular solvent. The general equation for the effect of solutes on the boiling point of the solvent is given as:

$$\Delta t_b = k_b \times m$$

$$\Delta t_b = k_b \times \frac{\text{wt solute}}{\text{mol wt (solute)}} \times \frac{1000}{\text{wt solvent}}$$

Δt_b = change in boiling point

k_b = molal boiling point elevation constant

wt solute = grams of solute

wt solvent = grams of solvent

mol wt = molecular weight of solute

m = molality

Freezing Point Depression.—The principle involved in depression of freezing point is similar to that described for boiling point elevation. At the freezing point of a solvent, there is an equilibrium between the tendency of the molecules to reduce the solid crystals to a liquid and the force of cohesion tending to bring the molecules into crystalline form. In solutions, the attraction of the solute molecules for those of the solvent has an effect on the equilibrium point and as a consequence the kinetic energy of the molecules must be reduced to a point lower than with the pure solvent.

If one were to freeze an aqueous solution, it would be observed that only ice forms at first, and as more and more ice accumulates, the remaining solution becomes more concentrated with an accompanying drop in the freezing point. Eventually a point is reached where a mixture of solute and ice separates out. The point at which this phenomenon occurs is referred to as the cryohydric point, and it reflects the formation of a new state (solid) of the solution. If one were to continue the freezing, the temperature would remain unchanged until the entire solution was solidified. This principle is used in food technology to concentrate solutions such as vinegar.

The freezing point of a solution is governed also by equilibrium conditions with the vapor phase. These principles are utilized in freeze-drying processes.

Since freezing point depression is due to the attraction of solute molecules for the solvent, the amount of this lowering will be proportional to the number of solute molecules present. Consequently, freezing point depression, boiling point rise, and osmotic pressure are related. The lowering of the freezing point by the addition of 1 mole of solute in 1000 gm of solvent will be the same regardless of the substance, provided the water does not act upon the solute to change its nature or form (ionization, etc.). The lowering of the freezing point by 1 mole of solute in 1000 gm of solvent is called the freezing point depression constant (k_f). The mathematical expression is identical for freezing point depression and boiling point rise.

$$\Delta t_f = k_f \times \frac{\text{wt solute}}{\text{mol wt (solute)}} \times \frac{1000}{\text{wt solvent}}$$

Thus, the depression of the freezing point may be used to determine the molecular weights of substances in solution. For example, if one dissolves 50 gm of a substance in 1000 gm of water ($k_f = -1.86°C$) and the freezing point is depressed 0.93°C, it is readily seen that 100 gm in the same volume would be required to depress the freezing point 1.86°C; hence 100 would be the molecular weight of the substance in question.

Surface Tension.—A needle may be made to float if it is carefully placed on the surface of the water, but the slightest disturbance of the surface causes the needle to sink. Thus the surface of the water behaves like an elastic film surrounding the body of the water, and it has different physical properties than the body of water. This phenomenon is called surface tension, and it may be defined as the resistance of a surface film to rupture. In the interior portion of a liquid a molecule is attracted equally in all directions by surrounding molecules. It is free to move in any direction. However, if a water molecule were to enter the surface of a body of liquid, the downward and lateral forces of attraction are greater than the force of attraction between the water molecules in the liquid and vapor state. The downward and lateral pull causes the surface of the film to contract. The force with which the surface molecules are held together is called surface tension.

The surface tension of a liquid (γ) can be quantitatively defined as the force per centimeter on the surface which opposes the expansion of the surface area. This can be illustrated by the simple diagram shown below (Fig. 2.2) in which a moveable bar is pulled with

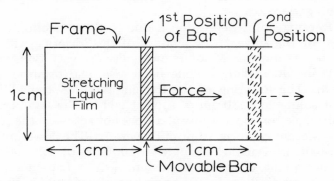

FIG. 2.2. SURFACE TENSION APPARATUS

a force (dynes) to cause the liquid film to stretch like a protein film on a wire frame. When the moveable bar is moved with a force (f) to expand the liquid film, the surface tension then can be calculated by the equation

$$\gamma = \frac{\text{force (dynes)}}{2 \text{ cm}}$$

The 2 is included because there are 2 liquid surfaces, one at the front and one at the back. The equation dictates that the unit of surface tension (γ) be dynes/cm.

Another technique of measuring surface tension is the capillary rise method. In this method the rise occurs if the liquid wets the interior of the capillary tube. This rise continues until the upward force due to surface tension is counterbalanced by the force of gravity pulling it downward. As shown in Fig. 2.3, the liquid capillary rises height (h) to the lower level of the meniscus plus $\frac{1}{3}$ the radius of the capillary (in very small capillaries h is essentially the lower level of the meniscus). The downward force on the capillary is $\pi r^2 hdg$, where r is the radius of the capillary, g is the acceleration of gravity, and d is the density of the liquid. The upward force is $2\pi r\gamma \cos \theta$. When the capillary stops rising, the forces are equal, and

$$\pi r^2 hdg = 2\pi r\gamma \cos \theta$$

rearranging, $\gamma = \dfrac{h \cdot d \cdot g \cdot r}{2 \cos \theta}$

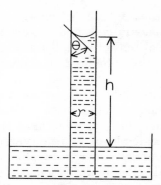

FIG. 2.3. SURFACE TENSION MEASURED BY CAPILLARY
RISE

For aqueous media and other liquids, the angle of contact of the liquid to the glass is very small, thus θ approaches 0 and $\cos \theta$ = one. The expression then reduces to

$$\gamma = \tfrac{1}{2} h \cdot d \cdot g \cdot r$$

expressed in proper units, $\gamma = \frac{1}{2}$ (cm) (g/cm^3) (cm/sec^2) (cm)

$$\gamma = \frac{1}{2} \frac{g \; cm/sec^2 \times cm^2}{cm^3}$$

$$\gamma = \frac{1}{2} \frac{dyne}{cm}$$

The Du Noüy instrument for measuring surface tension utilizes a platinum wire loop which is dipped into the liquid and the force, in dynes, required to separate the loop from the surface is measured. The instrument is calibrated to give a direct reading of surface tension. Typical examples of surface tension values are given in Table 2.1.

Surface tension, or interfacial tension, exists not only at the boundary between a liquid-air, but also between a liquid-liquid or liquid-solid interface. Thus, it will be evident that the surfaces which exist in biological materials (e.g., protoplasm) are enormous

TABLE 2.1

SURFACE TENSION OF LIQUIDS (DYNES/CM)

Temperatures, °C	H$_2$O	Ethanol	Acetic Acid	Mercury
0	76.64	24.0	29.5	480.3
25	72.00	21.8	27.1	—

and interfacial tension is a form of energy. Many of the energy changes which take place in cells and tissues may be accounted for by changes in interfacial tension; i.e., if interfacial tension is reduced in a system, the energy liberated becomes available for other purposes.

Substances in solution alter the surface tension of the solvent. In general, polar substances will increase surface tension. Substances of biological importance, e.g., proteins and lecithins, lower surface tension. There is a principle of thermodynamics which states that the amount of free energy (energy capable of doing work) in a system will decrease if possible. Since surface tension is such a form of energy, it is not surprising to learn that substances which lower the surface tension of water will concentrate at the surface so as to lower the surface energy as much as possible. This concentration at a surface is called positive adsorption. Conversely, substances which increase surface tension do not orient at the surface film (interface). This is referred to as negative adsorption.

Chemical Properties of Solutions

Acids and Bases.—Acidity and alkalinity are often spoken of as the reaction of a solution. They are extremely important factors in the proper functioning of living organisms. For example, biological fluids are maintained fairly constant at a definite acid or alkaline value; pronounced changes usually result in an unhealthy condition. The color of foodstuffs, texture, and preservation of foods are sensitive to changes in hydrogen ion concentration. Thus, it is necessary to know what is meant by hydrogen ion concentration, and to do this one should be familiar with some of the theories that are applicable.

An explanation of acids and bases presupposes that the base is an OH^- donor. However, in biological systems the bases encountered are rarely OH^- donors. Thus the classical theory of acids and bases must be modified. Bronsted proposed that reactions involving the transfer of H^+ be called acid-base reactions; the proton being the acid and the proton acceptor being the base. An example of a Bronsted acid-base is

$$NH_4^+ \longrightarrow NH_3 + H^+$$

Acid   Conjugate base
(Proton donor)

$$HCO_3^- \longrightarrow H^+ + CO_3^{2-}$$

Acid   Conjugate base

Dissociation of an acid in aqueous solution involves not only the proton donor but water molecules as well.

$$HOH + HCl \longrightarrow H_3O^+ + Cl^-$$

The H^+ reacts with the water molecules to produce a hydronium ion (H_3O^+), but in this discussion only the H^+ will be used.

When an acid is dissolved in water, some of the molecules or ions dissociate into H^+ ions and its conjugate base. The concentration of H^+ depends upon the degree of this dissociation. For example, hydrochloric acid dissociates or ionizes in the following manner:

$$HCl \rightleftharpoons H^+ + Cl^-$$

In this case, practically all of the hydrogen of the hydrochloric acid exists as H^+ at any given instant. In contrast, for acetic acid:

$$CH_3COOH \rightleftharpoons CH_3COO^- + H^+$$

only about 1.3% of the available hydrogen ions of a $0.1M$ solution exists as H^+ in solution. The titratable acidity of the two acids are similar, but when the acids are judged by properties dependent upon hydrogen ion concentration, the HCl is much stronger than the CH_3COOH.

When dissolved in water, the molecules of strong acids such as HCl or H_2SO_4 undergo almost complete dissociation to H^+ and their conjugate base, e.g., Cl^- or HSO_4^-. Hydroxide-containing bases undergo similar dissociations. However, biological systems contain weaker acids and bases which do not undergo complete dissociation in an aqueous solution. In these weaker acids and bases, the proton donor exists in equilibrium with its conjugate base, the proton acceptor.

In order to develop the concept of equilibrium as related to hydrogen ion concentration, one must first consider the Law of Mass Action. The law states that the rate of a chemical reaction is proportional to the concentration of the reacting substances. The law may be explained in the following terms: assume that two compounds, A and B, in solution, react to form C and D. Assume also that C and D when formed are able to react to form A and B. In time both combinations will be reacting at the same rate and are then in equilibrium. This reaction is illustrated by means of an equilibrium equation:

$$A + B \rightleftharpoons C + D$$

At equilibrium the rates of reaction are equal, but the concentration of the reactants are not necessarily the same. The velocity of the reaction to the right is proportional to the product of $[A] \times [B] \times k$, where k is a constant whose value depends on factors such as temperature. In like manner, the velocity of reaction to the left is proportional to $[C] \times [D] \times k$. When equilibrium is achieved the rates must be equal,

$$V_1 = V_2 \text{ or, } [A] \times [B] \times k = [C] \times [D] \times k_1$$

The mathematical relationship then is

$$\frac{[C] \times [D]}{[A] \times [B]} = \frac{k}{k_1}$$

A constant divided by a constant is equal to a constant, thus we have

$$\frac{[C] \times [D]}{[A] \times [B]} = K \text{ equilibrium } (K_{eq})$$

K is the equilibrium constant. The value of K depends on the reacting substances, i.e., for any one reaction the ratio of the reactants is unchangeable provided the temperature is held constant. Consequently, if K_{eq} is large the product of the concentrations of C and D at equilibrium is high relative to the product of the concentration of A and B, and the direction of the reaction is to the right. If K_{eq} is small the reverse relationship exists.

Water is a weak electrolyte which dissociates into H^+ and OH^- ions. The equation for the dissociation of water is

$$HOH \rightleftharpoons H^+ + OH^-$$

If one applies the Law of Mass Action to the above reaction, one obtains the following equation:[1]

$$\frac{[H^+] \times [OH^-]}{[H_2O]} = \frac{k}{k_1} = K_{\text{dissociation}}$$

Water ionizes only slightly, thus concentration of undissociated water molecules is substantially unaltered, and for all practical purposes may be considered a constant. We may rewrite the above equation as follows:

$$[H^+] \times [OH^-] = K_{\text{dis}} \times [H_2O] = K_w$$

---

[1] When we express concentrations of the reacting substances in moles per liter, we are keeping all substances on a comparable basis in terms of molecules. For this reason concentration, as applied to equilibrium, is always expressed in terms of molar concentration and the conventional method of indicating this fact is to enclose the formula in brackets, $[H^+]$.

Since [H$_2$O] is a constant, we may combine it with K_{dis} to give a new constant, K_w, which is the ionization constant of water. Its value varies widely with temperature but is constant at a given temperature. This is shown in Table 2.2.

TABLE 2.2

VALUES OF K_w AT DIFFERENT TEMPERATURES

Temperature, °C	K_w	$\dfrac{\sqrt{K_w}}{[H^+] \text{ or } [OH^-]}$
0	0.05×10^{-14}	0.22×10^{-7}
2	0.16×10^{-14}	0.40×10^{-7}
16	0.63×10^{-14}	0.79×10^{-7}
20	0.86×10^{-14}	0.93×10^{-7}
22	1.01×10^{-14}	1.00×10^{-7}
25	1.27×10^{-14}	1.13×10^{-7}
37	3.13×10^{-14}	1.77×10^{-7}
40	3.80×10^{-14}	1.95×10^{-7}
75	16.90×10^{-14}	4.11×10^{-7}
100	48.00×10^{-14}	6.93×10^{-7}

The value of K_w at 22°C is approximately 1×10^{-14}. This temperature is commonly used as a basis for our understanding of the true neutral point. Values for [H$^+$] and [OH$^-$] can be derived from the K_w as follows:

$$[H^+] \times [OH^-] = K_w$$

at the neutral point

$$[H^+] = [OH^-] \text{ or } [H^+]^2 = 10^{-14} \text{ or } [H^+] = \sqrt{10^{-14}} = 1 \times 10^{-7}.$$

Thus, we say that [H$^+$] of 1×10^{-7} is the true neutral point, and by common consent the temperature is ignored.

If one adds a dilute acid to water, the hydrogen ion concentration, [H$^+$], will increase. Assume the solution becomes 0.01N after the addition of the acid, the [H$^+$] of the solution will be 0.01 or 10^{-2} moles per liter. The [OH$^-$] can then be determined as follows:

$$[OH^-] = \frac{1 \times 10^{-14}}{1 \times 10^{-2}} = 1 \times 10^{-12}$$

Similarly, if one were to add a base to water so that the [OH$^-$] is 10^{-2} moles per liter, the [H$^+$] will be 10^{-12}.

Thus, it is seen that there is an inverse relationship between [H$^+$] and [OH$^-$] in solutions of acids and bases, they become equal in concentration when both are 10^{-7} moles per liter.

It should be apparent that it is difficult to express [H⁺] and [OH⁻] in terms of moles per liter. A convenient method for expressing hydrogen ion concentrations is pH. The latter term may be defined as the logarithm of the reciprocal of the hydrogen ion concentration. Therefore, if a solution has a [H⁺] of 10^{-7}, the pH of the solution is 7. The pH scale covers 0–14. Solutions with a pH less than 7 are acid, and solutions with a pH more than 7 are basic.

The concentration of hydrogen ions is not always an even decimal fraction of a molar, or normal solution. For example: assume a solution has a hydrogen ion concentration of 5×10^{-4} moles per liter. This value is a fractional number 5 times larger than 1×10^{-4}, but only half as large as 1×10^{-3}. Such a [H⁺] is not pH 3.5, and can be illustrated as follows

$$pH = -\log(5 \times 10^{-4}) = -(\log 5 + \log 10^{-4})$$
$$= -(\log 5 + (-4))$$
$$= -(0.699 - 4)$$
$$= 3.30$$

It should also be noted that pH values can not be averaged. One must first convert the pH values to hydrogen ion concentration, average these values, then convert back to pH values. The average of pH 4 and pH 5 is not pH 4.5, but rather 4.26.

$$pH\ 5 = 1 \times 10^{-5}$$
$$pH\ 4 = 1 \times 10^{-4}$$
$$\text{average} \quad 5.5 \times 10^{-5}$$
$$\log 5.5 = 0.740$$
$$pH = -(10^{0.740} \times 10^{-5}) = -(0.740 - 5)$$
$$= 4.26$$

Two general methods are commonly used for determining the pH of a solution: the colorimetric and the potentiometric method.

The colorimetric method is based upon the fact that an indicator behaves like a weak acid or base and forms different colors when present in the undissociated and dissociated forms. As a consequence, the behavior of indicators can be explained in terms of mass action. An indicator has a definite dissociation constant at a definite temperature, and the pH of a solution will determine the ratio of the acid to alkaline form of the indicator (or color). In practice, a measured volume of an indicator is added to a measured volume of an unknown solution. The color obtained is compared to a standard. The same shade of color indicates the two solutions have the same pH because the [H⁺] determines the ratio of concentration of (acid form/alkaline form) of the indicator.

The potentiometric method is based on the principle that two electrodes, one sensitive to hydrogen ions and a reference electrode, partially immersed in a test solution, will develop a voltage related to the pH of the unknown solution ($V - v = 0.059\ pH$). A glass electrode generates a potential (V) according to the hydrogen ion concentration of the solution, while a calomel electrode has a constant potential (v). The voltage of the cell is the algebraic sum of these two potentials ($V - v$). A potentiometer involving electronic amplification is necessary for measuring the change in voltage. Commercial pH meters are constructed so that the developed voltage may be read directly as pH values.

Buffers.—Buffers are defined as solutions which resist changes in pH when small amounts of acid or base are added. Buffers exist in all living systems, and are essential in all systems in maintaining a H^+ concentration that is compatible with the proper functioning of the living system. Typical examples of environments that must have controlled pH's are the blood of animals, reptiles, and birds, sap of plants, and water, since it is the essential aqueous media for numerous forms of life. The buffering capacity of natural water, however, is generally quite limited.

In order to understand a buffer, one must apply the same principles of dissociation that have previously been applied to weak acids and weak bases. Buffers are composed of a weak acid and its salt, or a weak base and its salt.

A more general view of a buffer would be to consider a buffer system composed of a H^+ donor and a H^+ acceptor existing in equilibrium. Acetic acid in equilibrium with acetate is such an example:

$$CH_3COOH \rightleftharpoons CH_3COO^- + H^+$$

$$\text{(H}^+\text{ donor)} \qquad \text{(H}^+\text{ acceptor)}$$

Salts also exhibit these properties, e.g. dihydrogen phosphate and hydrogen phosphate.

$$H_2PO_4^- \rightleftharpoons HPO_4^= + H^+$$

$$\text{(H}^+\text{ donor)} \qquad \text{(H}^+\text{ acceptor)}$$

Bases and their salts function similarly

$$NH_4^+ \rightleftharpoons NH_3 + H^+$$

$$\text{(H}^+\text{ donor)} \qquad \text{(H}^+\text{ acceptor)}$$

All buffer solutions must have both a H^+ donor and a H^+ acceptor in order to maintain a constant pH.

Mathematically, the pH of a buffer solution can be derived from the equilibrium expression for the dissociation of the H^+ donor to give a H^+ ion and the H^+ acceptor:

$$HA \rightleftharpoons H^+ + A^-$$

$$(H^+ \text{ donor}) \ (H^+ \text{ acceptor})$$

$$Ka = \frac{[H^+] \ [A^-]}{[HA]}$$

rearranging,

$$[H^+] = Ka \ \frac{[HA]}{[A^-]}$$

taking the $-\log$ of both sides of the equation gives $-\log [H^+] = -\log K_{eq} = \log \frac{[HA]}{[A^-]}$ since $-\log [H^+] = pH$ and $-\log Ka = pKa$

$$pH = pKa - \log \frac{[HA]}{[A^-]} \quad \text{or} \quad pH = pKa + \log \frac{[A^-]}{[HA]}$$

pKa for all common H^+ donors (acids) have been determined and can be found in appropriate handbooks, thus only the $\frac{[A^-]}{[HA]}$ ratio need be known to calculate the pH of a buffer solution.

This familiar equation for calculating the pH of a buffer solution is known as the Henderson-Hasselbach equation.

It should be observed that when the $\frac{[A^-]}{[HA]} = 1$ the pH of a buffer is numerically equal to the pKa. A buffer is most effective at a $pH = pKa$ and is generally considered usable ±1 pH unit on either side of the pKa. One pH unit above the pKa would have a $\frac{[A^-]}{[HA]} = 10$, while 1 pH unit below the pKa would correspond to a $\frac{[A^-]}{[HA]} = 0.1$.

One should remember that a $0.1M$ "acetate" buffer would be $0.1M$ in "total acetate," e.g., acetic acid plus acetate, not just acetate alone. This is true for all buffers.

The buffer capacity of a buffer is based on how many equivalents of acid or base are required to change the pH of the buffer solution one pH unit below or above the pH of the buffer. More concentrated buffers of course would have greater buffering capacity since more of both the proton (H^+) donor and acceptor are present.

Oxidation-Reduction Reactions.—The principal sources of energy for all living cells are sugars, fatty acids, and amino acids. These substances are relatively stable outside the cell, but within the cell they are readily oxidized to meet the energy needs of the cells. The oxidation process is not spontaneous, but instead is controlled by enzymes. The energy that is not liberated as heat is used by the cell. The oxidative process involves several enzymes acting in a connected series of reactions. Consequently, before one considers the reactions and enzymes of biological oxidations, it seems appropriate to review the principle of oxidation-reduction.

The term oxidation originally denoted reactions involving oxygen with another element or compound, while the term reduction described reactions involving the removal of oxygen from a compound. The terms are now used to describe a number of different reactions, many of which do not involve oxygen. Oxidations involve one or more of the following reactions:

(a) Reaction of oxygen with another atom

Example: $2H_2O + O_2 \longrightarrow 2H_2O_2$

(b) Dehydrogenation

Example:

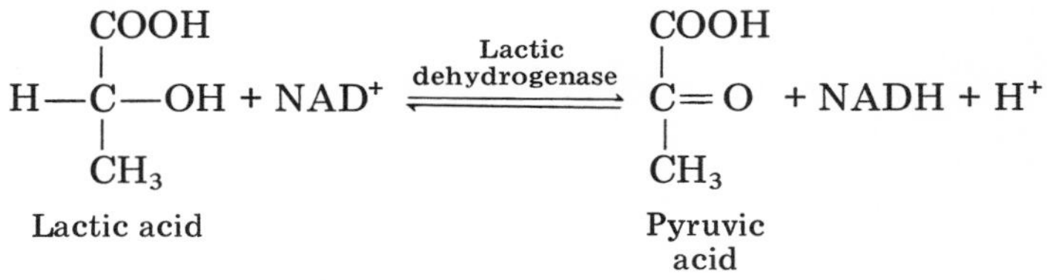

$$
\begin{array}{ccc}
\text{COOH} & & \text{COOH} \\
| & \text{Lactic} & | \\
\text{H—C—OH} + \text{NAD}^+ \underset{\text{dehydrogenase}}{\rightleftharpoons} & \text{C}=\text{O} + \text{NADH} + \text{H}^+ \\
| & & | \\
\text{CH}_3 & & \text{CH}_3 \\
\text{Lactic acid} & & \text{Pyruvic} \\
& & \text{acid}
\end{array}
$$

(c) Electron transfer

Example: $2FeCl_2 + Cl_2 \longrightarrow 2FeCl_3$ or
$2Fe^{2+} \longrightarrow 2Fe^{3+} + 2e^-$

The above examples illustrate that all the reactions have one common feature; i.e., oxidation corresponds to a loss of electrons, reduction corresponds to a gain of electrons, and that an oxidation and reduction reaction always occurs simultaneously and is equivalent. The overall process is called an oxidation-reduction system, and can be expressed by the reaction

Electron donor $\rightleftharpoons ne^-$ + electron acceptor
(reductant)   (oxidant)

where n = number of electrons dissociated per molecule reductant.

The tendency of a reductant to transfer electrons is expressed in terms of its standard reduction potential (redox potential). The redox potential does not show the relative amount of substance being oxidized, rather it shows the potential level at which electrons are available to the system. The tendency of a substance to gain or lose electrons is determined by the nature of the substance and, as a consequence, it is necessary to have some standard electrode for comparison. By convention, the standard is the hydrogen electrode, which has been assigned an oxidation-reduction potential E_o of 0.00 v at pH 0 and 1 atm pressure. In quantitative terms, the following relationship exists:

$$E(\text{volts}) = E_o(\text{volts}) + \frac{RT}{nF} \ln \frac{[\text{oxidized form}]}{[\text{reduced form}]}$$

in which R is the gas constant (1.987 cal/$^\circ$K/mole); T is the absolute temperature; n is the number of electrons per gram equivalent transferred in the reaction; F is the Faraday (23,000 cal/volt/gram-equivalent); E is the observed potential difference in volts; and E_o is the standard oxidation-reduction potential of the electrode. It is interesting to note that the potential will vary with the ratio of oxidant to reductant and not with absolute concentrations.

If the reference electrode is a hydrogen electrode and if the number of electrons transferred is unity, then the above equation can be written:

$$E = E_o + 0.06 \log \frac{[\text{oxidized form}]}{[\text{reduced form}]}$$

In biological systems, it is convenient to compare data which refer to reactions at pH 7.0 and 30°C. Because a proton is produced when hydrogen has become oxidized, the potential

$$H_2 \rightleftharpoons 2H^+ + 2e^-$$

will vary with pH. Hence, the above equation is rewritten

$$E = E_o' + 0.06 \log \frac{[\text{oxidized form}]}{[\text{reduced form}]}$$

and E_o' refers to the reference hydrogen electrode at pH 7 and 30°. On this scale, the reference electrode has a value of -0.42 volt.

Systems having a more negative oxidation-reduction potential (E_o or E_o') have a greater tendency to donate electrons. The more positive the oxidation-reduction potential, the greater the tendency to gain electrons (acceptor). A list of oxidation-reduction potentials, which includes several coenzymes and substrates to be included in subsequent chapters, is presented in Table 2.3.

From the above discussion, it is clear that oxidation-reduction reactions require both an electron donor and an electron acceptor. Hence, when two half-cells are coupled so as to react under standard

TABLE 2.3

OXIDATION-REDUCTION POTENTIALS FOR
SELECTED BIOCHEMICAL REACTIONS

System	E_o' (pH 7, 30°) Volts
Oxygen/water	+0.82
Ferric/ferrous	0.77
Cu^{2+}/Cu^+, hemocyanin	0.54
Cytochrome a, oxidation-reduction	0.29
Cytochrome c, oxidation-reduction	0.25
Cytochrome b, oxidation-reduction	0.04
Fumarate/succinate	0.03
Flavoprotein, oxidation/reduction	−0.06
Oxalacetate/malate	−0.17
Pyruvate/lactate	−0.19
Riboflavin, oxidation/reduction	−0.21
$NAD^+/NADH$	−0.32
Acetoacetate/β-hydroxybutyrate	−0.35
H^+/H_2	−0.42

conditions, one can calculate free energy changes for oxidation-reduction reactions.

The above discussion considers only the oxidation-reduction of a single component compared to a reference system. More commonly, two systems are coupled together to give some overall change in potential (volts) which ultimately leads to energy changes. These changes can be enzymatic or nonenzymatic. Typical of such a system would be the reversible oxidation-reduction of pyruvate to form lactate which is coupled to NAD^+ — $NADH + H^+$.

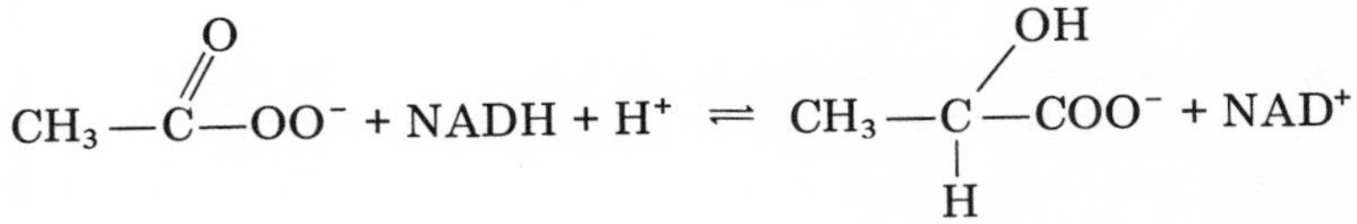

$$CH_3-\overset{O}{\overset{\|}{C}}-OO^- + NADH + H^+ \rightleftharpoons CH_3-\overset{OH}{\underset{H}{\overset{/}{C}}}-COO^- + NAD^+$$

In this reaction, E for pyruvate-lactate can be calculated

$$E = E_{o\,(\text{pyruvate})}' + \frac{RT}{nF} \ln \frac{[\text{pyruvate}]}{[\text{lactate}]}$$

while E for NAD^+ — $NADH$ is

$$E = E_{o\,(\text{NAD}^+)}' + \frac{RT}{nF} \ln \frac{[\text{NAD}^+]}{[\text{NADH}]}$$

combining these equations

$$E'_{o\,(\text{pyruvate})} - E'_{o\,(\text{NAD}^+)} = \frac{RT}{nF}\left[\ln\frac{[\text{NAD}^+]}{[\text{NADH}]} - \ln\frac{[\text{pyruvate}]}{[\text{lactate}]}\right]$$

$$E'_{o\,(\text{pyruvate-NAD}^+)} = \frac{RT}{nF}\ln\frac{[\text{NAD}^+]\ [\text{lactate}]}{[\text{NADH}]\ [\text{pyruvate}]}$$

since

$$\Delta G^\circ = -RT\ln K_{eq}$$

and

$$\Delta E_o = \frac{RT}{nF}\ln K_{(\text{oxid-red})}$$

$$nF\,\Delta E_o = RT\ln K_{(\text{oxid-red})}$$

Thus,

$$\Delta G^\circ = -nF\,\Delta E_o$$

The standard free energy (ΔG°) for a redox system as calculated using reduction potentials compared to the hydrogen electrode at pH = 0 ([H] = $1M$). Thus, ΔG° must be modified in order to compare data which refer to biological reactions at pH 7. For this convention, $\Delta G^{o'}$ is used to designate the modified standard free energy.

For the pyruvate-NAD$^+$ reaction:

$$\begin{aligned}\Delta G^{o'} &= -nF \times [\text{pyruvate-NAD}^+]\\ &= -(2)\,(23{,}000)\,[-0.19-(-0.32)]\\ &= -(2)\,(23{,}000)\,(0.13\,v)\\ &= -(5.98 \times 10^3\ \text{cal/mole})\end{aligned}$$

Thus, the reaction is thermodynamically feasible as written.

It should be pointed out that these calculations assume the reactants and products are at 1:1 ratio of concentration, but in actual biological systems such as cells or mitochondria, these concentrations would not likely be at unity ratio.

BIBLIOGRAPHY

BLACKBURN, T. R. 1969. Equilibrium—A Chemistry of Solutions. Holt, Rinehart and Winston, New York.

DANIELS, F., and ALBERTY, R. A. 1966. Physical Chemistry, 3rd Edition. John Wiley & Sons, New York.

EDSALL, J. T., and WYMAN, J. 1958. Biophysical Chemistry. Academic Press, New York.

LEHNINGER, A. L. 1964. The Mitochondrion. W. A. Benjamin, New York.

LOACH, P. A. 1970. Oxidation-reduction potentials, absorbance bands and and molar absorbance of compounds used in biochemical studies. *In* The Handbook of Biochemistry, 2nd Edition, H. A. Sober (Editor). Chemical Rubber Co., Cleveland, Ohio.

RACKER, E. 1965. Mechanisms in Bioenergetics. Academic Press, New York.

WEST, E. S. 1963. Textbook of Biophysical Chemistry, 3rd Edition. Macmillan Co., New York.

WILLIAMSON, A. G. 1967. An Introduction to Non-Electrolyte Solutions. John Wiley & Sons, New York.

CHAPTER 3

The Colloid State

The science of colloid chemistry was founded about 1861 when Thomas Graham published a summary of his work on the diffusion of substances in solution. He observed that the solutions of crystallizable substances diffused readily through parchment and other membranes whereas solutions of uncrystallizable substances did not diffuse through parchment and other membranes. To the first class he gave the name "crystalloids" and to the other the name "colloids."

The work of succeeding investigators showed that the failure of colloids to diffuse through parchment and other membranes was due to the size of the dissolved substances. Thus, colloids represent a state of matter and not a kind of matter as Graham had concluded from his work. We now know that it is possible to alter the particle size of some substances in solution so that they will not pass through a membrane. In fact, this kind of process exists in nature itself wherein glucose, "a crystalloid," is converted to starch, cellulose, or glycogen (a colloid). Conversely, starch or glycogen can be converted to glucose.

If one were to place a finely ground substance in water, one of three things may happen. First, it may form a true solution. In this case we have a molecular dispersion of the substance in water. The second possibility is that the substance may form a colloidal solution. The third possibility is that the particles will settle on standing. Thus it is apparent that matter can be classified according to particle size or degree of dispersion. Arbitrarily, we define colloidal particles as those ranging in size from 1–100 mμ (10–1000Å). Particles less than 1 mμ are particles in true solution, and particles greater than 100 mμ will form a coarse suspension.

Some Properties of Colloids

There are at least two phases to a colloidal system: the dispersed phase, and the dispersion medium. The colloidal material, which is suspended or dispersed, is known as the dispersed phase, or internal phase, or micelles. These particles are discontinuous and are distributed throughout another medium known as the continuous phase, or dispersion medium, or intermicellar liquid.

Perhaps it should be emphasized at this point that solids in liquids are not the only type of colloidal system, for it is possible to have other colloidal systems. For example: liquids suspended in liquids (homogenized milk); solids in gases (smokes); solids suspended in solids (colors in precious stones); and liquid in solid (pearl). If the suspended particle is of such a nature that it has no affinity for the dispersion medium, and does not tend to go into solution, it is referred to as a suspensoid or lyophobic colloid. If the suspended particle has an affinity for the dispersion medium, and tends to become hydrated, it is referred to as an emulsoid or lyophilic colloid.

When solutions of substances like salts or sugars are separated from water by a semipermeable membrane, osmotic pressure is observed. When colloidal solutions are studied under the same conditions it is found they do not diffuse, and as a result, they exert little or no osmotic pressure.

Methods of Preparing Colloidal Solution

The preparation of a colloidal solution may be accomplished in one of two ways. Either the degree of dispersion must be decreased or it must be increased. In the former case, the colloidal state is produced by aggregation of either molecules or ions in true solution. Heat denaturation of proteins is an example of a decrease in degree of dispersion. This process is known as condensation. When particles are large, they can be made small or more thoroughly dispersed in a number of ways, i.e. by mechanical grinding, electrical methods, or by chemical methods. This process is known as peptization. When coagulated egg albumin is treated with acid pepsin, a portion of the egg white forms a colloidal solution.

The diagram below shows the above relationships:

Dispersion Methods

Coarse Dispersions	Colloidal Solution	True Solution
>100 mμ	100 to 1 mμ	<1 mμ

Condensation Methods

Charge on Colloidal Particles

All colloids possess an electrical charge which may be either positive or negative. In a given colloidal system all particles have like charges and hence tend to repel one another and remain in suspension. To meet this condition, the colloidal particles distribute themselves uniformly throughout the liquid in which they are dispersed.

The charge upon colloidal particles arises in several ways.

(1) Direct ionization of the substances composing the micelle. This is especially true in the case of protein solutions. Proteins are

considered amphoteric electrolytes. The micelle might be mono-molecular or polymolecular. Whichever it is, let us consider the micelle of a protein as a polymolecular unit and each molecule as an amphoteric species as given below:

$$\begin{array}{c}
\overset{NH_3^+}{\underset{H}{R_1-C}}\!\!-\!\!\overset{O}{\underset{R-C-COOH}{C-NH}} \\
\underset{H}{}
\end{array}
\quad\underset{H^+}{\overset{-H^+}{\rightleftharpoons}}\quad
\begin{array}{c}
\overset{NH_3^+}{\underset{H}{R_1-C}}\!\!-\!\!\overset{O}{\underset{R-C-COO^-}{C-NH}} \\
\underset{H}{}
\end{array}$$

(Portion of protein structure having positive charge, thus is in cationic form)

($pH < IpH$)

Charge is zero, thus zwitterionic form

($pH = IpH$)

$$\underset{H^+}{\overset{-H^+}{\Updownarrow}}$$

R_1 = polypeptide chain

IpH = isoelectric pH where molecule has no charge

$$\begin{array}{c}
\overset{NH_2}{\underset{H}{R_1-C}}\!\!-\!\!\overset{O}{\underset{R-C-COO^-}{C-NH}} \\
\underset{H}{}
\end{array}$$

Charge is negative, thus anionic form

($pH > IpH$)

In a medium acid to the isoelectric pH the protein is positively charged, at the isoelectric point zero charged and in a dispersion medium alkaline to the isoelectric point, the polypeptide is negatively charged.

(2) Capture of an ion by adsorption. According to this theory the charge on the colloidal particle is due to selective adsorption of ions from solution. Proteins can acquire a charge by the association of ions or molecules with charged or uncharged sites on the protein molecule. Metal ions, particularly the transition metals, complex with side chain imidazole groups of the amino acid histidine. Factors such as pH, ionic strength and temperature have an effect on binding.

(3) Orientation. If polar molecules are adsorbed upon the surface of a colloidal particle, the charge of the particle surface will be dependent upon the orientation of the polar molecule on the particle. Thus, if the positively charged portion of a molecule is oriented toward the surface of the micelle, the negative portion of the molecule will be directed toward the dispersion medium and the micelle

is negatively charged. Conversely if the orientation is such that the negative portion of the molecule is adsorbed or oriented by the micelle, the micelle has a positive charge. Actually orientation is an extension of the capture of an ion by adsorption in which an oriented layer makes a gradual transition from the particle to the dispersion medium.

There are, of course, many cases in which it is difficult to form an opinion as to which of the above mechanisms were operative in the formation of the surface charge. Adsorption and ionization are the most frequently used methods but it should be remembered that several methods may operate in a given case.

The Double Layer of Colloidal Particles

The Helmholtz-Gouy double-layer theory gives the best explanation of the charge relations at the surface of a colloidal particle. According to this theory the charged surface of the colloid is surrounded by a layer of oppositely charged ions. The inner layer of ions is adsorbed upon the surface of the micelle from the liquid followed by a more diffuse layer which is mobile, the mobility increasing with distance from the surface. The outer layer possesses a charge opposite to that of the inner layer. The net charge surrounding the colloidal micelle, therefore, is zero since the fixed charges in the inner layer are exactly equal and opposite the mobile charges in the outer layer. Figure 3.1 shows a diagrammatic conception of the electrical double layer. The cross-hatched area indicates the wall of a colloidally dispersed particle to which adhere negatively-charged ions. We observe that the positive ions are attracted to the negative ions by electrostatic forces but in a diffuse manner. We have, therefore, a diffuse double layer in which the positive charges (17) are equivalent to the negative charges (17). Only part of the diffuse layer is mobile under the influence of an applied electromotive force; the area adhering to the wall is immobile. If the colloid particle is oppositely charged, the double-layer relations are reversed and the surrounding liquid contains negative ions.

The potential drop across all ionic layers from the surface of the particle into the solution is called epsilon (ϵ) potential. The potential between the charged surface of the particle (immobile layer) and the ions surrounding the particle (mobile layer) is called the electrokinetic or zeta (ζ) potential.

The electrokinetic, or zeta (ζ), potential between the immobile and mobile layers is of primary importance for some properties of colloids. It is a function of the concentration of the electrolyte, the valence and absorbability of its ions. When the zeta potential is

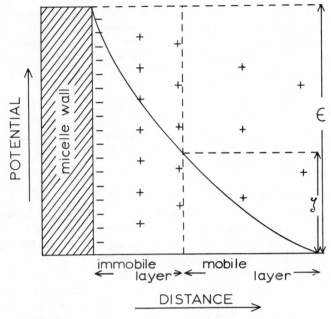

FIG. 3.1. DIAGRAM OF THE ELECTRICAL DOUBLE LAYER
OF COLLOIDAL PARTICLES

lowered to a definite value by the addition of electrolytes, the double layers of the colloid particles collapse, and the particles aggregate and precipitate.

Electrophoresis

Colloidally dispersed particles are most frequently negatively charged on their surface. The fact that these particles are charged can be demonstrated by electrophoresis. For example, if one puts a colloidal solution in the bottom of a U tube then carefully adds the dispersion medium (water) in each arm of the tube, and in the arms of the tube place platinum electrodes connected to a DC voltage, it will be noted that the colloidal particles will migrate to the electrode having a charge opposite to that of the colloidal particle. This migration of charged particles in an electric field is called electrophoresis (see Fig. 3.2).

The velocity of migration (cm/sec) can be determined by the following equation:

$$V = \frac{(\zeta)ED}{4\eta}$$

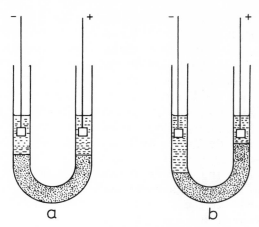

FIG. 3.2. ELECTROPHORESIS SYSTEM

a. Prior to application of dc voltage.   b. After migration of negatively charged particles.

Thus, the velocity of migration is directly proportional to the zeta (ζ) potential, the fall of potential in volts/cm (E), and the dielectric constant (D), and inversely proportional to the viscosity (η). If all factors are held constant, then the equation shows that the electrophoretic velocity is directly proportional to the zeta (ζ) potential. The higher the zeta (ζ) potential of a colloidal particle the faster it moves. At the isoelectric point, where the zeta (ζ) potential is zero, there is no migration in an electric field.

Precipitation of Colloids

In a preceding section it was pointed out that there are two types of colloidal systems, namely hydrophobic colloids and hydrophilic colloids. Hydrophobic colloids, which are more readily precipitated, are much less stable than hydrophilic colloids. In a hydrophobic system the colloidal particles have no affinity for water and remain dispersed because of the electric charge present. In a hydrophilic system the colloidal particles have an affinity for water and as a consequence they might be considered as being combined with a layer of the water. Thus, there are two factors favoring stability in a hydrophilic system, namely electric charge (zeta (ζ) potential) and the solvent layer (degree of solvation). Electrolytes in small concentration affect chiefly the zeta (ζ) potential whereas in large concentrations they affect chiefly the degree of hydration. If these stability factors are decreased sufficiently, the colloidal state is destroyed and precipitation will occur. The relationship between these two systems and precipitated particles is diagrammatically represented in Fig. 3.3.

In Fig. 3.3 are presented the various forms in which the micelles of a common milk protein (β-lactoglobulin) can exist. Micelles 1 to 3 represent hydrophilic micelles stabilized by the degree of hydration but only micelles 1 and 3 have both stability factor of zeta (ζ) potential and hydration. One can move horizontally by using acids, bases, and/or suitable concentrations of electrolytes. One can move vertically from micelle 2 to micelle 4 by removing water of hydration (e.g., heat, salt, or alcohol).

Note that when the micelles have lost their "hydration" and their charge as in 4, they agglomerate and form 5, a precipitate which can be repeptized. If the process of agglomeration has proceeded too far and the individual micelles have lost their identity, the precipitation becomes irreversible as 6 is formed.

When electrolytes in high concentration are used to bring about precipitation of a hydrophilic colloid, the process is called "salting out." The first addition of the salt reduces the charge of zeta (ζ) potential; subsequent additions of ions and molecules in solution compete with the protein for its water of hydration. Thus, when sufficiently concentrated, the salt not only deprives the colloid of its electrical charge (zeta potential) but also lowers its degree of hydration to such an extent that the colloid, precipitates, i.e., "salts out."

It should be remembered that the solubility of a salt is not the only factor to be considered in the salting out process. For example, $MgSO_4$ is less soluble than the chloride, yet the chloride is not suitable for salting out proteins. Thus, the salting out ability of an electrolyte depends on the nature of the anion as well as the cation series. Ionic strength of salt solutions has an effect on the solubility of hydrophilic colloids in this solution. Ionic strength is defined as

$$\mu = \tfrac{1}{2} \sum c_i z_i^2$$

where c_i is the concentration of each ion and z_i is the charge on the ion. For example a $0.01M$ solution of $MgSO_4$

$$\mu = \tfrac{1}{2}[(.01)(+2)^2 + (.01)(-2)^2]$$
$$= \tfrac{1}{2}[(.04) + (.04)]$$
$$\mu = .04$$

In a salt such as KCl the ionic strength would be $\mu = M$ where $M =$ molarity.

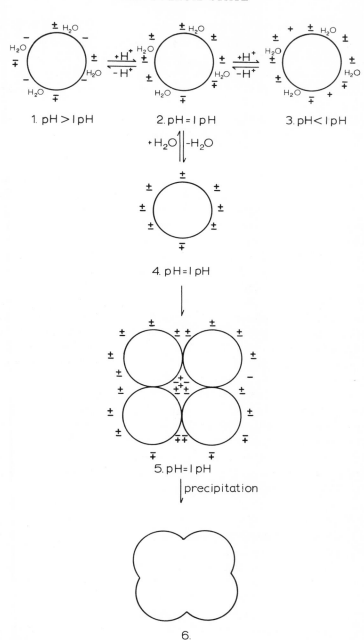

FIG. 3.3. EFFECT OF PHYSICAL AND CHEMICAL ENVIRONMENT ON
THE CHARGE AND STABILITY OF PROTEIN MICELLES

Protective Colloids

Hydrophilic colloids are much more stable than hydrophobic colloids. If one were to add a small amount of the former colloid to the latter, it would be observed that the hydrophobic colloid becomes much more stable. A colloid used in this manner is spoken of as a protective colloid.

Proteins (gelatin and egg albumin) and gums (gum acacia) are frequently used as protective colloids for hydrophobic sols.

Gels

Gels may be defined as semisolid systems having high yield values or high viscosities. They are similar to solids in that they maintain their form under the stress of their own weight and they show the phenomena of strain under any mechanical stress. They are different from solids in the following ways: (a) chemical reactions can occur in gels at a rate little affected by the gel state, (b) substances soluble in the liquid phase can diffuse through a gel with the same rate of diffusion as the rate of diffusion in the pure solvent.

Many theories have been advanced to explain the rigid properties of a gel. The most generally accepted theory, with regard to the structure is that in gels the colloidal particles arrange themselves in the form of fibrils which assume what is called a "brush-heap" arrangement. A gel, then is a mass of these fibrils with the dispersion liquid enmeshed between them.

Factors Affecting Gel Formation.—There are several factors which affect the formation of gels. (1) The nature of the colloid. Hydrophilic colloids form gels more readily than hydrophobic gels. Pectins and carrageens are widely used in the food industry to form gels. (2) A definite concentration is necessary under a definite set of conditions for a gel to set. In most cases gel strength and quality must be done by adjustment of ingredients of the gel. For example, a 2% gelatin sol will set within 30 min at 15°C and a 1% sol will set at 0°C. (3) Lowering of temperature of a solution favors the setting of a gel, whereas increasing temperature will cause a gel to liquefy. (4) Factors such as pH, salt and nonelectrolyte concentrations are important in the degree of hydration of the colloid. In the preparation of jams and jellies a pH range of 3.0–3.8 is preferred. Salts either retard or accelerate gelation, depending on the ions which compose them. For example, carrageenan requires a potassium salt. No general rule governs the effect of nonelectrolyte, (e.g., sucrose), concentration on gelation. (5) The temperature at which a gel liquifies is usually higher than that at which it sets. This lag is called hysteresis. (6) Mechanical treatment will affect the setting of a gel. If agitation is applied after setting, the gel structure will be broken and the fluidity increases. This tendency of certain colloidal systems to change their state on being shaken or stirred is called thixotropy. (7) The degree of hydration can be altered by changing the pH, salt and nonelectrolyte concentration. The addition of relatively high concentrations of acids and alkalies ($>.05N$) retards gelation. Salts either retard or accelerate gelation depending on the ions which compose them and on their selective adsorption.

Coagulation.—Gels may be classified into heat reversible and nonheat reversible. For example, an agar gel on being heated will pass from a gel to a sol and then back to a gel again on cooling. It is said to be reversible. Conversely many sols form gels which on heating cannot be readily converted back to the sol. Such a gelation is often spoken of as a coagulation. A good example of coagulation occurs in heating egg white. Coagulated egg white cannot be readily reversed.

Syneresis.—Syneresis is defined as the exudation of the aqueous phase constituent of gels irrespective of the vapor pressure imposed upon the system. The liquid which exudes is a very dilute sol. Common occurrences of syneresis are the accumulation of liquid around gelatin desserts kept in a refrigerator, the curdling of sour milk, the deposition of water droplets on butter, the exudation of serum over blistered skin, and the separation of fluid when lean meat is heated.

Syneresis is influenced by several factors. (1) It is dependent on pH since syneresis reaches a maximum when a gel is at its isoelectric point. In jelly making a proper pH is necessary for a proper set. A stiff jelly is not palatable and is subject to syneresis. (2) The influence of temperature on syneresis cannot be formulated by any general rule since hydration and temperatures do not run parallel. One would expect the phenomenon to take place to a greater extent with a rise in temperature. (3) Pressure influences syneresis. (4) The nature of the dispersed phase has an effect on syneresis, e.g., silicic acid exhibits more intense syneresis as concentration is increased, whereas starch exhibits the opposite.

Imbibition.—Many solid substances, such as are obtained from proteins (gelatin, albumins), and polysaccharides (pectin and "soluble" starches), will absorb water with the result that they increase in volume. This is called imbibition. In many ways imbibition may be looked upon as the opposite of syneresis. The rate of imbibition of the dispersion medium is greater at first but gradually decreases. The extent to which a gel imbibes a liquid is dependent upon a number of factors. (1) pH has a great influence on the amount of water which certain gels will imbibe. A small degree of acidity greatly increases the ability of proteins to imbibe water. (2) Temperature is another major factor in imbibition. When gels such as gelatin-water or agar-water are held below 30°C swelling does not occur. At higher temperatures these gels continue to swell until they liquefy.

Emulsions

An emulsion is a system composed of two liquid phases, one of which is dispersed as droplets in the other liquid. These systems are intrinsically unstable and as a consequence need an emulsifying agent to prevent coalescence of droplets into a continuous liquid. The emulsifying agent must be adsorbed at an interface between the two phases and as a consequence surface orientation will determine the kind of emulsion one obtains, i.e., oil-in-water (o/w), or water-in-oil (w/o) emulsions.

The type of orientation at the interface of two liquids is determined primarily by the character of the molecules involved, i.e., polar or apolar (nonpolar). Molecules that have an unequal distribution of shared electrons such as those containing —COOH, —CHO, —OH, ester, amine (ammonium), nitro and other radicals will always show some polar character. Extremes of these are water with a very high dielectric constant (see Chap. 1) and hydrocarbons such as hexane which has a relatively low dielectric constant. Molecules such as alcohols can have both polar and apolar groups in the same molecule, e.g.,

$$\underbrace{CH_3(CH_2)_n}_{\text{apolar}}\underbrace{CH_2OH}_{\text{polar}}$$

Thus, a molecule of this type is capable of being attracted to both a polar medium, such as water, and an apolar medium, such as an oil. The alcohol is oriented at the surface of water so that the —OH groups are directed into the water and the alkyl radicals are above the surface. If one uses higher members of the alcohols series, the apolar property of the alkyl radical will be increased, the polar character of the hydroxy group decreases, water solubility decreases, and an increasing solubility in fat solvents is observed.

Next consider what happens when two immiscible liquids, oil and water, are shaken or otherwise agitated. An emulsion is produced which is usually unstable. Coalescence occurs when agitation ceases with a concomitant separation into two layers. A third substance, called an emulsifying agent, is necessary if a stable emulsion is to be obtained. If sodium stearate is added before the immiscible liquids are agitated, a stable emulsion will be obtained. A diagrammatic

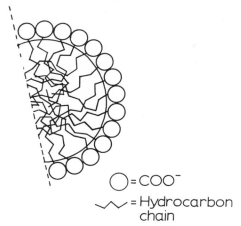

$\bigcirc$ = COO⁻

$\sim\!\!\sim$ = Hydrocarbon chain

FIG. 3.4. ORIENTATION OF AN EMULSIFYING AGENT IN A
FAT OR OIL DROPLET

explanation (Fig. 3.4) will aid in understanding the action of the sodium ion stabilizing the emulsion. The ionized soap molecules contain the hydrocarbon radical, $C_{17}H_{35-}$ which is soluble in oil but not in water, and the $-COO^-$ groups, which are soluble in water but not in oil. The hydrocarbon chain of the soap molecule will have a tendency to orient toward the oil phase, whereas the polar group, consisting of the carboxyl group, will have a tendency to orient in the direction of the water phase. Furthermore, as a result of orientation, the negative carboxyl group gives the droplet a negative surface charge and this is balanced by the sodium ions in the surrounding water. Consequently the emulsion droplets will have a Helmholtz double layer, across which there is a potential difference (zeta potential). The droplets possess the same charge, thus they will repel each other and remain in suspension. The soap (sodium stearate) thus stabilizes an oil-in-water emulsion by orienting the soap ions so that the droplets are attracted by water (hydrophilic) and by imparting a charge to the droplet.

It is interesting to note that oil-soluble substances such as calcium oleate, and cholesterol, favor w/o emulsions, while water-soluble substances such as proteins, dextrins, and lecithin favor o/w emulsions. Thus, a general statement might be made that the liquid which gives the higher degree of wetting of an emulsifying agent will exist as the external phase.

Factors Affecting Emulsification.—Emulsification is dependent upon several factors. (1) The ratio of the two phases will have an effect on the type of emulsion obtained. If oil and water are shaken, both w/o and o/w emulsions are formed. One will be very unstable and one will stabilize. If the oil concentration is much less than the water, the o/w emulsion would be the more stable of the two. (2) The chemical composition of the emulsifying agent will determine the type of emulsion. Water peptized substances favor o/w emulsions. (3) The mechanics of emulsification are important. Intermittent shaking is more effective than continuous shaking because a "rest period" is necessary for adsorption of the emulsifying agent at the newly formed surface. Emulsification is accomplished more readily at higher temperatures because a rise in temperature decreases viscosity and surface tension.

De-Emulsification (Breaking of Emulsions).—A knowledge of the factors which will destroy emulsions is important not only because those conditions must be avoided when preparing stable emulsions, but also because undesirable emulsions are sometimes formed and measures must be taken to "break them." Various methods have been used for breaking emulsions but no method is universally applicable. However, from the above discussion of emulsions, and the nature of emulsifying agents, it becomes apparent that the breaking of an emulsion involves the removal or destruction of the adsorbed film, and the neutralization of the electric charge carried by the dispersed phase. The methods used can be classified as physical, chemical, and electrical.

Physical Methods.—These methods depend on the use of centrifugation, filtration, lowering viscosity by heating, dehydration, stirring or churning, freezing, addition of an excess of dispersed phase followed by agitation, addition of a third liquid in which each of the liquid phases of the emulsion are soluble and agitation with 2 different solids each preferentially wetted by 1 phase.

Chemical Methods.—These methods might make use of: (1) the addition of oppositely charged electrolytes or colloids to decrease the electric charge of the dispersed phase, dehydrate the emulsifying agent, or chemically react with the emulsifier to alter its efficiency; (2) the addition of a o/w emulsifying agent to a w/o emulsion will bring about destabilization. The opposite will also occur.

Foams

Foams may be defined as a colloidal system consisting of a gas, or a mixture of gases, suspended in a very viscous liquid. In a foam an interface must exist between the liquid and gas much the same as the interface between the liquid phases of an emulsion. Consequently, the characteristics of the interfacial film must be similar to those of an emulsion if a stable foam is to be formed. In foam formations there is an increased concentration of the dissolved substance at the interface accompanied by a lowering of the surface tension. If this increase in concentration at the interface will impart sufficient viscosity to the film, the foam will be stable without the addition of a third substance. A colloidal substance is usually needed to give stability to a foam and must be concentrated at the interface. All protein solutions will ordinarily produce stable foams, e.g., meringues (egg albumin) and marshmallow (gelatin).

The foam of beer owes its rigidity and stability to the concentration at the surface film of a substance from the added hops.

Viscosity

Viscosity can be defined as a resistance due to internal friction which viscous matter offers to deforming forces, hence, as resistance to shear or flow. Hydrophobic sols deviate but little from that of the dispersion medium while lyophilic sols have viscosities which differ from that of the dispersion medium. This may be caused by hydration of the micelle. Consequently, viscosity can be a measure of the degree of hydration.

The absolute unit of viscosity is the poise. A poise, in cm-gm-sec units, is the force which, when exerted on a unit area between 2 parallel planes 1 sq cm in area and 1 cm apart, produces a difference in the velocity of streaming between the 2 planes of 1 cm per sec. The centipoise is 0.01 of a poise.

It is customary to determine specific viscosity rather than absolute viscosity. Specific viscosity expresses viscosity in terms of some standard. Water, whose absolute viscosity at 20°C is 1.0050 cp, is generally used as the standard.

There are some colloidal systems wherein the ratio of applied force to the rate of flow is not constant, but varies with the conditions such as force, rate of flow, and time. In these systems it is not appropriate to speak of the viscosity of the sol, but rather of apparent viscosity or consistency. The latter term represents the ratio between applied force and the rate of flow under the conditions of the determination. Many of these systems behave like "soft" solids and pastes rather than fluids which flow upon the application of pressure. They are called plastic systems, and have a property called the yield value. The latter term may be defined as the force necessary to initiate flow. This relationship is shown diagrammatically in Fig. 3.5. The line AB represents a truly viscous system in which the increase in the rate of flow, with increase of force applied, is a straight line which passes through the origin. In the case of plastic systems, the line CD intersects the force axis at C to the right of A.

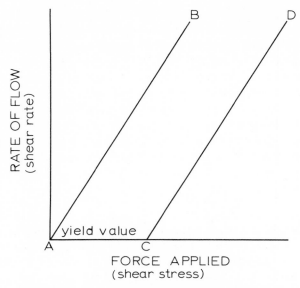

FIG. 3.5. DIAGRAM SHOWING VISCOUS VERSUS PLASTIC SYSTEM

This means that it is necessary to apply a force AC, equal to the yield value, before plastic flow begins. Thus, when dealing with a plastic system one must determine the rate of flow per unit of force applied and the yield value.

A simple and convenient method for determining viscosity utilizes the Ostwald viscometer. The viscometer is a capillary tube of known cross-section wherein one measures the time of flow of a given volume of liquid through the tube. Viscosity is calculated using the Poiseuille equation

$$\eta = \frac{Pr^4\pi}{8vl}$$

Where η (eta) = viscosity, v = volume of liquid flowing through a capillary tube of length, l, and radius, r, under pressure, P in unit time. If the times of flow of equal volumes of two liquids through the same capillary tube are measured under the same head of liquid, the ratio of viscosities is given by:

$$\frac{\eta_1}{\eta_2} = \frac{d_1 t_1}{d_2 t_2}$$

where η_1 and η_2 represent the coefficients of viscosity of the two liquids, d_1 and d_2, their densities, and t_1 and t_2 their times of flow.

If one chooses water as a standard with a viscosity of one, the viscosities of other liquids relative to water may be determined by obtaining the time of flow of water and another liquid through a capillary. The relative viscosity is obtained by using the equation:

$$\frac{\eta_1}{1} = \frac{d_1 t_1}{d_w t_w}$$

in which η_1 is the relative viscosity of the liquid, d_1 its density, and t, its time of flow. The viscosity of water is one, its density d_w and its time of flow t_w. The relative viscosity values obtained in this way may be converted to absolute viscosities by multiplying by the absolute viscosity of water at the temperature of the experiment.

Fluidity expresses the tendency of a liquid to flow and is equal to the reciprocal of viscosity. It is expressed by the Greek letter phi, thus

$$\phi = \frac{1}{\eta}$$

Factors Affecting Viscosity.—There are several factors which affect the viscosity of solutions. (1) Hydrophilic colloids in general have a viscosity that differs little from that of medium in which it is dispersed. Viscosity increases only slightly with increasing concentration of dispersed particles. In contrast, the viscosity of hydrophilic colloid sols is generally relatively high (Fig. 3.6) as the concentration of the dispersed phase is increased. (2) The viscosity of a hydrophilic sol increases with an increase in hydration. The micelles are much increased in size due to the bound water or other dispersion medium, and are pushed past each other with greater difficulty. (3) The viscosity of a colloidal system decreases with an increase of temperature. The decrease in viscosity of a hydrophobic colloid is much less than is the case for a hydrophilic colloid. The latter phenomenon is due not only to a decrease in the degree of hydration of the micelle with a rise in temperature, but also to a decrease in viscosity of the dispersion medium with increase in temperature. (4) Sols with the smaller particles show a higher viscosity for a given concentration than the coarser particles of the same concentration (degree of dispersion). (5) Hysteresis is a term which may be defined as the influence of previous treatment of a colloid system on its present behavior. Preliminary heat treatments, mechanical treatments, hydrolysis on standing with concomitant lowering of viscosity, etc., are examples of previous treatment. (6) In general, small quantities of nonelectrolytes may increase viscosity,

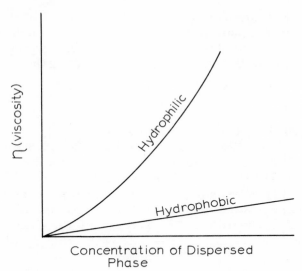

FIG. 3.6. VISCOSITY AS A FUNCTION OF THE CONCENTRA-
TION OF THE DISPERSED PHASE

Hydrophobic system is distinguished from the hydrophilic system.

while small amounts of electrolytes decrease viscosity. The solution
of large quantities of solids generally causes an increase in viscosity.

BIBLIOGRAPHY

BULL, H. B. 1964. An Introduction to Physical Biochemistry. F. A. Davis
    Co., Philadelphia.
JERGENSONS, B., and STRAUMANIS, K. E. 1962. A Short Textbook of
    Colloid Chemistry. Macmillan Co., New York.
McBAIN, J. W. 1950. Colloid Science. D. C. Heath & Co., Lexington, Mass.
MOORE, W. J. 1956. Physical Chemistry. Prentice-Hall, New York.
MYSELS, J. J. 1959. Introduction to Colloid Chemistry. John Wiley & Sons,
    New York.
SHELUDKO, A. 1966. Colloid Chemistry. Elsevier Publishing Co., Amsterdam.
VOLD, M. J., and VOLD, R. D. 1964. Colloid Chemistry. Van Nostrand
    Reinhold Co., New York.
WARD, A. G. 1946. Colloids. John Wiley & Sons, New York.

CHAPTER 4

Carbohydrates

The word "carbohydrate" was originally derived from the fact that the greater part of the compounds in this class had the empirical formula $C_n(H_2O)_n$. The values of n ranged from three to many thousands. The above formula is now considered to be extremely restrictive, and a more useful definition might be "polyhydroxy aldehydes or ketones and their derivatives." The latter definition would include deoxy sugars, sugar alcohols, sugar acids, and amino sugars.

Carbohydrates occur in fruits and vegetables; as storage reserves in seeds, roots, and tubers; in the sap; and as constituents of the structural tissues. They are also found in the milk, blood, and tissues of animals.

Carbohydrates are the most abundant food in the world and the most economical as an energy food source. In the American diet, carbohydrate foods constitute approximately 50% of the daily caloric intake. However, carbohydrates make up a greater proportion of the diet of peoples of other countries where cereals are a staple food.

Carbohydrates are important for reasons other than as an inexpensive source of energy. The body needs carbohydrates in order to use fat efficiently. Many foreign substances are removed from the body through the intermediate formation of glycosides of glucuronic acid. Diseases such as diabetes develop when the body is unable to utilize sugar properly. Some carbohydrates have an effect on the type of bacteria which will grow in the intestine. In some of the lower animals (crab and lobster), a major constituent of the exoskeleton is a polymer of glucosamine.

Certain industries (such as milling, baking, brewing, syrup, and sugars) are based on carbohydrates. Thus, it is readily seen that carbohydrates are at the very foundation of the economic structure of our society.

Classification

The carbohydrates are divided into two large groups, simple sugars and compound sugars. This classification is based upon the number of sugars one obtains when the various carbohydrates undergo hydrolysis. Carbohydrates such as glucose and fructose, which cannot be hydrolyzed into simpler compounds, are called monosaccharides. The compound sugars are made up of two or more molecules of monosaccharides. The latter group is further divided into two broad categories—oligosaccharides and polysaccharides. Oligosaccharides are composed of two or more monosaccharides. Examples of the latter group are sucrose (a disaccharide) and raffinose (a trisaccharide). The polysaccharides consist of many units of monosaccharides. The polysaccharides may be separated into three broad groups, homopolysaccharides (one kind of monosaccharide unit); heteropolysaccharides (two or more kinds of monosaccharides); and nitrogen containing polysaccharides. The monosaccharides and disaccharides are sweet tasting and soluble in water. In contrast, the polysaccharides are colloidal, dispersible under certain conditions in water, tasteless and vary greatly in digestibility.

The carbohydrates of interest to the food chemist include:

A. *Simple Sugars or Monosaccharides*
  - I.   Pentoses—arabinose, xylose, ribose
  - II. Hexoses
    - 1. Aldohexoses—galactose, glucose
    - 2. Ketohexose—fructose
B. *Oligosaccharides*
  - I.   Disaccharides
    - 1. Reducing—maltose, lactose
    - 2. Nonreducing—sucrose
  - II. Trisaccharides
    - 1. Nonreducing—raffinose, gentianose
C. *Polysaccharides*
  - I.   Homo—(one kind of monosaccharide unit)
    - 1. Pentosans—xylan, araban
    - 2. Hexosans
      - a. Glucosans—starch, dextrin, glycogen, cellulose
      - b. Fructosan—inulin
      - c. Mannan
      - d. Galactan
  - II. Hetero—(two or more kinds of monosaccharide units)
          pectins, gums, mucilages
  - III. Nitrogen-containing—chitin

The Monosaccharides

These simple carbohydrates are essentially polyhydroxy aldehydes and ketones and are classified according to the length of the carbon chain and according to the nature of the carbonyl group. Of this group only two types are of sufficient biological importance to merit detailed discussion, viz., the pentoses and hexoses. However, before we consider these sugars in detail, there are a number of properties and reactions of sugars that merit emphasis.

Optical Activity.—One very important property possessed by sugars is that of optical activity. It will be recalled that some organic compounds such as lactic and tartaric acids possess the property of rotating rays of polarized light. This property is referred to as optical rotation, and such compounds are said to be optically active.

The instrument used for measuring optical activity is called a polarimeter. The polarimeter employs monochromatic light from a sodium light; and in its simplest form, consists of two Nicol prisms. The prism nearest the light source is in a fixed position and is known as the polarizing prism; the prism nearer the eye of the observer is movable and is called the analyzer. If the two prisms are arranged so that their optical axes are in the same plane, essentially all of the radiation will pass through. If the optical axis of the analyzer is at right angles to that of the polarizing prism, the radiation will be totally absorbed. This is termed total extinction. The instrument is also equipped with a scale to indicate the number of degrees through which the analyzer is rotated. The zero point may be set at the point where the two Nicol prisms are crossed without the sample in the polarized beam. If an optically active compound is placed between the prisms, the plane of polarized light is rotated either to the right or to the left. It is necessary to rotate the analyzer until the prisms are again crossed. The angle through which the analyzer is turned is equal to the angular rotation of the optically active compound. If it is necessary to rotate the analyzer to the right to accomplish total extinction, the optically active compound is dextrorotatory (+). If, on the other hand, the analyzer was rotated to the left, the compound is said to be levorotatory (−).

The angular rotation of an optically active compound in solution is directly proportional to the concentration of the compound, the length of the column of solution through which the light passes, and the rotating power of the substance. The term specific rotation, $[\alpha]$, was introduced to define this relationship and may be defined as the angular rotation in degrees of a solution containing 100 gm of solute in 100 ml of solution when read in a tube 1 decimeter long.

$$[\alpha] = \frac{100A}{lc}$$

where A is the rotation (plus or minus), l is the length of the tube in decimeters, and c is the concentration in grams per 100 ml of solution. Specific rotation is a function of temperature as well as the wavelength of light. Therefore, in order to standardize data, specific rotation is indicated as follows:

$$[\alpha]_D^{20} = \text{rotation value (solvent used)}$$

which means specific rotation at 20°C, and the D line of the spectrum was used.

The optical activity of monosaccharides is due to asymmetry of the molecule. An asymmetric carbon atom may be defined as an atom which has four different atoms or atomic groups attached to it. For example, D-glyceraldehyde, represented by the following formula, contains an asymmetric carbon atom to which are attached four different radicals, the asymmetric carbon atom being indicated by bold-face type:

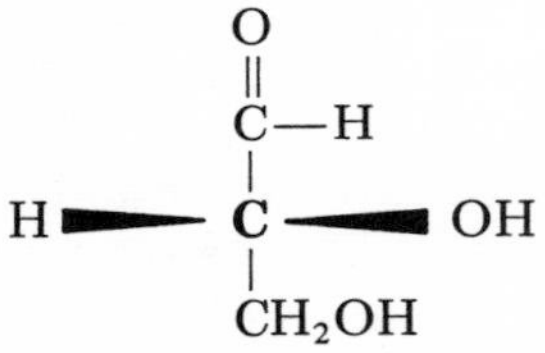

D(+)-Glyceraldehyde 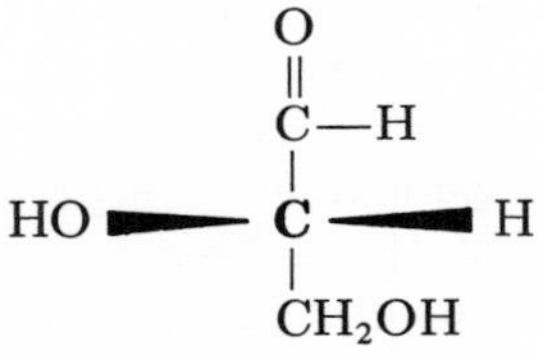   L(−)-Glyceraldehyde

Molecules possessing an asymmetric carbon atom exist in two mirror images, one of which is dextrorotatory and the other levorotatory. The above figures represent the two forms of glyceraldehyde. Since these sugars are isomeric with each other, they are said to be stereoisomers. This term refers to the geometrical arrangement of the atoms and atomic groups in space. The stereochemistry is designated D and L and will be discussed later.

A mixture of equal parts of the above isomers is optically inactive because the isomers rotate polarized light the same number of degrees in opposite directions, the net effect being zero. The mixture is referred to as a racemic mixture and is an example of external compensation.

When a molecule contains more than one asymmetric carbon atom, it is optically active if the rotatory effects of the asymmetric carbon atoms do not neutralize one another. If the molecule is symmetrical in structure, that is, if a plane of symmetry can be passed through it, the molecule is optically inactive.

With the above discussion as a background, we may now write the formulas of the different forms of tartaric acid.

$$
\begin{array}{ccc}
\text{COOH} & \text{COOH} & \text{COOH} \\
| & | & | \\
\text{H—C—OH} & \text{HO—C—H} & \text{H—C—OH} \\
| & | & | \\
\text{HO—C—H} & \text{H—C—OH} & \text{H—C—OH} \\
| & | & | \\
\text{COOH} & \text{COOH} & \text{COOH} \\
\text{L(+)-Tartaric acid} & \text{D(-)-Tartaric acid} & \textit{meso}\text{-Tartaric acid} \\
\text{I} & \text{II} & \text{III}
\end{array}
$$

If one constructs models of I, II, and III it may be noted that III possesses a plane of symmetry; i.e., the molecule can be divided into two mirror image halves and is optically inactive. Conversely, I and II are asymmetrical and thus are optically active.

Levo, *dextro*, and *meso*-tartaric acids are stereoisomers; that is, they have exactly the same functional groups but these groups are arranged differently in space. *Dextro* and *levo*-tartaric acids are optical isomers (enantiomorphs) which means they have these groups exactly reversed in space as mirror images and rotate polarized light equally and oppositely.

Racemic tartaric acid is composed of an equal mixture of the *dextro* and *levo* acids. It is optically inactive because of the external compensation. Whenever organic compounds, which contain asymmetric carbon atoms, are synthesized a racemic mixture of optical isomers is produced.

We have used for our discussion of optical activity glyceraldehyde and tartaric acids, both of which are rather simple compounds. Most organic compounds of biological importance, are much more complicated, usually having several asymmetric carbon atoms. Thus, the possibilities for optical isomerism are greatly increased. In a simple compound like a hexose there are 4 asymmetric carbon atoms and the number of optical isomers is 16.

Carbohydrate Structure.—A discussion of the determination of carbohydrate structure would be involved and beyond the scope of this book. For such information, the reader is referred to texts on carbohydrates (Pigman and Horton 1972). The food chemist is primarily concerned with the identification of carbohydrates because the properties and reactions are dependent on the structure of the molecule. For example, the properties and reactions of monosaccharides depend partly on the position of the hydroxyl groups within the molecule, the presence of an aldehyde or ketone group, and the number of carbon atoms in the molecule. Similarly, the properties and reactions of complex carbohydrates depend on the number of units in the chain, the kind of units in the chain, and the position of the linkages that join the individual units together. This involves some knowledge of carbohydrate structure; consequently, structural formulas will be given under the discussion of individual carbohydrates.

When the structures of the monosaccharides were first determined, they were pictured as aldehyde or ketone polyols. For example, D-glucose and L-glucose were assigned the following formulas:

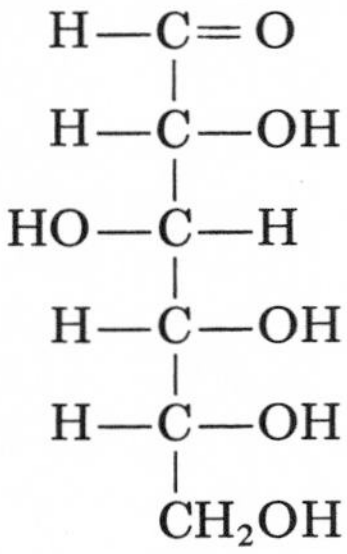

D-Glucose 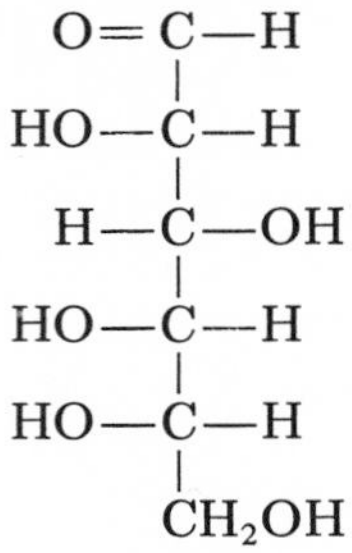   L-Glucose

When the structure of the glucose molecule is arranged and projected according to the Fischer system (aldehyde on top and primary alcohol at bottom; hydrogens and hydroxyl groups on the other carbon atoms projecting up out of the plane of the paper) we find that the assignment to the D or L series of compounds depends on whether the hydroxyl group of the asymmetric carbon atom farthest from the aldehyde group is projected to the right (D) or to the left (L).[1] Stereoisomers that are structurally related to D-glyceraldehyde are designated D-sugars,

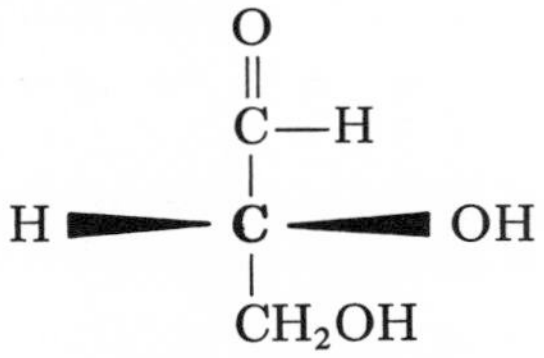

D-Glyceraldehyde 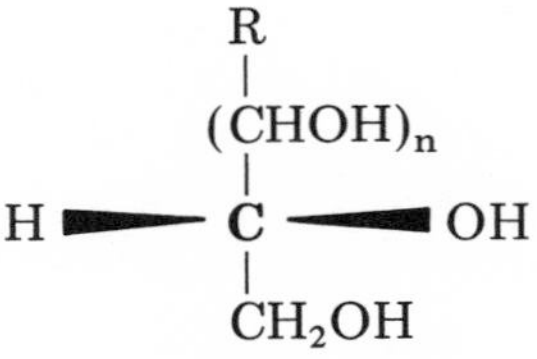   D-Sugar

and the corollary L-sugars are related to L-glyceraldehyde. These D- and L- designations do not indicate the direction in which the sugar rotates the plane of polarized light. If it is desired to indicate

---

[1] According to the Cahn-Ingold-Prelog conventions, R and S are used rather than D and L, respectively. Thus, D-glyceraldehyde is designated as R-glyceraldehyde and L-glyceraldehyde is designated S-glyceraldehyde. The convention is particularly useful when a compound contains several asymmetric carbon atoms. The configuration of each group around a specific asymmetric carbon atom can be specified. For example, D-erythrose becomes 2(R),3(R)-erythrose. Thus, the configuration of both hydroxyl groups are designated.

the direction of optical rotation, (+) indicates to the right or dextro-rotatory, (−) to the left or levorotatory.

The straight chain structure for the sugars did not account for all the reactions: (1) the sugars failed to respond to Schiff's reagent (test for aldehydes) under the usual conditions of the test, thus no appreciable amount of free or potential aldehyde was present; (2) freshly prepared solutions of the sugars exhibited a change in optical rotation on standing, indicating changes in the asymmetry of the sugar. Further evidence was the isolation of two crystalline isomers of both D and L forms of the sugars. When the two isomers of D-glucose were dissolved in water they were found to have different optical rotations:

$$\alpha\text{-D-glucose}, [\alpha]_D^{20} = +112.2, \beta\text{-D-glucose}, [\alpha]_D^{20} = +18.7.$$

When the aqueous solutions of either α- or β-forms were allowed to stand the specific rotations of each changed to a common rotation of $[\alpha]_D^{20} = +52.7$. Thus the β-form increased in positive rotation while the α-form decreased in positive rotation. It was established that the above forms were interconverted in aqueous solution to an equilibrium mixture represented by the final rotation. It should be noted that $[\alpha]_D^{20} = +52.7$ represents approximately 63%-β and 37%-α with probably minute amounts of free aldehyde form. The interconversion of α-form of any sugar to its β-form, or vice versa, is termed mutarotation. This phenomenon is catalyzed by the addition of dilute acid or alkali. An enzyme, mutarotase, present in extracts from the mold *Penicillium notatum* also catalyzes the mutarotation of glucose. This led to the representation of the sugars in the Fischer-Tollens cyclic formulas, which permitted an additional asymmetric carbon atom in the chain at the functional group. It should be noted, however, that the functional group still exists as a potential aldehyde or ketone group. Two isomeric D-glucoses are possible by this representation:

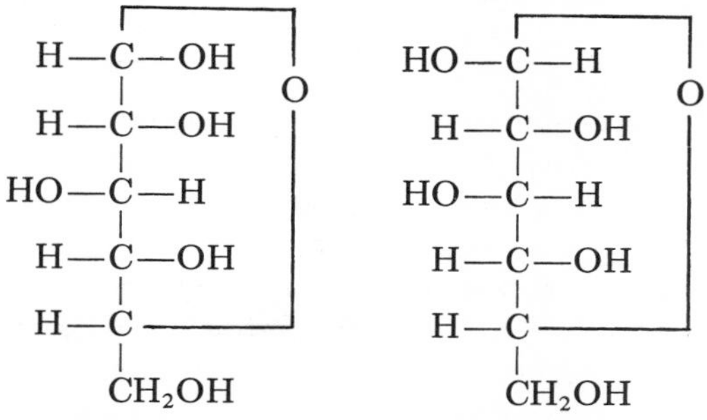

α-D-Glucose
$[\alpha]_D^{20} = +112.2$

β-D-Glucose
$[\alpha]_D^{20} = +18.7$

In depicting the structure of an α-isomer, we place the hydroxyl group of the hemiacetal carbon on the same side of the carbon chain as the hydroxyl group which determines whether the sugar is D or L. In practical terms, for sugars of the D-series, the hydroxyl group would be written to the right for the α-isomer. Similarly, the β-isomer would be shown with the hydroxyl group projecting to the left. The potential aldehyde or ketone carbon is called the anomeric carbon and α and β isomers thus are referred to as anomers.

The use of the cyclic formula introduced the question of ring size into the chemistry of the sugars. It is known that a cyclic hemiacetal can be formed which involves either carbon-4 or carbon-5. In the first case a ring is created consisting of four carbon atoms and one oxygen atom; this is called a furanose ring. In the second case, the resulting ring consists of 5 carbon atoms and 1 oxygen atom; this is a pyranose ring. These names were derived from the 5 and 6 membered cyclic ethers, furan and pyran. The pyranose form is the more stable of the two and is the one most frequently found in nature.

The cyclic Fischer formula, while useful to indicate differences in structure at the different asymmetric centers, does not properly represent the actual molecular configuration (bond angles and distances) of the sugars. For example, in D-glucose, carbons 1 and 5, which are involved in the oxygen bridge, must be close together for the existence of this bridge. In an attempt to illustrate better the structure and configuration of the sugar molecule, Haworth proposed a system of symmetric rings that avoids the impossible stretching of the electron pairs of the oxygen in the ring. The basic structures of the two forms are:

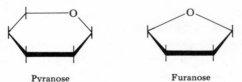

Pyranose   Furanose

In this system, the plane of the ring is conceived to be perpendicular to the plane of the page, and the attached groups lie either above or below the plane of the ring. The thin lines of the ring are conceived as being behind the plane of the page while the thick lines are in front of the plane of the page. We may apply certain rules to translate the Fischer projection to the Haworth form. The first rule is that any group to the right of the carbon chain is written below the plane of the ring; those to the left are written above the plane of the ring. For example:

α-D-Arabinose

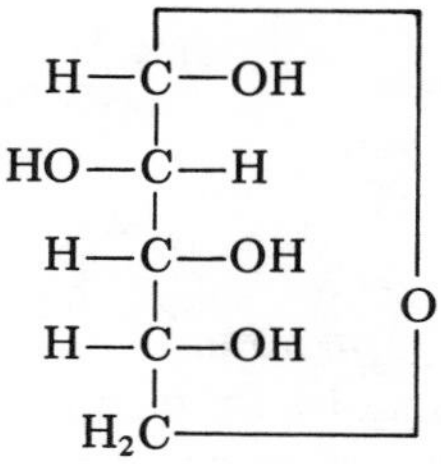

$$
\begin{array}{c}
\mathrm{H-C-OH} \\
\mathrm{HO-C-H} \\
\mathrm{H-C-OH} \\
\mathrm{H-C-OH} \\
\mathrm{H_2C}
\end{array}
\quad \text{becomes}
$$

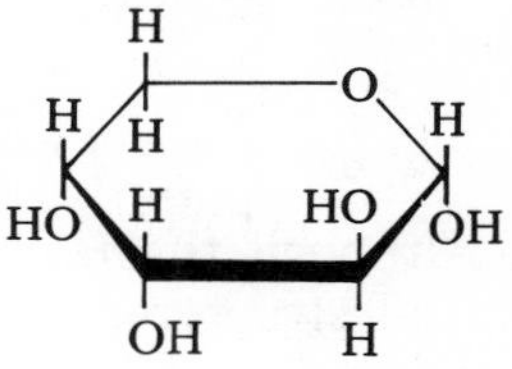

When there are more carbon atoms in the sugar than are involved in ring formation (e.g., hexose), it will be necessary to determine whether these atoms should be written above or below the plane of the ring. If the ring is to the right, the extra carbon will be up; conversely, if the ring is to the left, the extra carbon will be down (i.e., below the plane of the ring). For example:

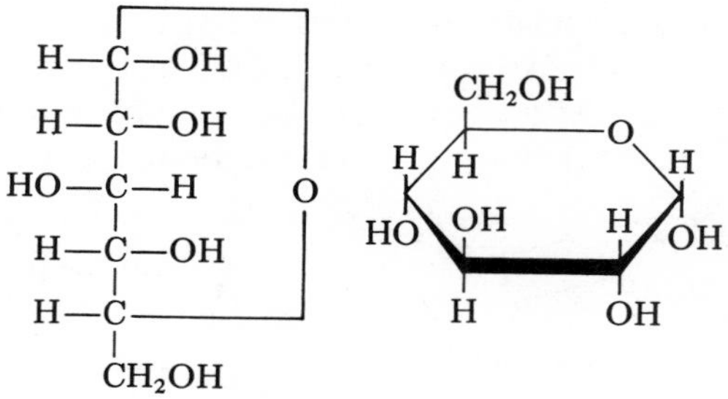

$$
\begin{array}{c}
\mathrm{H-C-OH} \\
\mathrm{H-C-OH} \\
\mathrm{HO-C-H} \\
\mathrm{H-C-OH} \\
\mathrm{H-C} \\
\mathrm{CH_2OH}
\end{array}
$$

α-D-Glucopyranose

$$
\begin{array}{c}
\mathrm{H-C-OH} \\
\mathrm{HO-C-H} \\
\mathrm{H-C-OH} \\
\mathrm{HO-C-H} \\
\mathrm{C-H} \\
\mathrm{CH_2OH}
\end{array}
$$

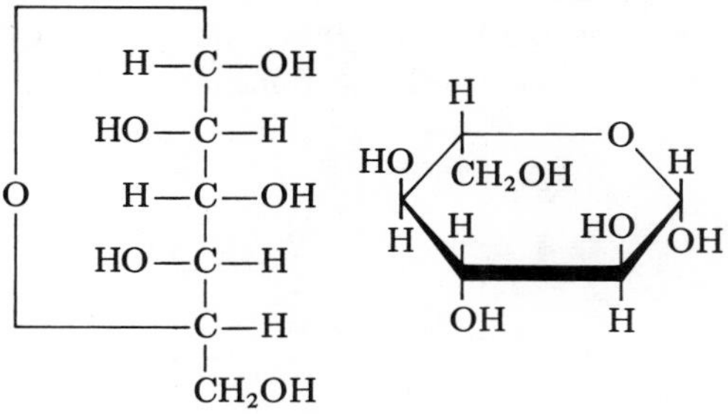

β-L-Glucopyranose

In the case of a ketohexose in the furanose form, the position of the 6-carbon will be determined as above; the 1-carbon will be up or down depending upon whether the sugar is in the α or β form:

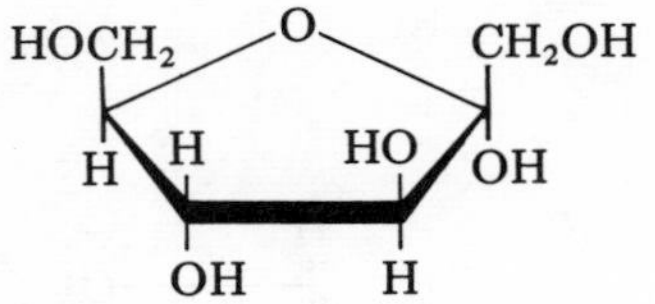

HOCH₂ — O — CH₂OH
H   H   HO   OH
      OH   H

α-D-Fructofuranose

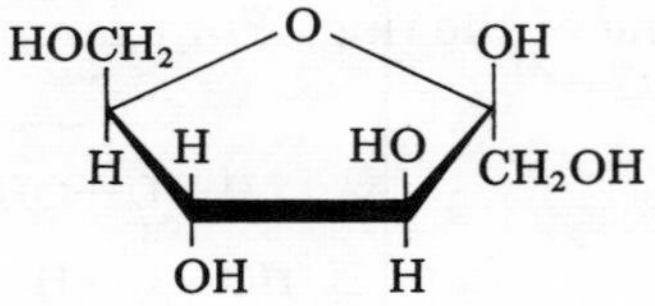

HOCH₂ — O — OH
H   H   HO   CH₂OH
      OH   H

β-D-Fructofuranose

Although the Haworth type of formula gives a better illustration of the structure of a sugar molecule than does the Fischer type formula, it does not reveal the true picture of the pyranose rings or furanose rings. The Haworth type formula is oversimplified in that it places all atoms in a single plane; whereas, the normal valence angle of the carbon atom prevents a stable planar arrangement for the atoms. Studies of molecular models have shown that the 5-membered furanose ring was strained and nonplanar while the 6-membered pyranose ring was strainless and existed in 2 different types of arrangements in space, the "chair" and "boat" forms. The chair form is the structure of lower energy and thus more stable. In contrast, the boat form is flexible and has an unlimited number of conformations. The pyranose ring can be compared to cyclohexane which can exist in both chair and boat forms.

chair form   boat form

Examination of structural models of cyclohexane reveals that hydrogen atoms are arranged on the ring in two different ways; those on C-H bonds parallel to an imaginary plane of the ring (equatorial); and those on C-H bonds perpendicular to this plane (axial). These relationships are shown in the following chair form of cyclohexane.

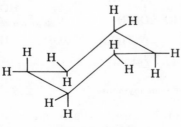

Cyclohexane

The conformational representation for α-D-glucopyranose according to this presentation would be:

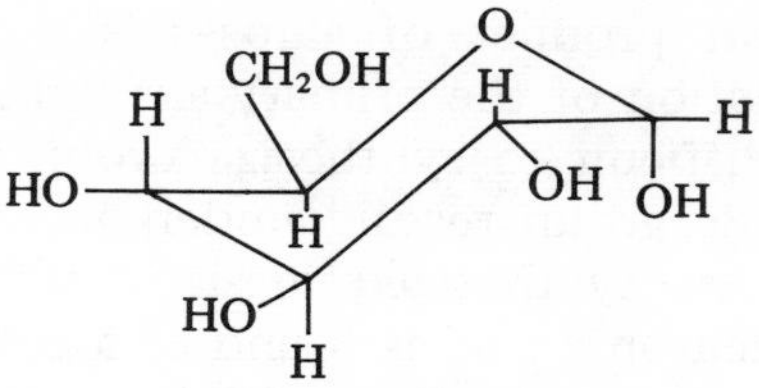

α-D-Glucopyranose

Reactions of Carbohydrates

Oxidation.—Since sugars contain alcohol groups, plus an aldehyde or a ketone group, it is evident that the oxidation of a sugar may, under various conditions, yield different products. Complete oxidation will yield CO_2 and H_2O.

The aldehyde group of an aldose may be oxidized to a carboxyl group with bromine water forming an aldonic acid.

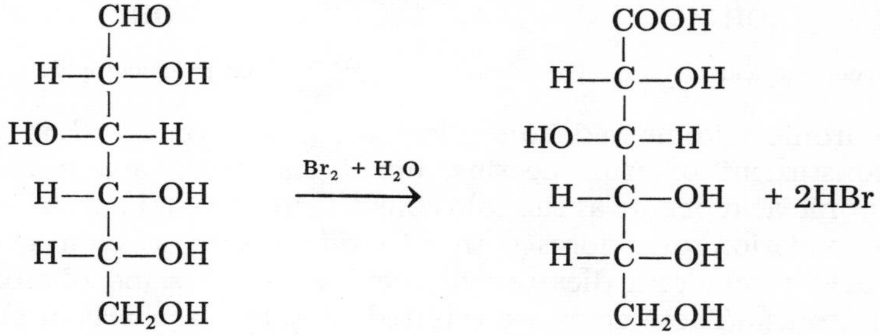

D-Glucose   D-Gluconic acid

The aldonic acids, when heated, readily lose water to form an equilibrium mixture of gamma (γ) and delta (δ) lactones:

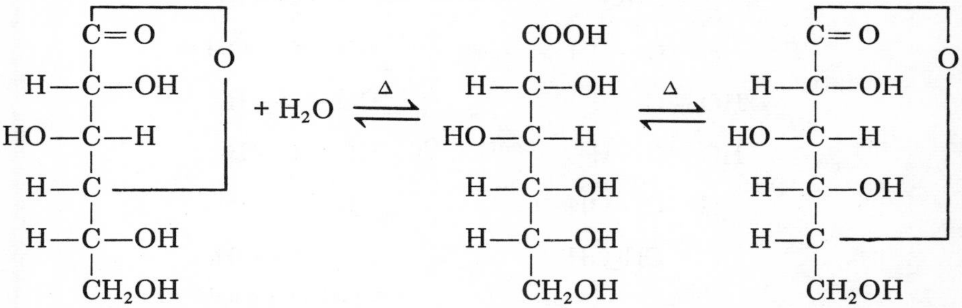

γ-Gluconolactone   D-Gluconic acid   δ-Gluconolactone

The aldonic acids are important as cation sequestering agents for the purpose of introducing metal ions into the body in a neutral and easily assimilable form. Calcium gluconate is valuable as a dietary supplement for the oral administration of calcium.

Another oxidation product of aldoses is a uronic acid. It is formed by the oxidation of the primary alcohol group to a carboxyl group. It is very difficult to synthesize uronic acids from aldoses because the aldehyde group readily undergoes oxidation. In contrast, uronic acids are synthesized in significant quantities by enzyme systems. Glucuronic acid is found as a constituent of certain polysaccharides (e.g., chondroitin sulfate). It occurs combined as monomethyl ethers in plant materials such as straws, saponins, and various woods. Its importance in the body arises out of the detoxication of substances such as phenol by the formation of glucuronides.

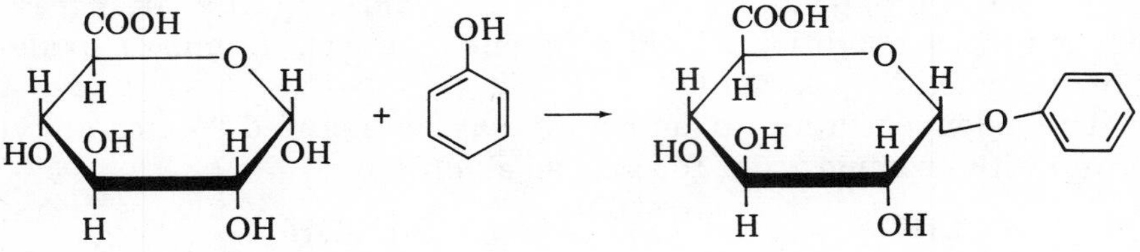

D-Glucuronic acid   Phenol   α-Phenylglucuronide

The uronic acid derived from galactose, galacturonic acid, is found as a constituent of fruit pectins, mucilages, and plant gums. D-mannuronic acid occurs as the sole constituent of alginic acid.

The oxidation of aldoses with an oxidant such as concentrated nitric acid produces a dicarboxylic acid with the same number of carbon atoms. These acids are referred to as the saccharic or aldaric acids. The latter reaction can be used to distinguish galactose from its isomers because mucic acid is insoluble in acidic solutions whereas the acids produced from the other hexoses are soluble.

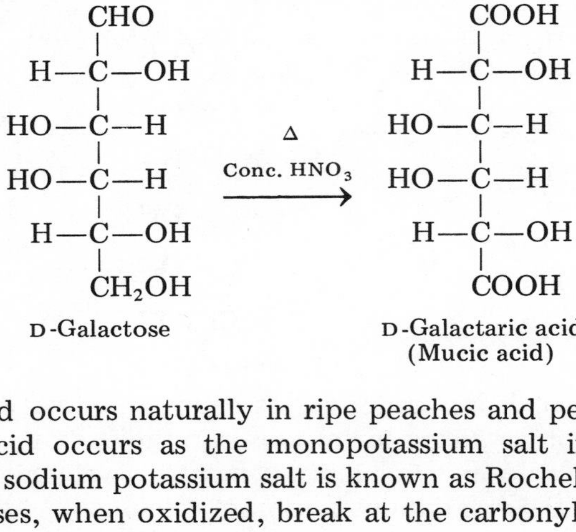

D-Galactose   D-Galactaric acid
                     (Mucic acid)

Mucic acid occurs naturally in ripe peaches and pears. Similarly, L-tartaric acid occurs as the monopotassium salt in the juice of grapes. The sodium potassium salt is known as Rochelle salt.

The ketoses, when oxidized, break at the carbonyl group to form two acids; fructose, for example, yields glycolic acid and trihydroxybutyric acid.

Reduction.—The reduction of the carbonyl group of a monosaccharide leads to the corresponding polyol. This may be accomplished by electrolysis of an acidified solution of the sugar or with sodium amalgam and water. The polyols formed from the hexoses are:

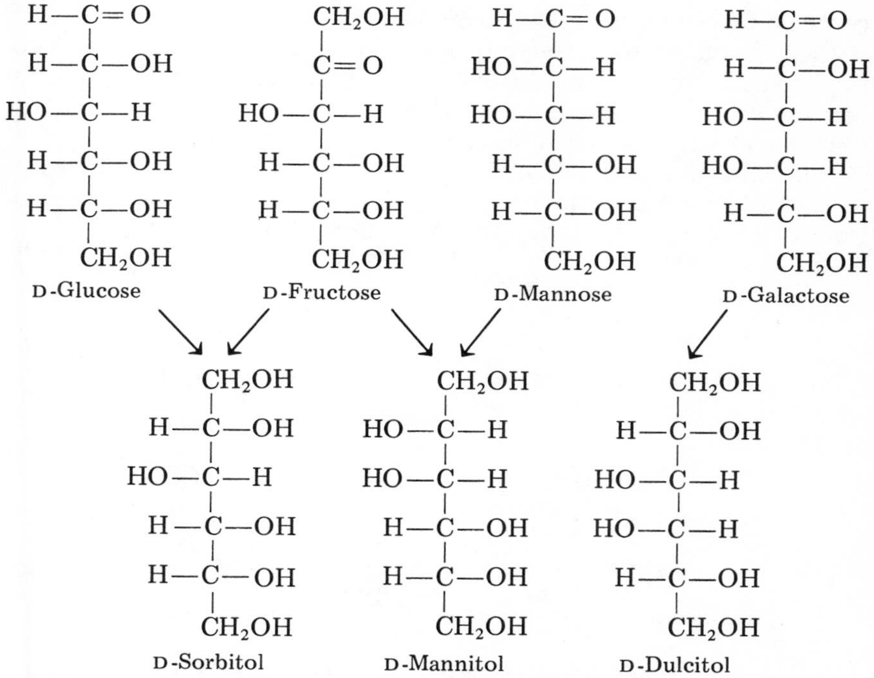

$$
\begin{array}{cccc}
\text{H—C=O} & \text{CH}_2\text{OH} & \text{H—C=O} & \text{H—C=O} \\
\text{H—C—OH} & \text{C=O} & \text{HO—C—H} & \text{H—C—OH} \\
\text{HO—C—H} & \text{HO—C—H} & \text{HO—C—H} & \text{HO—C—H} \\
\text{H—C—OH} & \text{H—C—OH} & \text{H—C—OH} & \text{HO—C—H} \\
\text{H—C—OH} & \text{H—C—OH} & \text{H—C—OH} & \text{H—C—OH} \\
\text{CH}_2\text{OH} & \text{CH}_2\text{OH} & \text{CH}_2\text{OH} & \text{CH}_2\text{OH} \\
\text{D-Glucose} & \text{D-Fructose} & \text{D-Mannose} & \text{D-Galactose}
\end{array}
$$

$$
\begin{array}{ccc}
\text{CH}_2\text{OH} & \text{CH}_2\text{OH} & \text{CH}_2\text{OH} \\
\text{H—C—OH} & \text{HO—C—H} & \text{H—C—OH} \\
\text{HO—C—H} & \text{HO—C—H} & \text{HO—C—H} \\
\text{H—C—OH} & \text{H—C—OH} & \text{HO—C—H} \\
\text{H—C—OH} & \text{H—C—OH} & \text{H—C—OH} \\
\text{CH}_2\text{OH} & \text{CH}_2\text{OH} & \text{CH}_2\text{OH} \\
\text{D-Sorbitol} & \text{D-Mannitol} & \text{D-Dulcitol}
\end{array}
$$

Fructose forms both sorbitol and mannitol because of the formation of an additional asymmetric carbon atom during the reduction process. Thus, sorbitol and mannitol are epimers; i.e., they are optical isomers having different configurations on the second carbon atom.

The polyols are crystalline solids, soluble in water and ranging in taste from faintly sweet to very sweet. Their distribution in nature is limited to plants and they occur in both free and combined form. Glycerol occurs in fats and other lipids. Erythritol occurs combined as esters in algae and grasses. Ribitol occurs universally in the form of its derivatives—riboflavin, flavin mononucleotide, and flavin adenine dinucleotide.

D-Sorbitol (glucitol) is one of the most widespread of the naturally occurring polyols. It is found in many fruits including apple, pear, cherry, plum, and peach. D-mannitol is widely distributed in plant tissues but rarely occurs in fruits. Dulcitol is found in Madagascar manna. Sorbitol and mannitol are prepared in large quantities and have widespread commercial applications. Sorbitol is used in the manufacture of sorbose, ascorbic acid, and detergents (Tweens and Spans). It is used as a humectant in foods and in candy manufacture. Medically, it is used as a diuretic, as a cathartic, and as a sugar substitute for diabetics. Mannitol is important as a pharmaceutical, especially the nitrate esters.

Closely related to the glycitols are the cyclic inositols. The most important compound of this group is myo-inositol, which is widely distributed in plants and animals. It often occurs as the hexaphosphoric acid ester (phytate) in seeds.

Condensation with Phenylhydrazine.—Aldoses and ketoses react with phenylhydrazine in two steps, the first step being a condensation with the carbonyl group to form a phenylhydrazone:

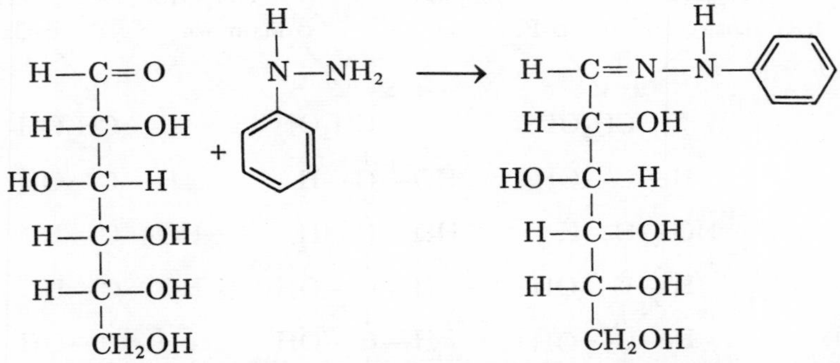

D-Glucose   Phenylhydrazine   D-Glucose phenylhydrazone

Heating with an excess of reagent rapidly converts the hydrazones into the yellow osazones:

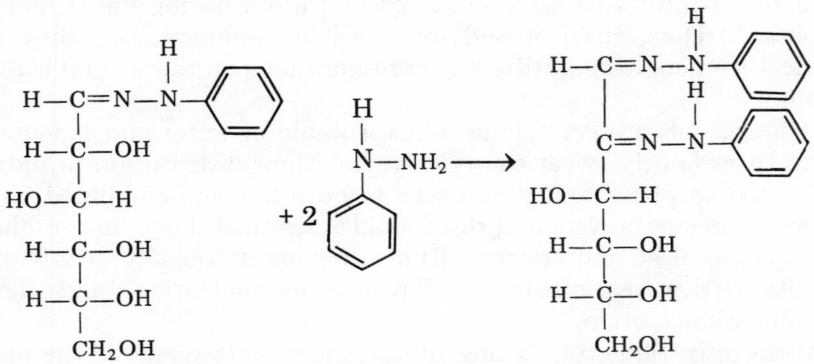

D-Glucose phenylhydrazone   Phenylhydrazine   D-Glucose phenylosazone

The conversion of an aldose to a ketose is a synthetic reaction of some importance. This conversion is effected by hydrolysis of the osazone to yield an osone with subsequent reduction of the aldehyde group to form a ketose. The conversion of D-glucose osazone to D-fructose is an example of this reaction.

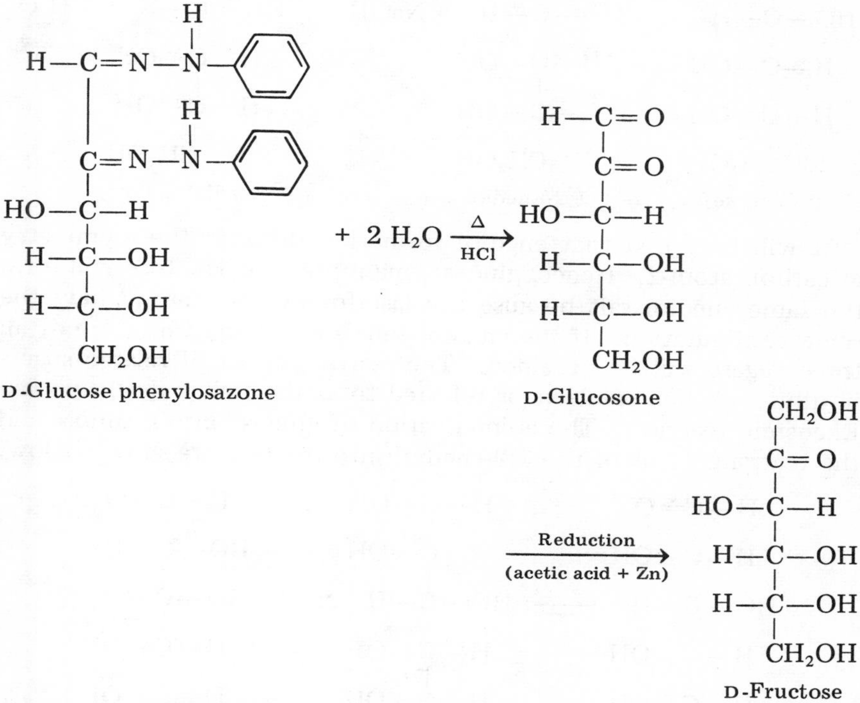

$$
\begin{array}{l}
\text{H}-\text{C}=\text{N}-\overset{\displaystyle \text{H}}{\underset{}{\text{N}}}-\bigcirc \\
\quad\ \ \ \overset{\displaystyle \text{H}}{\underset{}{\text{C}}}=\text{N}-\overset{\displaystyle \text{H}}{\underset{}{\text{N}}}-\bigcirc \\
\text{HO}-\text{C}-\text{H} \\
\text{H}-\text{C}-\text{OH} \\
\text{H}-\text{C}-\text{OH} \\
\quad\ \ \ \text{CH}_2\text{OH}
\end{array}
$$

D-Glucose phenylosazone

$+\ 2\ \text{H}_2\text{O} \xrightarrow[\text{HCl}]{\Delta}$

$$
\begin{array}{l}
\text{H}-\text{C}=\text{O} \\
\quad\ \ \ \text{C}=\text{O} \\
\text{HO}-\text{C}-\text{H} \\
\text{H}-\text{C}-\text{OH} \\
\text{H}-\text{C}-\text{OH} \\
\quad\ \ \ \text{CH}_2\text{OH}
\end{array}
$$

D-Glucosone

$\xrightarrow[\text{(acetic acid + Zn)}]{\text{Reduction}}$

$$
\begin{array}{l}
\text{CH}_2\text{OH} \\
\text{C}=\text{O} \\
\text{HO}-\text{C}-\text{H} \\
\text{H}-\text{C}-\text{OH} \\
\text{H}-\text{C}-\text{OH} \\
\text{CH}_2\text{OH}
\end{array}
$$

D-Fructose

In osazone formation only the first two carbon atoms of the sugar are involved. The osazones of D-glucose, D-mannose and D-fructose are identical; this indicates these sugars have the same arrangement on the last four carbon atoms. The osazone of D-galactose differs from that of the above three sugars.

If one substitutes methyl phenylhydrazine for phenylhydrazine in the preparation of osazones it will be observed that only ketoses will react. This reaction often serves to distinguish between an aldose and a ketose.

Action of Alkalies upon Sugars.—Three types of reactions can take place in alkaline solutions of sugars. They are: (a) isomerization, (b) cleavage into smaller fragments, and (c) internal oxidation-reduction and rearrangement.

(a) Reducing sugars tautomerize to form an enediol salt when allowed to stand for several hours in a dilute alkaline solution (0.05N).

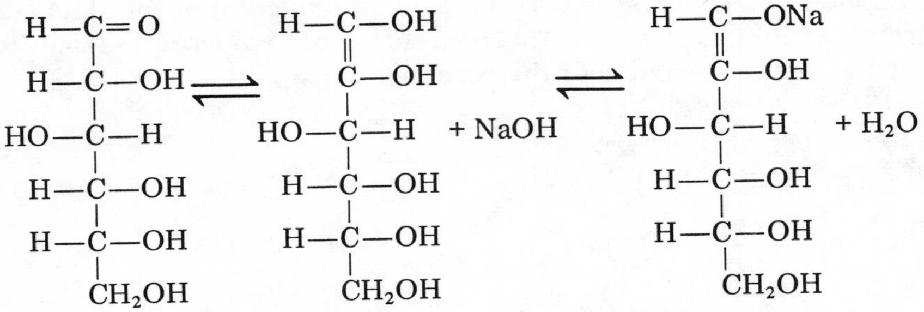

$$
\begin{array}{ccc}
\begin{array}{l}
\text{H—C}=\text{O} \\
\text{H—C—OH} \\
\text{HO—C—H} \\
\text{H—C—OH} \\
\text{H—C—OH} \\
\text{CH}_2\text{OH}
\end{array}
&
\begin{array}{l}
\text{H—C—OH} \\
\text{C—OH} \\
\text{HO—C—H} \quad +\text{NaOH} \\
\text{H—C—OH} \\
\text{H—C—OH} \\
\text{CH}_2\text{OH}
\end{array}
&
\begin{array}{l}
\text{H—C—ONa} \\
\text{C—OH} \\
\text{HO—C—H} \quad +\text{H}_2\text{O} \\
\text{H—C—OH} \\
\text{H—C—OH} \\
\text{CH}_2\text{OH}
\end{array} \\
\text{D-Glucose} & \text{1,2-Enediol} & \text{Enediol salt}
\end{array}
$$

It will be noted that enediol formation destroys the asymmetry at carbon atom-2. Hence, glucose, mannose, and fructose will form the same enediol salt because the last four carbon atoms have the same configuration. If the enediol salt is acidified, a mixture of all three sugars will be obtained. The rearrangement of related sugars in dilute alkaline solutions is referred to as the Lobry de Bruyn-van Ekenstein reaction. The epimerization of glucose into mannose and the rearrangement of the 1,2-enediol into fructose are shown below:

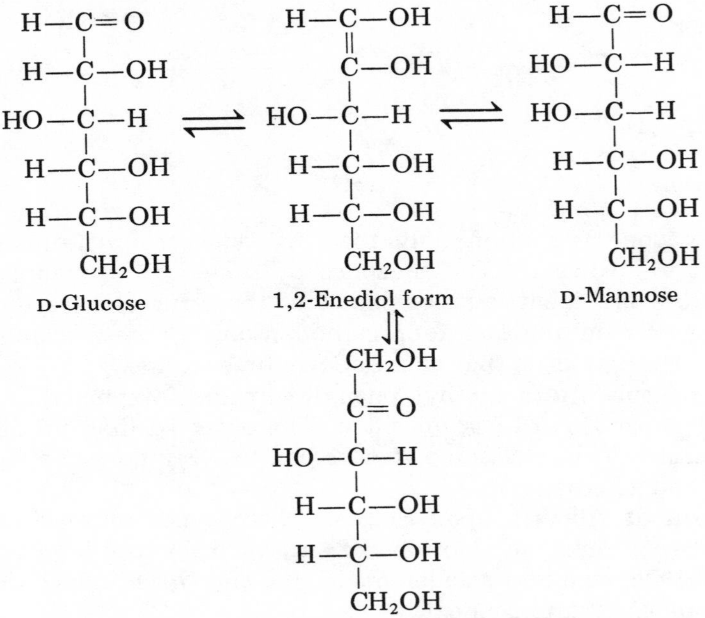

$$
\begin{array}{ccc}
\begin{array}{l}
\text{H—C}=\text{O} \\
\text{H—C—OH} \\
\text{HO—C—H} \\
\text{H—C—OH} \\
\text{H—C—OH} \\
\text{CH}_2\text{OH}
\end{array}
&
\begin{array}{l}
\text{H—C—OH} \\
\text{C—OH} \\
\text{HO—C—H} \\
\text{H—C—OH} \\
\text{H—C—OH} \\
\text{CH}_2\text{OH}
\end{array}
&
\begin{array}{l}
\text{H—C}=\text{O} \\
\text{HO—C—H} \\
\text{HO—C—H} \\
\text{H—C—OH} \\
\text{H—C—OH} \\
\text{CH}_2\text{OH}
\end{array} \\
\text{D-Glucose} & \text{1,2-Enediol form} & \text{D-Mannose}
\end{array}
$$

$$
\begin{array}{l}
\text{CH}_2\text{OH} \\
\text{C}=\text{O} \\
\text{HO—C—H} \\
\text{H—C—OH} \\
\text{H—C—OH} \\
\text{CH}_2\text{OH}
\end{array}
$$

D- Fructose

The rearrangement of a sugar into several other products is of little practical value but it indicates the detrimental effect of an alkali on a sugar. However, the isomerization of glucose ⇌ fructose and mannose ⇌ fructose are important enzymatic reactions in the intermediary metabolism of sugars.

(b) When reducing sugars are treated with a stronger alkali ($0.5N$ and stronger), additional isomerization occurs by a continuation of the enolization process along the carbon chain. The probable process is as follows:

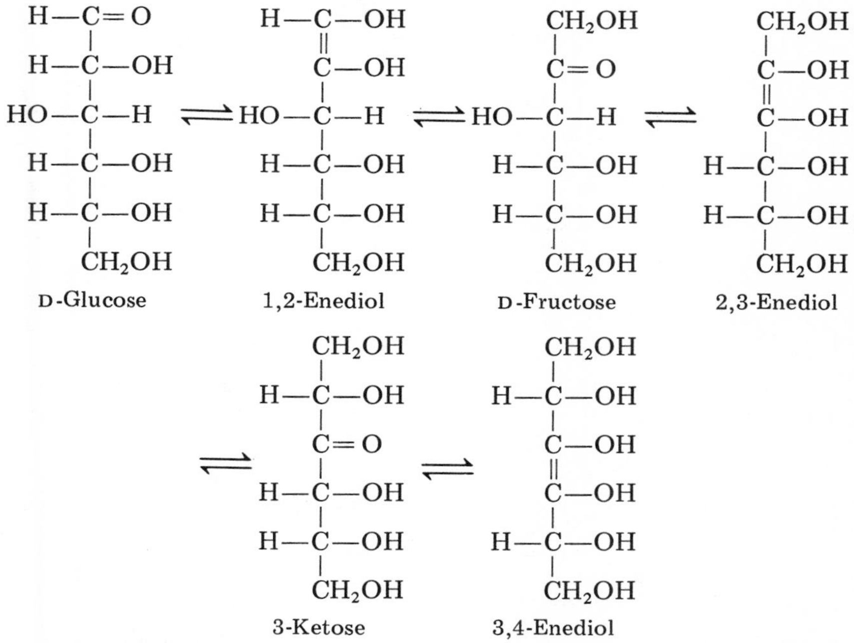

$$
\begin{array}{ccccc}
\text{H—C=O} & \text{H—C—OH} & \text{CH}_2\text{OH} & \text{CH}_2\text{OH} \\
\text{H—C—OH} & \text{C—OH} & \text{C=O} & \text{C—OH} \\
\text{HO—C—H} \rightleftharpoons & \text{HO—C—H} \rightleftharpoons & \text{HO—C—H} \rightleftharpoons & \text{C—OH} \\
\text{H—C—OH} & \text{H—C—OH} & \text{H—C—OH} & \text{H—C—OH} \\
\text{H—C—OH} & \text{H—C—OH} & \text{H—C—OH} & \text{H—C—OH} \\
\text{CH}_2\text{OH} & \text{CH}_2\text{OH} & \text{CH}_2\text{OH} & \text{CH}_2\text{OH} \\
\text{D-Glucose} & \text{1,2-Enediol} & \text{D-Fructose} & \text{2,3-Enediol}
\end{array}
$$

$$
\begin{array}{cc}
\text{CH}_2\text{OH} & \text{CH}_2\text{OH} \\
\text{H—C—OH} & \text{H—C—OH} \\
\rightleftharpoons \quad \text{C=O} \quad \rightleftharpoons & \text{C—OH} \\
\text{H—C—OH} & \text{C—OH} \\
\text{H—C—OH} & \text{H—C—OH} \\
\text{CH}_2\text{OH} & \text{CH}_2\text{OH} \\
\text{3-Ketose} & \text{3,4-Enediol}
\end{array}
$$

The enediols break at the double bonds to give a complex mixture of products. For example, cleavage between C-1 and C-2 gives rise to formaldehyde and a pentose; cleavage between C-2 and C-3 gives rise to glycolic aldehyde and a tetrose; cleavage between C-3 and C-4 forms glyceric aldehyde. The aldoses, formed as a result of cleavage of the enediol, may also undergo enolization and rearrangement to form a complex mixture of products. The effective reducing power of a sugar is thereby increased many times and it is this knowledge that permits one to increase the speed of reaction with cations such as Cu^{2+} and Bi^{2+} (solutions used for reducing sugars).

(c) In addition to epimerization and cleavage into units with a smaller number of carbon atoms, sugars are converted in a strongly alkaline solution in the absence of an oxidizing agent into carboxylic acids which in their total composition do not differ from the original sugar. This is due to intramolecular oxidation and rearrangement. The resulting acids are referred to as saccharinic acids and several types are possible.

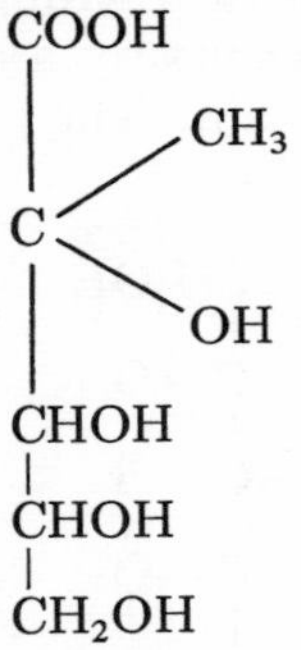

$$
\begin{array}{cc}
\text{COOH} & \text{COOH} \\
| & | \\
\text{C}\diagup^{\text{CH}_3}_{\diagdown\text{OH}} & \text{C}\diagup^{\text{CH}_2\text{OH}}_{\diagdown\text{OH}} \\
| & | \\
\text{CHOH} & \text{CH}_2 \\
| & | \\
\text{CHOH} & \text{CHOH} \\
| & | \\
\text{CH}_2\text{OH} & \text{CH}_2\text{OH} \\
\text{Saccharinic acid} & \textit{iso}\text{-Saccharinic acid}
\end{array}
$$

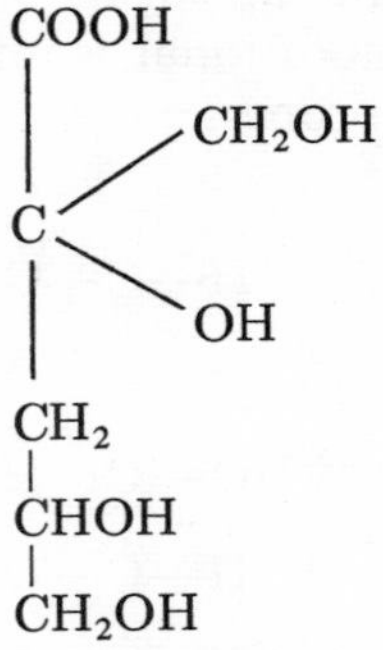

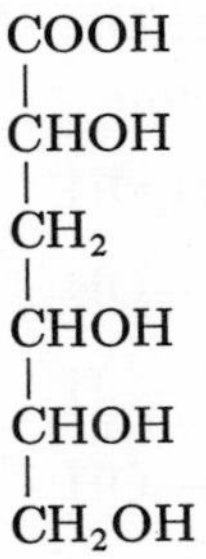

$$
\begin{array}{cc}
\text{COOH} & \text{CH}_2\text{OH} \\
| & | \\
\text{CHOH} & \text{CH}_2 \\
| & | \\
\text{CH}_2 & \text{C}\diagup^{\text{COOH}}_{\diagdown\text{OH}} \\
| & | \\
\text{CHOH} & \text{CHOH} \\
| & | \\
\text{CHOH} & \text{CH}_2\text{OH} \\
| & \\
\text{CH}_2\text{OH} & \\
\textit{meta}\text{-Saccharinic acid} & \textit{para}\text{-Saccharinic acid}
\end{array}
$$

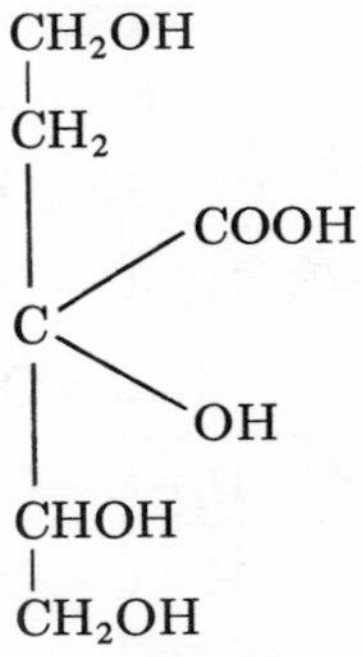

Carbohydrates which do not contain a free carbonyl group are not enolized by alkali and are relatively stable in alkaline solutions.

Reducing Action of Sugars in Alkaline Solution.—All sugars which contain a free aldehyde or ketone group may be classified as reducing sugars. It will be recalled that reducing sugars enolize in alkaline solutions, the enediol forms of sugars are highly reactive, and they are easily oxidized by oxygen or other oxidizing agents. Thus, sugars in alkaline solution readily reduce oxidizing ions such as Ag^+, Hg^{2+}, Cu^{2+}, and $Fe(CN)_6^{3-}$ and the sugars are oxidized to complex mixtures of acids. This reducing action of sugars is utilized for both their qualitative and quantitative determination.

Copper II (Cu^{2+}) is the most common ion used in sugar analysis. It is used in combination with sodium citrate or sodium potassium tartrate and sodium hydroxide, potassium hydroxide, or sodium carbonate. The citrate or tartrate prevents precipitation of cupric hydroxide by forming soluble, slightly dissociated complexes with the copper ion. However, the copper complex dissociates adequately to provide a continuous supply of cupric ions for oxidation.

The alkali in the reagents enolizes the sugars and thereby causes them to break into a number or reactive fragments. For example, it is believed several reactive fragments are produced when glucose is heated with Fehling's solution:

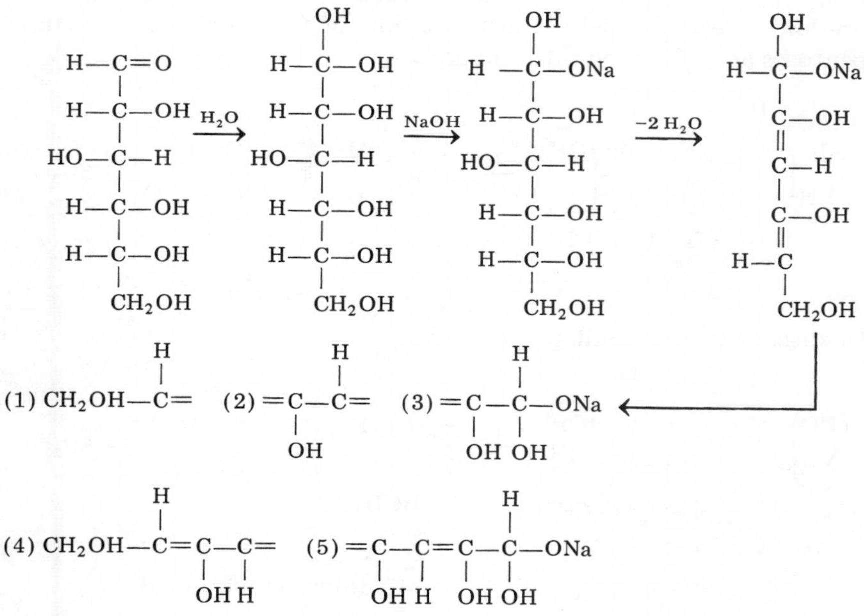

$$
\begin{array}{ccccc}
& & \overset{\displaystyle OH}{|} & \overset{\displaystyle OH}{|} & \overset{\displaystyle OH}{|} \\
H-C=O & H-C-OH & H-C-OH & H-C-ONa & H-C-ONa \\
| & | & | & | \\
H-C-OH & \xrightarrow{H_2O} & H-C-OH & \xrightarrow{NaOH} & H-C-OH & \xrightarrow{-2H_2O} & C-OH \\
| & | & | & || \\
HO-C-H & HO-C-H & HO-C-H & C-H \\
| & | & | & | \\
H-C-OH & H-C-OH & H-C-OH & C-OH \\
| & | & | & || \\
H-C-OH & H-C-OH & H-C-OH & H-C \\
| & | & | & | \\
CH_2OH & CH_2OH & CH_2OH & CH_2OH
\end{array}
$$

$$
(1)\ CH_2OH-\overset{\displaystyle H}{\underset{}{C}}= \qquad (2)\ =\overset{\displaystyle H}{\underset{\displaystyle OH}{C}}-C= \qquad (3)\ =\overset{\displaystyle H}{\underset{\displaystyle OH}{C}}-\underset{\displaystyle OH}{C}-ONa \longleftarrow
$$

$$
(4)\ CH_2OH-\overset{\displaystyle H}{\underset{\displaystyle OH}{C}}=\underset{\displaystyle H}{C}-C= \qquad (5)\ =\overset{\displaystyle H}{\underset{\displaystyle OH}{C}}-\underset{\displaystyle H}{C}=C-\underset{\displaystyle OH}{\overset{}{C}}-ONa
$$

These fragments are readily oxidized and the copper II (Cu^{2+}) ion is reduced to the copper I (Cu^+) ion. The course of the reaction, which is very complex, may be shown schematically:

Sugar + alkali $\longrightarrow$ reducing sugar fragments
                                    +
$$Cu(OH)_2 \longleftarrow \text{copper complex of tartrate or citrate}$$
$$\downarrow$$
$$H_2O + Cu_2O \xleftarrow{\Delta} CuOH \xleftarrow{OH^-} Cu^+ + \text{mixture of sugar acids}$$

As the copper II ions (Cu^{2+}) are reduced by the sugar fragments, the copper (I) ions combine with hydroxyl ions to form yellow copper (I) hydroxide. The reduced copper (I) hydroxide loses water in the presence of heat to give insoluble Cu_2O. The determination of the reduced copper may be accomplished by gravimetric, volumetric, colorimetric, or electrolytic methods.

Alkaline solutions of potassium ferricyanide are also used in the quantitative determination of reducing sugars. The reduced ferricyanide may be precipitated as the zinc salt and the excess ferricyanide determined iodometrically.

Action of Acids.—Dilute solutions of inorganic acids have relatively little effect on the structure of monosaccharides. However, when a monosaccharide is heated in a strongly acid solution, dehydration takes place with the formation of furan derivatives. Aldopentoses are converted into furfural:

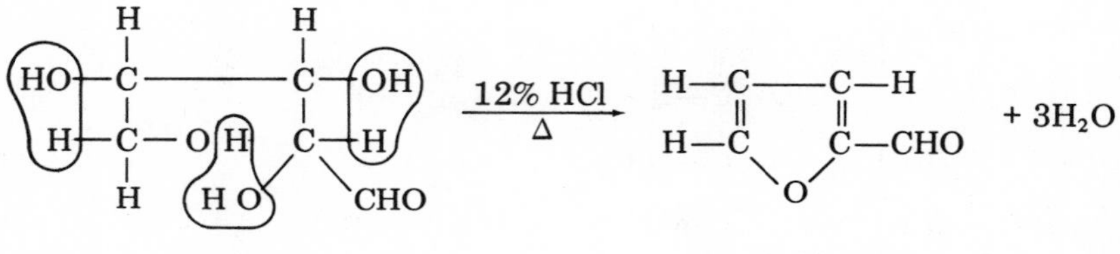

Pentose   Furfural

Hexoses react in a similar way:

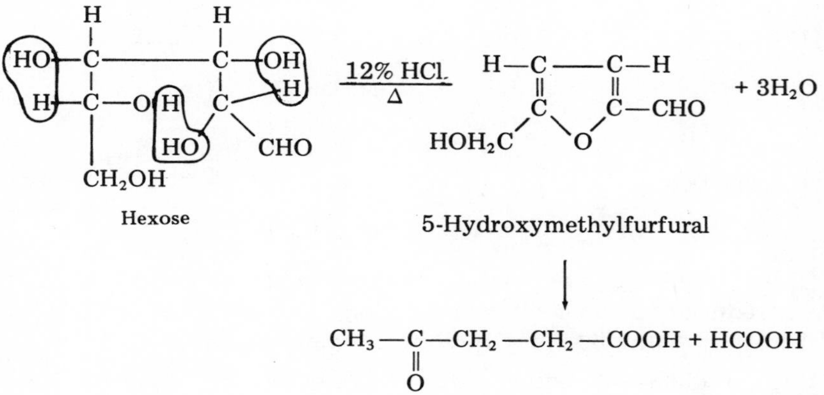

Hexose   5-Hydroxymethylfurfural

$$CH_3-\underset{\underset{O}{\|}}{C}-CH_2-CH_2-COOH + HCOOH$$

Levulinic acid   Formic acid

5-Hydroxymethylfurfural is not the final product of hexoses; it is further degraded with the formation of levulinic acid and formic acid. Ketohexoses react with acids more rapidly than the aldohexoses. The furfurals readily undergo further reactions with the formation of brown colors (humins). It is probable that many of the brown colors produced in food processing result from the intermediary formation of furfurals.

Polysaccharides and compound carbohydrates are generally hydrolyzed to monosaccharides by boiling with dilute (0.5–1.0 N) mineral acids.

Reactions of Sugars Due to Hydroxyl Groups

Most of the reactions of sugars previously discussed were concerned directly or indirectly with the carbonyl groups though a few reactions involving hydroxyl groups were considered. However, the dominant functional group of carbohydrates is the hydroxyl group, particularly if the hemiacetal group is included.

Formation of Glycosides.—One of the most common reactions of hydroxyl groups is that of glycoside formation. This is generally accomplished by treating the sugar with the appropriate alcohol and an acid catalyst.

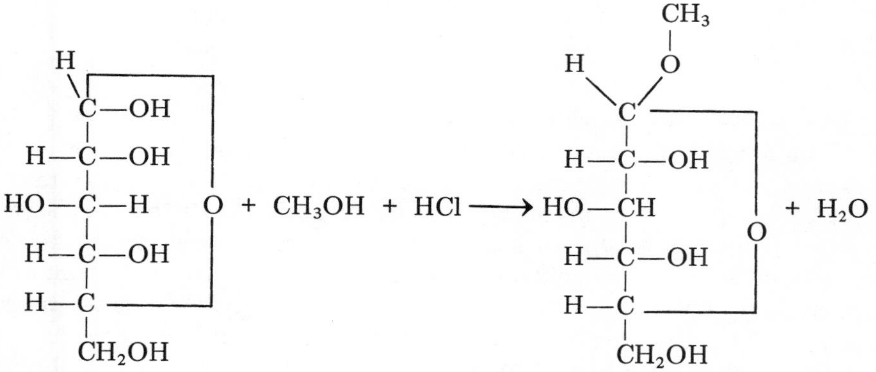

α-D-Glucose   α-Methyl-D-Glucoside

Both α and β anomers of methylglucoside are formed since both α and β forms exist in the original glucose. A general term for this type of compound is glycoside, and it may be defined as a derivative of a sugar in which the hydrogen atom of the potential aldehyde or ketone (hemiacetal) is replaced by an organic group to form an acetal. The glycoside, or acetal, bond is the basic linkage through which all oliogo- and polysaccharides are formed.

Aqueous solutions of glycosides are stable, exhibit mutarotation, and are nonreducing. The glycoside bond is not hydrolyzed by dilute alkali solutions, but is readily cleaved in acid solutions.

Formation of Esters.—The sugar esters have special significance because sugars are metabolized almost exclusively as the phosphorylated sugar. Although the sugar phosphate ester can be synthesized *in vitro*, the biochemical origin of the sugar phosphate esters is via enzymatic synthesis, e.g.

$$\alpha\text{-D-Glucose} + \text{ATP} \xrightarrow{\text{hexokinase}} \alpha\text{-D-Glucose-6-phosphate}$$

$$\text{Starch} + \text{Pi} \xrightarrow{\text{phosphorylase}} \alpha\text{-D-Glucose-1-phosphate}$$

Different phosphates of the same sugar (e.g. glucose-1-phosphate and glucose-6-phosphate; see formulas) behave differently in biochemical reactions.

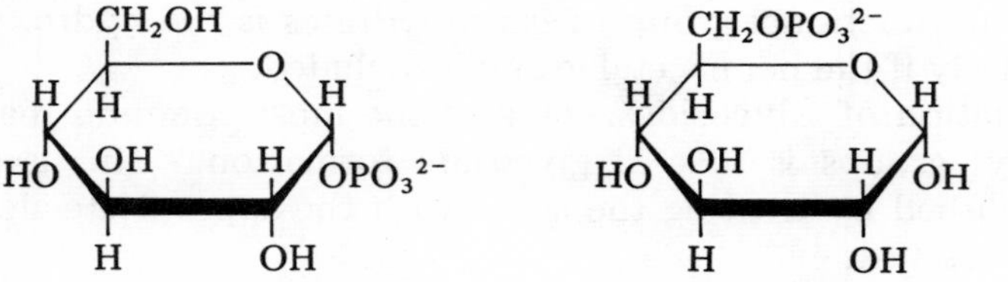

Glucose-l-phosphate

(Cori ester)

Glucose-6-phosphate

(Robison ester)

Color Reactions of Carbohydrates

The action of mineral acids on sugars leads to the formation of a number of volatile products such as furfural and 5-hydroxymethylfurfural. As noted in a previous discussion, the furan derivative depends upon the type of sugar used. The decomposition products (levulinic acid, formic acid, and furfural) will condense with aromatic phenols or amines to form colored substances. This fact is the basis of several qualitative and quantitative determinations for sugars.

Color reactions of this type include the Molisch test with alcoholic α-naphthol and concentrated sulfuric acid and the anthrone reaction (anthrone + sulfuric acid). The latter type of reaction can be used for the quantitative determination of sugars. The ketoses and pentoses usually form colored products under conditions milder than those required for aldohexoses. The Seliwanoff reaction (resorcinol + HCl) permits one to distinguish ketoses from aldoses. The Bial test (orcinol + HCl) and the Tollens phloroglucinol reaction can be used to distinguish pentoses from hexoses.

All mono- and some oligosaccharides are reducing sugars. Although the tests for reducing sugars are nonspecific, they are used frequently to detect and determine sugars. The reduction of Cu(II) ions in alkaline solution is the basis of Benedict's and Fehling's solutions.

Individual Sugars

Pentoses.—Pentoses occur only in limited amounts as free monosaccharides but they are widely distributed as component units of complex polysaccharides. These complex substances are known as pentosans and on hydrolysis will yield pentose sugars.

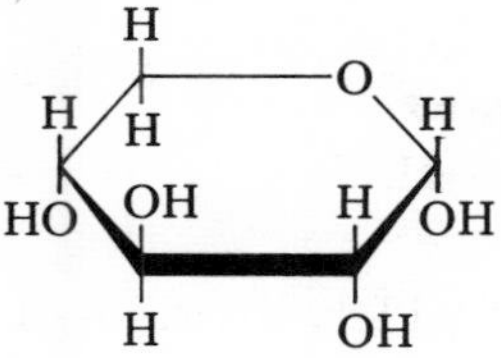

α-D-Xylopyranose 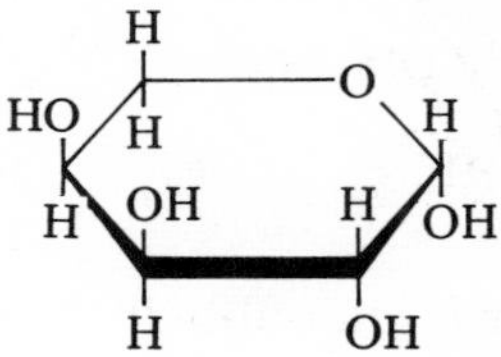   β-L-Arabinopyranose 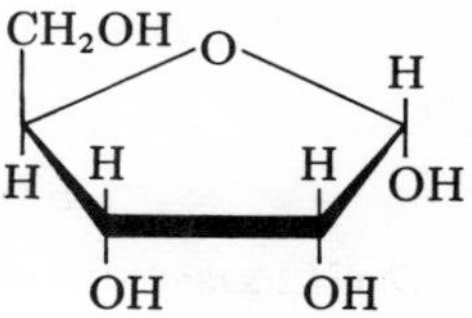   α-D-Ribofuranose

These sugars are not fermented by yeasts and they are utilized only to a limited extent by most mammals. Therefore, they are of little value as a source of energy in humans.

D-*Xylose (Wood Sugar)*.—This sugar is found as a pentosan (xylan) in corn cobs, straw, bran, wood gum, and the bran of seeds. The sugar can be obtained from any of the above materials by dilute acid hydrolysis. Xylose has been identified in fruits such as cherry, peach, pear, and plum. Industrially, waste materials such as corn cobs are converted into furfural through dehydration with concentrated sulfuric acid.

L-*Arabinose (Pectin Sugar)*.—This pentose occurs as a component of many gums, pectins, mucilages, and hemicelluloses. It is obtained principally by hydrolysis of gum arabic, cherry gum, mesquite gum, or beet pulp with dilute sulfuric acid. L-Arabinose has been identified in a number of fruits including apple, fig, grapefruit, lime, and some varieties of grape.

D-*Ribose*.—Ribose occurs as a component of nucleic acids and the nucleotide coenzymes. D-Ribose is an important pentose sugar because it is a part of riboflavin, vitamin B_2. A very important derivative of ribose is 2-deoxyribose, which is a part of deoxyribonucleic acid (DNA).

Hexoses.—These monosaccharides occur naturally in many types of plant materials and one of them, glucose, is the circulating sugar of both plants and animals. At least four hexose sugars merit consideration, i.e., glucose, fructose, galactose, and mannose. The cyclic formulas are shown below:

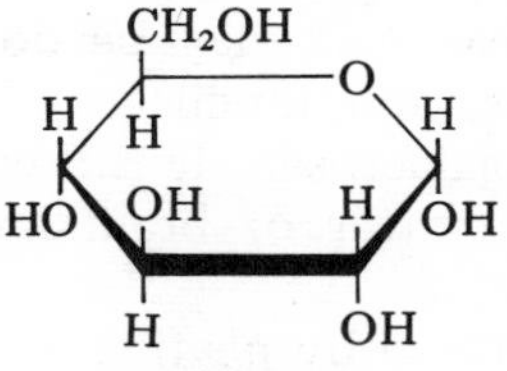

α-D-Glucose 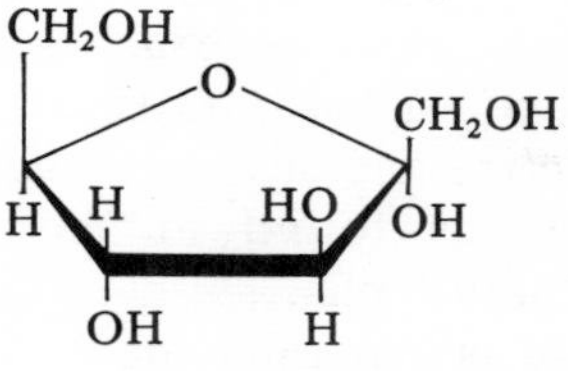   α-D-Fructose

$$CH_2OH$$

α-D-Galactose

$$CH_2OH$$

α-D-Mannose

D-Glucose.—This sugar is undoubtedly the most widely distributed sugar in nature because of its role in biochemical processes.

In the free state, it occurs in ripe fruits, flowers, leaves, roots, and the sap of plants. It is the principal sugar in the blood of most animals. In the combined state, it forms a part of or the whole of a number of oligosaccharides and polysaccharides (e.g., maltose, sucrose, lactose, raffinose, dextrins, starch, cellulose, and glycogen). Glucose also occurs in the combined form as glucosides such as salicin and arbutin.

D-Glucose is commonly prepared by the hydrolysis of starch. Crude dextrose, refined dextrose (Cerelose), and corn syrup are commercial glucose products. They may contain other carbohydrates as impurities, e.g., corn syrup contains, in addition to glucose, considerable oligosaccharides including maltose.

D-Fructose (Levulose).—Fructose is a ketose which is present in syrups, honey, molasses, and ripe fruits. It also occurs in small amounts in blood. Fructose is obtained from the hydrolysis of the polysaccharide inulin. It is the only ketose sugar of importance in foods.

In most fruits the glucose concentration exceeds that of fructose, but in apples and pears the fructose concentration may exceed the glucose concentration whereas in oranges, grapes, and strawberries there are equal amounts of both sugars.

Fructose exists in two structural forms, depending upon whether it is in the free state or combined. In the free state it exists principally as a pyranose structure, while in the combined form (e.g., sucrose, inulin, and several phosphate esters) it exists as a furanose.

D-Galactose.—Galactose occurs most frequently as a constituent of oligosaccharides and polysaccharides rather than as a monosaccharide. Galactose has been reported to be present in grapes, olives, and possibly in peaches and pears. It may be obtained by hydrolysis of lactose, raffinose, gums, and mucilages. Legumes, impure pectin, and agar also contain galactose. It is a constituent of galactolipids found in the white matter of brain and myelin sheaths of nerve cells.

Galactose is generally made from lactose by heating with 2% sulfuric acid. α-D-Galactose is the stable isomer obtained under most conditions whereas the β-form may be obtained by crystallization from cold alcoholic solution.

D-Mannose.—Mannose has been detected in oranges, olives, germinating seeds, and sugar cane molasses. It is more widely distributed in the polymeric form, as mannosans. Polysaccharides containing mannose are found in yeast and other microorganisms. In animals, mannose is a component of glycolipids, glycoproteins, and serum albumin.

Mannitol, the alcohol derived from mannose, is widely distributed in nature. It has been identified in the green bean, cauliflower, onion, pineapple, and in the bark and leaves of many trees.

Sugar Derivatives of Biological Importance

Amino Sugars.—The amino sugars are formed by the substitution of an amino group for hydroxyl group, usually the C-2 carbon. Two amino sugars occur frequently in organisms: 2-amino-2-deoxy-D-glucosamine and 2-amino-2-deoxy-D-galactosamine or their *N*-acetyl derivatives.

Glucosamine.—This amino sugar occurs in mucoproteins and mucopolysaccharides. It is the chief component of fungi cell walls and the shells of insects and crustaceans (lobster, crabs, etc.).

Galactosamine.—This amino sugar occurs as a constituent of the mucopolysaccharide, chondroitin sulfate.

Sialic Acids.—These compounds are naturally occurring amino-sugar derivatives consisting of a six-carbon amino sugar linked to pyruvic acid or lactic acid. Two of the more common of these are *N*-acetylneuraminic acid and *N*-acetylmuramic acid.

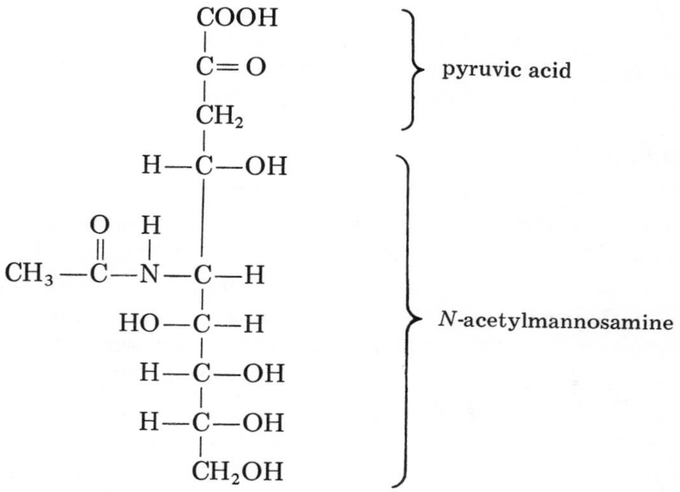

$$
\begin{array}{l}
COOH \\
| \\
C=O \\
| \\
CH_2
\end{array} \left.\rule{0pt}{3.5em}\right\} \text{pyruvic acid}
$$

$$
\begin{array}{l}
H-C-OH \\
\quad\quad | \\
CH_3-C-N-C-H \\
\quad\quad HO-C-H \\
\quad\quad H-C-OH \\
\quad\quad H-C-OH \\
\quad\quad CH_2OH
\end{array} \left.\rule{0pt}{6em}\right\} \text{\textit{N}-acetylmannosamine}
$$

N-acetylneuraminic acid

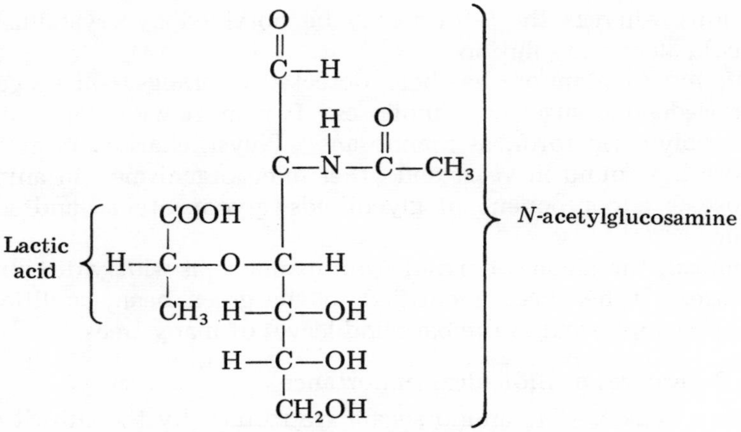

$$
\begin{array}{c}
O \\
\parallel \\
C-H \\
| \\
H \quad O \\
| \quad \parallel \\
C-N-C-CH_3 \\
\end{array}
$$

COOH

H—C—O—C—H *Lactic acid* { }

CH₃ H—C—OH

H—C—OH

CH₂OH

N-acetylglucosamine

N-acetylmuramic acid

These acids are important constituents of structural polysaccharides of cell walls and membranes.

Deoxy Sugars.—Deoxy sugars are most important in biochemical processes due to their incorporation into deoxyribonucleic acids. 2-Deoxy-D-ribose is the outstanding deoxy sugar of this group.

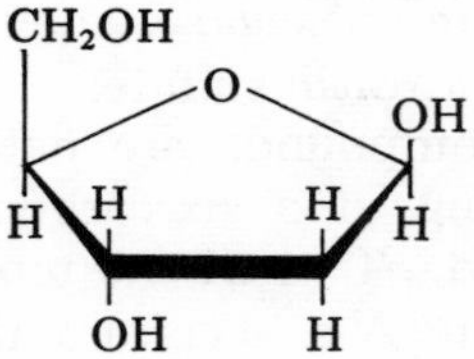

CH₂OH

O   OH

H H   H H

OH   H

β-2-Deoxy-D-ribose

Other deoxy sugars include L-rhamnose and L-fucose which are important constituents of bacterial cell walls.

Disaccharides

The disaccharides are formed by linking two monosaccharides via a glycosidic bond. Hydrolytic cleavage of the disaccharides may be brought about by acids or by enzymes which act specifically on each sugar. Disaccharides are important as food components. Sucrose, maltose, and lactose are the most important disaccharides.

Sucrose.—This disaccharide is known under various names such as saccharose, cane sugar, beet sugar, or simply sugar. It is the most widely distributed of all sugars, ranging in amounts from 0.1 to 25% of the fresh material. Ripe fruits are especially rich in sucrose. It is obtained commercially from sugar cane and sugar beets. The sugar of commerce, granulated sugar, is available as a relatively pure food product.

Sucrose upon mild hydrolysis (inversion) yields an equimolar mixture of glucose and fructose. The hydrolysis reaction is catalyzed by enzymes (invertases) and dilute acids. Sucrose is dextrorotatory (+66.5 degrees) whereas invert sugar is levorotatory (-19.8 degrees), hence the term inversion for the hydrolysis reaction and invert sugar for the product obtained. Since fructose is sweeter than sucrose, invert sugar is commonly used in candies and similar food products. Invert sugar is the principal component of honey.

Sucrose is a nonreducing sugar, as can be seen from the formula below, because the anomeric carbonyl groups of both glucose and fructose are used in the formation of a glycosidic linkage. Sucrose does not exhibit mutarotation and is unaffected by boiling sodium hydroxide. Sucrose loses water when heated to 210°C and forms a brown syrup known as caramel. It is readily fermented by yeast.

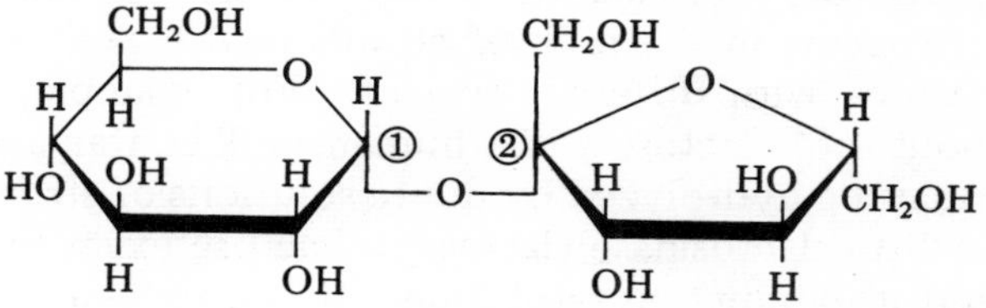

Sucrose (α-D-glucopyranosyl-(1 → 2)-β-D-fructofuranoside)

Maltose.—Maltose derived its name from the fact that it occurred in the extracts from sprouted barley or other cereals (malt liquors). Maltose is composed of two glucose units and is formed when the enzyme amylase hydrolyzes starch. The enzyme maltase, which is specific for the α-linkage, splits maltose into two glucose units. Maltose is an important constituent of corn syrups which are prepared by the partial hydrolysis of starch with acids or enzymes. The principal saccharides in commercial starch hydrolysates are D-glucose, maltose, trisaccharides, and higher saccharides.

Starch hydrolysates are used in many food applications. For example, they are used in soft drinks, bread, confections, coffee substitutes, and infant foods.

Technology is now available for preparing starch hydrolysates that contain 90% or more maltose (Hodge *et al.* 1972). This involves the use of a multiple enzyme process coupled with β-amylase i.e., iso-amylases (amylo-α-1,6-glucosidases) which debranch the amylopectin fraction of gelatinized starch to linear segments.

Maltose is a reducing sugar and it exhibits mutarotation. Consequently, the hemiacetal group of one glucose unit is involved in the glycoside linkage while the hemiacetal linkage of the other glucose unit is free.

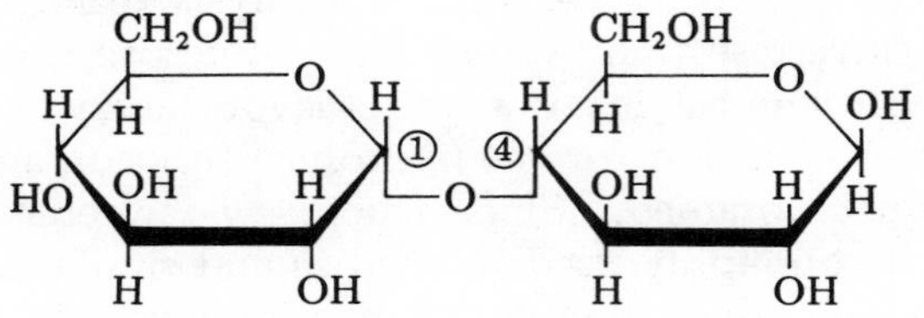

β-Maltose (O-α-D-glucopyranosyl-(1 → 4)-β-D-glucopyranose)

Maltose is obtained as a monohydrate of the β-isomer: mp 102–103°; $[\alpha]_D^{20}$ = 111.7 → 130.4 (H_2O). The structure of a α-maltose differs from the above structure only in the position of the groups on the unsubstituted hemiacetal group.

Lactose.—Lactose consists of 1 unit of glucose and 1 unit of galactose. It occurs in the milk of all mammals. The concentration of lactose varies with different species. For example, cow's milk contains about 4.5% lactose while human milk contains about 6.0%.

Lactose may be hydrolyzed by dilute solutions of strong acids and the enzyme β-D-galactosidase (lactase). Lactose exists in two forms, α and β, and it exhibits mutarotation. It is a reducing sugar and is decomposed by alkali. The common crystalline form of lactose is alpha-lactose monohydrate, or simply alpha-hydrate. It is prepared by allowing a supersaturated solution of lactose to crystallize at a temperature below 93.5°C. The alpha-hydrate loses water of hydration at about 130°C and caramelizes at 160–180°C. Other crystalline forms may be prepared, but they will change to the hydrate form in the presence of a small amount of water at temperatures below 93.5°C.

Of all the common sugars, lactose has the lowest relative sweetness, and it is the least soluble (17 gm per 100 gm at 20°C). Ingestion of lactose in moderate amounts is tolerated by most people, but excessive amounts may result in gastrointestinal disturbances in certain individuals. Moreover, there are some individuals who cannot tolerate lactose and are made ill whenever they ingest lactose.

The unique chemical and physical properties of lactose are used to advantage in the food industry. Lactose readily absorbs flavors, aromas, and coloring materials. Hence, it is used as a carrier for such substances. Lactose is a component in biscuit and other baking mixes. In baked goods, lactose readily reacts with proteins via the Maillard reaction to form the golden brown color found in the crusts.

Lactose is not fermented by yeast so its functional properties are effective throughout the baking process, i.e., its emulsifying properties promote greater efficiency from the shortening.

Lactose is used in infant foods, as a coating agent for foods, and for the production of lactic acid. It is also used as a preservative for flavor, color, and consistency in meat products.

Lactose has the following configuration:

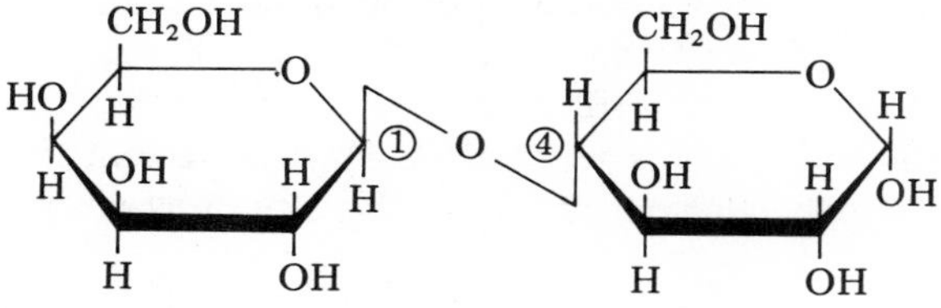

α-Lactose (O-β-D-galactopyranosyl-(1 → 4)-α-D-glucopyranose)

Physical properties of lactose are: monohydrate of α-isomer, mp 202°C; $[\alpha]_D^{20}$ = +85.0 → +52.6. Anhydrous α-isomer, mp 223°C; $[\alpha]_D^{20}$ = +90.0 → +55.3. Anhydrous β-isomer, mp 252°C; $[\alpha]_D^{20}$ = +34.9 → +55.3.

Trisaccharides

Raffinose.—Several trisaccharides occur in nature but raffinose is the most important. It occurs in small quantities in sugar beets, cottonseed meal, soybeans, and coconut meats. It is a nonreducing sugar and has a specific rotation of +104 degrees. Raffinose contains fructose, glucose, and galactose and it can be hydrolyzed by strong acid into these three monosaccharides. Hydrolysis by weak acids yields fructose and a disaccharide called melibiose (galactose, glucose). The enzyme maltase, an α-glucosidase, hydrolyzes raffinose to form galactose and sucrose. Raffinose contains water of hydration which it loses at 100 to 100°C. The structure of raffinose is as follows:

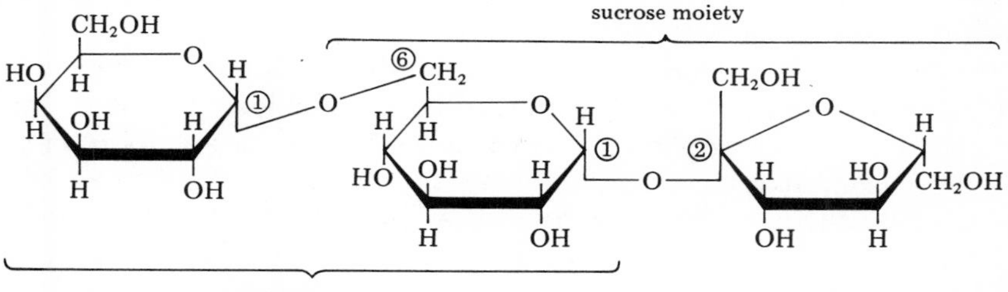

Raffinose (α-D-galactopyranosyl-(1 → 6)-α-D-glucopyranosyl-(1 → 2)-β-D-fructofuranoside)

Polysaccharides

Carbohydrates composed of ten or more monosaccharide units are referred to as polysaccharides. These substances are amorphous, colorless, and almost tasteless. Some polysaccharides possess low molecular weights, but the majority of the substances are large molecules composed of several hundred or even thousands of monosaccharide units.

Polysaccharides form colloidal solutions rather than true solutions, which is characteristic of the sugars. It is for this reason that they are purified with much difficulty. For example, the empirical formula for the hexosans is written $(C_6H_{10}O_5)_x$ to indicate that the number of monosaccharide units in the condensation polymer is not known.

Polysaccharides are an important group of carbohydrates. Some are constituents in structural tissues (cellulose in plants, chitin in marine life, muramic acid in bacterial cell walls), while others constitute storage reserves (starch in plants, glycogen in animals).

The chemical structure of polysaccharides permits the following classifications: (1) homopolysaccharides, which are composed of many units of a single monosaccharide and include cellulose, starch and glycogen; (2) heteropolysaccharides (analogous to copolymers) composed of two or more different components and include hemicelluloses, pectins, mucilages, and resins; (3) conjugated compounds composed of saccharides, lipids, or proteins. For convenience of discussion, we shall consider the polysaccharides in relation to their products of hydrolysis.

Homopolysaccharides

Cellulose.—This polysaccharide is the major constituent of the structural tissues of plants, being present in the walls of cellular tissue combined with xylans and lignins. Cellulose differs in toughness and strength, depending on the age and type of plant. Wood fiber, flax, and cotton are excellent sources of cellulose; e.g., cotton contains more than 90% cellulose.

Cellulose is insoluble in water. It is quite resistant to the action of most enzymes, dilute acids, and dilute alkalies. Cellulases are absent in the digestive enzymes of animals and, as a consequence, cellulose cannot be used directly by the animal. Herbivorous animals can utilize appreciable quantities of cellulose because of the rumen microflora which hydrolyze the cellulose. The indigestible carbohydrate of foods is often referred to as "crude fiber."

Cellulose is a chain structure consisting of glucose units linked by β-$(1 \rightarrow 4)$ glycosidic linkages which is in contrast to the α-$(1 \rightarrow 4)$ glycosidic linkages found in starch. The cellulose structure is as follows:

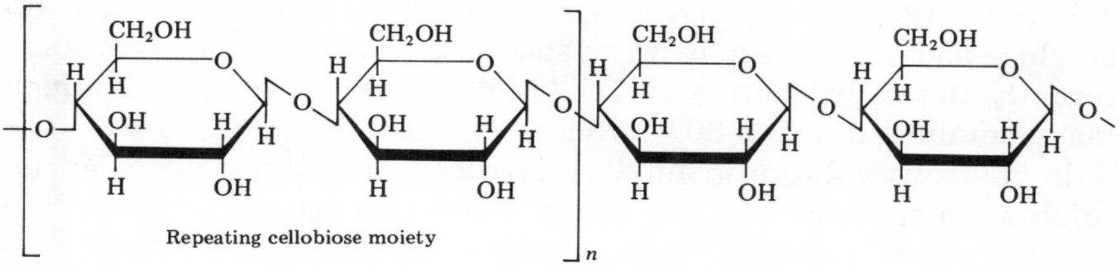

Repeating cellobiose moiety

Cellulose type structure

Evidence indicates that the high molecular weight substance is not branched, but is arranged in bundles of long parallel chains. The chains are held together horizontally by hydrogen bonds between the hydroxyl groups. The molecular weights of native cellulose may vary between 100,000 and 2,000,000.

Starch.—The exact molecular formula is not known. It occurs as the main reserve carbohydrate in most plants, being found in roots, tubers, seeds, stems, and in many fruits. Starch is found in layers within a granule that is surrounded by a thin protein layer. Although the starches are polymers of glucose, the granules of different plant species differ in size, shape, and other physical characteristics. Thus, starch grains from a given source can be identified by microscopic examination. Starch granules are insoluble in cold water, but they will absorb water and swell slightly. The swelling is reversible; i.e., the granules will shrink on drying. In contrast, when starch granules are treated with boiling water, the granules swell until ultimately they rupture, collapse, and yield a paste. This process of swelling is referred to as gelatinization. The dispersion or paste contains two kinds of starch, amylose and amylopectin. Partial acid hydrolysis of starch yields a complex mixture of dextrins (higher saccharides), maltose, and glucose. Complete acid hydrolysis yields D-glucose. Colloidal dispersions of starch are hydrolyzed by enzymes, amylases, to maltose and glucose units. The above two kinds of starch can be distinguished by chemical methods.

a. Amylose is a linear polymer consisting of 250–2000 glucose residues linked by a α-D-(1 → 4) glucosidic bonds. The repeating unit is maltose.

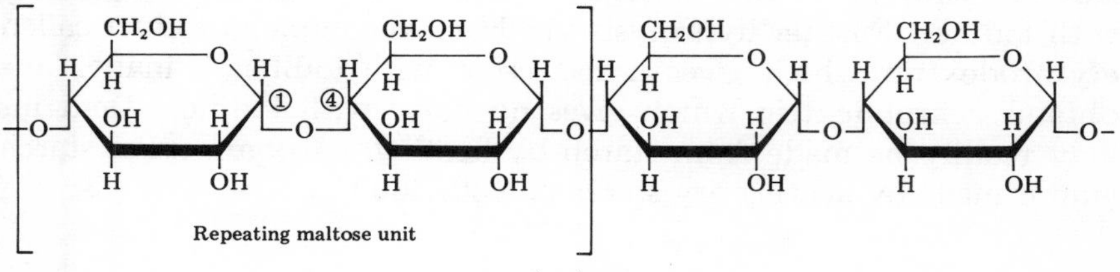

Repeating maltose unit

Amylose

Common starches (corn, wheat, potato) contain from 10 to 30% amylose. Certain varieties of corn, sorghum, and rice contain no amylose and are known as waxy starches. On the other hand, some recently developed corn varieties (amylomaize) have starches which may contain as much as 80% amylose.

In aqueous solutions, amylose readily associates to form an insoluble precipitate; i.e., the linear molecules have a tendency to become oriented parallel to one another to the extent that association occurs through hydrogen bonding with the net result that the affinity for water decreases, the aggregate size increases, and ultimately a precipitate is formed. This phenomenon is called retrogradation and the precipitate is called retrograded starch.

Amylose has an affinity for iodine. It has been discovered that amylose complexes with iodine by forming a helical structure around the iodine and, in such an enclosure, the iodine exhibits a strong absorption of light (intense blue). Amylose also complexes with fatty acids, surfactants, and polar agents such as butyl alcohol, amyl alcohol, thymol, and nitroparaffins. The latter complexing property provides a method for separating amylose from amylopectin.

b. Amylopectin, the other component of grain starch (70–100%) is a highly branched polymer consisting of glucose units joined to each other by α-glucosidic linkages. Each branch contains about 15–25 glucose units occurring periodically in the chain. The residues are joined to each other by α-(1 $\rightarrow$ 4) linkages, with the branch point formed by α-(1 $\rightarrow$ 6) linkages. Amylopectin is usually the larger molecule. The minimum molecular weight is approximately 1,000,000. In contrast to amylose, amylopectin gives a red-violet color with iodine. Retrogradation from aqueous solution is very slow. Consequently, amylopectin starches may be characterized as being resistant to gelling and change in water-holding properties. The structure of the amylopectin molecule at the branch point may be represented as shown in Fig. 4.1.

c. Dextrins are the partial degradation products resulting from the action of enzymes, acid, and heat upon starch. Three kinds of dextrins are recognized as intermediate products in the hydrolysis of starch. The most complex degradation product is referred to as amylodextrin or soluble starch. This substance gives a blue color with iodine. Further hydrolysis yields a less complex product called erythrodextrin which gives a red color with iodine. Finally, one obtains achroödextrin which gives no color with iodine. Dextrins may readily be made from starch by heating. A commercial starch gum is made by heating dry starch at 230–260°C.

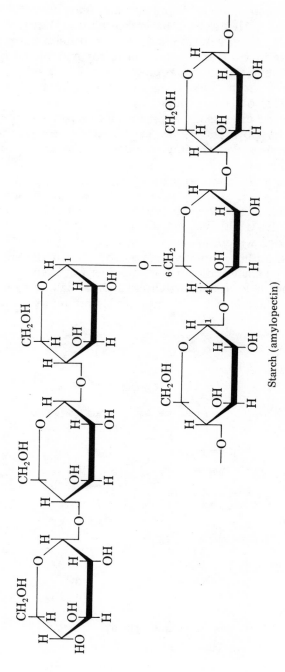

Starch (amylopectin)

FIG. 4.1. AMYLOPECTIN STRUCTURE

Dextrin is water-soluble and is precipitated from aqueous solution by adding alcohol. All dextrins have free carbonyl groups and, as a result, reduce Fehling's solution and undergo other sugar reactions.

Dextrins occur in fruit and vegetable juices and in the leaves of many plants. These substances represent the intermediates in the synthesis of starch from glucose or the breakdown from starch to glucose. Dextrins also occur in honey.

Dextrins are used extensively in encapsulating water-soluble flavor oils for use in dry powders, mixes, etc. Dextrins are also used extensively as adhesives and are important constituents of food products such as corn syrups.

Inulin.—Inulin is a linear polyfructosan composed of D-fructose units formed together with β-(2 → 1) glycosidic linkages. It is only slightly soluble in cold water but is readily soluble in hot water. Inulin does not give a blue color with iodine solution. It is a white amorphous powder which is readily hydrolyzed by acids. In contrast to dextrins, inulin is not hydrolyzed by any of the enzymes in the gastrointestinal tract and cannot be used as a nutrient.

Inulin is found in Jerusalem artichoke and dahlia bulbs, in chicory and dandelion roots, and in the bulb of garlic and onion.

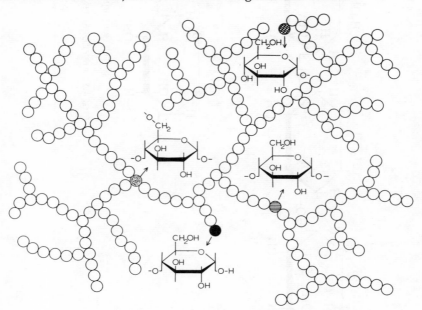

FIG. 4.2. GLYCOGEN STRUCTURE

Glucose units are shown at various points in the molecule.

Inulin can be used as a source of D-fructose, the sweetest simple sugar.

Glycogen.—This polysaccharide is the principal storage form of carbohydrate in animals; the chief storage sites of glycogen are liver and muscles. The structure of glycogen is similar to amylopectin except it is more branched and is higher in molecular weight (Fig. 4.2). Glycogen from different sources shows different degrees of branching and different molecular weights. Like amylopectin, glycogen consists of repeating glucose units joined to each other by α-(1 → 4) linkages with the branched point joined by α-(1 → 6) linkages. In contrast to amylopectin, glycogen has shorter linear chains (12–18 units) and there is more frequent branching.

Glycogen is a white, amorphous, tasteless substance which may be hydrolyzed to yield dextrins, maltose, and glucose. It is water-soluble yielding a dextrorotatory solution. Glycogen gives a violet-brown color with iodine and forms an opalescent dispersion in water.

Glycogen is one of the most important biochemical substances found in the body. Liver glycogen is the principal reserve for maintaining a normal blood level of glucose. Muscle glycogen is a source of energy for the contraction of muscle fibers.

Heteropolysaccharides

Mucilages.—These polysaccharides are well-known for their properties of forming gels. Agar is an example of a sulfated polysaccharide occurring in marine plants. The structure of this substance is not completely known. It is composed of D-galactose, 3,6-anhydro-L-galactose, and small amounts of an ester sulfate. Agar is insoluble in cold water and alcohol. The agar, on heating, forms a viscous solution which, on cooling, forms a gel. A firm gel is formed with as little as 1.5 gm of agar per 100 ml of water. The free sugar acid is a relatively strong acid (a 1% solution having a pH 2.0), and it will not form a gel. In the presence of specific metal ions, such as Na^+, K^+, Ca^{2+} and Mg^{2+}, agar will form thermally reversible gels. Agar is nondigestible and is at times used as a bulk laxative.

Agar is used as a gelling agent in meat products and in dairy products.

Carrageenan, (Irish moss), which is similar to agar in composition and properties has many applications in the food industry. It is used: in chocolate milk to suspend cocoa particles; to improve body in soups and sauces; and in pie fillings as a gelling agent.

Gums.—The plant gums are polysaccharides containing hexoses and pentoses in combination with a uronic acid. For example, gum arabic is a complex calcium, magnesium, and potassium salt of arabic acid, which on acid hydrolysis, yields D-galactose, L-arabinose, L-rhamnose, and D-glucuronic acid. Gum arabic is soluble in water and its aqueous solutions are slightly acidic within a pH range of 4.5–5.5. It has many commercial applications such as an adhesive in icings and toppings and as a foam stabilizer in beer.

Hemicelluloses.—This generic term includes a number of complex polysaccharides which are extracted by dilute alkali from the insoluble plant residue that remains after extraction with hot and cold water. Evidence indicates that the hemicelluloses occur in combination with lignin and cellulose in the cell walls of fibrous tissues. The hemicelluloses are polyuronides (D-glucuronic acid) in combination with xylose, arabinose, glucose, mannose, and galactose.

Pectins.—Pectins are structural polymers which occur in combination with cellulose in the cell walls of fruits and vegetables. Chemically, the pectins are linear polymers of D-galacturonic acid, joined in α-(1 → 4) glycosidic linkages in which the carboxyl groups of the galacturonic acid are partly esterified with methanol, and the remaining free carboxyl groups are partly neutralized. Some of the hydroxyl groups on C-2 and C-3 may be acetylated. Many pectins have neutral sugars covalently linked to them as side chains. Included among the sugars are arabinose, galactose, and to a lesser extent, glucose, xylose, and rhamnose. The molecular weight of pectic substances range from 10,000–400,000.

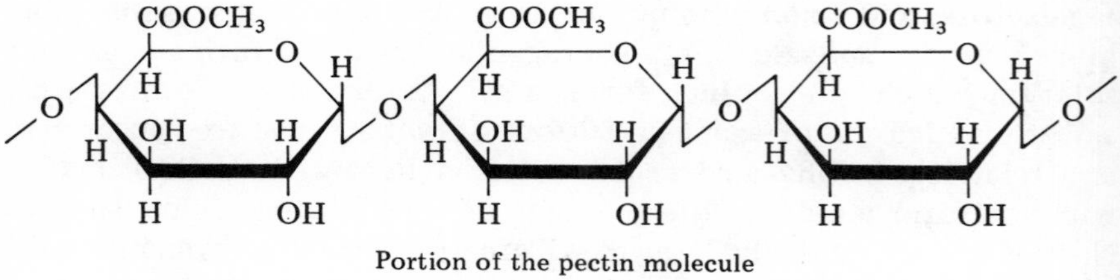

Portion of the pectin molecule

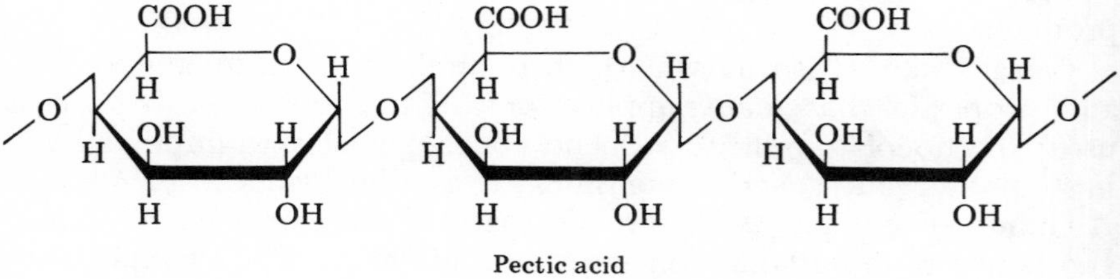

Pectic acid

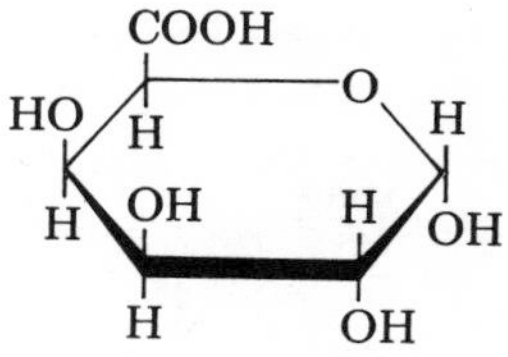

$$\text{D-Galacturonic acid}$$

COOH

HO H O H

H OH H OH

H OH

D-Galacturonic acid

Various terms have been used to identify pectic substances and their derivatives. The nomenclature adopted by the American Chemical Society (Kertesz 1951) has been widely used to define the pectic substances.

"Pectic substances. Pectic substances is a group designation for those complex, colloidal carbohydrate derivatives which occur in or are prepared from plants and contain a large proportion of anhydrogalacturonic acid units which are thought to exist in chain-like combination. The carboxyl group of these polygalacturonic acids may be partly esterified by methyl groups and partly or completely neutralized by one or more bases."

"Protopectin. The term protopectin is applied to the water-insoluble parent pectic substance which occurs in plants and which, upon restricted hydrolysis, yields pectinic acids."

"Pectinic acids. The term pectinic acids is used for colloidal polygalacturonic acids containing more than a negligible proportion of methyl ester groups. Pectinic acids, under suitable conditions, are capable of forming gels (jellies) with sugar and acid or, if suitably low in methoxyl content, with certain metallic ions. The salts of pectinic acids are either normal or acid pectinates."

"Pectic Acid. The term pectic acid is applied to pectic substances mostly composed of colloidal polygalacturonic acids and essentially free from methyl ester groups. The salts of pectic acid are either normal or acid pectates."

The following discussion relates only to pectic substances as related to foods and food products. Many excellent texts on pectins are available. The books by Kertesz (1951) and Doesburg (1965) adequately cover the various aspects of pectin chemistry.

Pectins are soluble in water. They may be precipitated with polyvalent cations, proteins, and water-miscible organic solvents. Dilute acids hydrolyze the ester and the glycosidic linkages of pectin. At low temperatures, the removal of the methyl ester yields pectic acid. At high temperatures, depolymerization takes place. Alkali hydrolyzes the methyl ester group. However, with increasing temperature, the glycosidic linkage in the β-position to the ester group of pectin is cleaved following the formation of a double bond between C-4 and C-5. This reaction

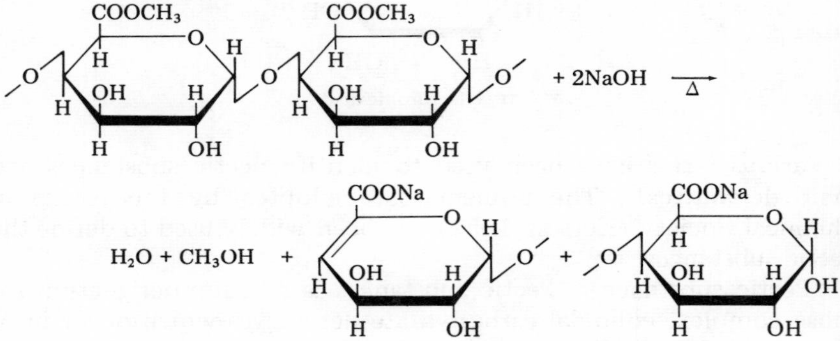

is referred to as transeliminative cleavage of pectin. The above reaction can also be catalyzed by enzymes (lyases).

High viscosity is a characteristic of pectin solutions. There are several factors which will influence the viscosity: molecular weight of the pectin, the degree of esterification, the electrolyte concentration, and pH. Thus, the higher the molecular weight, the greater the viscosity; an increase in degree of esterification will increase viscosity; the addition of salts of calcium and aluminum will increase viscosity; and pH optimum for highest viscosity is related to the degree of esterification.

Pectins form stable gels and it is this property which makes them an important additive to jams, jellies, and marmalades. There are two types of pectin gels: high sugar-pectin-acid gels and low sugar gels (calcium pectinate gels). The first type of gel utilizes a pectin with a high methoxyl content (60–75% esterification), whereas the latter gel utilizes a pectin of low methoxyl content (20–45% esterification). In the high sugar-pectin-acid gel, the three components can replace each other within limits. The lower limit of sugar is approximately 55° Brix; the upper pH limit is determined by degree of esterification. Gel strength is also influenced by the molecular weight and concentration of pectin.

The reactivity of low-methoxyl pectin with Ca^{2+} is used to form a low sugar gel. This type of gel is obtained by adding calcium salts (soluble) under boiling conditions and then allowing the solution to cool. This kind of gel is used commercially to make low-calorie jams and jellies.

Commercial pectins are standardized in terms of an arbitrary unit called "jelly grade." The unit may be defined as the proportion of sugar which one part of solid pectin or pectin extract is capable of turning, under prescribed conditions, into a jelly with suitable characteristics. Thus, if 1 lb of pectin is capable of turning 100 lb of sucrose under prescribed conditions into a standard jelly, it is 100 grade pectin.

Changes occur in the pectin content and structure during growth, maturation, handling, and storage of plant material as well as in preserved products. There is limited information regarding the synthesis of pectic substances; however, information relative to the action of pectic enzymes on its substrate during processing is well-known.

There are two groups of enzymes which catalyze changes in pectic substances: depolymerizing enzymes and pectin esterases (Doesberg 1965).

(1) Depolymerizing enzymes are hydrolases which split the α-$(1 \rightarrow 4)$ glycosidic linkages in pectin and pectic acids. These enzymes are referred to as polygalacturonases. These enzymes may be subdivided into enzymes which act primarily on pectin (poly-methylgalacturonases, pectin-trans-eliminases), and enzymes which act on pectic acid (polygalacturonases and pectic acid-trans-eliminases).

(2) The pectin esterases are highly specific enzymes which hydrolyze methanol from esterified groups of pectinic acids. These enzymes will not hydrolyze the methyl ester of galacturonic acid and esters of the dimers and trimers of galacturonic acid.

Pectic enzymes are widely used in the food industry. They are used, for example, to clarify fruit juices, especially those used for jelly manufacture and wine making. It should also be noted that pectic enzymes may have an adverse effect as well as a beneficial effect. Changes in texture of a good product may be related to the activity of the pectic enzymes on their substrates.

Glycoproteins.—The glycoproteins are composed of simple proteins covalently bonded to carbohydrate moieties. These substances are widely distributed in nature, and include: soybean hemagglutenen, human transferrin, gamma globulin, egg ovalbumin, hormones and ribonuclease B. Some of the structural characteristics are:

(1) Seven sugars comprise the dominant portion of the carbohydrate moiety; namely, mannose, N-acetylglucosamine, galactose, fucose, N-acetylneuraminic acid, N-acetylgalactosamine and glucose.

(2) The carbohydrate moieties are generally linked to the protein via the amide nitrogen of asparagine. However, there are some glycoproteins in which the carbohydrate is linked to the protein through the hydroxyl group of serine, threonine, or hydroxyproline.

(3) The carbohydrate chain length is relatively short, ranging from 6–29 residues per mole of glycopeptide.

(4) Molecular weights of the glycoproteins range from 660 to 4500.

Acid Mucopolysaccharides.—Chondroitin sulfate, keratin sulfate, hyaluronic acid, and heparin are mucopolysaccharides which occur in connective tissue covalently bonded to protein. These substances are commonly referred to as glycoproteins or protein-polysaccharides and differ from typical glycoproteins in that they contain greater carbohydrate chains.

Enzymatic Degradation of Polysaccharides

Polysaccharides are stored better than low molecular weight substances because they are less soluble and when they are in solution their osmotic pressure is so low their accumulation within the cell does not result in hypertonicity. However, before the polysaccharides can fulfill their established role in the body they must first be converted into monosaccharide units.

Cleavage of glycosidic linkages is carried out in biological systems by two general mechanisms. One mechanism involves the hydrolytic cleavage of the glycosidic bond while the second mechanism involves the "phosphorolysis" of the glycosidic bond. The process by which starch (polymeric substances) is reduced to its component unit is referred to as hydrolysis or digestion. Virtually all of these changes are brought about by the amylases of which there are two broad groups: α- and β-amylase. The designation α- or β- does not refer to the configuration of the glycosidic bond that is hydrolyzed; both kinds hydrolyze α-(1 → 4)-glucosidic linkages.

α-Amylases.—These enzymes occur in many plant tissues and in the ptyalin of saliva and amylopsin of pancreatic juices of animals. The initial products resulting form α-amylase activity are oligosaccharides of 6 or 7 glucose units. Thus, the cleavage occurs at the glycosidic linkage in the interior of the chain (Fig. 4.3). This shortening of chain length is manifested by a rapid loss in viscosity of a colloidal starch solution and the iodine color reaction disappears without the appearance of reducing sugars. When acting on the amylose fraction of starch, the fragments are degraded largely to maltose. Since α-amylases cannot cleave α-(1 → 6) glycosidic linkages, the final products of starch hydrolysis are maltose, small amounts of higher saccharides (malto-oligosaccharides), glucose, and panose (trisaccharide). The latter sugar contains the α-(1 → 6) linkage of the branching of amylopectin.

β-Amylases.—The β-amylases occur in higher plants, particularly

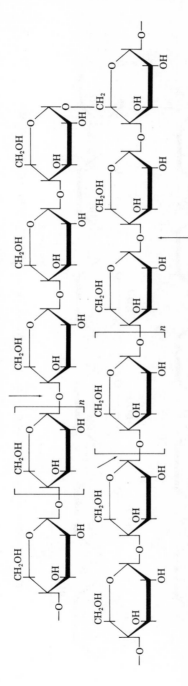

FIG. 4.3. SCHEMATIC DIAGRAM OF THE ENZYMATIC HYDROLYSIS OF STARCH BY α-AMYLASE

Points of hydrolysis are shown by arrows.

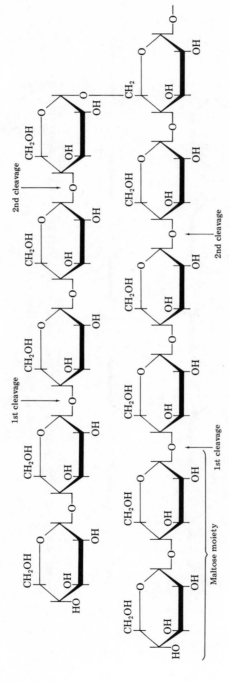

FIG. 4.4. SCHEMATIC DIAGRAM OF THE ENZYMATIC HYDROLYSIS OF STARCH BY β-AMYLASE

Points of hydrolysis are shown by arrows.

in cereals and potatoes. These enzymes attack starch from the non-reducing end of the polymeric chain, cleaving alternate α-(1 → 4) glycosidic linkages to yield maltose in its β-form (Fig. 4.4). This hydrolytic cleavage is practically quantitative and negligible amounts of dextrin are formed from the straight-chain amylose. Within the branched-chain amylopectin approximately 50–60% of the polysaccharide is hydrolyzed since enzymatic cleavage stops at the points of branching (α-(1 → 6) glycosidic linkage), leaving the "beta-limit dextrins." Hydrolysis will cease unless debranching enzymes (α-(1 → 6) glucosidases) are present. Breakdown will occur only if an α-amylase is active at the same time.

The amylases have a wide variety of uses in the food industry; e.g., the baking industry, the brewing industry, dextrose manufacture, sugar products, and starch removal from fruit extracts. An extremely important use for amylases is in the production of syrups of superior flavor and sweetness as compared to regular acid conversion syrups. Technology has developed to the point whereby enzyme preparations of the different amylases (α-amylase, β-amylase, and glucoamylase) can be used with either acid-liquefied or amylase-liquefied corn starch to produce corn syrups of widely differing composition to meet the demands of different food industries (Table 4.1). For example, commercial processes are now available for producing syrups with a maltose content of about 52%, or a fructose content of 42%, or a glucose content of 39%. The above syrups possess a number of properties other than sweetness which represents a specific contribution to many foods. Some of the properties or functional uses of corn syrups are shown in Fig. 4.5.

Maltase.—An intestinal α-glucosidase, maltase, splits maltose to form glucose and thereby completes the digestion of starch.

Phosphorolysis of Polysaccharides.—The enzyme, phosphorylase, is found in animals, plants, and microorganisms. In animals it occurs in muscle, liver, heart, and brain. Peas, beans, and potatoes are good sources of phosphorylase in higher plants.

Intracellularly, the storage polysaccharides are reduced to their component units by a different process; namely, phosphorolysis. The latter term describes the enzyme catalyzed reaction whereby the terminal (nonreducing) glucose group of a polysaccharide chain is transferred to an inorganic phosphate group (Fig. 4.6). The chain is thus shortened and glucose-1-phosphate is formed. By this process, amylose is converted completely into glucose-1-phosphate; amylopectin is converted only to dextrin because the reaction stops near the branching point. Here another enzyme, amylo-1,6-glucosidase

TABLE 4.1

RELATIVE SWEETNESS AND CARBOHYDRATE CONTENT OF SEVERAL CORN SYRUPS

Product[1]	Baume	Relative Sweetness (Dry Basis)	Pounds/Pound Dry Substance	Carbohydrate Composition (Dry Basis)				
				Monosaccharides		Disaccharides (Maltose)	Tri-saccharides	Higher Saccharides
				Dextrose	Fructose			
28 DE Corn Syrup	42°	30%	1.29	6%	—	9%	12%	73%
36 DE Corn Syrup	43°	45%	1.25	15%	—	12%	11%	62%
42 DE Corn Syrup	43°	50%	1.25	19%	—	14%	12%	55%
52 DE Corn Syrup	43°	60%	1.23	28%	—	17%	13%	42%
62 DE Corn Syrup	43°	70%	1.22	39%	—	28%	14%	19%
High Maltose 42 DE Corn Syrup	43°	55%	1.25	6%	—	45%	15%	36%
High Maltose 50 DE Corn Syrup	43°	65%	1.24	9%	—	52%	15%	24%
Glucose	—	80%	1.09	99.5%	—	—	—	—
High Fructose Corn Syrup	37°	100%	1.41	50%	42%	—	—	—
Liquid Sucrose	36.2°	100%	1.49	—	—	100%	—	—

Source: Clinton Corn Processing Co., Clinton, Iowa.
[1] DE = Dextrose equivalent = total reducing value expressed as glucose.

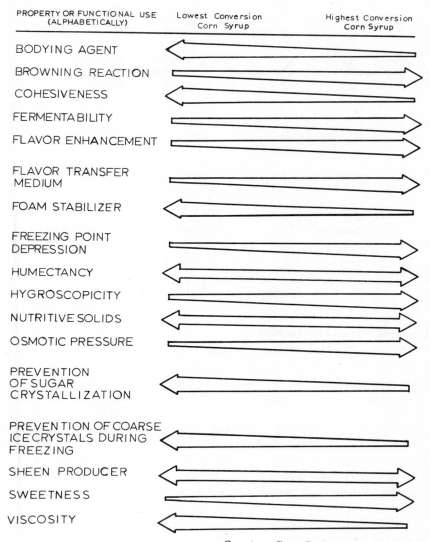

PROPERTY OR FUNCTIONAL USE (ALPHABETICALLY)	Lowest Conversion Corn Syrup	Highest Conversion Corn Syrup
BODYING AGENT		
BROWNING REACTION		
COHESIVENESS		
FERMENTABILITY		
FLAVOR ENHANCEMENT		
FLAVOR TRANSFER MEDIUM		
FOAM STABILIZER		
FREEZING POINT DEPRESSION		
HUMECTANCY		
HYGROSCOPICITY		
NUTRITIVE SOLIDS		
OSMOTIC PRESSURE		
PREVENTION OF SUGAR CRYSTALLIZATION		
PREVENTION OF COARSE ICE CRYSTALS DURING FREEZING		
SHEEN PRODUCER		
SWEETNESS		
VISCOSITY		

Courtesy Corn Refiners Association

FIG. 4.5. PROPERTIES AND FUNCTIONAL USES OF CORN SYRUPS

(debranching enzyme), splits off the α-(1 → 6) linkage by simple hydrolysis, forming a molecule of glucose instead of glucose-1-phosphate. With the 2 enzymes, the final product is about 29% glucose-1-phosphate and 8% glucose.

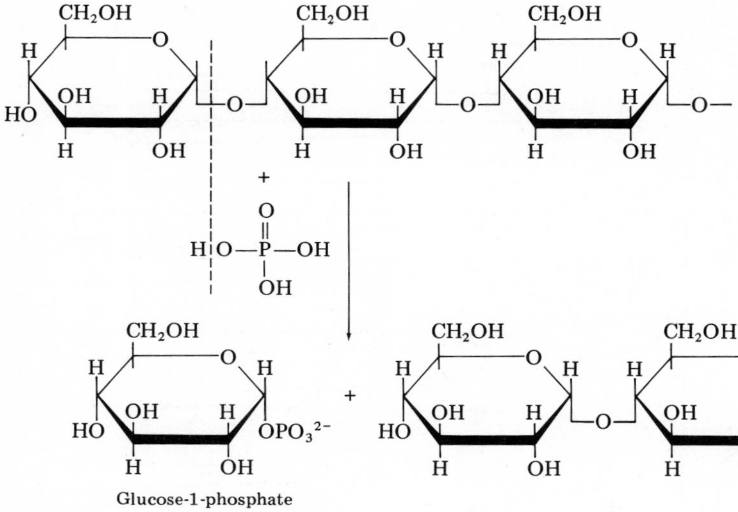

FIG. 4.6. SCHEMATIC DIAGRAM OF THE ACTION OF PHOSPHORYLASE AT THE NONREDUCING END OF A POLYSACCHARIDE

Biosynthesis of Saccharides

Monosaccharides.—The biosynthesis of monosaccharides in animals arises mainly out of hydrolysis reactions, e.g. starch → glucose and maltose, sucrose → fructose + glucose, and glycolysis (gluco-neogenesis) in which glucose-6-phosphate and fructose-6-phosphate are key intermediates. Plants produce monosaccharides by the photosynthetic process utilizing ribulose-1,5-diphosphate which accepts CO_2 and forms 3-phosphoglyceric acid. Glucogenesis follows this carboxylation leading to the formation of glucose-6-phosphate which can be converted to a variety of monosaccharides. Disaccharide synthesis is possible due to the synthesis of the necessary monosaccharides.

The enzymes capable of converting monosaccharides to other monosaccharides are:

(1) Isomerases—These enzymes reversibly convert aldoses to ketoses.

Glucose-6-phosphate $\rightleftharpoons$ Fructose-6-phosphate

Ribose-5-phosphate $\rightleftharpoons$ Ribulose-5-phosphate

Glyceraldehyde-3-phosphate $\rightleftharpoons$ Dihydroxyacetone phosphate

Mannose-6-phosphate $\rightleftharpoons$ Fructose-6-phosphate

(2) Epimerases—These enzymes function mainly by utilizing uridine diphosphosugars. These derivatives are synthesized via:

$$\text{UTP + sugar-1-phosphate} \rightleftharpoons \text{UDP-sugar + PPi}$$

Examples of these are:

$$\text{UTP + Glucose-1-phosphate} \rightleftharpoons \text{UDP-Glucose + PPi}$$

$$\text{UTP + Galactose-1-phoshate} \rightleftharpoons \text{UDP-Galactose + PPi}$$

The UDP-sugar can then be converted to another monosaccharide epimerization as follows:

$$\text{UDP-Galactose} \rightleftharpoons \text{UDP-Glucose}$$

$$\text{UDP-Glucuronate} \rightleftharpoons \text{UDP-Galacturonate}$$

$$\text{UDP-D-Xylose} \rightleftharpoons \text{UDP-L-Arabinose}$$

Epimerization of the sugar phosphate, Xylulose-5-phosphate, can occur without being mediated by UDP-sugars.

$$\text{Xylulose-5-phosphate} \rightleftharpoons \text{Ribulose-5-phosphate}$$

Lactose.—Lactose is synthesized in the mammary gland by the enzyme-lactose synthetase. The galactose moiety is formed by two reactions. UDP Glucose-epimerase catalyzes the conversion of UDP-glucose to UDP-galactose. The epimerase reaction is as follows:

$$\text{Glucose-1-phosphate + UTP} \xrightarrow{\text{transferase}} \text{UDP-glucose + PPi}$$

$$\text{UDP-Glucose} \xrightarrow{\text{epimerase}} \text{UDP-galactose}$$

Since galactose and glucose differ only at C-4, these sugars are interconvertible. Glucose-1-phosphate from metabolism serves as a ready source of galactose. UDP-Galactose may also be formed by the reaction:

$$\text{Galactose + ATP} \longrightarrow \text{galactose-1-phosphate}$$

$$\text{Galactose-1-phosphate + UTP} \rightleftharpoons \text{UDP-galactose}$$

The reaction for the biosynthesis of lactose is:

$$\text{UDP-Galactose + glucose} \rightleftharpoons \text{lactose + UDP}$$

Sucrose.—The synthesis of sucrose in plants involves a reaction similar to lactose synthesis. Fructose-6-phosphate which is formed in glycolysis reacts with UDP-glucose to form sucrose-phosphate (the phosphate remains on the C-6 position of fructose). Sucrose phosphate is hydrolyzed to sucrose.

$$\text{Fructose-6-phosphate + UDP-glucose} \xrightarrow{\text{synthetase}} \text{sucrose-6-phosphate + UDP}$$

$$\text{Sucrose-6-phosphate} \xrightarrow{\text{phosphatase}} \text{sucrose + Pi}$$

Sucrose is also synthesized by the reaction of UDP-glucose and fructose.

$$\text{UDP-glucose} + \text{fructose} \longrightarrow \text{sucrose} + \text{UDP}$$

Maltose.—Maltose production occurs mainly from the degradation of starches.

Glycogen.—One of the most important biochemical substances in the body is glycogen. It occurs in liver and muscle of vertebrates and is found in some plants, yeasts, oysters, and clams. It is a nonlinear polymer of glucose, each unit being joined by an α-glycosidic linkage either to carbon 4 or carbon 6 of another glucose unit. Glycogen is a highly branched substance with an average chain length of about 12 glucose units. Figure 4.2 shows in a diagrammatic way the structure of glycogen and the kind of glucosidic units involved. Glycogen is broken down to glucose which can pass into the bloodstream. The glucose units on the branch exhibit a more rapid turnover than the glucose units in the interior portion, or shorter portion of the chain.

The synthesis of glycogen begins with the conversion of glucose 6-phosphate to glucose 1-phosphate, catalyzed by the enzyme phosphoglucomutase. The mechanism of the reaction is shown below.

glucose-6-phosphate + phosphoenzyme $\rightleftharpoons$

glucose-1,6-diphosphate + dephosphoenzyme

$\Updownarrow$

glucose-1-phosphate + phosphoenzyme

The concentration of glucose-1,6-diphosphate is less than that of glucose 1-phosphate which in turn is lower than that of glucose-6-phosphate.

It was once thought glycogen phosphorylase catalyzed both the synthesis and degradation of glycogen. This latter enzyme catalyzes the making and breaking of α-1,4 but not α-1,6 glucosidic bonds.

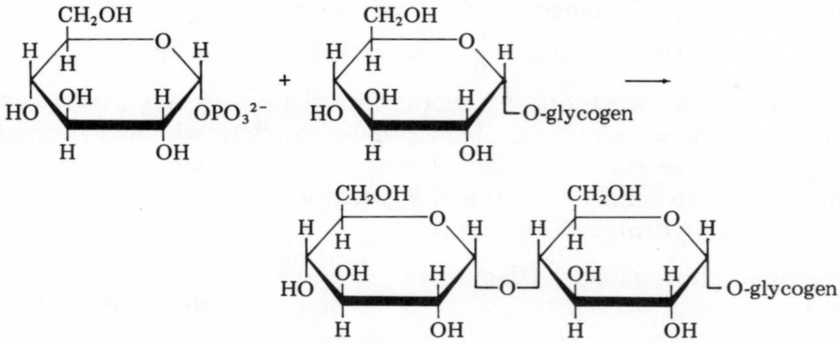

(Note that a glucosyl rather than a glucoside transfer takes place)

It is now known that the biosynthesis pathway for the conversion of glucose-1-phosphate to glycogen involves a reaction catalyzed by the enzyme uridine diphosphoglucose pyrophosphorylase. The reactants are glucose-1-phosphate and uridine triphosphate (UTP).

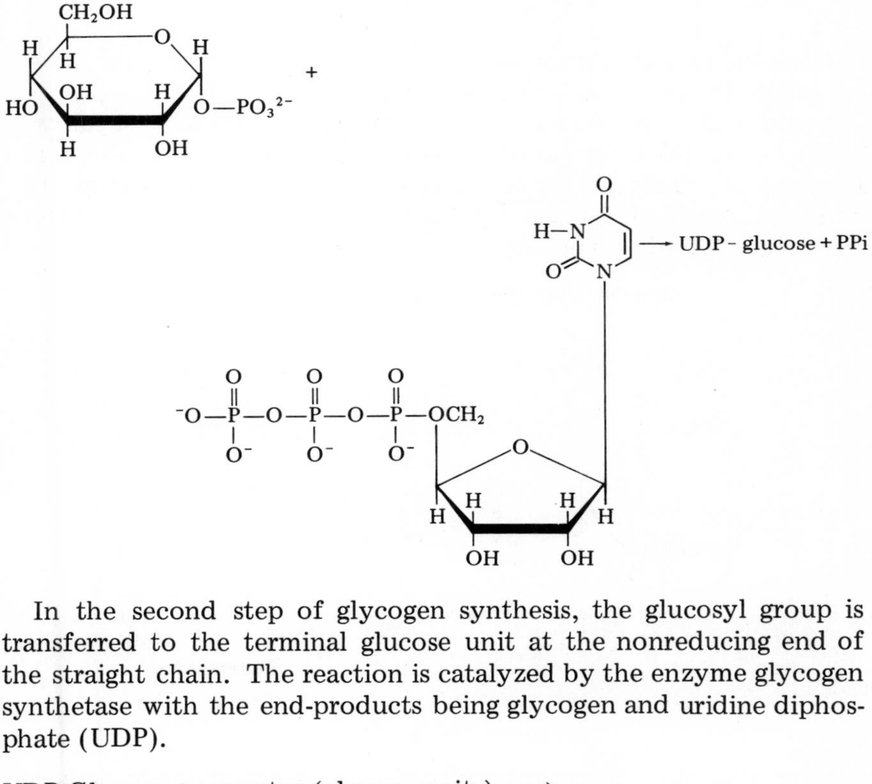

In the second step of glycogen synthesis, the glucosyl group is transferred to the terminal glucose unit at the nonreducing end of the straight chain. The reaction is catalyzed by the enzyme glycogen synthetase with the end-products being glycogen and uridine diphosphate (UDP).

UDP-Glucose + acceptor (glucose units)$_n \longrightarrow$

UDP + glycogen (glucose units)$_{n+1}$

UDP is converted to UTP by reaction with ATP (thus the UTP/UDP ratio is maintained in the cell).

In the foregoing discussion of glycogen synthesis, only the formation and hydrolysis of α-1,4-glucosidic linkages have been considered. A glycogen branching enzyme, amylo (1,4 → 1,6) transglycosylase, has been isolated from liver and other tissues and has been shown to catalyze the formation of α-1,6 bonds. In the reaction there is a transfer of an oligosaccharide fragment from the end of a chain to the 6-hydroxyl group of a glucose residue of the same or another glycogen chain. The action of branching enzyme on glycogen is shown on page 98.

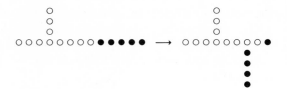

In all likelihood, intramolecular rearrangements occur with the extension of the branches by transglycosylation.

Starch.—The synthesis of starch in plant tissues follows a pathway analogous to the synthesis of glycogen. In plants, the glycosyl donor is adenosine diphosphoglucose (ADPG) which is formed from ATP and α-glucose-1-phosphate by the action of the enzyme ADPG-pyrophosphorylase. The latter

$$\text{glucose-1-phosphate} + \text{ATP} \rightleftharpoons \text{ADPG} + \text{PP}_i$$

Adenosine diphosphoglucose

enzyme is specific for starch synthesis and is not active in glycogen synthesis. The second step of starch synthesis involves the enzyme amylose synthetase.

$$\text{ADP-glucose} + \text{acceptor (glucose)}_n \longrightarrow \text{ADP} + \text{starch (glucose)}_{n+1}$$

As was noted in glycogen synthesis, only the formation of α-1,4-glucosidic linkages have been considered. The formation of the branched structure of the starch molecule is accomplished by the branching enzyme, amylo-$(1,4 \rightarrow 1,6)$ transglycosylase.

Cellulose.—It has been observed that each of the major homopolymers of glucose has as a precursor a characteristic nucleoside diphosphate glucoside. In the glycogen synthesis the α-1,4 bonds were from adenosine diphosphoglucose. The same holds true for cellulose wherein the glycosyl group donor is guanosine diphosphoglucose.

Cellulose, which is a β-$(1 \to 4)$ glucan, is synthesized in a manner similar to the linear polyglucose molecules, glycogen and amylose. The general reactions are:

$$\text{GDP-glucose} + \text{acceptor (glucose)}_n \longrightarrow \text{GDP} + \text{cellulose-(glucose)}_{n+1}$$

Other structural polysaccharides are synthesized by similar reactions. For example, xylans (α-1,4 linkages) are formed from UDP-D-xylose.

Relationship of Structure to Sweetness

Acceptance of food by an individual is determined by such aesthetic properties as taste, color, odor, texture, etc. Our perception of flavor depends on both taste and odor. We are reminded of this when a head cold reduces one's sense of smell to the extent that most of the flavor of food disappears. It tastes flat because we are responding to the sense of taste alone and we are left with only a distinction between sweet, salty, sour and bitter or combinations of these four basic tastes.

The raised portions of the tongue, the papillae, are the organs of taste. The taste buds, containing the receptors, are located in the papillae on the tongue and a few may be in the mucosa of the soft palate. Different tastes are sensed at different places on the tongue. A sweet taste is sensed at the tip of the tongue, a salty taste at the tip and edge of the tongue, a sour taste at the edge of the tongue, and a bitter taste at the back of the tongue.

The salt taste and the sour taste are produced by well-defined compounds. The salt taste is due to soluble inorganic salts, while the sour taste is related to the hydrogen-ion centration of a solution. In contrast, the sweet and bitter tastes cannot be associated with any single class of compounds. In fact, sweet and bitter responses may be found in the same class of compounds. The sweet taste is produced by a variety of organic compounds, including alcohols, glycols, sugars, and sugar derivatives.

The mechanism of sweet taste response is not well-understood However, it is known that sensory responses to sweet substances are related to chemical specificity. Minor changes in the structure of a molecule can result in a new compound which is tasteless or bitter rather than sweet. For example, p-ethoxyphenylurea (Dulcin) is very sweet, o-ethoxyphenylurea is tasteless, and if oxygen of the urea group is replaced by sulfur, one obtains a bitter compound (p-ethoxyphenylthiourea).

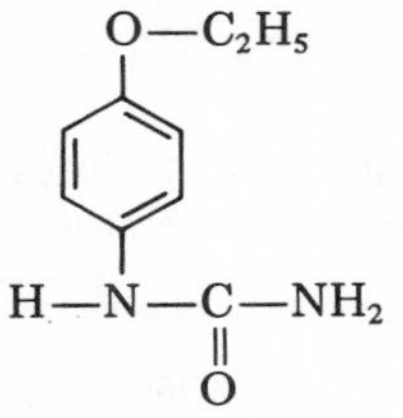

$O-C_2H_5$

H—N—C—NH$_2$
‖
O

p-Ethoxyphenylurea

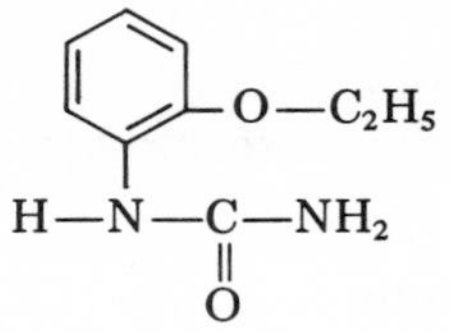

$O-C_2H_5$

H—N—C—NH$_2$
‖
O

o-Ethoxyphenylurea

$O-C_2H_5$

H—N—C—NH$_2$
‖
S

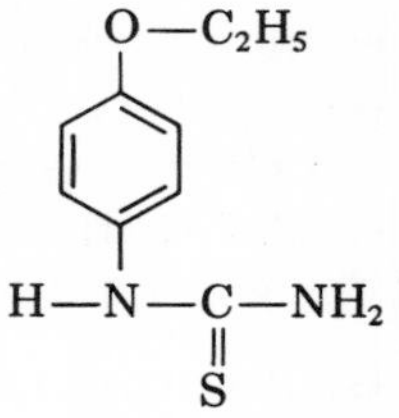

p-Ethoxyphenylthiourea

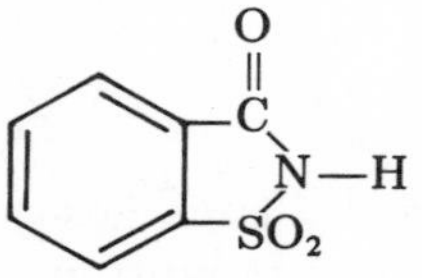

O
‖
C
N—H
SO$_2$

Saccharin

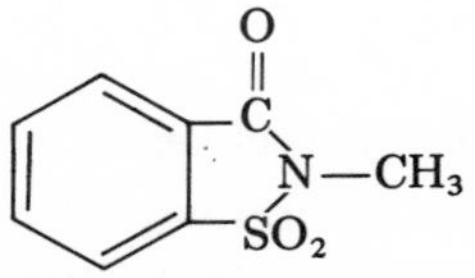

O
‖
C
N—CH$_3$
SO$_2$

N-Methylsaccharin

O
‖
C
N—Na
SO$_2$

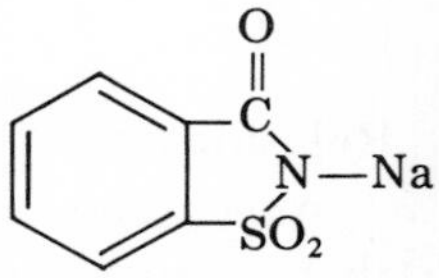

Sodiumsaccharin

Similarly, saccharin is very sweet but if a methyl group replaces the hydrogen of the imido nitrogen a tasteless compound is formed. Sodium saccharin is very sweet. Stereoisomers and anomers may have different tastes. L-glucose has a slight salty taste, while D-glucose is sweet. Similarly, the two anomers of D-mannose have different tastes, α-D-mannose is sweet, whereas β-D-mannose is bitter. Many of the D-isomers of amino acids are sweet, while the L-isomers generally are tasteless (Table 4.2). These differences in taste are due to a change in structure of the molecule and indicate that discrimination between tastes is in part a recognition of the spatial structure of molecules.

TABLE 4.2

TASTE OF STEREOISOMERS OF AMINO ACIDS

Amino Acid	L-Isomer	D-Isomer
Glutamic acid	Unique	Almost tasteless
Phenylalanine	Faintly bitter	Sweet with bitter aftertaste
Leucine	Flat, faintly bitter	Strikingly sweet
Valine	Slightly sweet, yet bitter	Strikingly sweet
Serine	Faintly sweet, stale aftertaste	Strikingly sweet
Histidine	Tasteless to bitter	Sweet
Isoleucine	Bitter	Sweet
Methionine	Flat	Sweet
Tryptophan	Flat	Very sweet
Tyrosine	Bitter	Sweet

Source: Berg (1953).

An unusual source of sweetness has been observed in an African fruit known as the miracle berry. The flavor principle, miraculin, has been isolated and identified as a glycoprotein. The sweetness induced by this substance abolishes the taste response to acidic materials.

Sweetness of Sugars.—Since sweetness is of primary interest in sugars, a knowledge of their relative sweetening ability is important. The intensity of sweetness cannot be determined quantitatively in absolute physical or chemical terms. Sweetness can only be measured by subjective sensory methods and must always represent averages of opinion. Sucrose is usually accepted as the standard. Other sweeteners, either natural or nonnutritive, are then compared with sucrose and their sweetening power is expressed with sucrose as a base. Glucose, for example, is assigned a relative sweetness value of 69 (Table 4.3) when compared to 10% sucrose, while D-fructose has a relative sweetness value of 114.

TABLE 4.3

RELATIVE SWEETNESS OF
VARIOUS SWEETENERS

Sugar	Relative Sweetness
Lactose	39
Maltose	46
D-Mannose	59
Galactose	63
Invert sugar	65
D-Xylose	67
α-β-D-Glucose	69
Sucrose	100
D-Fructose	114

Source: Nieman (1958); Amerine *et al.* (1965).

Synthetic Sweeteners.—The sweet taste is produced by a wide variety of chemical compounds. Some of the compounds which have been reported as sweet-tasting have been collected and discussed by Moncrieff (1967). The relative sweetness of some synthetic sweetners, relative to sucrose, is presented in Table 4.4. One of the best known synthetic sweeteners is saccharin, being 200–300 times as sweet as sucrose. Other sweet substances are sodium cyclamate (cyclohexylsulfamate), Dulcin (*p*-ethoxy-phenylurea) and the alkoxy-2-amino-4-nitrobenzenes. Cyclamate is 15 to 30 times as sweet as sucrose and the *n*-propyl derivative of 2-amino-4-nitrobenzene is over 4000 times as sweet as sucrose.

TABLE 4.4

SWEETNESS OF SYNTHETIC SUBSTANCES COMPARED TO SUCROSE

Sweetener	Relative Sweetness Weight Basis
Sucrose	1
Cyclohexylsulfamate (Sodium cyclamate)	15–31
p-ethoxyphenylurea (Dulcin)	70–350
2,3-Dihydro-3-oxobenzisosulfonate (Saccharin)	240–350
L-aspartyl-L-phenylalanine methyl ester	250
1-n-propoxy-2-amino-4-nitrobenzene	4100

Source: Inglett (1970).

A dipeptide sweetener, L-aspartyl-L-phenylalanine methyl ester, has been found to be 250 times as sweet as sucrose.

The dihydrochalcones of the naturally occurring flavanones (prunin, naringin, and neohesperidin) are intensely sweet.

In addition to the above sweeteners, other intensely sweet-tasting substances have been isolated from plant materials. Glycyrrhizin is a sweetener present in licorice root (*Glycyrrhiza glabra*). It is a triterpenoid glycoside and its relative sweetness is about 15,000 as compared to 10% sucrose. Another naturally occurring, intensely sweet, organic compound is steviosid which is found in the leaves of a small shrub native to Paraguay. It is a steroid glycoside that has a relative sweetness of 30,000 compared to 10% sucrose.

BIBLIOGRAPHY

AKAZAWA, T. 1965. Starch, insulin, and other reserve polysaccharides. *In* Plant Biochemistry, J. Bonner, and J. E. Varner (Editors). Academic Press, New York.

ALBERSHEIM, P. 1965. Biogenesis of the cell wall. In Plant Biochemistry, J. Bonner, and J. E. Varner (Editors). Academic Press, New York.

AM. CHEM. SOC. 1955. Use of Sugars and Other Carbohydrates in the Food Industry. Advances in Chemistry Series *12*, Washington, D.C.

AM. CHEM. SOC. 1966. Flavor Chemistry. Advances in Chemistry Series *56*, Washington, D.C.

AMERINE, M. A., PANGBORN, R. M., and ROESSLER, E. B. 1965. Principles of Sensory Evaluation of Food. Academic Press, New York.

ASPINALL, G. O. 1969. Gums and mucilages. *In* Advances in Carbohydrate Chemistry and Biochemistry, Vol. 24, M. L. Wolfram, and R. S. Tipson (Editors). Academic Press, New York.

AXELROD, B. 1965. Mono- and oligosaccharides. *In* Plant Biochemistry, J. Bonner, and J. E. Varner (Editors). Academic Press, New York.

BERG, C. 1953. Physiology of the D-amino acids. Physiol. Rev. *33*, 145–189.

CAHN, R. S., INGOLD, C., and PRELOG, V. 1966. Specification of molecular chirality. Angew. Chem. *5*, 385–415.

CAMERON, A. T. 1947. The Taste Sense and the Relative Sweetness of Sugars and Other Sweet Substances. Sci. Rept. *9*. Sugar Res. Found., New York.

CLAMP, J. R. *et al.* 1961. Lactose. *In* Advances in Carbohydrate Chemistry, Vol. 16, M. L. Wolfram (Editor). Academic Press, New York.

DOBY, G. 1965. Plant Biochemistry. John Wiley & Sons, London.

DOESBURG, J. J. 1965. Pectic Substances in Fresh and Preserved Fruits and Vegetables, Communication *25.* Institute for Research on Storage and Processing of Horticultural Produce, Wageningen, Netherlands.

DYKE, S. F. 1960. The Carbohydrates. John Wiley & Sons, London.

FURIA, T. E. (Editor). 1968. Handbook of Food Additives. Chemical Rubber Co., Cleveland, Ohio.

GINSBURG, V., and NEUFELD, E. F. 1969. Complex heterosaccharides of animals. Ann. Rev. Biochem. *38*, 371–388.

GUTHRIE, R. D., and HONEYMAN, J. 1968. An Introduction to the Chemistry of Carbohydrates, 3rd Edition. Clarendon Press, Oxford.

HASSID, W. Z. 1967. Biosynthesis of complex saccharides. *In* Metabolic Pathways, 3rd Edition, Vol. 1, D. M. Greenberg (Editor). Academic Press, New York.

HEUSER, E. 1944. The Chemistry of Cellulose. John Wiley & Sons, New York.

HODGE, J. E., RENDLEMAN, J. A., and NELSON, E. C. 1972. Useful properties of maltose. Am. Assoc. Cereal Chem. *17*, 180–184.

HORSTEIN, T., and TERANISHI, R. 1967. The chemistry of flavor. Chem. Eng. News, *45*, No. 17, 92–108.

INGLETT, G. E. 1970. Natural and synthetic sweetners. J. Hort. Sci. *5*, 139–141.

JONES, J. K. N., and SMITH, F. 1949. Plant gums and mucilages. *In* Advances in Carbohydrates, Vol. 4, W. W. Pigman, and M. L. Wolfrom (Editors). Academic Press, New York.

KERTESZ, Z. D. 1951. The Pectic Substances. John Wiley & Sons, New York.

MAHLER, H. R., and CORDES, E. H. 1971. Biological Chemistry, 2nd Edition. Harper and Row, New York.

MANNERS, D. J. 1957. The molecular structure of glycogens. *In* Advances in Carbohydrate Chemistry, Vol. 12, M. L. Wolfrom (Editor). Academic Press, New York.

MONCRIEFF, R. W. 1967. The Chemical Senses, 3rd Edition. L. Hill Books, London.

NIEMAN, C. 1958. Relative sweetness of various sugars. Zucker-u. Sussenwarenwirtsch. *11*, 420–422; 465–467; 505–507; 632–633; 670–671; 974; 1051–1052; 1088–1089.

PIGMAN, W. 1967. The Carbohydrates: Chemistry, Biochemistry, Physiology. Academic Press, New York.

PIGMAN, W., and HORTON, D. (Editors). 1972. The Carbohydrates, Chemistry/Biochemistry. Academic Press, New York.

SCRUTTON, M. C., and UTTER, M. F. 1968. The regulation of glycolysis and gluconegensis in animal tissues. Ann. Rev. Biochem. *37*, 249–302.

SHARON, N. 1966. Polysaccharides. Ann. Rev. Biochem. *35*, No. 2, 485–520.

SPIRO, R. G. 1970. Glycoproteins. Ann. Rev. Biochem. *39*, 599–638.

WEST, E. S., and TODD, W. R. 1954. Textbook of Biochemistry. Macmillan Co., New York.

WHISTLER, R. L., and SMART, C. L. 1953. Polysaccharide Chemistry. Academic Press, New York.

CHAPTER 5

Lipids

Lipids have been defined as a heterogeneous group of naturally occurring substances which are insoluble in water but soluble in organic solvents such as ether, chloroform, benzene, and acetone. Lipids contain carbon, hydrogen, and oxygen, while some contain phosphorus and nitrogen. Most lipids are soft solids or liquids at room temperature and are difficult to crystallize.

Types of Lipids

The major classes of lipids are listed below.

I. Simple lipids—esters of fatty acids and alcohols
   a. Fats and oils—esters of glycerol and monocarboxylic acids (fatty acids)
   b. Waxes—esters of long-chain monohydroxy alcohols and fatty acids

II. Compound lipids—simple lipids conjugated with nonlipid molecules
   a. Phospholipids—esters containing phosphoric acid in place of one mole of fatty acid, combined with a nitrogenous base
      1. Phosphatidic acids—glycerides composed of 1 mole of phosphoric acid and 2 moles of fatty acids
      2. Lecithins—phosphatidyl choline
      3. Cephalins—phosphatidyl enthanolamine (or serine)
   b. Glycolipids—compounds of carbohydrate, fatty acids, and sphingosinol
   c. Lipoproteins—complexes of various lipids and proteins

III. Derived lipids—products of hydrolysis of lipids
   a. Fatty acids
   b. Alcohols—long chain or cyclic; insoluble in water (e.g., sterols, vitamin A)
   c. Hydrocarbons (carotenoids)
   d. Fat-soluble vitamins (D, E, and K)

Edible fats are complex mixtures of triglycerides and small amounts of other substances occurring naturally or are derived through processing and storage of the fats. In general, edible fats and oils contain the following:

Triglycerides	Phospholipids	Hydrocarbons
Diglycerides	Sterols	Oxidation products
Monoglycerides	Fat-soluble vitamins	Trace metals
Fatty acids	Pigments	Water

The natural fats are made up mostly of mixed triglycerides with only trace amounts of the mono- and diglycerides and little or no free fatty acids. In contrast, processed fats may contain up to 20% of the mono- and diglycerides. The associated substances are important. As examples: The fat-soluble vitamins, sterols, and phospholipids are of nutritional importance; the free fatty acids are an index of the degree of hydrolysis of a triglyceride; the presence of peroxides, aldehydes, and ketones are indicative of the amount of oxidative deterioration that has taken place in the fat. Furthermore, certain of the sterols, phospholipids, carotenoid pigments, metallic impurities may contribute to the oxidative deterioration of the fat. Thus, it is necessary to understand the composition and structure of lipids in order to know their role in the biological chemistry of foods.

Triglycerides.—Triglycerides are esters of monocarboxylic acids, the fatty acids, and glycerol (a trihydroxy alcohol):

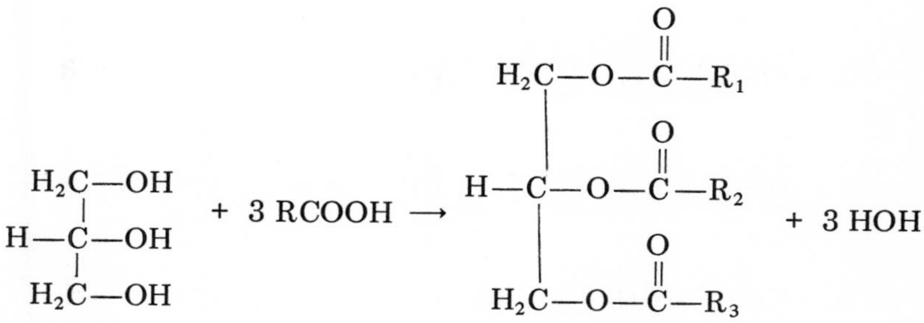

$$
\begin{array}{c}
H_2C-OH \\
| \\
H-C-OH \\
| \\
H_2C-OH
\end{array}
\; + \; 3\,RCOOH \; \rightarrow \;
\begin{array}{c}
\quad\quad O \\
\quad\quad \| \\
H_2C-O-C-R_1 \\
| \quad\quad O \\
\quad\quad \| \\
H-C-O-C-R_2 \\
| \quad\quad O \\
\quad\quad \| \\
H_2C-O-C-R_3
\end{array}
\; + \; 3\,HOH
$$

Glycerol   Fatty acids   Fat or oil

Naturally occurring fats are always mixtures of different triglycerides and the individual triglyceride may have three different fatty acids. Such molecules are known as mixed glycerides. The system of nomenclature for triglycerides is illustrated in the following:

A

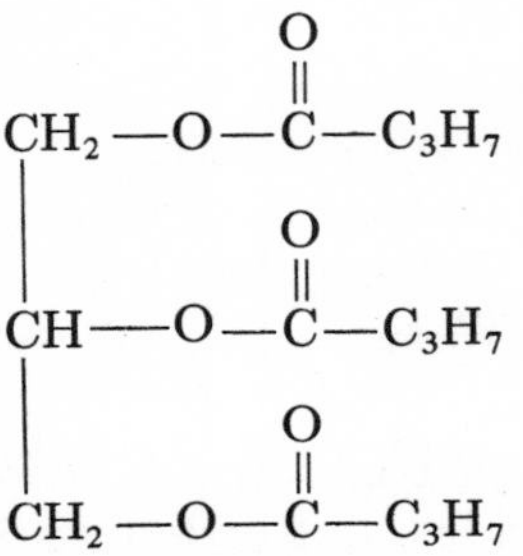

$$CH_2—O—\overset{\overset{\displaystyle O}{\|}}{C}—C_3H_7$$

$$CH—O—\overset{\overset{\displaystyle O}{\|}}{C}—C_3H_7$$

$$CH_2—O—\overset{\overset{\displaystyle O}{\|}}{C}—C_3H_7$$

Tributyrin

B

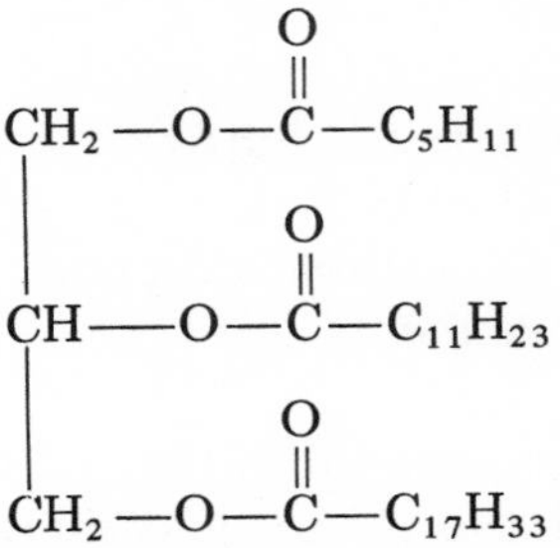

$$CH_2—O—\overset{\overset{\displaystyle O}{\|}}{C}—C_5H_{11}$$

$$CH—O—\overset{\overset{\displaystyle O}{\|}}{C}—C_{11}H_{23}$$

$$CH_2—O—\overset{\overset{\displaystyle O}{\|}}{C}—C_{17}H_{33}$$

α-caproyl-β-lauryl-α'-olein

C

$$CH_2—O—\overset{\overset{\displaystyle O}{\|}}{C}—C_{17}H_{35}$$

$$CH—O—\overset{\overset{\displaystyle O}{\|}}{C}—C_{15}H_{31}$$

$$CH_2—O—\overset{\overset{\displaystyle O}{\|}}{C}—C_{17}H_{35}$$

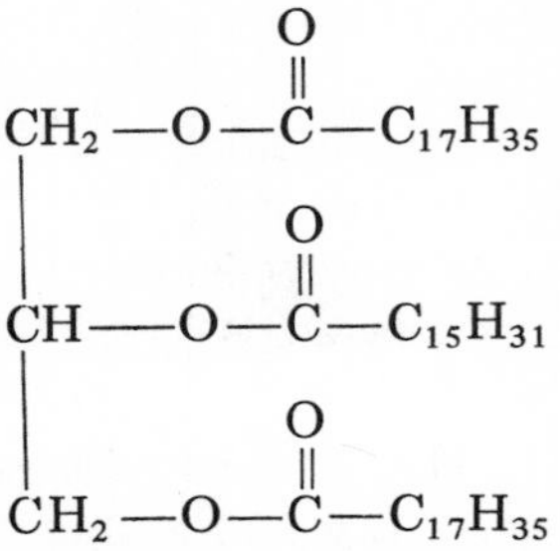

β-palmityl-α,α'-distearin

Simple triglycerides usually bear the name of the component acid with a prefix of *tri-* and a suffix of *-in* replacing the terminal *-ic* (e.g., tributyrin). With mixed triglycerides, in which there are 3 different fatty acids the names of the first 2 single acids end with the suffix *-yl*, the third single acid ends with the suffix *-in*, as in formula B above. If the mixed triglyceride has two molecules of the same acid, the prefix *di-* and suffix *-in* are given to this acid, see formula C. The glycerol carbons may be numbered as 1,2,3 or designated as α,β,α'. Thus, in the formula above, β-palmityl-α,α' distearin could be designated 2-palmityl-1,3-distearin.

Mixed glycerides can exist in several isomeric forms. For example, a triglyceride containing two different fatty acids could have the following structures:

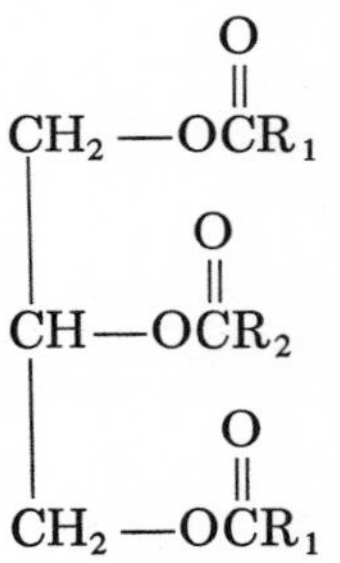

$$CH_2—O\overset{\overset{\displaystyle O}{\|}}{C}R_1$$
$$CH—O\overset{\overset{\displaystyle O}{\|}}{C}R_2$$
$$CH_2—O\overset{\overset{\displaystyle O}{\|}}{C}R_1$$
(1)

$$CH_2—O\overset{\overset{\displaystyle O}{\|}}{C}R_1$$
$$CH—O\overset{\overset{\displaystyle O}{\|}}{C}R_1$$
$$CH_2—O\overset{\overset{\displaystyle O}{\|}}{C}R_2$$
(2)

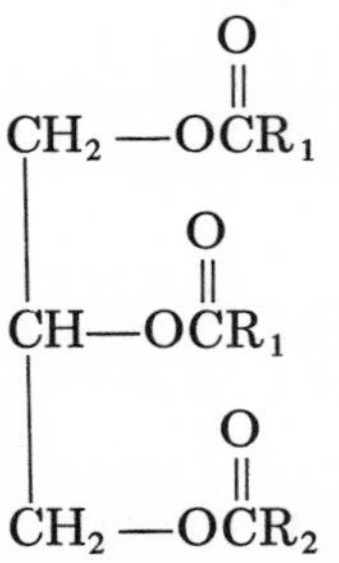

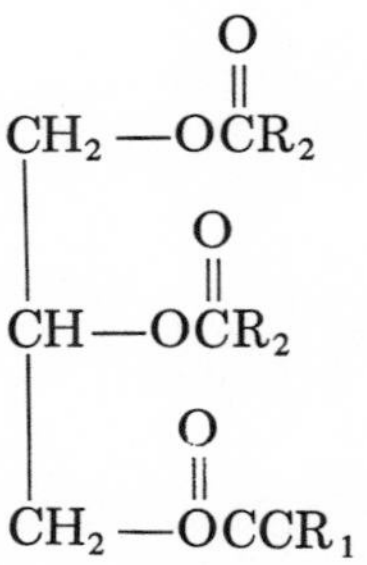

$$CH_2—O\overset{\overset{\displaystyle O}{\|}}{C}R_2$$
$$CH—O\overset{\overset{\displaystyle O}{\|}}{C}R_2$$
$$CH_2—O\overset{\overset{\displaystyle O}{\|}}{C}CR_1$$
(3)

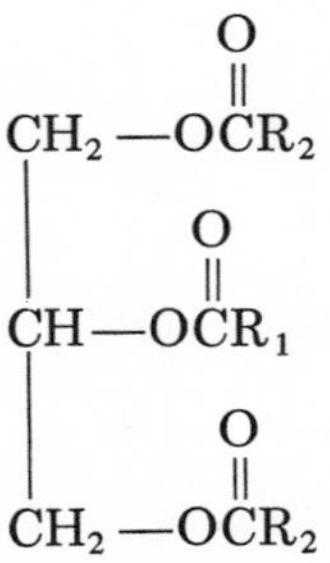

$$CH_2—O\overset{\overset{\displaystyle O}{\|}}{C}R_2$$
$$CH—O\overset{\overset{\displaystyle O}{\|}}{C}R_1$$
$$CH_2—O\overset{\overset{\displaystyle O}{\|}}{C}R_2$$
(4)

In compounds (2) and (3), the β-carbon atom is asymmetric because two different acyl groups are attached to the α and α'-carbon positions. As a consequence, optical isomers of these two compounds exist. However, the naturally occurring fats do not exhibit an observable optical rotation.

Di- and Monoglycerides.—Triglycerides, on standing, may undergo partial hydrolysis to form diglycerides and monoglycerides. The extent of hydrolysis is dependent upon the presence of water, heat, and hydrogen or hydroxide ions. Partial hydrolysis of a glyceride can form the following hydrolytic products.

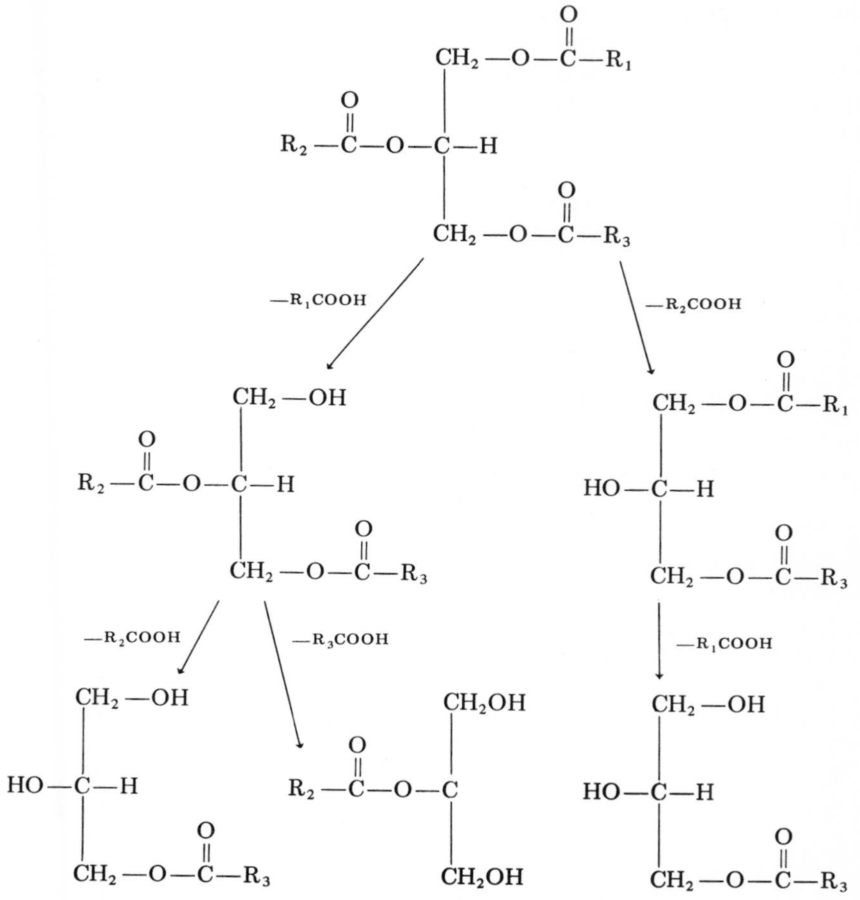

$$
\begin{array}{c}
\quad\quad\quad\quad\quad\quad\quad\quad\quad\overset{\displaystyle O}{\overset{\displaystyle \|}{CH_2-O-C-R_1}} \\
\overset{\displaystyle O}{\overset{\displaystyle \|}{R_2-C-O-C-H}} \\
\quad\quad\quad\quad\quad\overset{\displaystyle O}{\overset{\displaystyle \|}{CH_2-O-C-R_3}}
\end{array}
$$

$-R_1COOH$ $-R_2COOH$

$$
\begin{array}{c}
CH_2-OH \\
\overset{\displaystyle O}{\overset{\displaystyle \|}{R_2-C-O-C-H}} \\
\quad\quad\overset{\displaystyle O}{\overset{\displaystyle \|}{CH_2-O-C-R_3}}
\end{array}
\qquad
\begin{array}{c}
\quad\quad\overset{\displaystyle O}{\overset{\displaystyle \|}{CH_2-O-C-R_1}} \\
HO-C-H \\
\quad\quad\overset{\displaystyle O}{\overset{\displaystyle \|}{CH_2-O-C-R_3}}
\end{array}
$$

$-R_2COOH$ $-R_3COOH$ $-R_1COOH$

$$
\begin{array}{c}
CH_2-OH \\
HO-C-H \\
\quad\overset{\displaystyle O}{\overset{\displaystyle \|}{CH_2-O-C-R_3}}
\end{array}
\quad
\begin{array}{c}
CH_2OH \\
\overset{\displaystyle O}{\overset{\displaystyle \|}{R_2-C-O-C}} \\
CH_2OH
\end{array}
\quad
\begin{array}{c}
CH_2-OH \\
HO-C-H \\
\quad\overset{\displaystyle O}{\overset{\displaystyle \|}{CH_2-O-C-R_3}}
\end{array}
$$

Complete hydrolysis will yield glycerol and free fatty acids.

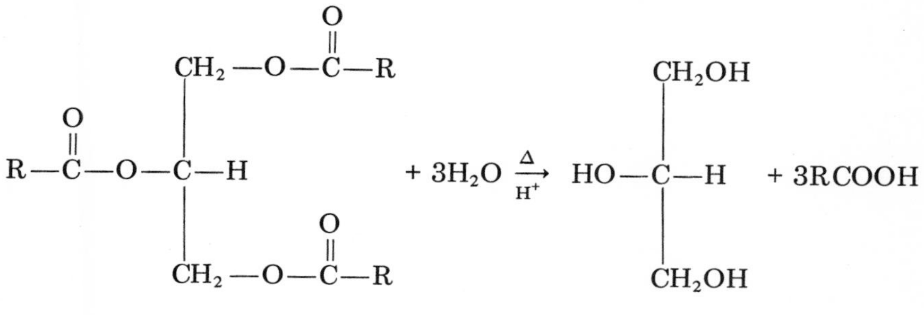

$$
\begin{array}{c}
\quad\quad\overset{\displaystyle O}{\overset{\displaystyle \|}{CH_2-O-C-R}} \\
\overset{\displaystyle O}{\overset{\displaystyle \|}{R-C-O-C-H}} \\
\quad\quad\overset{\displaystyle O}{\overset{\displaystyle \|}{CH_2-O-C-R}}
\end{array}
\quad + 3H_2O \xrightarrow[H^+]{\Delta} \quad
\begin{array}{c}
CH_2OH \\
HO-C-H \\
CH_2OH
\end{array}
\quad + 3RCOOH
$$

Triglycerides in contact with plant and animal lipases (esterases) may undergo appreciable hydrolysis. In contrast to nonenzymatic hydrolysis, lipases catalyze the hydrolysis of the ester linkage at the primary hydroxyl groups of the glycerol moiety of the molecule (α or α' positions). Thus the initial product is an α,β-diglyceride. The latter is hydrolyzed to a monoglyceride, the β-monoglyceride. Most lipases do not hydrolyze the acyl group from the β-position. The β-monoglycerides rapidly isomerize to give a mixture of approximately 12% β-monoglyceride and 88% α-monoglyceride. The reaction sequence for complete enzyme hydrolysis of a triglyceride is as follows:

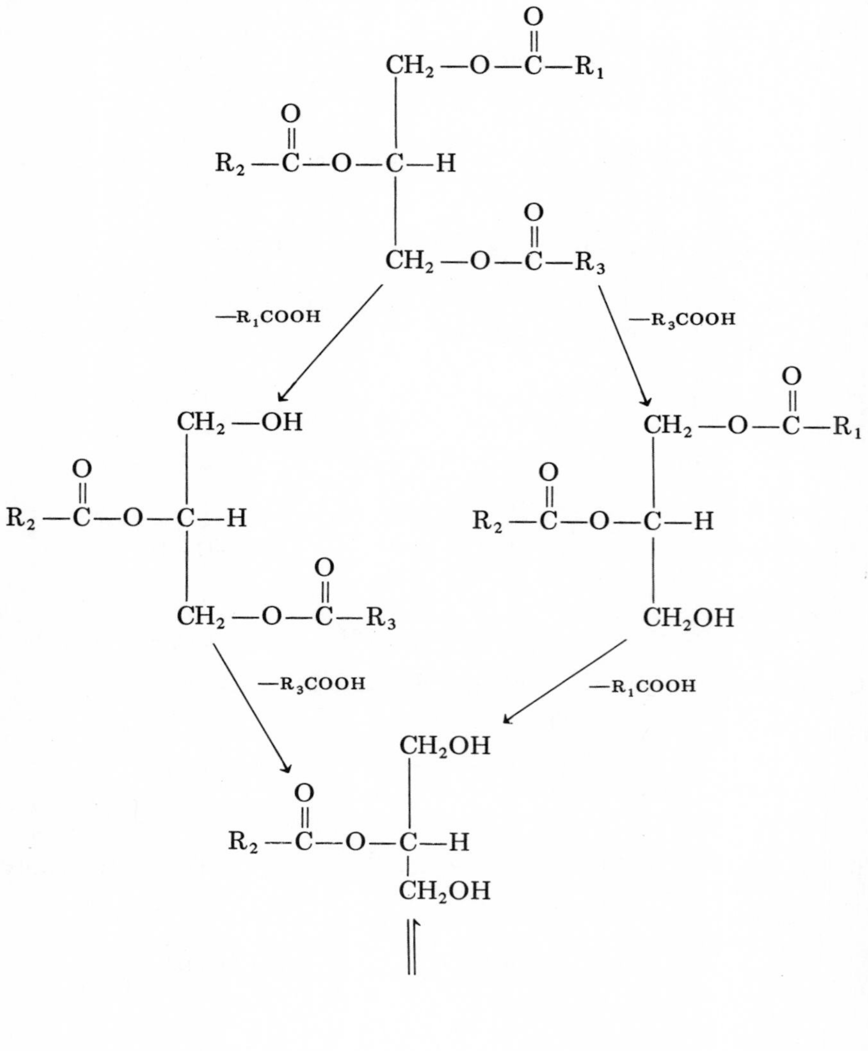

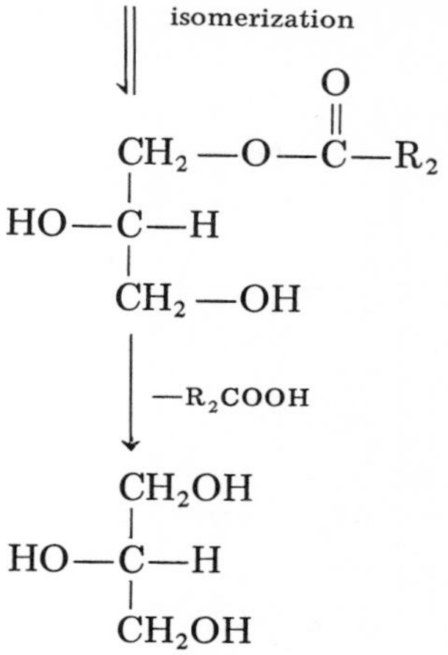

$$\Big\Downarrow \text{isomerization}$$

$$
\begin{array}{l}
\qquad\qquad\qquad\quad\;\; \overset{\displaystyle O}{\overset{\|}{}} \\
CH_2-O-C-R_2 \\
\;\; | \\
HO-C-H \\
\;\;\;\;\;\; | \\
CH_2-OH
\end{array}
$$

$$\Big\downarrow \;\; -R_2COOH$$

$$
\begin{array}{l}
CH_2OH \\
\;\;\; | \\
HO-C-H \\
\;\;\;\;\;\; | \\
CH_2OH
\end{array}
$$

Mono- and diglycerides are prepared by interesterification of fats with glycerol and an alkaline catalyst. The interesterification process is generally carried out at atmospheric pressure under a blanket of nitrogen or other inert gas to protect fats from oxidation. Heating is continued to a temperature of 200–235°C for 1 to 2 hr. Various alkaline catalysts (caustic soda, caustic potash, sodium alcoholates, trisodium phosphate, and lime) in concentrations of 0.05 to 0.20% are employed.

The reaction mixture consists of mono-, di, and triglycerides together with unreacted glycerol. This mixture, which is commonly referred to as monoglycerides, contains 50 to 60% monoglycerides and 30 to 45% diglycerides. Molecular distillation of the technical monoglycerides will yield a distillate containing 90 to 95% monoglycerides.

Fatty Acids.—Most fatty acids are unbranched monocarboxylic acids which vary in length and degree of saturation or unsaturation. There are a limited number of fatty acids containing cyclic groups, hydroxyl groups, and branched chains. As a consequence, the fatty acids may be divided into classes according to their structure: saturated, hydroxy, and cyclic acid (see classification in Table 5.1).

The vast majority of the naturally occurring fatty acids have an even number of carbon atoms in the molecule. The physiological processes involved in the catabolism and anabolism of fatty acids in the plant and animal are so constituted that only this type of acid is produced in major quantities.

The saturated fatty acids range from C_4 to C_{30}, but fatty acids of greater than C_{20} are comparatively rare. The most common saturated fatty acids found in animal fats are palmitic ($C_{15}H_{31}COOH$)

TABLE 5.1

CLASSIFICATION OF FATTY ACIDS PRESENT AS GLYCERIDES IN FOOD FATS

Common Name	Systematic Name	Formula	Common Source
I. Saturated Fatty Acids			
A. Straight-Chain Series			
Butyric	Butanoic	$CH_3(CH_2)_2COOH$	Butterfat
Caproic	Hexanoic	$CH_3(CH_2)_4COOH$	Butterfat, coconut, and palm nut oils
Caprylic	Octanoic	$CH_3(CH_2)_6COOH$	Coconut & palm nut oils, butterfat
Capric	Decanoic	$CH_3(CH_2)_8COOH$	Coconut & palm nut oils, butterfat
Lauric	Dodecanoic	$CH_3(CH_2)_{10}COOH$	Coconut & palm nut oils, butterfat
Myristic	Tetradecanoic	$CH_3(CH_2)_{12}COOH$	Coconut and palm nut oils, most animal and plant fats
Palmitic	Hexadecanoic	$CH_3(CH_2)_{14}COOH$	Practically all animal and plant fats
Stearic	Octadecanoic	$CH_3(CH_2)_{16}COOH$	Animal fats and minor component of plant fats
Arachidic	Eicosanoic	$CH_3(CH_2)_{18}COOH$	Peanut oil
Behenic	Docosanoic	$CH_3(CH_2)_{20}COOH$	Mustard, peanut, and rapeseed oil
Lignoceric	Tetracosanoic	$CH_3(CH_2)_{22}COOH$	Small amounts in peanut oil and most natural fats
Cerotic Acid	Hexacosanoic	$CH_3(CH_2)_{24}COOH$	Wool fat
B. Branched-Chain Series			
Isovaleric	3-methylbutanoic	$(CH_3)_2CHCH_2COOH$	Dolphin and porpoise fat
	11-methyldodecanoic	$(CH_3)_2CH(CH_2)_9COOH$	Butterfat
	13-methyltetradecanoic	$(CH_3)_2CH(CH_2)_{11}COOH$	Butterfat
II. Unsaturated Fatty Acids			
A. Monoethenoic Acids[1]			
Caproleic	9-decenoic	$C_9H_{17}COOH$	Milk fat
Lauroleic	9-dodecenoic	$C_{11}H_{21}COOH$	Milk fat
Myristoleic	9-tetradecenoic	$C_{13}H_{25}COOH$	Animal fat, milk fat
Physeteric	5-tetradecenoic	$C_{13}H_{25}COOH$	Sardine and dolphin oils
Palmitoleic	9-hexadecenoic	$C_{15}H_{29}COOH$	Marine animal oils, minor component plant and animal fats
Oleic	cis-9-Octadecenoic	$C_{17}H_{33}COOH$	Plant and animal fats
Elaidic	trans-9-Octadecenoic	$C_{17}H_{33}COOH$	Animal fats

Name	Systematic name	Formula	Occurrence
Petroselenic	6-Octadecenoic	$C_{17}H_{33}COOH$	Parsley seed & coriander seed oils
Vaccenic	trans-11-Octadecenoic	$C_{17}H_{33}COOH$	Minor component of animal fats & hydrogenated plant oils
Vaccenic	12-Octadecenoic	$C_{17}H_{33}COOH$	Minor component of hydrogenated plant oils
Gadoleic	9-Eicosenoic	$C_{19}H_{37}COOH$	Fish and marine animal oils
Cetoleic	11-Docosenoic	$C_{21}H_{41}COOH$	Marine oils
Erucic	13-Docosenoic	$C_{21}H_{41}COOH$	Rapeseed, mustard, and fanweed oils
Selacholeic	15-Tetracosenoic	$C_{23}H_{45}COOH$	Marine animal and fish liver oils
B. Diethenoid Acids			
Linoleic	9,12-Octadecadienoic	$C_{17}H_{31}COOH$	Peanut, linseed, and cottonseed oils
C. Triethenoid Acids			
Linolenic	9,12,15-Octadecatrienoic	$C_{17}H_{29}COOH$	Linseed and other seed oils
Eleostearic	9,11,13-Octadecatrienoic	$C_{17}H_{29}COOH$	Peanut seed fats
D. Tetraethenoid Acids			
Moroctic	4,8,12,15-Octadecatetraenoic	$C_{17}H_{27}COOH$	Fish oils
Arachidonic	5,8,11,15-Eicosatetraenoic	$C_{19}H_{31}COOH$	Traces in animal fats
E. Polyethenoid Acids			
Clupanodonic	4,8,12,15,19-Docosapentaenoic	$C_{21}H_{33}COOH$	Fish oil
Nisinic	4,8,12,15,18,21-Tetracosahexaenoic	$C_{23}H_{35}COOH$	Sardine and other fish oils
III. Unsaturated Monohydroxy Fatty Acids			
Ricinoleic	12-hydroxy-cis-9-Octadecenoic	$HO—C_{17}H_{32}COOH$	Peanut seed oils and castor oil
IV. Cyclic Fatty Acids			
Lactobacillic acid	ω-(2-n-Octylcyclopropyl)-octanoic acid		Microorganisms
Sterculic acid	ω-(2-n-octylcycloprop-1-enyl)-octanoic acid		Plant seed oil
Malvalic acid	ω-(2-n-octylcycloprop-1-enyl) heptanoic acid		Plant seed oil

[1] In designating the position of the double bond it is customary to number the fatty acid chain in accordance with I.U.P.A.C. system beginning with the C of the carboxyl group and to give only the lower number of each pair of carbon atoms that are in the unsaturated linkage. The symbol Δ is occasionally used with a superscript denoting both carbon atoms formed by the double bond. In the nomenclature, cis-trans configuration is usually not indicated and in these cases the cis form is implied.

and stearic acid ($C_{17}H_{35}COOH$). Saturated fatty acids of less than 16-carbon chain length are frequently found in plant fats. In animal fats, fatty acids containing less than 16 carbons occur only in small quantities. Higher fatty acids such as arachidic acid ($C_{19}H_{39}COOH$) may also occur in animal fats but branched-chain acids are uncommon.

The saturated acids, C-4 through C-8, are liquid at ordinary temperatures (20°C); above C-10 the fatty acids are solids.

Butyric acid is miscible with water in all proportions. As the molecular weight increases solubility diminishes rapidly; caproic, caprylic and capric acids are slightly soluble in water whereas lauric acid and higher homologues are water-insoluble.

In addition to saturated fatty acids, unsaturated fatty acids are found in the fats of animals, plant, and marine animals. Those occurring in animal fats are principally monoethenoic acids (oleic and palmitoleic) because animal cells are unable to synthesize unsaturated fatty acids containing more than one double bond. In contrast di- and triethenoic acids (linoleic and linolenic) are found primarily in plant fats and oil while polyunsaturated acid (arachidonic) are found in fish oils.

Unsaturated fatty acids are more chemically reactive than the saturated fatty acids. The presence of a double bond permits the addition of hydrogen atoms to the double bond, in the presence of a suitable catalyst (palladium, platinum, nickel, and copper) to give the corresponding saturated fatty acid. Thus, oleic, linoleic and linolenic acids give stearic acid upon hydrogenation. Since the melting point of a fat is increased by this procedure, vegetable oils can be hydrogenated to yield semisolid creamy products that are used extensively as shortening agents for pies, cakes, and other bakery products. The hydrogenation process must be controlled in order to yield the type of product desired.

In addition to hydrogenation, unsaturated fatty acids are susceptible to oxidation because of the double bond. Exposure to oxygen of the air causes a fat containing polyunsaturated fatty acids to undergo gradual formation of peroxides together with a mixture of volatile aldehydes, ketones, and acids. The reaction is catalyzed by trace metals or the enzyme lipoxidase.

Unsaturated fatty acids show two types of isomerism: geometric (*cis*, *trans*) and positional (difference in position of the double bond).

Geometric isomerism is due to a restricted rotation of 2 carbon atoms joined by a double bond and the presence of 2 different atoms or groups on the carbon atoms involved in the double bond. The term *cis* and *trans* refers to the geometry of groups (alkyl or others) attached to the carbons of a double bond. Since the carbons of the double bond are not free to rotate on their axis, a group attached to one of the carbons of the double bond can be on the same side of the double bond as a group attached to the other carbon (*cis*). When the groups are on opposite sides they are *trans* to each other. Fatty acids that contain more than 1 double bond can exist in more than 2 geometrical isomeric forms.   For example, linoleic acid can exist in four stereoisomeric forms: *cis-cis*, *cis-trans*, *trans-cis*, and *trans-trans*.

Most naturally occurring unsaturated fatty acids exist in the *cis* form; however, *trans* acids are high in ruminant fats and commercial hydrogenated fats. Upon heating with selenium or nitrous acid, the *cis* forms of unsaturated fatty acids are converted to a mixture of *cis* and *trans* isomers. For example, a portion of oleic acid (*cis* form), when heated with nitrous acid, is converted to elaidic acid (*trans* form).

Cis

$$\begin{array}{ccc} H & & H \\ \diagdown & & \diagup \\ & C=C & \\ \diagup & & \diagdown \\ CH_3(CH_2)_7 & & (CH_2)_7COOH \end{array}$$

Oleic acid (mp $14°C$)

Trans

$$\begin{array}{ccc} CH_3-(CH_2)_7 & & H \\ \diagdown & & \diagup \\ & C=C & \\ \diagup & & \diagdown \\ H & & (CH_2)_7COOH \end{array}$$

Elaidic acid (mp $44°C$)

Positional isomerism occurs in only a few of the naturally occurring unsaturated fatty acids, but it occurs in many derivatives of such acids as well as the synthetic acids. The isomerism depends on the relative position of the double bonds in the carbon skeleton. The 2 most common arrangements are (1) the conjugated system, with alternate single and double bonds:

$$-CH=CH-CH=CH-$$

and (2) the nonconjugated system, with 2 double bonds separated by 1 or more methylene groups:

$$-CH=CH-CH_2-CH=CH-$$

The naturally occurring polyunsaturated fatty acids are non-conjugated; however, upon heating with alkali the unconjugated form (1,4-system) rearranges to the conjugated form (1,3-system). A similar shift may occur when a nonconjugated system is heated to high temperatures or during autoxidation. The reaction is irreversible and the conjugated form is the more stable form. Consequently, the reaction can be made to go to completion. The conjugated system is usually more readily oxidized than the isolated system. Polyunsaturated fatty acids with a conjugated system occur in vegetable glycerides.   Eleosteric acid, the principal acid in tung oil, is one of the most common fatty acids with a conjugated system.

   Cyclic Fatty Acids.—Several acids containing cyclic groups have been isolated from natural sources.   The cyclopropenoid fatty acids, malvalic and sterculic acids, must be removed from cottonseed meal that is to be fed to laying birds, otherwise the acids will produce a pink-white disorder in eggs.

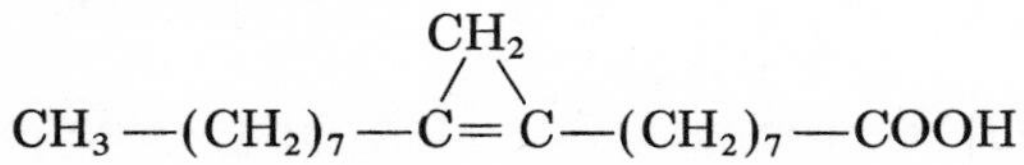

$$CH_3—(CH_2)_7—\overset{\displaystyle CH_2}{\overset{/\ \backslash}{C}}=C—(CH_2)_7—COOH$$

Sterculic acid

$$CH_3—(CH_2)_7—\overset{\displaystyle CH_2}{\overset{/\ \backslash}{C}}=C—(CH_2)_6—COOH$$

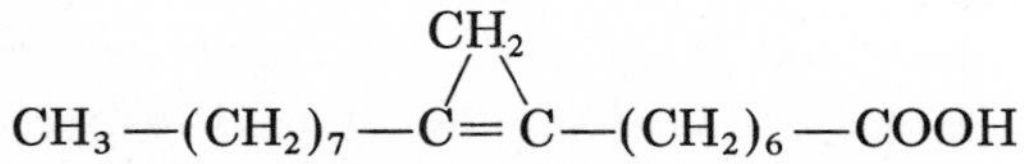

Malvalic acid

Lactobacillic acid, which is extracted from different species of bacteria, contains a cyclopropane ring.

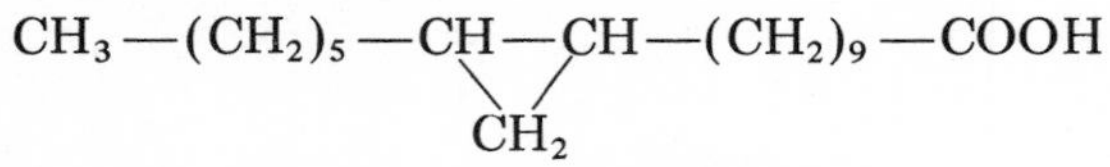

$$CH_3—(CH_2)_5—\underset{\underset{\displaystyle CH_2}{\backslash\ /}}{CH}—CH—(CH_2)_9—COOH$$

Lactobacillic

   Glycerol.—The common constituent of all fats and oils is glycerol. Since glycerol is a trihydric alcohol containing primary and secondary alcohol groups, the compound shows all the chemical reactions of alcohols. For example, on oxidation some of the compounds formed are represented in the following diagram:

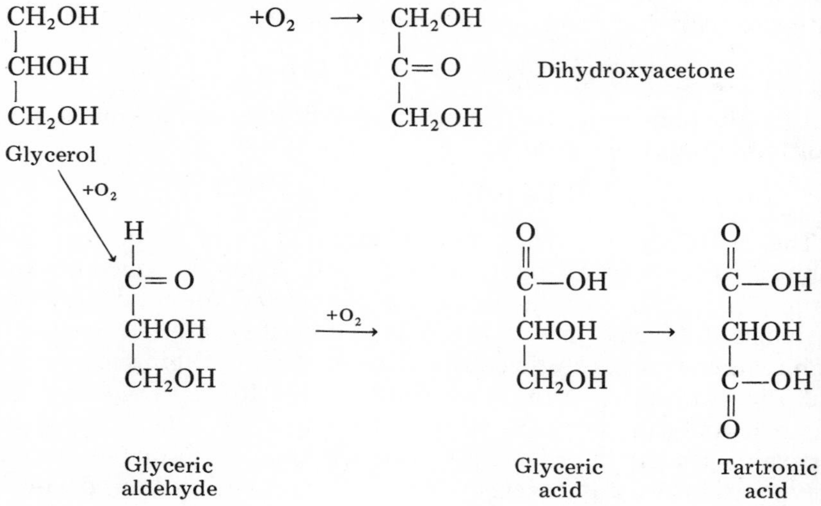

CH₂OH   +O₂   →   CH₂OH
| |
CHOH   C=O   Dihydroxyacetone
| |
CH₂OH   CH₂OH
Glycerol
        \ +O₂
         \
          \   H
           ↘ |
                    C=O   O   O
                    | ‖   ‖
                    CHOH   +O₂   C—OH   C—OH
                    | ⟶ | |
                    CH₂OH   CHOH   →   CHOH
                                                 | |
                                                 CH₂OH   C—OH
                                                                       ‖
                                                                       O

        Glyceric   Glyceric   Tartronic
        aldehyde   acid   acid

An interesting reaction takes place when glycerol is heated to high temperatures, as in the case of fats spilled on a hot stove; it loses two molecules of H_2O forming acrolein a compound with a very pungent odor and irritating action.

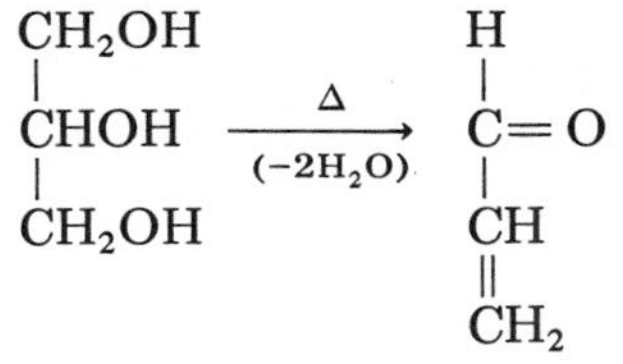

$$
\begin{array}{ccc}
CH_2OH & & H \\
| & & | \\
CHOH & \xrightarrow[(-2H_2O)]{\Delta} & C=O \\
| & & | \\
CH_2OH & & CH \\
& & \| \\
& & CH_2 \\
\text{Glycerol} & & \text{Acrolein}
\end{array}
$$

It forms esters with inorganic, as well as organic acids. Glycerol, which is a by-product of saponification of fats and oils is used commercially as a humectant in some food products. Glycerol forms a trinitrate when heated with concentrated nitric and sulfuric acid. The latter product is used medically as a vasodilator to increase the flow of blood through the coronary arteries.

Waxes.—In contrast to the triglycerides, waxes are esters of long-chained monohydroxy alcohols and fatty acids. Waxes are more resistant to hydrolysis than fats, requiring higher temperatures and stronger alkalies. Natural waxes also contain paraffins, hydroxylated and unsaturated fatty acids, secondary alcohols, and ketones. All of these compounds have high molecular weights and similar physical properties. They are widely distributed in nature, but as a general rule they never occur abundantly. In animals, they cover the surfaces of hair, wool, and feathers. In plants they cover the surface of stems, leaves, and fruits. Fruit waxes often contain cyclic compounds of triterpinoid types; for example, ursolic acid is found as the white coating on the surface of apples, grapes, etc. Some of the more common waxes are listed below:

$$
\begin{array}{cc}
O & O \\
\| & \| \\
C_{30}H_{61}-O-C-C_{15}H_{31} & C_{30}H_{61}-O-C-C_{25}H_{51} \\
\text{Beeswax (myricyl palmitate)} & \text{Carnauba wax (myricyl cerotate)}
\end{array}
$$

$$
\begin{array}{c}
O \\
\| \\
C_{16}H_{33}-O-C-C_{15}H_{31} \\
\text{Spermaceti (cetyl palmitate)}
\end{array}
$$

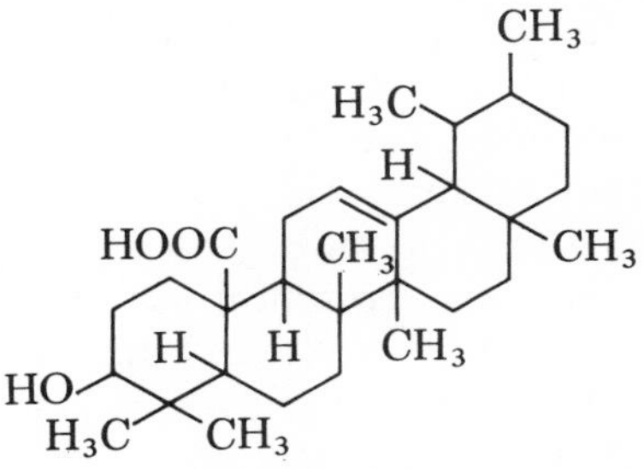

Ursolic acid

Sterols.—The sterols are high molecular weight alcohols occurring in the unsaponifiable fraction of fats. They are insoluble in water, sparingly soluble in cold alcohol or petroleum ether, and readily soluble in fats and the common fat solvents.

The fundamental carbon skeleton of the sterols is the cyclopentanoperhydrophenanthrene ring. The formula of cholesterol as shown gives the system used for designating the various rings and carbon atoms.

Stereoisomerism is an important property of the sterols since they contain a number of asymmetric carbon atoms; cholesterol contains asymmetric carbon atom at position 3,8,9,10,13,14,17, and 20.

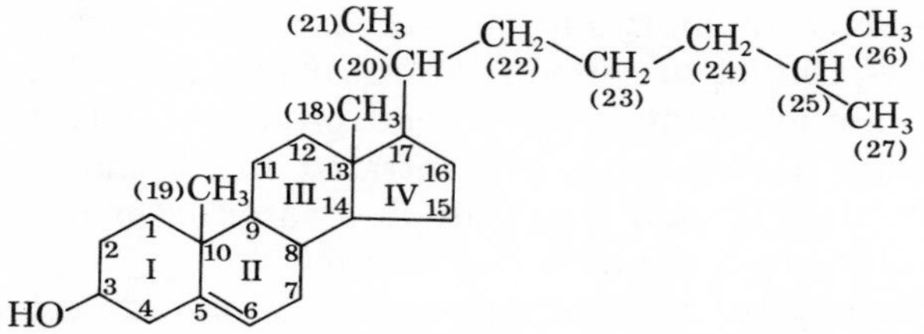

Sterols occur in the fats of plants and animals. The sterols are frequently classified on the basis of their origin; e.g., (1) plant sterols are referred to as phytosterols; (2) sterols from animals are referred to as zoosterols and (3) sterols from lower plants, such as fungi, are referred to as mycosterols.

A common sterol found in peanuts is ergosterol.

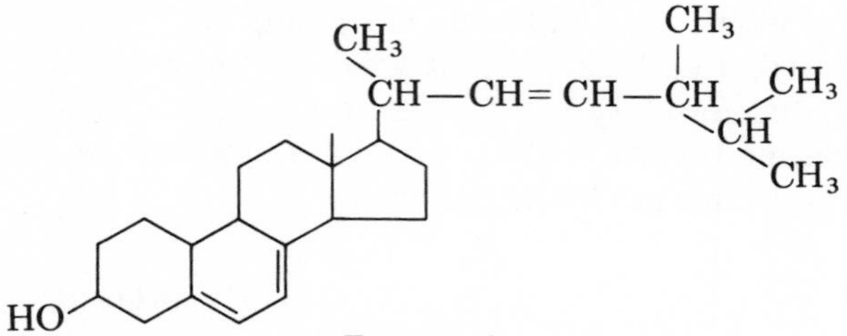

Ergosterol

The Liebermann-Burchard test is a very sensitive color test for sterols. A bluish-green to green color is obtained when a chloroform solution of the sterol is treated with acetic anhydride and concentrated sulfuric acid. The color varies in intensity with the amount of sterol present, and is the basis of a quantitative estimation.

The most common sterol in animals is cholesterol. It is present in all animal cells and has several important biological functions. It serves as the precursor of 7-dehydrocholesterol (vitamin D activity); and as a part of the bile acids, it aids in the emulsification of dietary fats. Cholesterol is utilized in the biosynthesis of the adrenocortical hormones which are important in the development of secondary male and female sex characteristics.

Phospholipids.—The phospholipids (phosphatides) are diglycerides containing phosphoric acid and a nitrogenous base, most commonly choline, ethanolamine, or serine. The phospholipids occur in varying amounts in vegetable and animal fats. Phospholipids make up about 1–2% of many crude vegetable oils and higher percentages in animal fats. Egg yolk contains approximately 20% phospholipids. Only small amounts of phospholipids are present in processed fats since they are essentially removed in the refining of the crude product. Phospholipids have several important biological functions: (1) as essential structural elements in living cells; (2) as intermediates in the transport, absorption, and metabolism of fatty acids; (3) as a storage form for fatty acids and phosphates; (4) as essential components in biological oxidations; (5) as intermediaries in the transport and utilization of sodium and potassium ions; and (6) are involved in the process of blood clotting.

The phospholipids include the phosphoglycerides (lecithin, cephalin, and plasmalogens), the sphinogolipids (sphingomyelins), and the phosphoinositides.

Lecithins.—Lecithins from various sources have the same general structure and can be represented as follows:

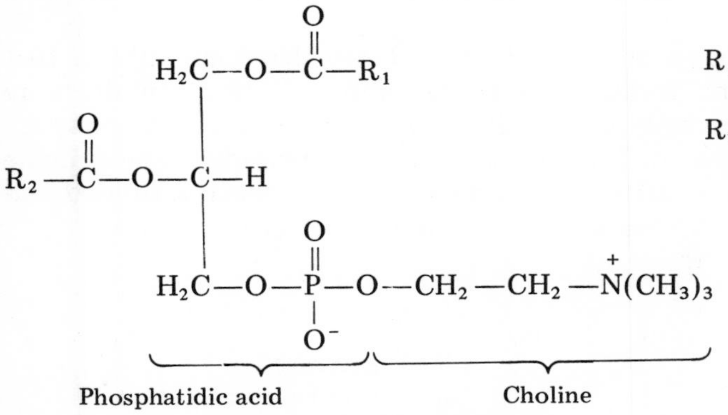

$$
\begin{array}{l}
\text{H}_2\text{C---O---C(=O)---R}_1 \\
\text{R}_2\text{---C(=O)---O---C---H} \\
\text{H}_2\text{C---O---P(=O)(O}^-)\text{---O---CH}_2\text{---CH}_2\text{---}\overset{+}{\text{N}}(\text{CH}_3)_3
\end{array}
$$

R_1 = saturated fatty acid
R_2 = unsaturated fatty acid

Phosphatidic acid   Choline

L-α-lecithin (phosphatidyl choline)

Theoretically, two isomers of lecithin may occur depending upon whether the phosphorylcholine group is attached to the α- or β-carbon of glycerol. The naturally occurring lecithins are primarily of the α-variety. Also, since the C-2 of the glycerol molecule is asymmetric, there are two possible isomers, however, the lecithins found in nature are of the L-variety.

Numerous variations are possible because of the wide variety of fatty acids that may be attached to the glycerol moiety. As a general rule, the fatty acid in the α-position (C-1) is saturated (palmitic or stearic acid) while that in the β-position (C-2) is unsaturated (oleic, linoleic, linolenic, and arachidonic acid).

Choline is an essential component of the diet. It is a quaternary ammonium base bearing a positive charge; and since a negative charge may appear on the phosphate, depending on pH, lecithin may be a dipolar ion. In addition to the importance of choline in the lecithin molecule, choline is also required for acetylcholine, a compound involved in the transmission of nerve impulses. The absence of choline in the diet leads to a fatty infiltration of the liver.

Lecithins are characterized as waxy, colorless solids, that turn yellow and then brown on exposure to light. In general, they are soluble in the usual fat solvents, are insoluble in acetone or methyl acetate, and dissolve in aqueous medium if bile salts are present. The lecithins are surface tension-active substances because of the presence of the strongly polar choline as well as the nonpolar fatty acids.

Lecithins occur in nervous tissue, egg yolk, liver, soybeans, and many crude vegetable oils. They function in tissues to keep non-polar molecules, such as sterols, in an emulsified state. Lecithins are used commercially as emulsifiers and antioxidants in food products.

Cephalins.—These compounds differ from lecithins only in that ethanolamine and serine replace the choline. They contain more unsaturated fatty acids than lecithin and have the L-α-configuration.

The distribution of fatty acids in the phosphatidyl ethanolamine molecule shows an almost equal distribution between saturated and unsaturated acids. Stearic acid is the only saturated fatty acid.

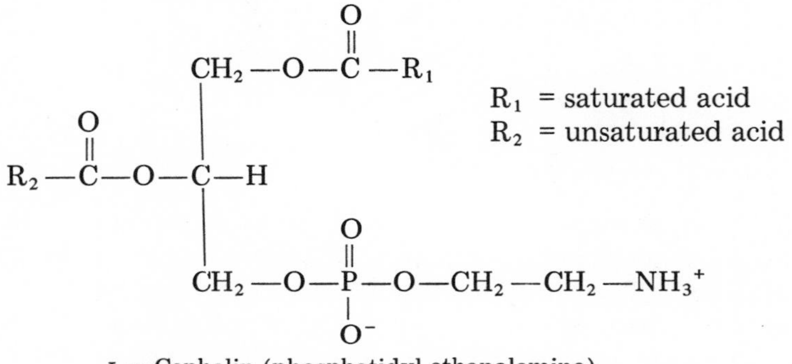

$$CH_2-O-\overset{\displaystyle O}{\overset{\|}{C}}-R_1$$

R_1 = saturated acid
R_2 = unsaturated acid

$$R_2-\overset{\displaystyle O}{\overset{\|}{C}}-O-\overset{|}{\underset{|}{C}}-H$$

$$CH_2-O-\overset{\displaystyle O}{\overset{\|}{\underset{\underset{O^-}{|}}{P}}}-O-CH_2-CH_2-NH_3^+$$

L-α-Cephalin (phosphatidyl ethanolamine)

Cephalin is a colorless solid which readily darkens to a reddish-brown color on exposure to air and light. It can be isolated from brain, liver, and yeasts. Cephalin is soluble in the usual fat solvents but is insoluble in alcohol.

Phosphatidyl serine is also classified as a cephalin. This compound has the following structure.

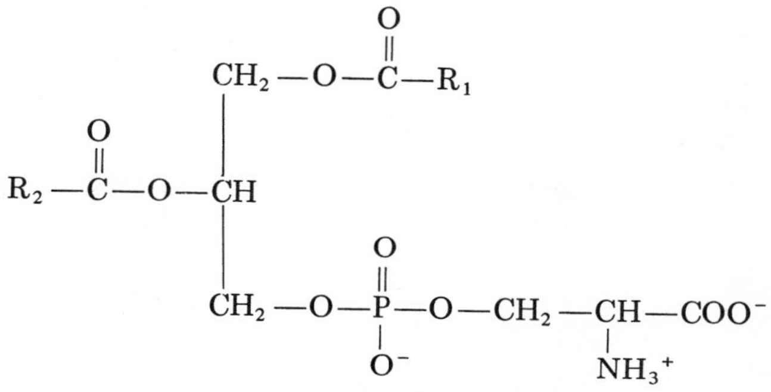

$$CH_2-O-\overset{\overset{\displaystyle O}{\|}}{C}-R_1$$

$$R_2-\overset{\overset{\displaystyle O}{\|}}{C}-O-CH$$

$$CH_2-O-\overset{\overset{\displaystyle O}{\|}}{\underset{\underset{\displaystyle O^-}{|}}{P}}-O-CH_2-\underset{\underset{\displaystyle NH_3^+}{|}}{CH}-COO^-$$

L-α-phosphatidyl serine

It should be noted that decarboxylation of phosphatidyl serine forms phosphatidyl ethanolamine.

Plasmalogens.—Plasmalogens are a subgroup of phosphatides which differ from lecithins and cephalins in that the fatty acid in the α-position is replaced by an α,β-unsaturated ether. These substances are present in the membranes of muscle tissue, brain, and heart.

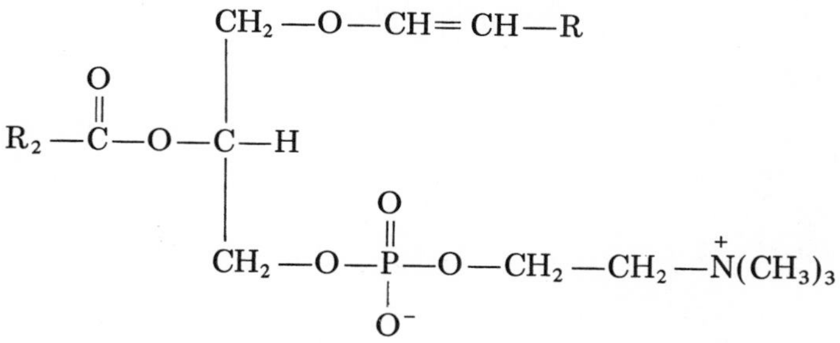

$$CH_2-O-CH=CH-R$$

$$R_2-\overset{\overset{\displaystyle O}{\|}}{C}-O-\underset{\underset{\displaystyle |}{|}}{C}-H$$

$$CH_2-O-\overset{\overset{\displaystyle O}{\|}}{\underset{\underset{\displaystyle O^-}{|}}{P}}-O-CH_2-CH_2-\overset{+}{N}(CH_3)_3$$

A plasmalogen (phosphatidyl choline)

Inositol phosphatides.—These compounds contain the cyclic hexahydroxy alcohol, inositol, attached to the phosphate. A relatively pure "inositide" can be prepared from soybean oil, in which as much as 16% inositol is present. These substances are found in brain tissue and there is evidence that they have an active role in transport processes in the cell.

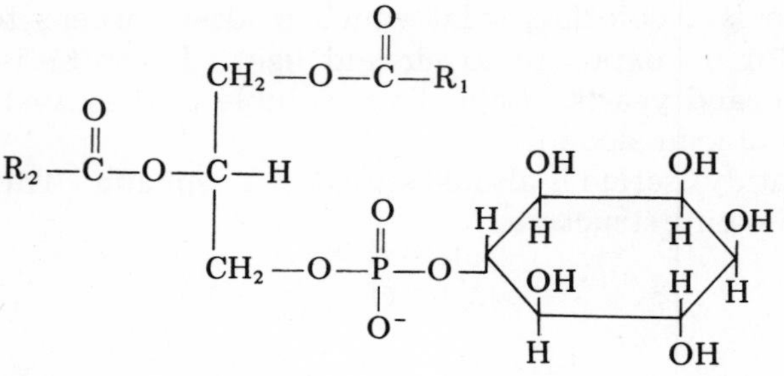

$$CH_2-O-\overset{\overset{\textstyle O}{\|}}{C}-R_1$$

$$R_2-\overset{\overset{\textstyle O}{\|}}{C}-O-\overset{|}{\underset{|}{C}}-H$$

$$CH_2-O-\overset{\overset{\textstyle O}{\|}}{\underset{\underset{\textstyle O^-}{|}}{P}}-O-$$

Phosphatidyl inositol

Other phosphoglycerides of biochemical importance are phosphatidyl glycerol and cardiolipin (diphosphatidyl glycerol). The monophosphatidyl glycerols are found in the cell membranes of

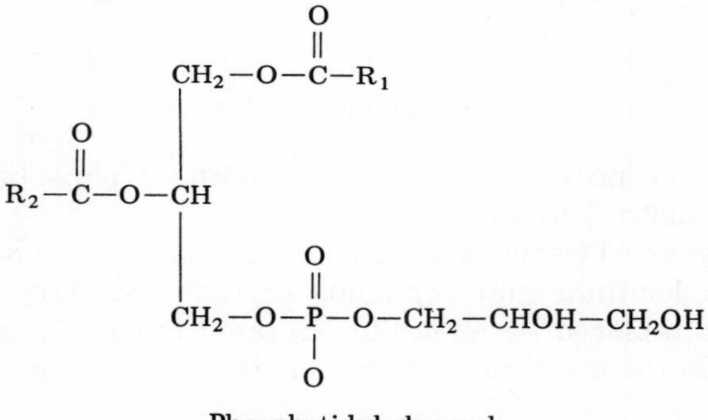

$$CH_2-O-\overset{\overset{\textstyle O}{\|}}{C}-R_1$$

$$R_2-\overset{\overset{\textstyle O}{\|}}{C}-O-CH$$

$$CH_2-O-\overset{\overset{\textstyle O}{\|}}{\underset{\underset{\textstyle O}{|}}{P}}-O-CH_2-CHOH-CH_2OH$$

Phosphatidyl glycerol

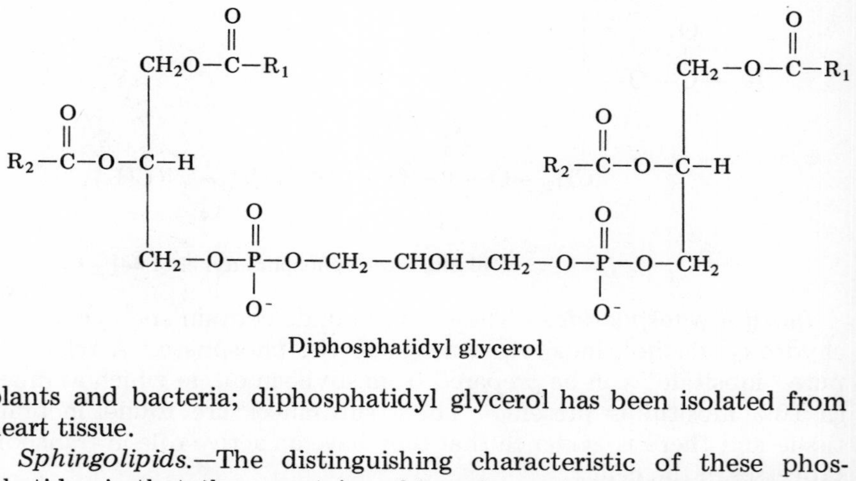

$$CH_2O-\overset{\overset{\textstyle O}{\|}}{C}-R_1 \qquad\qquad CH_2-O-\overset{\overset{\textstyle O}{\|}}{C}-R_1$$

$$R_2-\overset{\overset{\textstyle O}{\|}}{C}-O-\overset{|}{C}-H \qquad R_2-\overset{\overset{\textstyle O}{\|}}{C}-O-\overset{|}{C}-H$$

$$CH_2-O-\overset{\overset{\textstyle O}{\|}}{\underset{\underset{\textstyle O^-}{|}}{P}}-O-CH_2-CHOH-CH_2-O-\overset{\overset{\textstyle O}{\|}}{\underset{\underset{\textstyle O^-}{|}}{P}}-O-CH_2$$

Diphosphatidyl glycerol

plants and bacteria; diphosphatidyl glycerol has been isolated from heart tissue.

Sphingolipids.—The distinguishing characteristic of these phosphatides is that they contain sphingosine, a long-chain unsaturated amino alcohol in contrast to the other phosphatides which have glycerol as a part of their structure. Sphingolipids occur in the membranes of plants and animals. Sphingomyelin, the most common sphingolipid, is a component of nerve and brain tissue. The structure is as follows:

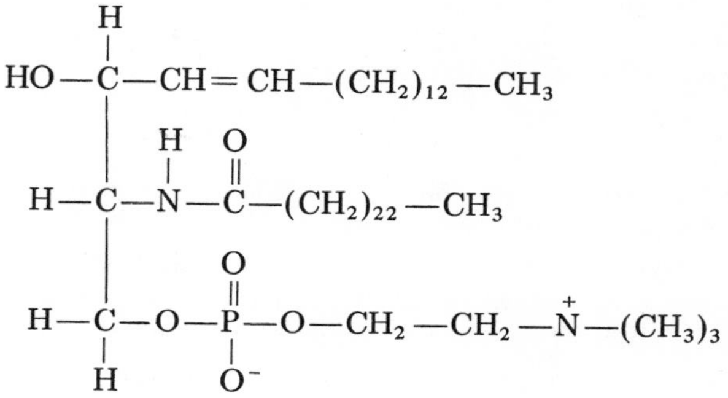

$$HO-\underset{\underset{H}{|}}{C}-CH=CH-(CH_2)_{12}-CH_3$$

$$H-\underset{|}{\overset{\overset{H}{|}}{C}}-N-\overset{\overset{O}{\parallel}}{C}-(CH_2)_{22}-CH_3$$

$$H-\underset{\underset{H}{|}}{C}-O-\overset{\overset{O}{\parallel}}{\underset{\underset{O^-}{|}}{P}}-O-CH_2-CH_2-\overset{+}{N}-(CH_3)_3$$

Sphingomyelin

Cerebrosides (Glycolipids).—The glycolipids are sphingolipids which contain a carbohydrate, usually galactose, in place of phosphorylcholine. Thus, they contain no phosphorus. These substances are abundant in the membranes of brain and nerve cells, but they are

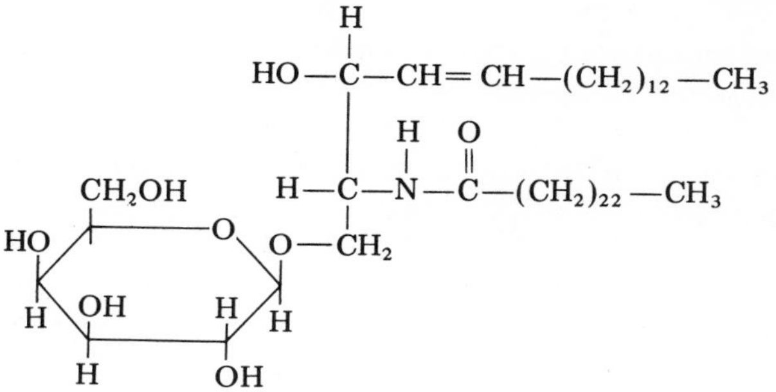

$$HO-\underset{\underset{H}{|}}{C}-CH=CH-(CH_2)_{12}-CH_3$$

$$H-\underset{|}{\overset{\overset{H}{|}}{C}}-N-\overset{\overset{O}{\parallel}}{C}-(CH_2)_{22}-CH_3$$

Cerebroside (β-galactolipid)

also found in the liver, kidney, spleen, and adrenal glands.

Pigments.—Carotene and carotenoid pigments, present in the unsaponifiable fraction of most fats and oils, are responsible for the yellow-red color of many fats and oils of plant origin. The biochemical role of carotenes as provitamin A will be discussed later in more detail.

Deterioration of Triglycerides

Deterioration of fats, or rancidity, constitutes one of the most important technical problems of the food industries. All of the chemical reactions can be explained on the basis of the ester linkage and the nature of the fatty acid glycerides. Deterioration will occur through the hydrolysis of the ester linkage by lipases and moisture (hydrolytic rancidity); through the autoxidation of unsaturated fatty acid glycerides in atmospheric oxygen (oxidative rancidity); through the enzymatic oxidation of unsaturated fatty acid glycerides (lipoxidase rancidity); or the enzymatic oxidation of certain saturated fatty acid glycerides (ketonic rancidity).

Hydrolytic Rancidity.—In hydrolytic rancidity the off-flavor is due to the hydrolysis of a fat with the liberation of free fatty acids. Hydrolytic rancidity is extremely noticeable in fats such as butter because the volatile fatty acids have a disagreeable odor and taste. In contrast, hydrolytic changes in fats which contain few volatile fatty acids, are not evident on the basis of odor and taste.

Oxidative Rancidity.—This is the most important type of fat spoilage because all edible fats, as such or as components of foods, contain unsaturated triglycerides. Oxidative deterioration of fat results in the destruction of vitamins (A, D, E, K, and C), destruction of essential fatty acids, and the development of a pungent and offensive off-flavor.

Fat autoxidation of all nonconjugated olefinic compounds, according to Farmer, proceeds through the formation of a hydroperoxide. Experimental evidence indicates that hydroperoxides are the predominating but not exclusive primary products of autoxidation of fats. Hydroperoxides are relatively unstable at or above 80°C, whereas at room temperatures they are relatively stable; therefore, different end products may be produced under different reaction temperatures. The chain or cyclic nature of autoxidation is well-established (viz. Swern 1960). The polyethenoic acids are more readily oxidized than the monoethenoic acids. The mechanism involves three types of reactions: (1) initiation of the chain reaction, (2) chain propagation, and (3) chain termination.

A mechanism for the autoxidation of a methylene-interrupted unsaturated system (e.g., linoleate) was proposed by Holman (1954). The various reactions which may occur are presented in Fig. 5.1. In the initiation step, a hydrogen atom (H) is abstracted from the methylenic carbon atom adjacent to a double bond. This reaction results in the formation of a free radical (II). The reaction is catalyzed by catalysts (trace metals, oxygen, light, etc.) or enzymes (lipoxidases). Catalysts are necessary; otherwise the reaction would be too slow to be significant. The free radical (II) is a resonance hybrid, the two extreme forms are shown as III. Molecular oxygen adds to the resonating radical, predominantly at the ends, to yield

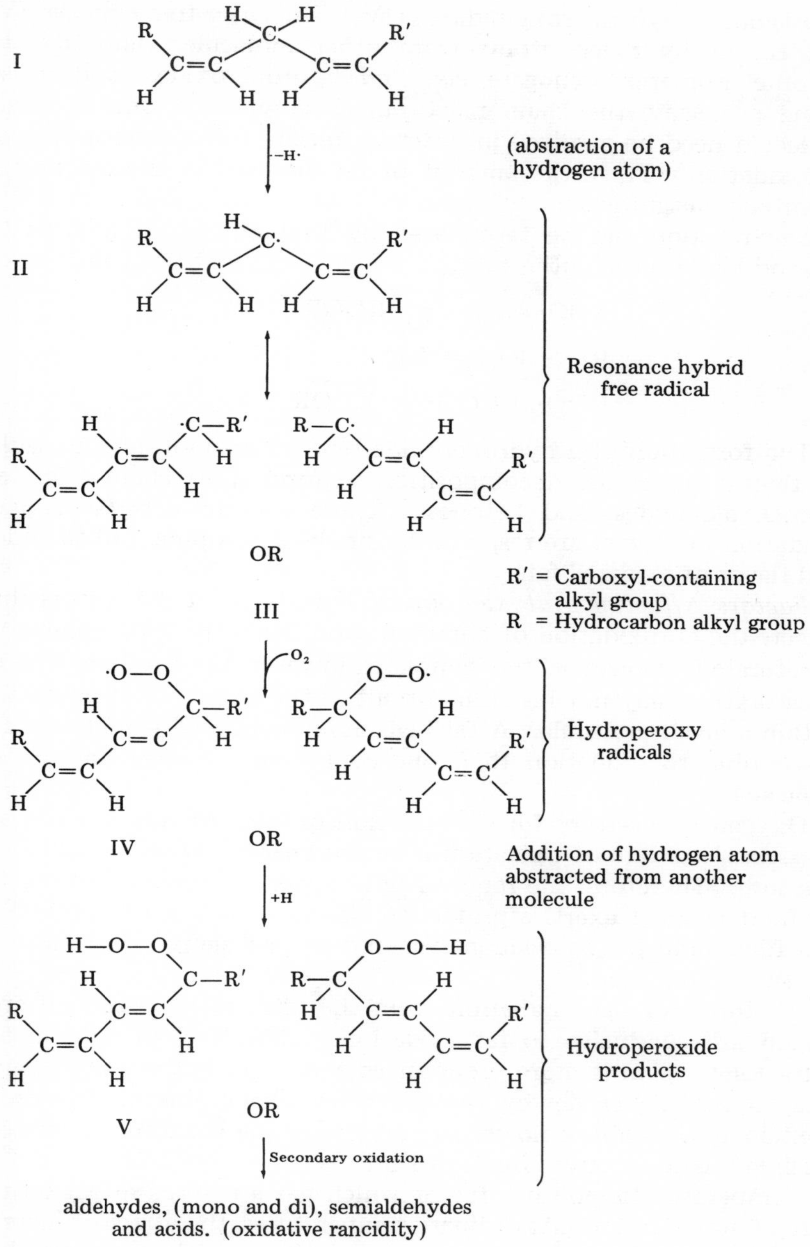

FIG. 5.1 REACTION MECHANISMS FOR THE AUTOXIDATION OF AN UN-
SATURATED FATTY ACID

two types of hydroperoxy radicals (IV). The latter free radicals (IV) can accept hydrogen atoms from other molecules (linoleate) to become isomeric conjugate *cis*, *trans*-hydroperoxides, and in so doing propagate the chain reaction. Theoretically, only a single molecule need be involved in order to initiate the chain reaction of autoxidation. Thus, the amount of fat involved in the reaction is essentially insignificant.

The reaction can be terminated by the collision of radicals II, III, and IV with each other.

$$ROO\cdot + R\cdot \longrightarrow ROOR$$

$$R\cdot + R\cdot \longrightarrow RR$$

$$ROO\cdot + ROO\cdot \longrightarrow ROOR + O_2$$

The formation of a hydroperoxide renders the molecule unstable, so that it undergoes decomposition to form short chain acids, alcohols, aldehydes, and ketones. These end-products (secondary oxidation products) are responsible for the development of the odor and flavor of oxidized fats.

Factors Affecting Autoxidation of Fats.—One of the factors that affects the autoxidation of common food fats is the total number of unsaturated linkages in the sample. However, the total amount of unsaturation may not be as important as the degree of unsaturation within a given molecule. A fat high in linolenic acid would be more susceptible to oxidation than one containing a similar amount of oleic acid.

Oxygen is necessary for autoxidation of fats. At very low oxygen pressures, the rate of oxidation is approximately proportional to the pressure. Therefore, the removal of atmospheric oxygen from a fat or food product exerts a protective effect. This is accomplished in the food industry by vacuum packing or packaging under an inert gas such as nitrogen.

All forms of light radiation from the ultraviolet to the infrared region are conducive to fat oxidation. The effect of light in the ultraviolet region is more pronounced than light in the visible region due to the higher energy of ultraviolet. Packaging in light-proof containers or amber-colored containers are the usual means of controlling the destructive effects of light.

Temperature is another factor which has a marked effect on the rate of autoxidation. At ordinary temperatures, the effect of increasing temperature on the rate of autoxidation is slightly greater than for most chemical reactions because increasing temperatures accelerates both the chain propagation reactions and peroxide decompositions. Consequently, the control of this factor is accomplished by low-temperature storage.

Moisture appears to prevent or inhibit fat autoxidation. It has been demonstrated that small amounts of water inhibit the absorption of oxygen. For example, in the preparation of dehydrated foods, it has been observed that moisture levels for optimal stability vary with the products. These levels vary from 6% moisture for starchy foods to trace moisture for high sugar foods.

Various trace metals, especially copper and iron, act as prooxidants in fat. Thus, in processing packaged fats, or food products containing fats, every precaution must be taken to eliminate contamination with these trace metals.

Antioxidants.—Antioxidants act primarily as hydrogen donors or free radical acceptors and the reaction may be represented as follows:

$$ROO\cdot + AH_2 \longrightarrow ROOH + AH\cdot$$

$$AH\cdot + AH\cdot \longrightarrow A + AH_2$$

Thus, the primary role of antioxidants is one of breaking the chain reaction of autoxidation by reacting with hydroperoxy radicals. The antioxidants may be classed as (1) natural, and (2) synthetic. Many fats and oils, particularly in the unrefined form, are quite stable to oxidative rancidity. This stability is due to the presence of natural antioxidants. The tocopherols (α, β, and γ) are the most important of the natural antioxidants and are widespread in both plant and animal tissues. Vegetable oils contain much higher concentrations than animal fats. The tocopherols are effective antioxidants for animal fats, but have little antioxidant effect when added to vegetable fats. The tocopherols are readily oxidized to tocoquinones which have no antioxidant properties. Too, the tocopherols are readily destroyed by heat, particularly at temperatures employed in the refining and processing of fats and oils.

Naturally occurring antioxidants exhibit relatively weak antioxidant properties. As a consequence, synthetic antioxidants have been developed for use in foods. These substances, to be allowed in foods, must have a low order of toxicity, should be effective in low concentrations in a wide variety of fats, should contribute no objectionable flavor, odor or color to the product, and should have approval by the Food & Drug Administration.

Since antioxidants vary in their effectiveness to stabilize fats of fat products, and in their mode of action, combinations of antioxidants are often used to stabilize fatty foods. The first satisfactory antioxidant combination was a mixture of butylated hydroxyanisole

(BHA), propyl gallate, and citric acid to stabilize lard for shortening purposes.   At the present time BHA, butylated hydroxytoluene (BHT) and propyl gallate (PG) constitute the major proportion of the total antioxidants used.   Other antioxidants are used in only limited amounts.   Citric acid or other metal chelators are usually added as insurance against trace quantities of metals often present in fats and oils.

Certain acidic compounds such as ascorbic, citric, and phosphoric acids, have been found to exert a synergistic effect when added along with polyphenolic antioxidants; consequently, they have been called synergists.   These acidic compounds are effective metal chelating agents which give rise to the theory that their only activity is that of metal chelation.   However, if citric acid were added alone, it would exhibit no antioxidant activity.   Privett (1961) has suggested a series of reactions which permit an explanation of the general characteristics of synergism.   These reactions are as follows:

Absence of Synergist

$$AH + ROOH \longrightarrow A + \begin{cases} RO \cdot + H_2O \\ R \cdot + H_2O_2 \end{cases}$$

$$A \cdot + ROOH \longrightarrow OxA + \begin{cases} RO \cdot + H_2O \\ R \cdot + H_2O \end{cases}$$

Presence of Synergist

$$AH + ROOH \longrightarrow A \cdot + \begin{cases} RO \cdot + H_2O \\ R \cdot + H_2O_2 \end{cases}$$

$$A + S \longrightarrow A \cdot S$$

$$A \cdot S + ROOH \longrightarrow \text{No reaction or very slow}$$

$$A \cdot S + ROO \cdot \longrightarrow OxA + ROOH + S$$

AH = original antioxidant   S = Synergist
ROOH = hydroperoxide $A \cdot S$ = antioxidant radical
A· = antioxidant radical   synergist complex
OxA = oxidized antioxidant   ROO· = peroxide radical formed
                                                          in autoxidation

According to the above theory, the synergist forms an antioxidant radical-synergist complex $(A \cdot S)$ and this chemical association suppresses the antioxidant's catalysis of peroxide composition.   By suppressing the catalysis, additional chain formation is stopped and consequently the antioxidant is spared from its function in stopping such chains.

Lipid Metabolism

Most people consider fat as a substance which does nothing more than accumulate at an alarming rate in certain well-defined regions of the body. Lipids, however, have many functions in the body other than as a means of storing utilizable energy. For example, adipose tissue acts as a padding for protecting organs such as the heart, kidney, lungs, and spleen. Triglycerides function as solvents for the fat-soluble vitamins. Phospholipids are important structural components of cell membranes.

Digestion and Absorption.—Very little breakdown of ingested fat occurs before the food reaches the small intestine. Fat entering the small intestine is emulsified into very small globules by the salts of the bile acids. Pancreatic lipase catalyzes the hydrolysis of the ester linkages of the triglyceride molecule in a specific manner. The hydrolysis occurs at the α or α' positions to yield an α,β-diglyceride. The latter product is then hydrolyzed to a monoglyceride, primarily the β-monoglyceride. It will be recalled the β-monoglycerides isomerize to give a mixture of α- and β-monoglycerides. The result of the hydrolysis is a heterogeneous mixture containing mainly fatty acids and glycerol, some β-monoglycerides, and small amounts of di- and triglycerides as well as fat-soluble compounds originally present in the fat.

Phospholipids are hydrolyzed by pancreatic phosphatidases to yield glycerol, fatty acids, phosphate, and nitrogenous bases.

A group of pancreatic esterases catalyze the hydrolysis of cholesterol esters and short-chain triglycerides. Complete hydrolysis of fats is not essential for absorption. The hydrolytic reactions by esterases are accelerated by the bile salts which promote the emulsification and solubilization of lipids. The products of lipid hydrolysis are absorbed through the intestinal wall. Fatty acids containing 12 or more carbon atoms together with the glycerides (mono-, di- and triglycerides) are resynthesized into triglycerides in the intestinal mucosa, released into the lymph which then enter the portal circulation via the thoracic duct. Fatty acids containing 10 carbon atoms or less together with glycerol appear in the portal circulation and are transported to the liver. Transport of the resynthesized glycerides in the lymph and portal circulation occur in the form of chylomicrons (lipoprotein complexes). It is these minute droplets which give a milky appearance to the blood following the ingestion of a meal high in fat. Triglyceride synthesis in the intestinal mucosa is similar to that which occurs in the liver. The glycerol used for triglyceride synthesis in the intestinal mucosa is not the same as that absorbed through the intestinal wall but is in the form of α-L-glycerophosphate from the glycolytic pathway.

Cholesterol is esterified in the epithelial cells and released in the lymph. Cholesterol is the only sterol found in foods which is absorbed. Plant sterols are not absorbed. The D-vitamins are absorbed as well as certain sex and adrenal hormones.

Storage and Transport of Lipids.—Foods ingested beyond the normal daily requirements are largely converted to triglyceride and distributed in all organs and adipose tissue. The latter tissues are located subcutaneously, abdominally, and intramuscularly. In these specialized tissues the lipid is stored as droplets in the cytoplasm of the cells. As a rule, the composition of the stored lipid is characteristic of the particular species. However, the composition of the lipid in animals may be altered by the composition of the dietary fats. Environmental temperature can have an effect on the composition of the storage fat.

The depot fats are in a state of dynamic equilibrium. As long as caloric intake is sufficient to meet the energy requirements of the organism, there will be no net gain or loss in depot fat. Failure to provide sufficient calories to meet energy needs will result in a net loss of depot fat; conversely, an excess of calories will result in a net increase in depot fat. Consequently, adipose tissue has two functions: (1) it has the capacity to synthesize and store lipids, and (2) it has the capacity to mobilize lipids for transport to the various tissues for oxidation.

As discussed above, there is an increase in blood concentration of fatty acids and glycerides (chylomicra) following introduction of fatty foods into the small intestine. The chylomicra give a milky appearance to the blood plasma. The milky emulsion disappears as the blood circulates through the liver and other organs because of the hydrolysis of the lipids by plasma lipoprotein lipase (or clearing factor). The fatty acids released from the glycerides in the blood are bound to plasma albumin. Thus, plasma proteins play a major role in the transport of free acids (FFA).

Hormones influence the concentration of plasma FFA. For example, concentrations of FFA are increased by epinephrine because of an increase in lipase activity in adipose tissue. Insulin acts in an opposite manner; i.e., an increase in blood glucose results in a decrease in FFA. Conversely, when the blood glucose level or liver glycogen is low, the plasma FFA increases, mainly from the breakdown of triglycerides stored in the liver and adipose tissue. Thus, the initial step in the utilization of either dietary fat or fat reserves is the hydrolytic breakdown by lipases to glycerol and fatty acids.

Intermediary Metabolism of Fatty Acids.—The fatty acids liberated from the depots into the blood are in the form of nonesterified fatty acids (FFA). The fatty acids are oxidized in the mitochondria of a variety of tissues including liver, heart, and kidney. The fatty acids are degraded by β-oxidation to acetyl-SCoA which may be oxidized in the tricarboxylic acid (TCA) cycle to carbon dioxide and water. Acetyl-SCoA may also be transported out of the mitochondria for biosynthesis (anabolism) of other compounds, including fatty acids.

β-Oxidation of Fats.—Before fatty acids can be oxidized, they must first be activated to the acyl-SCoA ester by a reaction involving ATP, Coenzyme ASH, and the enzyme thiokinase (Fig. 5.2, Reaction 1). All further reactions of the β-oxidation scheme take place on the fatty acyl-SCoA compound, which will ultimately degrade to units of acetyl-SCoA. The activated compound is first dehydrogenated by the enzyme, acyl-SCoA dehydrogenase; the product is the corresponding α,β-unsaturated acyl-SCoA compound (Reaction 2). The enzyme (acyl-SCoA dehydrogenase) contains flavin adenine dinucleotide (FAD) as the coenzyme. There are several acyl-SCoA dehydrogenases that are specific for fatty acids of different chain lengths. Carnitine has been observed to mediate the transfer of the extramitochondrial fatty acyl group through the mitochondrial membrane to the enzymes of β-oxidation present within the mitochondria. The enzymes of the electron transport system reoxidize the flavoproteins ($FADH_2$).

Water is added across the double bond of the unsaturated acyl-SCoA compound to yield L-β-hydroxyacyl-SCoA (Reaction 3). The enzyme, enoyl-SCoA hydrase, catalyzes the stereospecific addition of water to the *trans*-2 enoyl derivatives of CoASH to form the L-β-hydroxyacyl-SCoA derivatives. It also catalyzes the hydration of the *cis* isomer to form the L-β-hydroxyacyl-SCoA derivatives.

In the next step, the β-hydroxy compound is dehydrogenated to the corresponding β-keto compound (Reaction 4). The enzyme β-hydroxyacyl dehydrogenase is stereospecific for the L-isomer and acts on all chain lengths. This is the second oxidative step and requires NAD^+ as a hydrogen acceptor. Reoxidation of NADH is effected by the transport of hydrogen along the respiratory chain to become oxidized to water.

The dehydrogenated acid, β-ketoacyl-SCoA, undergoes cleavage with another molecule of CoA-SH to produce acetyl-SCoA and a fatty acid-SCoA derivative with two less carbon atoms (Reaction 5). The reaction is termed thioclastic cleavage and the enzyme involved is β-ketothiolase. The acyl-SCoA derivative, shortened by two carbon atoms, will return to Reaction 2. The feedback of an active acyl derivative will continue until the fatty acid molecule has been degraded to acetyl-CoA.

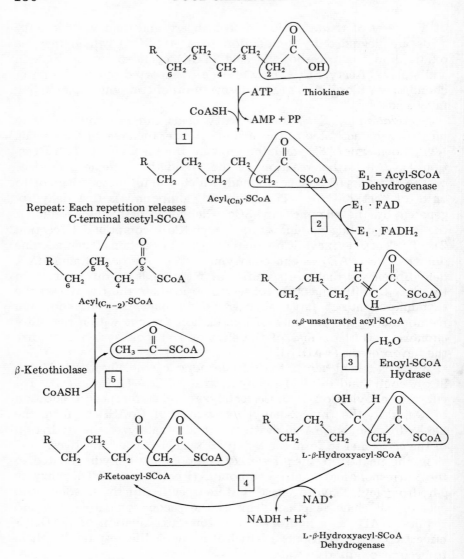

FIG. 5.2 SCHEME FOR THE β-OXIDATION OF FATTY ACIDS

Fatty acids that are branched or contain an odd number of carbon atoms can be metabolized by essentially the same pathway as described above. In the case of a branched-chain fatty acid, the respective branched acyl-SCoA is formed near the point of branching. Similarly, where an odd-numbered straight-chain fatty acid is involved, 2 carbon units in the form of acetyl-SCoA would be successively removed until the last 3 carbon atoms which become propionyl-SCoA. The propionyl-SCoA enters the tricarboxylic acid cycle in the form of succinyl-CoA. The series of reactions may be summarized as follows:

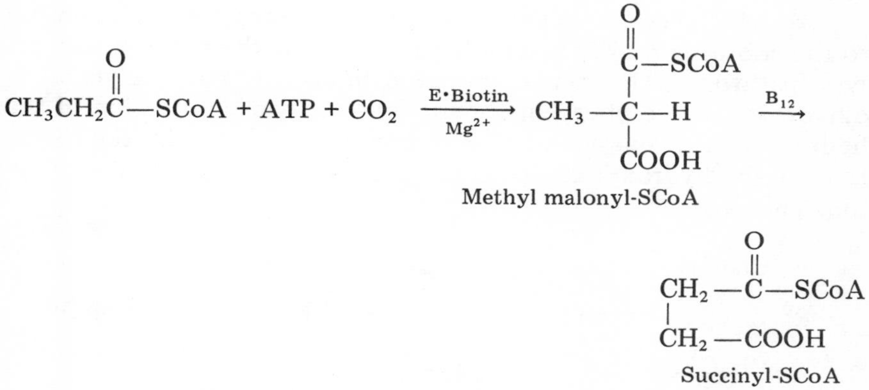

$$CH_3CH_2\overset{\overset{O}{\|}}{C}\text{—SCoA} + ATP + CO_2 \xrightarrow[Mg^{2+}]{E \cdot Biotin} CH_3\text{—}\underset{\underset{COOH}{|}}{\overset{\overset{O}{\|}}{\overset{C\text{—SCoA}}{\underset{|}{C}}}}\text{—H} \xrightarrow{B_{12}}$$

Methyl malonyl-SCoA

$$\underset{CH_2\text{—COOH}}{\overset{O}{\underset{|}{CH_2\text{—}\overset{\|}{C}\text{—SCoA}}}}$$

Succinyl-SCoA

The importance of this pathway lies in the fact that the breakdown of amino acids involves the intermediate formation of branched fatty acids, which are then metabolized as propionyl-SCoA or other acyl compounds such as methylmalonyl-SCoA, acetyl-SCoA, and acetoacetate.

The enzyme system involved in the β-oxidation of fatty acids is closely linked with the respiratory chain and tricarboxylic acid systems in the mitochondria. This association provides for the maximal yield of ATP from the β-oxidation of fatty acids. From each C_2 fragment, 1 molecule of $FADH_2$ (Reaction 2) and 1 molecule of NADH (Reaction 4) are formed. The reoxidation of these reduced coenzymes via the respiratory chain results in the formation of 2 molecules of ATP from $FADH_2$ and 3 molecules of ATP from NADH or a total of 5. Thus, the number of molecules of ATP produced per mole of long-chain fatty acid is considerable and the effectiveness of fats as a source of energy is evident.

The acetyl-SCoA produced by fatty acid oxidation follows two main pathways. (1) Under normal conditions most of the acetyl-SCoA condenses with oxaloacetate to form citrate, consequently it enters the tricarboxylic acid cycle for oxidation to CO_2 and H_2O. Each mole of acetyl-SCoA formed by β-oxidation would ultimately form 12 moles of ATP via the citric acid cycle and electron transport coupled with oxidative phosphorylation (see Chap. 12 for citric acid cycle). (2) When acetyl-SCoA is present in amounts greater than can be handled by the tricarboxylic acid cycle (e.g., starvation or diabetes), then acetoacetyl-SCoA is formed from acetyl-SCoA. Acetoacetyl-SCoA normally reacts with acetyl-SCoA in the synthesis of cholesterol. In abnormal conditions, e.g., diabetes, acetoacetyl-SCoA forms ketone bodies (acetoacetate, β-hydroxy-butyrate, and acetone).

Fate of Glycerol.—Glycerol, because of its structural relationship to the trioses is readily metabolized by way of the anaerobic glycolytic pathway. The steps involved in the conversion of glycerol to dihydroxyacetone phosphate are as follows: phosphorylation of the hydroxyl group on the alpha-carbon atom, followed by the oxidation of the hydroxyl group on the β-carbon to form dihydroxyacetone phosphate.

$$
\begin{array}{c}
\text{CH}_2\text{OH} \\
|\\
\text{CHOH} \\
|\\
\text{CH}_2\text{OH}
\end{array}
+ \text{ATP}
\xrightleftharpoons{\text{glycerokinase}}
\begin{array}{c}
\text{CH}_2\text{OH} \\
|\\
\text{HOCH} \\
|\\
\text{CH}_2\text{O}-\text{PO}_3{}^{2-}
\end{array}
+ \text{ADP}
$$

L-α-glycerophosphate

$$
\begin{array}{c}
\text{CH}_2\text{OH} \\
|\\
\text{C}=\text{O} \\
|\\
\text{CH}_2-\text{O}-\text{PO}_3{}^{2-}
\end{array}
\xleftarrow[\text{dehydrogenase}]{\text{Glycerophosphate}}
\quad \text{NADH}+\text{H}^+ \curvearrowright \text{NAD}^+
$$

It will be recalled that dihydroxyacetone phosphate is in the pathway for the formation of pyruvic acid (refer to glycolysis) and ultimately acetyl-SCoA. The reactions involved in the conversion of dihydroxyacetone phosphate to pyruvic acid generate 2 moles of ATP (1,3-diphosphoglyceric acid to 3-phosphoglyceric acid and phosphoenol-pyruvic to pyruvic acid. Since the phosphorylation of glycerol (see above) required a mole of ATP, the net production is one ATP molecule. Additionally, the NADH produced ultimately forms three moles of ATP via electron transport.

Fat as a Source of Energy for Work.—Energy must be supplied to the body both for its normal functioning and for the performance of work. It is known that during muscular work fats are oxidized. Evidence in support of this view has been obtained from respiratory quotient studies and from the fact that work causes a rise in serum lipids.

A total of five ATP molecules are produced each time the cycle of β-oxidation is traversed. Palmitic acid, for example, with 16 carbon atoms will be traversed 7 times to degrade it completely to acetyl-SCoA (in the final turn, 2 moles of acetyl-SCoA are produced). Thus, the conversion of palmitic acid to acetyl-SCoA will produce 35 molecules of ATP. The primary activation of palmitic acid required 1 molecule, ATP, or a net yield of 34 molecules of ATP is realized from each molecule of palmitic acid.

The eight molecules of acetyl-SCoA produced by the β-oxidation of palmitic acid now enters the tricarboxylic acid cycle (TCA).

Each molecule of acetyl-SCoA, degraded via the TCA cycle, yields 12 molecules of ATP or a total of 96 molecules of ATP. This sum added to the above figure (34) gives a total of 130 molecules of ATP formed by the complete oxidation of palmitic acid. For purpose of calculation, let us use tripalmitin as the triglyceride (Fig. 5.3).

There are three fatty acids in a triglyceride. A molecule of tripalmitin will yield 390 molecules of ATP. To this must be added the 7 molecules of ATP produced in the conversion of glycerol to pyruvic acid, and the 15 moles of ATP produced when pyruvic acid is degraded by the TCA cycle. Thus, a net yield of 412 molecules of ATP (energy rich bonds) is realized when tripalmitin is oxidized in the body. The total combustion of tripalmitin yields 7537 kilocalories. Assuming a value of 7.5 kilocalories per molecule of ATP, the efficiency of conversion of available energy to a utilizable form (ATP) becomes:

$$\frac{412 \times 7.5}{7537} \times 100 = 41.5\%$$

The remaining energy is lost, probably as heat. It becomes clear why body fat is an effective source of energy. If the diet is not to be very bulky, the intake of fat is required.

Since the site of β-oxidation is intramitochondrial and since much of the thiokinases for activating free fatty acids occurs in the cytosol of the cell, a mechanism must exist for the transfer of the fatty acyl-SCoA across the mitochondrial membrane. Carnitine, γ-trimethylamine-β-hydroxybutyrate, serves as the acyl group acceptor. In this mechanism, the free fatty acids is activated to the CoASH derivative, the fatty acyl-SCoA is transferred to the carrier molecule carnitine by carnitine transferase. The acylated carnitine ester crosses the mitochondrial membrane where it is reconverted to the fatty acyl-SCoA derivative and then oxidized by the β-oxidation system. The mechanism is as follows:

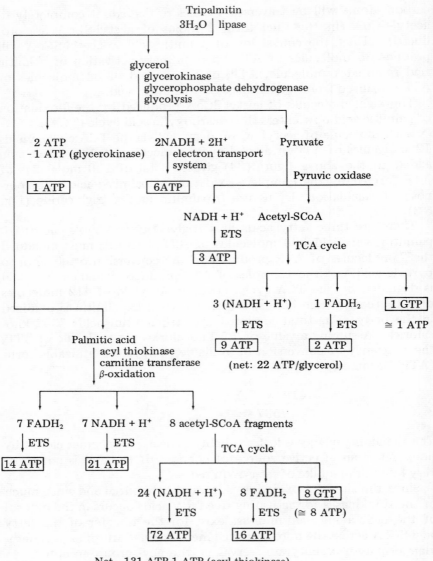

FIG. 5.3. SCHEME SHOWING ENERGY YIELD FROM DEGRADATION OF TRIPALMITIN

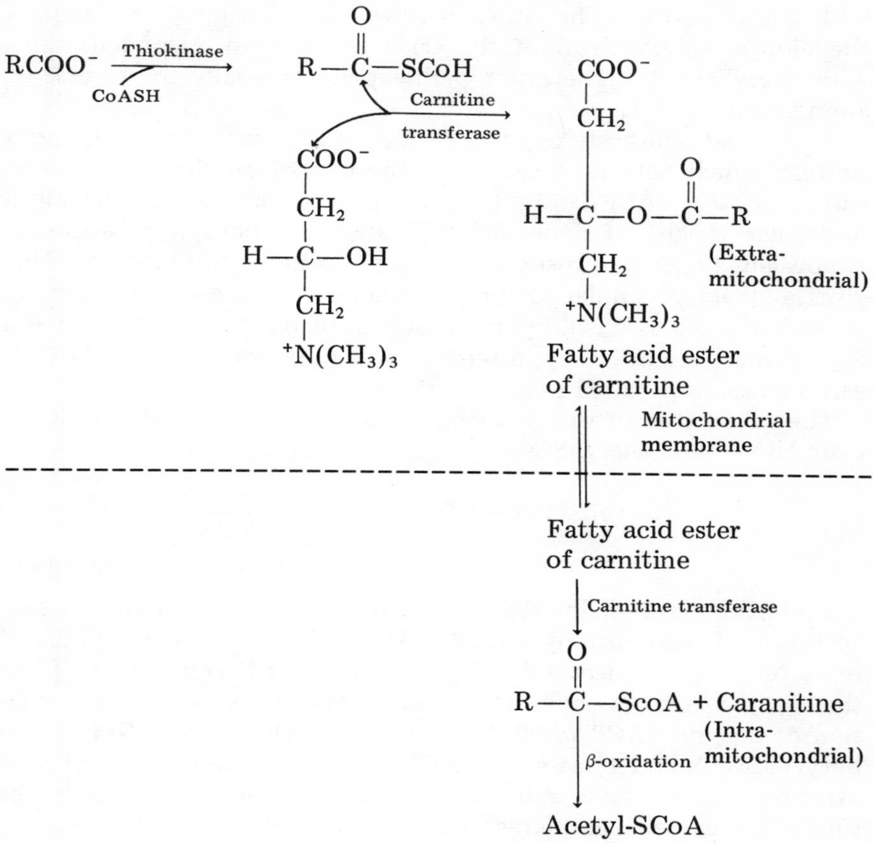

$$\text{RCOO}^- \xrightarrow[\text{CoASH}]{\text{Thiokinase}} R-\overset{\overset{\displaystyle O}{\|}}{C}-\text{SCoH}$$

Carnitine transferase

$$\begin{array}{c}\text{COO}^- \\ | \\ \text{CH}_2 \\ | \\ H-C-OH \\ | \\ \text{CH}_2 \\ | \\ ^+\text{N(CH}_3)_3\end{array}$$

$$\begin{array}{c}\text{COO}^- \\ | \\ \text{CH}_2 \\ | \\ H-C-O-\overset{\overset{\displaystyle O}{\|}}{C}-R \quad \text{(Extra-} \\ | \quad\quad\quad \text{mitochondrial)} \\ \text{CH}_2 \\ | \\ ^+\text{N(CH}_3)_3\end{array}$$

Fatty acid ester
of carnitine

Mitochondrial
membrane

- -

Fatty acid ester
of carnitine

Carnitine transferase

$$R-\overset{\overset{\displaystyle O}{\|}}{C}-\text{ScoA} + \text{Caranitine}$$
(Intra-
β-oxidation mitochondrial)

Acetyl-SCoA

Synthesis of Fatty Acids

Not all fat in the body comes from dietary fat because the consumption of carbohydrate alone can lead to an increase in body fat. Similarly, in peanut seeds there is an increase in fat content with an accompanying decrease in carbohydrate content. These observations imply that a mechanism exists for the synthesis of fatty acids from carbohydrate.

It was previously believed that fatty acid synthesis could be accounted for simply by reversing the sequence of reactions of β-oxidation. However, evidence now indicates that there are at least 3 pathways for the synthesis of fatty acids, 2 in the mitochondria and 1 in the microsomal portion of the cytoplasm. The cytoplasmic pathway is considered to be the major pathway. One of the pathways in the mitochondria is similar to the cytoplasmic pathway, which catalyzes synthesis of fatty acids, *de novo*, beginning with acetyl-SCoA. The other pathway in mitochondria catalyzes the elongation of certain fatty acids by successive condensations with acetyl-SCoA. The latter pathway is essentially the reverse of β-oxidation.

Fatty acid synthesis requires HCO_3^-, ATP, Mn^{2+}, NADPH, and a protein which acts as a carrier of the acyl-SCoA derivatives (acyl carrier protein; ACP). Acyl carrier protein is a protein having a molecular weight of approximately 9000. 4'-phosphopantotheine is covalent bonded to a serine hydroxyl group of the protein. This gives a structure similar to the phosphopantotheine of coenzyme A in which there is a sulfhydryl group available for bonding to the acyl group. Additionally, a biotin containing enzyme, acetyl-SCoA carboxylase, is required in the reactions.

The initial step of the synthesis is the formation of malonyl-SCoA from HCO_3^- and acetyl-SCoA:

$$\text{Acetyl-SCoA} + HCO_3^- + ATP \xrightarrow[\text{Enz·Biotin}]{Mn^{2+}}$$

$$\text{Malonyl-SCoA} + ADP + Pi$$

Acetyl-SCoA and malonyl-SCoA then react with ACP-SH to give acetyl-SACP and malonyl-SACP. Acetyl-SACP and malonyl-SACP react to give acetoacetyl-SACP where carbons 3 and 4 come from the acetyl-SACP. A series of enzymatic reactions lead to the formation of butyryl-SACP which then can react with CoASH to produce butyryl-SCoA and releases the ACP-SH. The cycle can be repeated utilizing butyryl-SACP and malonyl-SACP, adding two carbons per turn of the cycle until the reactions is terminated (Fig. 5.4).

The subsequent conversions (namely reduction, loss of water and a second reduction), yield an even-numbered saturated fatty acid-SCoA derivative, having two more carbon atoms than it started with. The long chain of fatty acids are synthesized in this manner. Available evidence has led to the view that the intermediate short chain fatty acids are not released in appreciable amounts by the enzyme complex (synthetase) involved in the biosynthesis of long chain acids. Only when a chain length of C_{16} or C_{18} is reached will the acyl-SCoA be released from the enzyme complex. This fact provides an explanation for the large amount of palmitic and stearic acid in neutral fats.

The acetyl-SCoA required for the synthesis of fatty acids in the cytoplasm of the cell is derived from the mitochondria via the transfer of acetyl carnitine through the mitochondrial membrane. Thus, carnitine functions as the acetyl group carrier in a manner

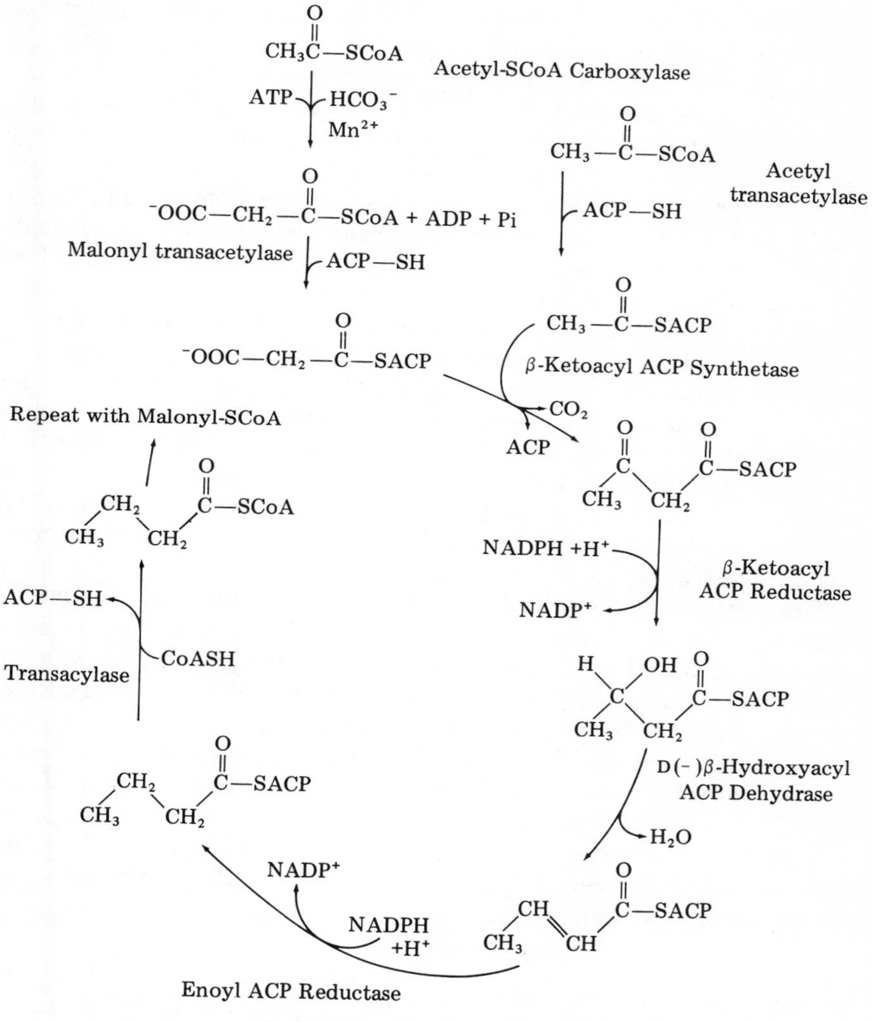

FIG. 5.4. SCHEME FOR THE BIOSYNTHESIS OF FATTY ACIDS

opposite to that discussed above. The principal sources of intra-mitochondrial acetyl-SCoA are the oxidation of pyruvate and the β-oxidation of long-chain fatty acids.

It is well-established that palmitoleic $(16:1\omega 7)$, oleate $(18:1\omega 9)$, linoleate $(18:2\omega 6)$, and linolenate $(18:3\omega 3)$ each serve as the initial precursor for the biosynthesis of all other unsaturated fatty acids (viz. Mead 1968).[1] Consequently, there are apparently additional pathways in mitochondria and microsomes for chain lengthening and shortening by C-2 units as well as for interconversion of mono- to polyunsaturated fatty acids. Two of the above precursors, palmitoleic and oleic acids, are synthesized from palmitic (16) and stearic (18) acid while linoleic and linolenic acids must be derived from the diet (linoleic and linolenic acid are synthesized *de novo* in higher plants and molds). The latter fatty acids are essential fatty acids because the animal cannot form a double bond within the terminal seven carbon atoms of the chain. In general, animals can synthesize palmitoleic, vaccenic, oleic, nervonic acids, and one series of polyunsaturated fatty acids (eicosatrienoic, 20:3). The biosynthesis of the various acids is carried out by reaction sequences in which the chain is alternately elongated, utilizing malonyl-SCoA, and dehydrogenated in which oxygen and reduced pyridine nucleotide (NADPH) are required cofactors. The stereochemistry of the double bond in the unsaturated fatty acid is *cis*. Sources of the essential fatty acids include grain and seed oils and fats from nuts, peanuts, green leafy vegetables, and legumes.

The prostaglandins, which have hormone-like activity, are derived from the essential fatty acids. The prostaglandins each contain 20 carbon atoms and have the same basic skeleton of prostanoic acid. Three fatty acids, (8,11,14-Eicosatrienoic acid, 5,8,11,14-Eicosatetraenoic acid and 5,8,11,14,17-Eicosapentaenoic acid) are converted to 6 primary prostaglandins by the oxidative closure of a 5-membered ring in the middle of the fatty acid chain (viz. Bergstrom *et al.* 1968, Samuelsson 1972). Different members of this family of compounds stimulate contraction of smooth muscle, control inflammation and lower blood pressure, and exert effects on action of such hormones as vasopressin.

---

[1] Another system for indicating structure of unsaturated fatty acids is the abbreviated formula (e.g., Guarnieri and Johnson 1970). In this system of nomenclature the chain length is given followed by a colon and by the number of double bonds in the molecule. The number following the letter ω (omega) indicates the number of carbon atoms between the terminal double bond and the methyl group. If more than one double bond is present in the molecule, advantage is taken of the fact that a divinyl methane rhythm ($= CH — CH_2 — CH =$) is maintained in polyenoic acids. Therefore the position of all double bonds is fixed relative to the terminal methyl group. Example, the abbreviated formula of linoleic acid is $18:2\omega6$. This is deciphered as:

  a. contains 18 carbons
  b. contains 2 double bonds
  c. contains 6 carbons between the terminal double bond and the methyl group.

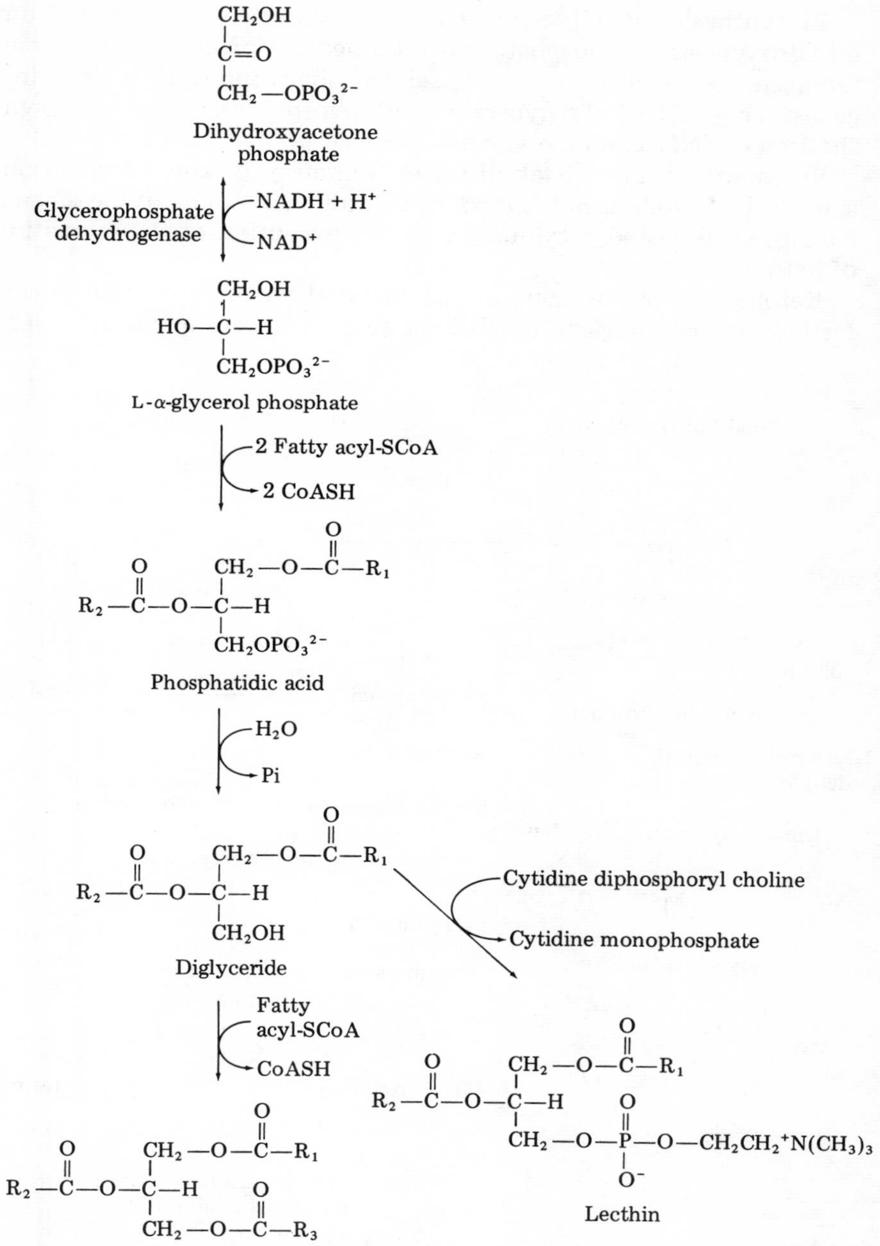

$$CH_2OH$$
$$|$$
$$C=O$$
$$|$$
$$CH_2-OPO_3{}^{2-}$$

Dihydroxyacetone
phosphate

Glycerophosphate
dehydrogenase

$\Big($ NADH + H$^+$

$\Big($ NAD$^+$

$$CH_2OH$$
$$|$$
$$HO-C-H$$
$$|$$
$$CH_2OPO_3{}^{2-}$$

L-α-glycerol phosphate

$\Big($ 2 Fatty acyl-SCoA

$\Big($ 2 CoASH

$$\begin{array}{c} & & O \\ & & \| \\ O & CH_2-O-C-R_1 \\ \| & | \\ R_2-C-O-C-H \\ & | \\ & CH_2OPO_3{}^{2-} \end{array}$$

Phosphatidic acid

$\Big($ H$_2$O

$\Big($ Pi

$$\begin{array}{c} & & O \\ & & \| \\ O & CH_2-O-C-R_1 \\ \| & | \\ R_2-C-O-C-H \\ & | \\ & CH_2OH \end{array}$$

Diglyceride

Cytidine diphosphoryl choline

Cytidine monophosphate

Fatty
acyl-SCoA

CoASH

$$\begin{array}{c} & & O \\ & & \| \\ O & CH_2-O-C-R_1 \\ \| & | \\ R_2-C-O-C-H & O \\ & | & \| \\ & CH_2-O-C-R_3 \end{array}$$

$$\begin{array}{c} & & O \\ & & \| \\ O & CH_2-O-C-R_1 \\ \| & | \\ R_2-C-O-C-H & O \\ & | & \| \\ & CH_2-O-P-O-CH_2CH_2{}^+N(CH_3)_3 \\ & & | \\ & & O^- \end{array}$$

Lecthin

FIG. 5.5. GENERAL OUTLINE FOR NEUTRAL FAT AND LECITHIN SYNTHESIS

Biosynthesis of Glycerol.—Glycerol can be synthesized from dihydroxyacetone phosphate, an intermediate of carbohydrate metabolism, by a reaction catalyzed by glycerophosphate dehydrogenase (Fig. 5.5). Triglycerides and phospholipids are then synthesized directly from L-α-glycerophosphate.

Summary of Fat Metabolism.—A summary of the interrelationships of fat metabolism is shown in Fig. 5.6. All points of the scheme have been discussed previously with the exception of the formation of ketone bodies.

Ketone bodies arise out of the metabolism of fatty acid during fasting or pathological conditions (e.g., diabetes mellitus). The

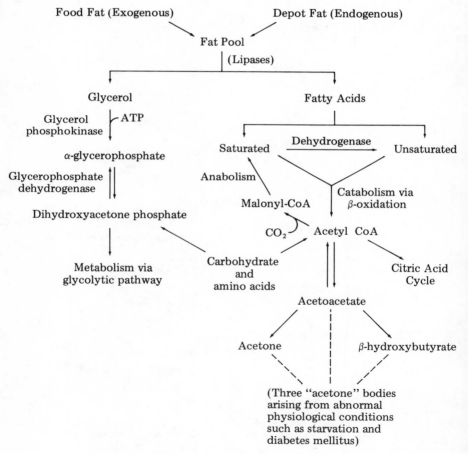

FIG. 5.6. SIMPLIFIED OUTLINE OF FAT METABOLISM

compounds commonly referred to as ketone bodies include aceto-acetate, β-hydroxybutyrate, and acetone. As the concentration of acetoacetic acid and β-hydroxbutyric acid increase, they lower the pH, thereby converting HCO_3^- to $CO_2 + H_2O$ and HPO_4^{2-} to $H_2PO_4^-$, thus acidosis develops in the blood. A mild acidosis frequently occurs during fasting and can be corrected by including in the diet small amounts of carbohydrate, thereby decreasing the accumulation of acetoacetate. This condition is magnified even more in diabetes mellitus which is due to the faulty oxidation of glucose resulting from a deficiency of insulin.

BIBLIOGRAPHY

BERGSTROM, S., CARLSON, L. A., and WEEKS, J. R. 1968. The prostaglandins. A family of biologically active lipids. Pharmacol. Rev. *20*, 1–48.

BLOCH, K. 1963. Lipid Metabolism. John Wiley & Sons, New York.

BOLLAND, J. L., TEN HAVE, P. 1947. Kinetic studies on the chemistry of rubber and related materials. IV. The inhibitory effect of hydrogen on the thermal oxidation of ethyl linoleate. Trans. Faraday Soc. *43*, 201–210.

BRAVERMAN, J. B. S. 1963. Introduction to the Biochemistry of Foods. Elsevier Publishing Co., New York.

FIESER, L. F., and FIESER, A. M. 1959. Steroids. Van Nostrand Reinhold Co., New York.

FURIA, T. E. (Editor). 1968. Handbook of Food Additives. Chemical Rubber Co., Cleveland, Ohio.

GIBSON, D. M. 1965. The biosynthesis of fatty acids. J. Chem. Educ. *42*, 236–243.

GUARNIERI, M., and JOHNSON, R. M. 1970. Nomenclature. Advances in Lipid Research, Vol. *8*. Academic Press, New York.

HOLMAN, R. T. 1954. Autoxidation of Fats and Related Substances. *In* Progress in the Chemistry of Fats and Other Lipids, Vol. 2, Holman, R. T., Lundberg, W. O., and Malkin, T. (Editors). Academic Press, New York.

KRITCHEVSKY, D. 1958. Cholesterol. John Wiley & Sons, New York.

LENNARZ, W. J. 1970. Lipid metabolism. Ann. Rev. Biochem. *39*, 359–388.

LUNDBERG, W. O. (Editor). 1961. Autoxidation and Antioxidants, Vol. I and II. John Wiley & Sons, New York.

MAHLER, H. R. 1964. Biological oxidation of fatty acids. *In* Fatty Acids, 2nd Edition, Part 3, K. S. Markeley (Editor). John Wiley & Sons, New York.

MAJERUS, P. W., and VAGELOS, P. R. 1967. Fatty acid biosynthesis and the role of the acyl carrier protein. *In* Advances in Lipid Research, Vol. *5*, R. Paoletti, and D. Kritchevsky (Editors). Academic Press, New York.

MARKLEY, K. S. 1961. Fatty Acids, Their Chemistry, Properties, Production and Uses, 2nd Edition, Parts 1 & 2. John Wiley & Sons, New York.

MEAD, J. F. 1968. The metabolism of the polyunsaturated fatty acids. *In* Progress in the Chemistry of Fats and Other Lipids, Vol. 9, Part 2, R. T. Holman (Editor). Pergamon Press, New York.

PRIVETT, O. S. 1961. Some observations on the course and mechanism of autoxidation and antioxidant action. *In* Proceedings Flavor Chemistry Symposium · Campbell Soup Co., Camden, N.J.

SAMUELSSON, B. 1972. Biosynthesis of Prostaglandins, Federation Proc. *31*, 1442–1450.

SCOTT, G. 1965. Atmospheric Oxidation and Antioxidants. Elsevier Publishing Co., New York.

SHAPITO, B. 1967. Lipid Metabolism. Ann. Rev. Biochem. *36*, 247–270.
SOBER, H. A. (Editor). 1970. Handbook of Biochemistry, 2nd Edition. Chemical Rubber Co., Cleveland, Ohio.
SWERN, D. 1960. Oxidation by atmospheric oxygen. *In* Fatty Acids, 2nd Edition, Part 2, K. Markley (Editor). John Wiley & Sons, New York.
WAKIL, S. J. (Editor). 1970. Lipid Metabolism. Academic Press, New York.
WILLIAMS, K. A. 1966. Oils, Fats, and Fatty Acids, 4th Edition. J. and A. Churchill-Little, London.

CHAPTER 6

Proteins

Proteins are essential components of every living cell, and are utilized in the formation and regeneration of tissue. Certain specific proteins serve as enzymes, some as antibodies, while others serve to provide indispensable functions in metabolic regulation and contractile processes. All things considered, proteins are concerned with virtually all physiological events.

Plants are able to synthesize proteins from inorganic sources of nitrogen, water, and carbon dioxide assimilated by the roots and leaves. In contrast, animals and man are dependent on plant and animal proteins in the diet to provide the necessary constituents for protein synthesis.

Since proteins are of such great importance to animals and man, many plants are grown because of the nutritional value of their proteins. Not all proteins have the same biological value. This difference lies in the fact that some proteins are rich in certain essential amino acids, whereas other proteins are devoid of some of these acids or contain them in very small amounts. For example, in many areas of the world, protein deficiency diseases occur, particularly in children, where the main protein source is vegetable protein in which certain amino acids are lacking.

Proteins contain nitrogen, carbon, hydrogen, and oxygen; many contain sulfur, some contain phosphorus, and, in a few cases, other elements such as zinc, iron, and copper. Although proteins vary in composition, most consist of nitrogen, 16%; carbon, 50%; hydrogen, 7%; oxygen, 22%; and sulfur, 0.5 to 3%.

If one were to attempt to define proteins, it would be necessary to consider the following: (1) they are polymeric materials of high molecular weight; (2) they are of colloidal dimensions and as such will not pass through semipermeable membranes; (3) they are amphoteric, i.e., they may act chemically both as acids and as bases; (4) following complete hydrolysis, the hydrolysate consists entirely of amino acids (except that additional groups, such as heme, iron, or copper, may also be found in the case of "conjugated" protein); and (5) in their polymeric structures the amino acid units are joined together in definite sequences and in definite three-dimensional conformations.

Amino Acids and the Peptide Bond

All proteins yield amino acids when hydrolyzed, and all but two of these are α-amino carboxylic acids. Proline and hydroxyproline are α-imino acids. In proteins, amino acids are united through amide linkages between the α-carboxyl and α-amino functional groups of adjacent amino acid residues. Such bonds are called peptide bonds and this linkage between the amino acids is shown below:

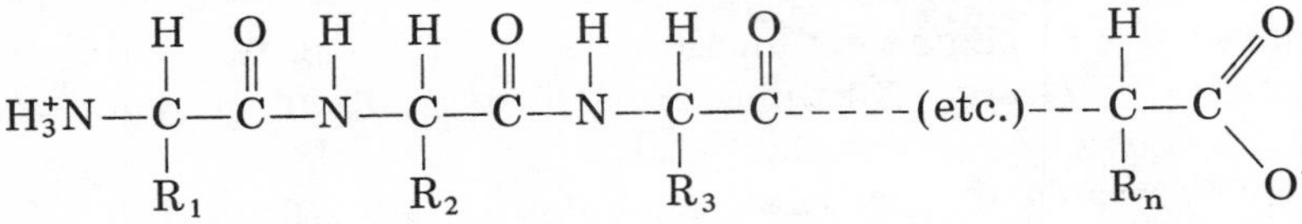

$$H_3^+N-\underset{\underset{R_1}{|}}{\overset{\overset{H}{|}}{C}}-\overset{\overset{O}{\|}}{C}-\underset{}{\overset{\overset{H}{|}}{N}}-\underset{\underset{R_2}{|}}{\overset{\overset{H}{|}}{C}}-\overset{\overset{O}{\|}}{C}-\overset{\overset{H}{|}}{N}-\underset{\underset{R_3}{|}}{\overset{\overset{H}{|}}{C}}-\overset{\overset{O}{\|}}{C}-----\text{(etc.)}---\underset{\underset{R_n}{|}}{\overset{\overset{H}{|}}{C}}-C\overset{\diagup O}{\diagdown O^-}$$

The substances resulting from the formation of peptide bonds are termed peptides, while the individual amino acid units of peptides are termed residues. Thus, a peptide containing two amino acid residues is referred to as a dipeptide; one containing many residues is referred to as a polypeptide. By convention, peptides are written with the terminal α-amino group (N-terminus) to the left and the terminal α-carboxyl group (C-terminus) to the right.

The peptide linkages of proteins are somewhat resistant to hydrolysis and, in the absence of enzymes, require prolonged heating with strong acids or alkalies for completion of the process. Acid hydrolysis is generally preferred because alkaline hydrolysis partly converts the optically active amino acids (L-isomers) into racemic mixtures (D and L forms). Total acid and alkaline hydrolyses present problems in that all of the glutamine and asparagine, most of the tryptophan, and some of the serine and threonine residues are destroyed by acid; whereas arginine, cystine and cysteine as well as asparagine and glutamine, are destroyed by alkali.

Proteolytic enzymes are frequently used for hydrolyzing proteins. A number of proteases will hydrolyze peptide bonds; they are divided into two broad classes, endopeptidases and exopeptidases. Endopeptidases act on one or more of the "internal" peptide bonds of protein substrates, whereas aminopeptidases and carboxypeptidases (exopeptidases) can be used for the sequential removal of N-terminal and C-terminal amino acids, respectively.

The α-amino acids, except glycine, have at least one asymmetric carbon atom and, as a consequence, may exist in optically active D- and L- forms or in optically inactive racemic mixtures. The configuration around the asymmetric carbon of most naturally occurring amino acids is the same as the configuration of the asymmetric carbon atom of L-glyceraldehyde; accordingly, they are classified as L-amino acids.

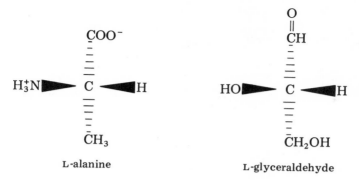

L-alanine   L-glyceraldehyde

Classification of the Amino Acids

The amino acids have been classified in various ways. One system classifies them according to their structure and another according to the number of amino and carboxyl groups they possess (Table 6.1).

Chemistry of the Amino Acids

Ionic Properties.—Typical free amino acids have at least two groups that can act as proton acceptors or donors; namely, the amino group and the carboxyl group. The high melting points and water solubilities of amino acids suggest that the amino acid is in the ionic form. Titration of a simple amino acid with both acid and base indicate that the α-amino group exists as an α-ammonium group (pK_a approximately 10) and the carboxyl group exists as a carboxylate group (pK_a approximately 2). The structure that satisfies the above observation is commonly called the Zwitterionic form:

$$H_3\overset{+}{N}-\overset{\overset{\displaystyle R}{|}}{\underset{\underset{\displaystyle H}{|}}{C}}-COO^-$$

This concept may be better understood by referring to the titration curve for glycine (Fig. 6.1). At low pH the cationic form of the amino acid is present:

$$H_3\overset{+}{N}-\overset{\overset{\displaystyle R}{|}}{\underset{\underset{\displaystyle H}{|}}{C}}-COOH$$

Cationic form

TABLE 6.1

CLASSIFICATION OF α-AMINO ACIDS

I. Aliphatic Amino Acids

A. Monoamino-monocarboxylic acids

	Structure	pK_a@25°
1. Glycine (Gly)	H_3^+N—CH_2—COO^-	2.35; 9.78
2. Alanine (Ala)	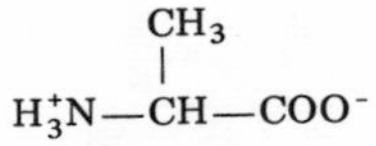 CH_3 $\mid$ H_3^+N—CH—COO^-	2.35; 9.83
3. Valine (val)	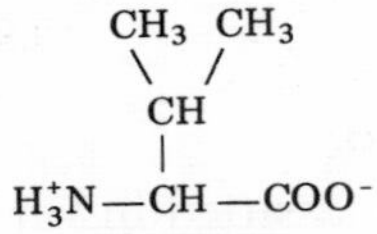 CH_3 CH_3 \ / CH $\mid$ H_3^+N—CH—COO^-	2.29; 9.72
4. Leucine (Leu)	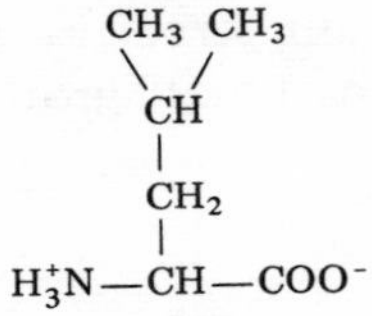 CH_3 CH_3 \ / CH $\mid$ CH_2 $\mid$ H_3^+N—CH—COO^-	2.33; 9.74
5. Isoleucine (Ile)	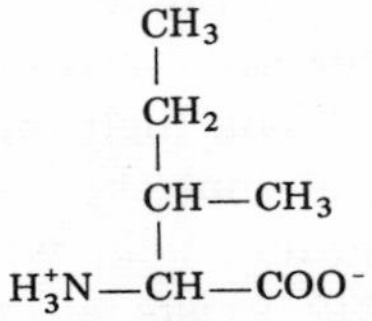 CH_3 $\mid$ CH_2 $\mid$ CH—CH_3 $\mid$ H_3^+N—CH—COO^-	2.34; 9.76
6. Serine (Ser)	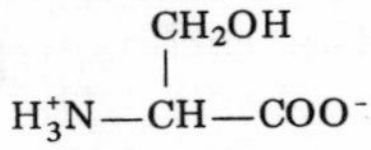 CH_2OH $\mid$ H_3^+N—CH—COO^-	2.19; 9.21
7. Threonine (Thr)	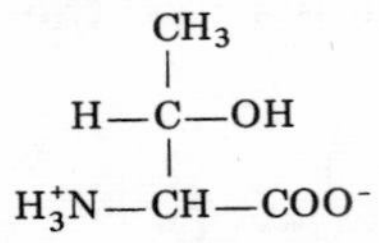 CH_3 $\mid$ H—C—OH $\mid$ H_3^+N—CH—COO^-	2.09; 9.10
8. Cysteine (Cys)	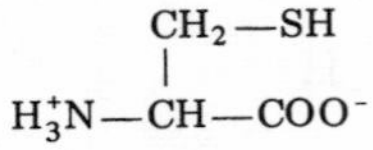 CH_2—SH $\mid$ H_3^+N—CH—COO^-	1.71 8.39 (sulfhydryl) 10.76 (α-amino)
9. Cystine (Cys Cys)	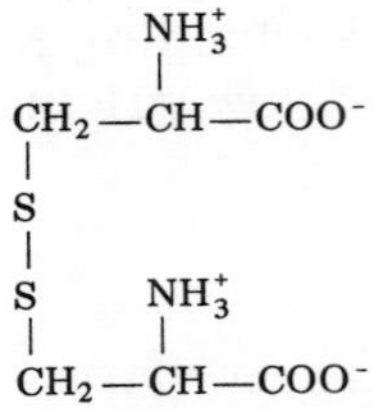 NH_3^+ $\mid$ CH_2—CH—COO^- $\mid$ S $\mid$ S NH_3^+ $\mid$ $\mid$ CH_2—CH—COO^-	1.65; 2.26 (carboxyls) 7.85; 9.85 (α-amino)
10. Methionine (Met)	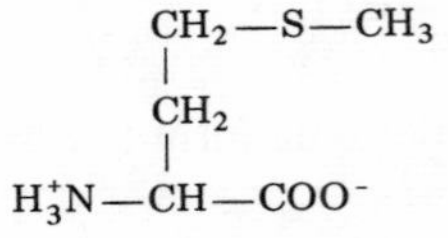 CH_2—S—CH_3 $\mid$ CH_2 $\mid$ H_3^+N—CH—COO^-	2.13; 9.28

TABLE 6.1 (*Continued*)

Structure	pK_a@ 25°

B. Monamino-dicarboxylic acids

1. Aspartic (Asp)

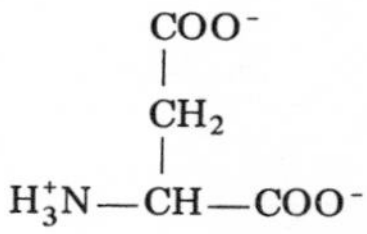

$$COO^-$$
$$|$$
$$CH_2$$
$$|$$
$$H_3^+N-CH-COO^-$$

2.05 (α-carboxyl)
3.87 (β-carboxyl)
10.00

2. Asparagine (Asn)

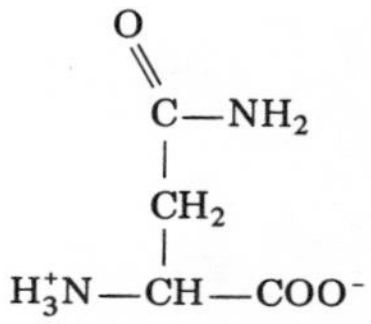

$$O$$
$$\diagdown$$
$$C-NH_2$$
$$|$$
$$CH_2$$
$$|$$
$$H_3^+N-CH-COO^-$$

2.02
8.80

3. Glutamic (Glu)

$$COO^-$$
$$|$$
$$CH_2$$
$$|$$
$$CH_2$$
$$|$$
$$H_3^+N-CH-COO^-$$

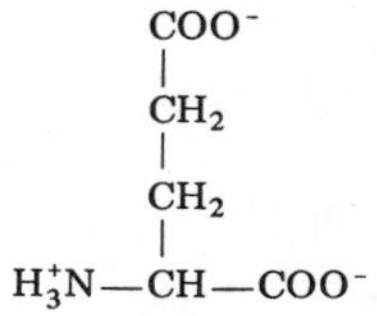

2.16 (α-carboxyl)
4.27 (γ-carboxyl)
9.36

4. Glutamine (Gln)

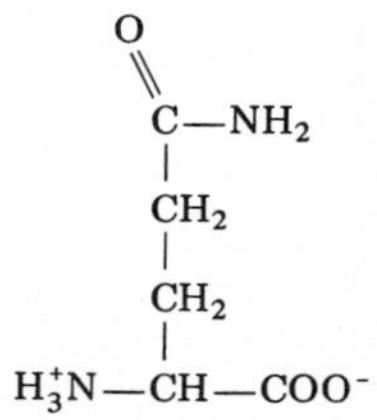

$$O$$
$$\diagdown$$
$$C-NH_2$$
$$|$$
$$CH_2$$
$$|$$
$$CH_2$$
$$|$$
$$H_3^+N-CH-COO^-$$

2.17; 9.13

C. Diamino-monocarboxylic acids

1. Arginine (Arg)

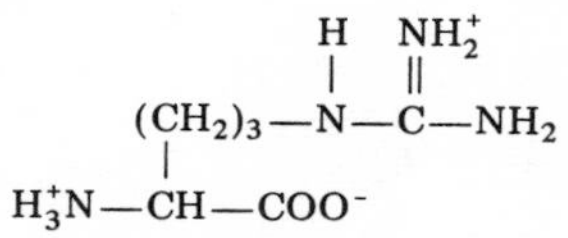

$$H \quad NH_2^+$$
$$| \quad ||$$
$$(CH_2)_3-N-C-NH_2$$
$$|$$
$$H_3^+N-CH-COO^-$$

1.82
8.99 (α-amino)
12.48 (guanido)

2. Lysine (Lys)

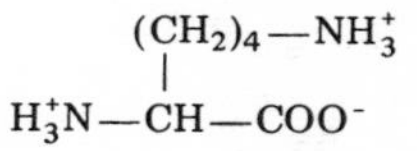

$$(CH_2)_4-NH_3^+$$
$$|$$
$$H_3^+N-CH-COO^-$$

2.18
8.95 (α-amino)
10.53 (ϵ-amino)

3. Hydroxylysine (Hyl)

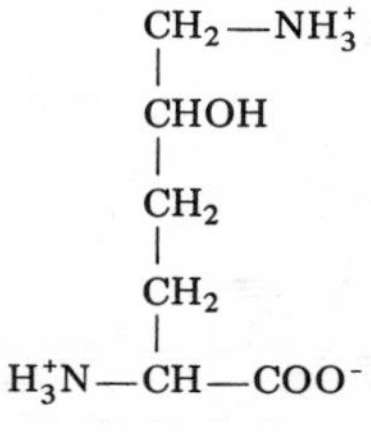

$$CH_2-NH_3^+$$
$$|$$
$$CHOH$$
$$|$$
$$CH_2$$
$$|$$
$$CH_2$$
$$|$$
$$H_3^+N-CH-COO^-$$

2.13
8.62 (α-amino)
9.67 (ϵ-amino)

TABLE 6.1 (*Continued*)

Structure	pK_a @25°

II. Aromatic Amino Acids

A. Monoamino-monocarboxylic acids

   1. Phenylalanine (Phe)   1.83; 9.31

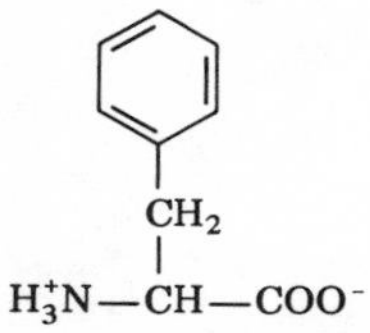

   2. Tyrosine (Tyr)   2.20
                                        9.11 (α-amino)
                                        10.03 (phenolic hydroxyl)

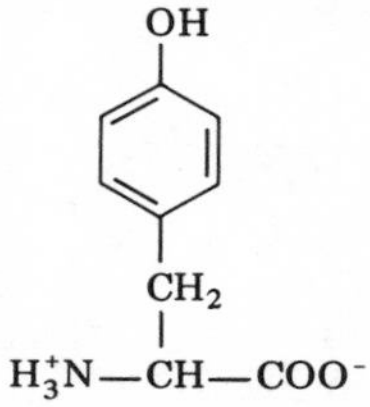

   3. Tryptophan (Trp)   2.46; 9.41

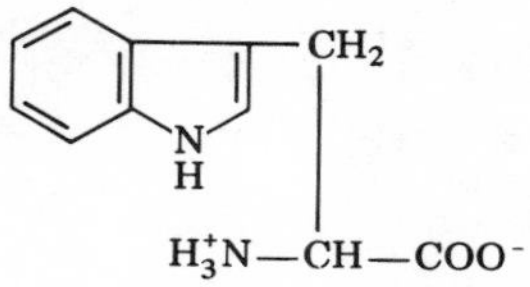

III. Heterocylic Aliphatic Amino Acids

A. Monoamino-monocarboxylic acid

   1. Histidine (His)   1.82
                                          6.04 (imidazole)
                                          9.17

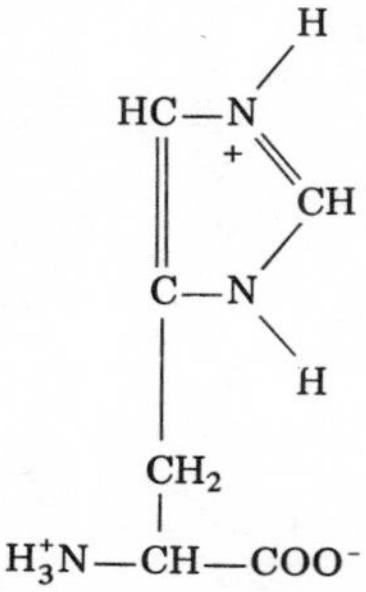

B. α-Imino acids

   1. Proline (Pro)   1.95; 10.64

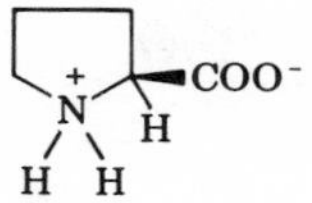

   2. Hydroxyproline (Hyp)   1.82; 9.66

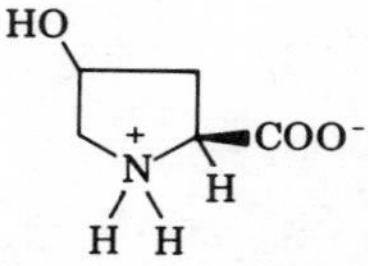

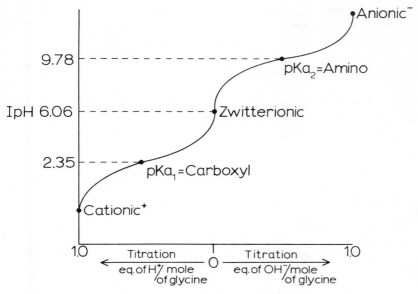

FIG. 6.1. TITRATION CURVE FOR GLYCINE

At intermediate pH, the amino acid exists as the Zwitterion, and at high pH, the amino acid is in the anionic form:

$$H_2N-\underset{\underset{\displaystyle H}{|}}{\overset{\overset{\displaystyle R}{|}}{C}}-COO^-$$

Anionic form

At a pH midway between the pK_a of the cationic and pK_a of the anionic form is the isoelectric point (pI) of the amino acid, at which it carries no net charge, being Zwitterionic.

Other functional groups of amino acids contribute to their acid-base properties. These are:

(1) Sulfhydryl of cysteine (pK_a = 8.39)

(2) β-carboxyl of aspartic acid (pK_a = 3.87)

(3) γ-carboxyl of glutamic acid (pK_a = 4.27)

(4) guanidino of arginine (pK_a = 12.48)

(5) ε-amino of lysine (pK_a = 10.53)

(6) phenolic hydroxyl of tyrosine (pK_a = 10.03)

(7) imidazole of histidine (pK_a = 6.04)

Color Reactions of Amino Acids and Proteins.—Generally speaking, the color reactions of proteins or amino acids can be divided into two classes: those which involve specific reactive side chains and those general reactions which occur at the amino or carboxyl groups of amino acids or at peptide bonds. Several of the color reactions are used for the qualitative and quantitative estimation of proteins and of their constituent amino acids.

(a) The ninhydrin reaction, undoubtedly the most widely used color reaction in protein chemistry, involves the reaction of ninhydrin with the amino groups of amino acids.

The reaction may be summarized as follows:

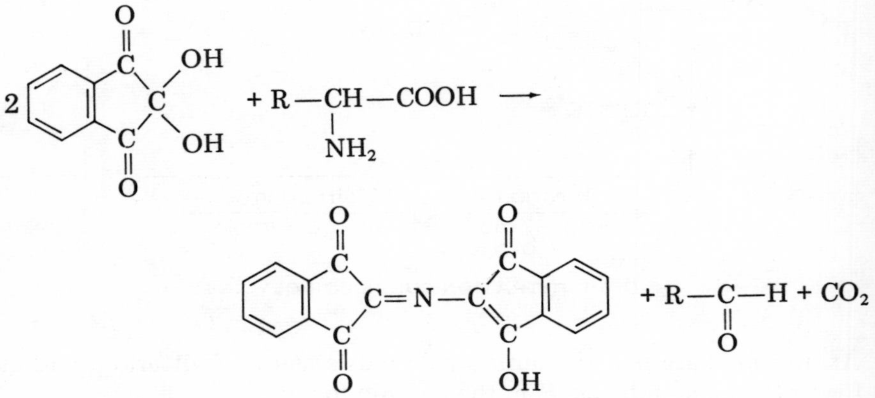

The test may be used for the qualitative detection of proteins and their hydrolytic products. Ninhydrin is used in the quantitation of separated amino acids, but cannot be used for the quantitative estimation of amino acids in mixtures because the colors given by different amino acids vary in shade and depth.

(b) Biuret reaction. When a protein is mixed with a solution of sodium hydroxide and a dilute solution of copper sulfate, a violet color is produced. The color is due to complexation of Cu^{2+} with the peptide bond to form a coordination compound. This reaction is a test for peptide linkages and will be positive when two or more peptide linkages are present. Thus, a dipeptide will not give the test.

Color reactions are useful in identifying proteins as well as in characterizing their reactive side chains. The phenolic side chain of tyrosine is responsible for the red color produced by the Millon reagent and the blue color given in an alkaline solution of phosphomolybdotungstate (Folin-Ciocalteau); the Xanthoproteic reagent gives a yellow color with proteins containing amino acids having a benzene ring (Trp, Phe, Tyr). The indole side chain of tryptophan reacts with the Hopkins-Cole reagent to give a purple color or with 2-hydroxy-5-nitrobenzylating reagents to incorporate a yellow color. The guanidino side chain of arginine reacts with α-naphthol and sodium hypochlorite (Sakaguchi) to give a red color.

Classification of Proteins

There are many ways of classifying proteins based on either their chemical or physical properties. A uniform system of classification has evolved wherein the proteins are divided into three main groups: simple, conjugated, and derived proteins. The first two groups represent proteins as they exist in nature; the third group contains those proteins which have been changed or modified by enzymes or chemical reagents.

A. **Simple Proteins.**—Substances which, on hydrolysis, yield only amino acids or their derivatives.

1. *Albumins.*—Soluble in water and salt solutions. Coagulated by heat. Examples: egg albumin, lactalbumin, serum albumin, legumetin of peas and leucosin of wheat.

2. *Globulins.*—Soluble in neutral solutions of salts of strong bases and strong acids but only sparingly soluble in water. Examples: serum globulin (blood), myosin (muscle), edestin (hemp seed), and legumin (peas).

3. *Glutelins.*—Soluble in very dilute acid or base, but insoluble in neutral solvents. These proteins occur only in plant materials. Examples: glutelin (wheat), oryzenin (rice).

4. *Prolamins.*—Soluble in 50 to 90% alcohol, but insoluble in water, absolute alcohol, and other neutral solvents. The prolamins occur only in plants. Examples: gliadin (wheat, rye), zein (corn), and hordein (barley).

5. *Scleroproteins.*—Are characterized by their insolubility in neutral solvents. They are found only in animals. Examples: collagen and keratin from connective tissue, bones, hair, horns, hoofs, etc.; fibroin from silk.

6. *Histones.*—Characterized by a high content of basic amino acids and are found in animals. They are soluble in water, dilute acids and alkali; insoluble in dilute ammonia. Examples: histones from calf thymus and pancreas.

7. *Protamines.*—The protamines are strongly basic proteins having a molecular weight lower than histones. They are soluble in water and ammonia, form stable salts with strong acids, are highly basic and not coagulated by heat. The protamines are rich in the basic amino acid arginine which may account for 70 to 80% of the total amino acid content. The protamines occur in combination with

nucleic acid in spermatazoa. Examples: protamines of the sperm of salmon, herring, and sardines.

B. Conjugated Proteins.—The conjugated proteins are more complex molecules in which the amino acid structure is similar to that of simple proteins, but in addition, the protein molecule is combined with nonprotein substances such as lipids, carbohydrates, organic prosthetic groups, and nucleic acids. The principal categories are indicated below:

1. *Nucleoproteins.*—Proteins which are combined with nucleic acids. The latter are strongly acidic polymers, frequently found in combination with the basic proteins of the histone and protamine classes. Nucleoproteins are the chromatin material of cell nuclei.

2. *Lipoproteins.*—Conjugates of protein with lipids; e.g., lecithin, cholesterol. Lipoproteins are found in cell nuclei, blood, egg yolk, milk, brain, nerve tissue and cellular and intracellular membranes.

3. *Glycoproteins.*—The nonprotein moiety of this category of conjugated proteins is a carbohydrate (Chap. 4).

4. *Chromoproteins.*—The chromophoric group of the chromoproteins is a colored prosthetic group. Flavoprotein is an example in which the prosthetic group is a derivative of riboflavin. Other protein-bound pigments include chlorophyll, heme and ferritin.

C. Derived Proteins.—This group contains all hydrolytic products of naturally occurring proteins. They can be obtained by chemical or physical methods and can be subdivided according to degree of hydrolysis. Those which have been changed least are called primary derivatives, while those which have undergone considerable cleavage are known as secondary derivatives.

1. *Primary Derivatives.*—The term protean refers to those proteins which have been slightly modified by water, dilute acids or alkalies, or by enzymes. They are insoluble in water. Examples: fibrin (coagulated blood), casein (curdled milk), edestin.

Products of the further action of acids and alkalies, which are soluble in acids and alkalies but not in neutral solvents are called metaproteins. Examples: acid-metaprotein, alkali-metaprotein.

Insoluble protein substances resulting from the action of heat, alcohol, etc., are commonly referred to as coagulated proteins. Example: cooked egg albumin.

2. *Secondary Derivatives.*—Secondary derivatives include proteoses, peptones, and peptides. Proteoses are soluble in water and not coagulated by heat, but are precipitated by saturated solutions of ammonium sulfate. Simpler products of protein hydrolysis are peptones. They are soluble in water, not coagulated by heat and not precipitated by saturated solutions of ammonium sulfate. Peptides

are much simpler than the peptones (combinations of two or more amino acids).

Structure of Proteins

Primary Structure.—Primary structure refers only to the structure imposed by the covalent peptide bonds; the amino acid residues are in ordered sequence proceeding from the N-terminal to the C-terminal position. Evidence for the peptide bond as the primary structural unit of all proteins is now unequivocal. Proteins contain few titratable α-amino and α-carboxyl groups but on hydrolysis the number of these groups increases markedly. Moreover, amino acids can be isolated from protein hydrolysates, and polypeptides can be synthesized chemically from amino acids (or their derivatives).

It was logical that theories should arise relative to the role of this linkage in protein structure. The simplest concept of a protein is that of a straight-chain (i.e., nonbranched) polymer consisting of several hundred amino acids possessing a variety of side chains. At one end of the polymeric chain is a free α-amino group, termed the N-terminal amino acid, and at the other end is a free α-carboxyl group or the C-terminal amino acid. The physical and chemical properties of proteins depend not only on the peptide bonds but also on the side chains which have a pronounced effect on the overall reactions and interactions of proteins.

It is obvious that if a peptide was defined only in terms of its constituent amino acids, one could not be certain of the sequential order of the residues in the peptide structure. A useful method for detecting and identifying N-terminal amino acids is the Sanger reaction, in which 2,4-dinitrofluorobenzene reacts with the amino groups of protein molecules. Following acid hydrolysis of the polypeptide, the α-N-dinitrophenyl derivative of the N-terminal amino acid can be extracted with ether and identified by chromatographic procedures.

An end group analysis known as the Edman degradation permits the sequential removal and identification of amino acids from the N-terminus of a protein molecule. In this method, the peptide is allowed to react with phenyl isothiocyanate in alkaline media to form an N-phenylthiocarbamyl peptide (PTC-peptide). Upon treatment with strong, anhydrous acid, the terminal peptide bond is broken and the derivative cyclizes to form a thiazolone which undergoes rearrangement to a phenylthiohydantoin of the terminal amino acid (PTH-amino acid); the cyclization is carried out in an anhydrous medium (e.g., hydrogen chloride in nitromethane) so as to prevent nonspecific acid hydrolysis of other peptide bonds. The overall process is shown on page 154.

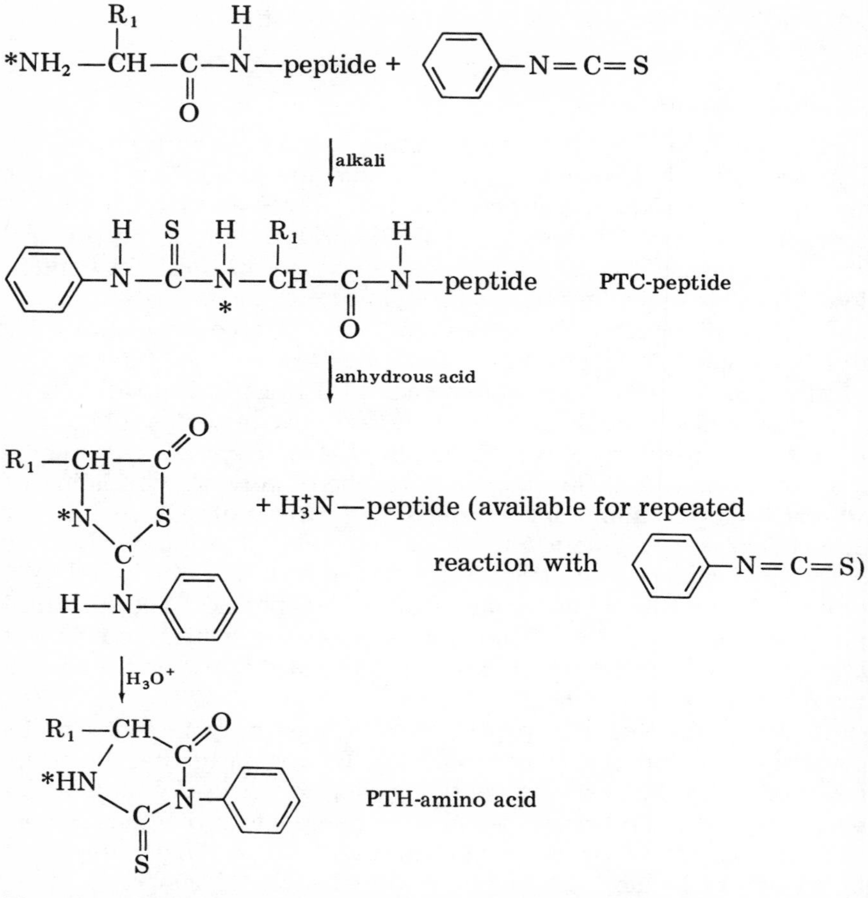

$$*NH_2-\underset{R_1}{\overset{}{CH}}-\underset{\overset{\|}{O}}{C}-\underset{H}{\overset{}{N}}-\text{peptide} + \langle\text{phenyl}\rangle-N=C=S$$

$$\downarrow \text{alkali}$$

$$\langle\text{phenyl}\rangle-\underset{H}{\overset{}{N}}-\underset{\overset{\|}{S}}{\overset{*}{C}}-\underset{H}{\overset{}{N}}-\underset{R_1}{\overset{}{CH}}-\underset{\overset{\|}{O}}{C}-\underset{H}{\overset{}{N}}-\text{peptide} \qquad \text{PTC-peptide}$$

$$\downarrow \text{anhydrous acid}$$

$$R_1-CH-C{\overset{O}{\diagup}} \quad \text{(ring with } *N, S, C, H-N-\langle\text{phenyl}\rangle) + H_3^+N-\text{peptide (available for repeated}$$

$$\text{reaction with } \langle\text{phenyl}\rangle-N=C=S)$$

$$\downarrow H_3O^+$$

$$R_1-CH-C{\overset{O}{\diagup}} \quad \text{(ring: } *HN, C{=}S, N-\langle\text{phenyl}\rangle) \qquad \text{PTH-amino acid}$$

The phenylthiohydantoin may be identified directly by gas chromatography or thin-layer chromatography.

The number and sequence of amino acid residues linked by peptide bonds is referred to as the primary structure of a protein. Thus, the only forces involved here are the covalent bonds which link the amino acids together.

Secondary Structure.—The chemical and physical properties of a protein depend on their three dimensional molecular shapes (conformation) as well as their amino acid sequence. Specific terms are used to discuss the several levels of structural organization of proteins and large peptides. The term secondary structure refers to the spatial relationship of extended, partially extended, or helically coiled polypeptide chains which is conferred by hydrogen bonding between peptide bonds. The α-helix (Fig. 6.2) is the most stable of

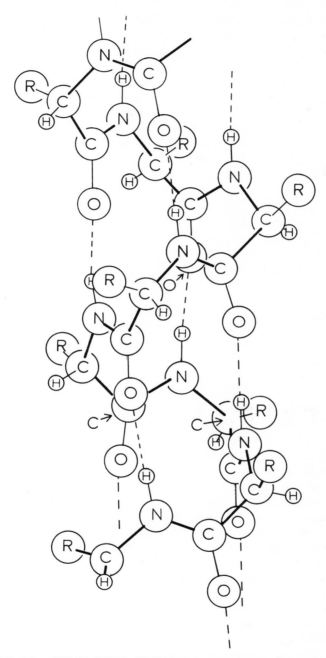

FIG. 6.2. α-HELIX FORM OF PROTEIN MOLECULE (RIGHT-
HANDED)

the various secondary structures that certain polypeptide chains (depending on the nature of the individual residues) might assume. There are approximately 5.4 Å per turn of the helix with each amino acid residue contributing approximately 1.5 Å translation along the helical axis. This gives 3.6 amino acid residues per turn and, thus, 100° rotation per residue. The factor that determines the secondary conformations that peptide chains may assume is the formation of hydrogen bonds between peptide linkages; i.e., the attractive force between a hydrogen atom attached to the N of one peptide bond, and the O atom of the carbonyl group of another peptide bond. An isolated hydrogen bond is relatively weak as compared to a

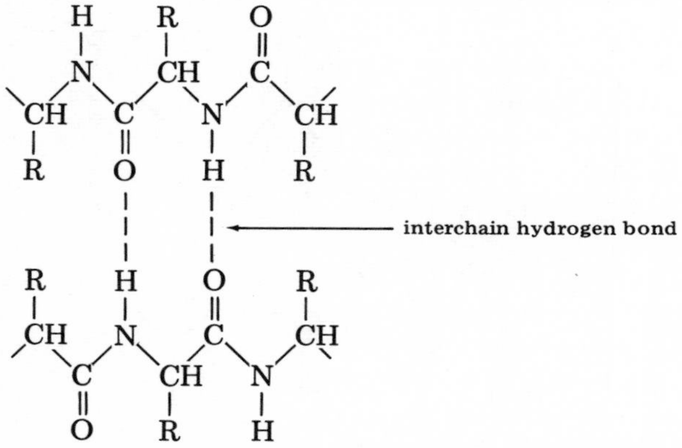

covalent bond, but there may be hundreds of such hydrogen bonds in a protein molecule, thereby resulting in overall strength. Factors such as heat, acids, bases, urea, sodium dodecylsulfate, and salts can interfere with hydrogen bonding, thus affecting the stability of secondary conformation of proteins.

Hydrogen bonding is particularly prevalent in fibrous proteins, generally holding the polypeptide chains together in bundles parallel to the fiber axis. Two such proteins are keratins (hair and wool) and myosin (a protein of muscle tissues). These proteins can exist in either the alpha form (helical, contracted form) or the beta form (stretched, pleated sheet form). Silk fibroin, on the other hand, naturally occurs in the β-pleated sheet secondary structural conformation.

Tertiary Structure.—Protein molecules containing only hydrogen bonds may be extremely flexible. A stable, globular three-dimensional structure requires other forces in order to compress the polypeptide chain into a more or less spherical form. The forces which contribute to the folding of the coiled chain (tertiary structure) are attributable to the properties of the side chains of the amino acid residues. Thus, tertiary structure may be imposed by a combination of various interactions: (1) hydrophobic interactions which constitute the major force stabilizing tertiary structures of all proteins; (2) disulfide bonds, present in some, but not all proteins; (3) hydrogen bonds between polar side chains (relatively infrequent) and (4) ionic bonds (salt linkages) which are also infrequent.

The basic amino acids such as lysine and arginine and the dicarboxylic amino acids, aspartic acid and glutamic acid, are in certain instances involved in salt linkages, but like other polar side chains are usually hydrated by solvent. Cysteine is the sole source of sulfhydryl groups which may form a disulfide bond. Disulfide bonds are covalent linkages. A number of amino acid residues have side chains which are made up of aliphatic or aromatic groups and, therefore, tend to be hydrophobic (e.g., leucine, valine, phenylalanine, methionine). When placed in an aqueous environment, the hydrophobic side chains are repelled by the polar water molecules and tend to associate together. Side chain hydrogen bonds may occur between aspartic and glutamic acids, asparagine, glutamine, and the phenolic hydroxyl group of tyrosine.

Quaternary Structure.—Quaternary structure is the association of individual polypeptide chains (monomeric units) via noncovalent bonding to form an oligomeric protein molecule. Hemoglobin, for example, consists of 4 subunits—2 α- and 2 β-chains—each chain having a molecular weight of about 16,000, and thus possesses quaternary structure. Myoglobin, on the other hand, consists of a single polypeptide chain (molecular weight ca 16,000), and thus lacks quaternary structure. Quaternary structural organization also occurs in certain enzymes that are made up of subunits. Thus, the enzyme glycogen phosphorylase contains four subunits which alone are catalytically inactive but when linked as a tetramer form the active enzyme.

Denaturation.—The term denaturation denotes the response of a native protein to heat, acid, alkali, or a variety of other chemical and physical agents which cause marked changes in the protein structure. Thus, the denaturation process involves an unfolding or at least an alteration of the folded structure of a protein without breaking its covalent peptide bonds.

Accordingly, protein denaturation can contribute to both flavor and texture of foods containing proteins. For example, in the dairy industry, the deciding factor in the choice of a particular temperature treatment is made on the basis of chemical changes produced by the heat treatment. Thus, temperatures in excess of 162°F for 15 sec in the pasteurization of milk are avoided; otherwise the milk serum (or whey proteins) becomes denatured and the milk acquires a cooked flavor and has a resistance to clotting by rennet. Such changes are of practical significance in the production of cheese.

The denaturation of proteins does not necessarily imply a decrease in digestibility by proteolytic enzymes. Denaturation increases the digestibility of egg albumin by trypsin. Native hemoglobin is not digested by trypsin, whereas denatured hemoglobin is readily digested.

Physical and Chemical Properties of Proteins

Molecular Weight of Proteins.—Proteins are complex substances, and thus it is extremely difficult to determine their molecular weights. The ultracentrifugal method developed by Svedberg *et al.* has proven to be the most generally satisfactory method for the determination of the molecular weights of proteins. When solutions of proteins are placed in a centrifuge, the rate of sedimentation of the protein molecules is determined by the molecular weight, shape and density of the molecule, by the density and viscosity of the dispersion medium, and by the centrifugal force developed in the ultracentrifuge. In addition to determining molecular weight, ultracentrifugation can be used to determine the purity of a protein solution because molecules of different molecular size sediment at different rates giving multiple boundaries.

Molecular weights can also be calculated from light scattering. This method is based on the fact that protein solutions opalesce. A measurement of the intensity of light scattered (sidewise) by a known weight of protein in solution allows computation of its molecular weight. Gel filtration chromatography has been used extensively for determining the molecular weights of proteins. This method is simple and inexpensive but the accuracy depends upon the particular protein being investigated.

Table 6.2 lists the molecular weights of some typical proteins, most of which were determined by the ultracentrifugal method.

A number of naturally occurring proteins exist in different micellar or aggregate forms. Casein has been shown to be a complex mixture of molecules varying in molecular weight from 75,000 to 375,000. Insulin is an example of a protein which naturally exists as a molecular aggregate. The molecular weight was first found to be approximately 36,000. However, upon dilution it dissociates to units of 12,000 which in turn are made up of 2 subunits, each with a molecular weight of 6,000.

Isoelectric Points of Proteins.—Since the charges of the α-carboxyl groups and the α-amino groups of internal amino acid residues were

TABLE 6.2

APPROXIMATE MOLECULAR WEIGHTS OF
SOME TYPICAL PROTEINS

Protein	Source	Approximate Molecular Wt
Myoglobin	Muscle	17,200
Lactalbumin	Cow's milk	17,400
Gliadin	Wheat	27,500
β-Lactoglobulin	Cow's milk	35,400
Zein	Corn	40,000
Egg albumin	Hen	44,000
Gelatins	Skins	10,000–100,000
Caseins	Cow's milk	75,000–375,000
Myosin	Muscle	1,000,000
Nucleohistone (thymus)	Calf	2,300,000

removed in the formation of the peptide bonds, the chemical nature of the side chains will determine the overall charge of a protein molecule. Carboxyl groups in the side chains of aspartic and glutamic acid residues bear negative charges, while the amino groups of lysine and arginine residues bear positive charges at physiological pH. The behavior of a protein toward acid or base is similar to the behavior of an amino acid. At a lower pH the H^+ ions protonate the side chain functional groups of basic amino acids and the carboxyl groups of acidic amino acids, so that the protein is positively charged. At a higher pH, the protons are removed from the functional groups of basic amino acids and acidic amino acids, so that the protein becomes negatively charged. At some intermediate pH the protein is electrically neutral, in that it possesses exactly the same number of positive and negative charges. This particular pH is called the isoelectric point (pI) and it has a characteristic value for each given protein. As a general rule, most of the physical properties of proteins are minimal at or near the isoelectric point. This is true for solubility, conductivity, degree of hydration, viscosity, osmotic pressure, stability, and electrokinetic phenomena.

Proteolytic Enzymes

A large number of enzymes catalyze the hydrolysis of proteins whereby peptides or amino acids are liberated. (In animals, the amino acids are absorbed via the small intestines and may be subsequently used to synthesize new body proteins and other essential nitrogenous metabolites, or broken down further to form urea, CO_2 and water.) The enzymes which catalyze protein hydrolysis are called proteolytic enzymes and the process of protein fragmentation is called proteolysis.

Proteolytic enzymes may be divided into two groups, endopeptidases and exopeptidases. Endopeptidases attack interior, as well as terminal peptide bonds, of polypeptide chains, and are also referred to as proteases. Examples of this group of enzymes are pepsin, elastase, trypsin, and chymotrypsin (from mammals) and papain and ficin (from plants). Exopeptidases are enzymes which attack only the terminal peptide bonds of peptide chains so as to sequentially remove amino acids. Carboxypeptidases act on the carboxyl-terminal peptide bonds of oligopeptides (tripeptides and longer) and polypeptides, and aminopeptidases act on the amino-terminal peptide bonds; there are also dipeptidases whose action is limited to dipeptides (i.e., C-terminal and N-terminal).

Many of the proteolytic enzymes have a relatively high degree of specificity although several can hydrolyze esters of L-amino acids. Denatured proteins are attacked more readily than are native proteins. The proteases cleave the peptide chain only at specific points; i.e., some enzymes act selectively on peptide bonds of basic amino acyl residues, others act on aromatic or acidic residues. For example, the specificity of trypsin is directed toward the hydrolysis of peptide bonds whose carbonyl group is contributed by lysine or arginine. The specificity of α-chymotrypsin is somewhat less. Its activity is directed towards the cleavage of peptide bonds in which the carbonyl group is derived from phenylalanine, tyrosine, or tryptophan, or residues with long aliphatic side chains. Pepsin has a specificity which is even broader (less selective) than that of chymotrypsin.

Pepsin, the proteolytic enzyme in gastric juice, initiates the breakdown of protein entering the digestive tract of monogastric animals. This enzyme is synthesized in the form of an inactive enzyme precursor (zymogen) by the chief cells of the stomach mucosa. The zymogen, known as pepsinogen, is converted to pepsin by the action of HCl secreted by parietal cells of the gastric mucosa, and once a small amount of pepsin is formed, the latter acts on additional pepsinogen molecules to generate additional pepsin. Such a process is known as autocatalysis. The optimum pH for peptic activity is at the normal acidity of gastric juice (pH 1.5–2.5), and the products of hydrolysis are mixtures of polypeptides.

As the contents of the stomach pass into the small intestine, they are neutralized by the pancreatic juice, which contains the zymogens, trypsinogen, three chymotrypsinogens, proelastase, and two procarboxypeptidases. Trypsinogen is activated by an enzyme present in the intestine called enterokinase. Once trypsin is formed, it catalyzes the further transformation of trypsinogen into active trypsin (autocatalysis), and also catalyzes activation of the other zymogens from the pancreas, namely, the chymotrypsinogens and procarboxypeptidases.

The intestinal mucosa furnished two exopeptidases; aminopeptidase, which hydrolyzes N-terminal peptide bonds, sequentially; and dipeptidase, which hydrolyses dipeptides to form free amino acids.

Thus, through the combined actions of the above enzymes, food proteins are ultimately broken down into their constituent amino acids and, as such, are absorbed and utilized. Absorption is not simply a diffusion process, since L-amino acids are absorbed more readily than are the D-isomers.

Large molecules such as polypeptides and even proteins can be absorbed only to a limited extent under certain conditions. If undigested or partly digested proteins are repeatedly injected into an animal's blood stream, the animal may undergo a severe shock or even die after reinjection of the same protein. Similarly, if the absorption process of a person is such that it allows polypeptides or proteins to be absorbed, shock or death may occur upon eating of certain food proteins. Asthma, eczema, and hayfever are hyperallergenic symptoms known to be intensified by certain protein foods.

Proteolysis is not limited to the gastrointestinal tract. There are intracellular proteases which digest necrotic tissue. These enzymes, called cathepsins, are usually localized in the lysosomes and, as long as the cell is undamaged in any way, the lysosomes remain intact. Cell damage or cell death results in the destruction of the lysosomal membrane so that there is a release of these intracellular proteases with subsequent autolysis of the cell tissue. The increase in tenderness of beef following storage at temperatures just above freezing for 1 to 4 weeks is attributed to the catheptic enzymes present in the muscle. Today proteolytic enzyme preparations (papain, bromelain, microbial proteases, etc.) added in the form of powders, are routinely used to increase the tenderness of meat, especially beef.

Microorganisms must frequently fragment proteins in their media, which they accomplish by secreting extracellular enzymes. In general, the proteases and peptidases from microorganisms hydrolyze a wider variety of bonds than do the individual proteolytic enzymes of the gastrointestinal tract. The proteolytic enzymes of microorganisms are used extensively in the ripening of special cheeses (i.e., Liederkranz, Limburger, Camembert, and Cheddar).

Rennin is the proteolytic enzyme found in the gastric juice of calves.   Its substrate is the κ-casein of milk, which is converted by the enzyme to insoluble para-κ-casein.   The casein micelle can also be hydrolyzed by pepsin, trypsin, and other proteases.   The formation of paracasein is an important step in the manufacture of cheeses.

Metabolism of Amino Acids

The absorbed amino acids may undergo one of two fates: (1) they are used to build endogenous proteins and other nitrogenous metabolites essential to the organism (nucleotides, nucleic acids, porphyrins, amino sugars, etc.), or (2) they are degraded further into CO_2 and H_2O or other catabolites with the elimination of nitrogen either in the form of urea or uric acid.

Living organisms contain many different kinds of proteins. Proteins serve as catalysts in cellular reactions, as structural materials, and as antibodies which act in the defense of the body against intrusion of foreign organisms.   Since the individual proteins are characteristic for each species of living organism, the mechanism of protein synthesis must provide for not only the synthesis of the peptide bonds from amino acids, but also the synthesis of specific protein structures.   Most plants and microorganisms have the ability to synthesize all the amino acids required for protein generation. Some of the amino acids required for protein synthesis in animals are formed from α-keto acids (pyruvate, oxaloacetate, α-ketoglutarate, and others).   Consequently, they need not be ingested in foods.   These amino acids have been named endogenous or nonessential amino acids.   Other amino acids can also be synthesized by mammalian cells at rates sufficient to meet metabolic needs, and are thus nonessential.   In contrast, there are certain amino acids which must be present in food either as free amino acids or as constituents of the dietary proteins.   These amino acids have been termed essential amino acids.   Amino acid requirements vary from species to species.   The term essential amino acids is thus used to designate those amino acids which cannot be synthesized at a rate sufficient to meet metabolic requirements and therefore must be supplied in the diet.   The essential and nonessential amino acids for man are listed in Table 6.3.

It should be stressed that the terms essential and nonessential amino acids relate only to dietary intake. However, the role of the nonessential amino acids should not be underemphasized since they participate in many diverse metabolic reactions and thus are key intermediates in both anabolism and catabolism; i.e., while they are not "essential nutrients," they are essential metabolites.

TABLE 6.3

AMINO ACIDS REQUIRED BY MAN FOR THE
BIOSYNTHESIS OF PROTEIN

Essential		Non-essential	
Lysine	Threonine	Alanine	Histidine[1]
Isoleucine	Tryptophan	Arginine[1]	Proline
Leucine	Valine	Aspartic acid	Serine
Methionine	Phenylalanine	Cysteine	Tyrosine
		Glutamic acid	Asparagine
		Glycine	Glutamine

[1] In the young growing child, L-histidine and L-arginine are essential amino acids, although in adults they are apparently synthesized at rates sufficient to meet metabolic needs.

DNA, RNA and Protein Synthesis

Three of the more important macromolecules of all microorganisms, plants, and animals are deoxyribonucleic acids (DNA), ribonucleic acids (RNA), and proteins. These molecules, either directly or indirectly, control essentially all life processes. The involvement of DNA in genetic duplication is one of the outstanding discoveries of all times. Subsequent studies of the involvement of DNA and RNA in protein synthesis have opened new avenues of insight into chemotherapy, nutrition, and a host of other biochemical phenomena.

Both DNA and RNA are made up of subunits called nucleotides which contain a purine or pyrimidine base, a sugar (either D-ribofuranose or 2-deoxy-D-ribofuranose) and phosphate (esterified on the 5′-hydroxyl of the sugar molecule). The sugar is attached to either the N-1 position of pyrimidine moieties or to the N-9 position of purine moieties via β-N-glycosidic linkages, e.g.

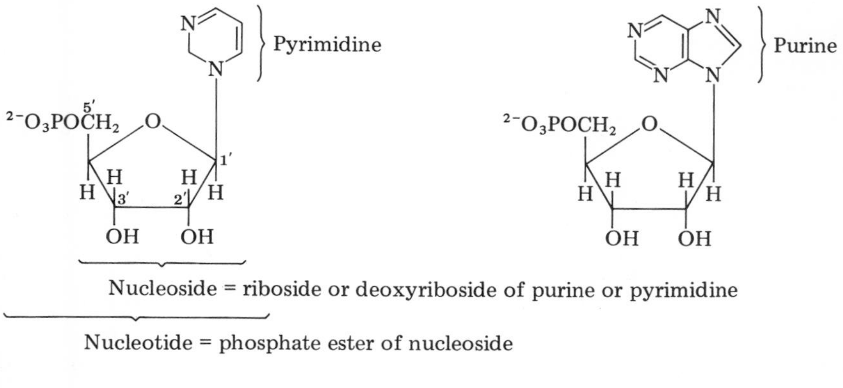

Nucleoside = riboside or deoxyriboside of purine or pyrimidine

Nucleotide = phosphate ester of nucleoside

Free purine or pyrimidine, or their nucleosides or nucleotides, are not found in nature; rather, purines and pyrimidines involved in living cells all contain one or more nitrogen and/or oxygen substituents.

DNA Structure.—Deoxyribonucleic acids are found primarily in the nucleus of eucaryotic cells and are responsible for the "passing on" of genetic characteristics of a parent cell to the daughter cell. The structure of DNA is the well-known double-helix which is comprised of two strands of polydeoxyribonucleotide. The monomeric deoxyribonucleotides are predominantly deoxyadenylate, deoxyguanylate, deoxycytidylate, and deoxythymidylate, as shown:

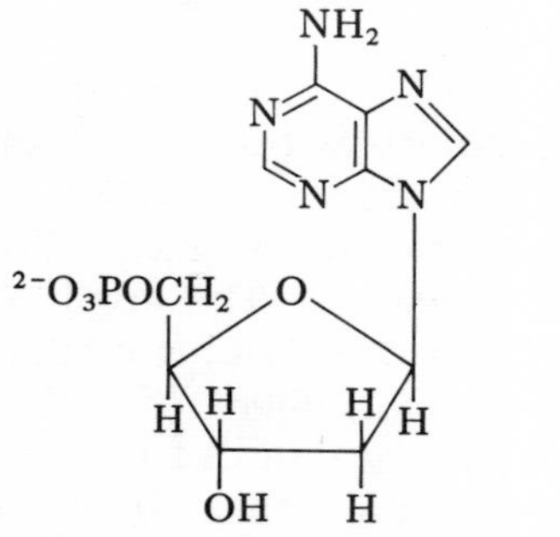

2'-Deoxyadenosine-5'-monophosphate
(deoxyadenylate; dAMP)

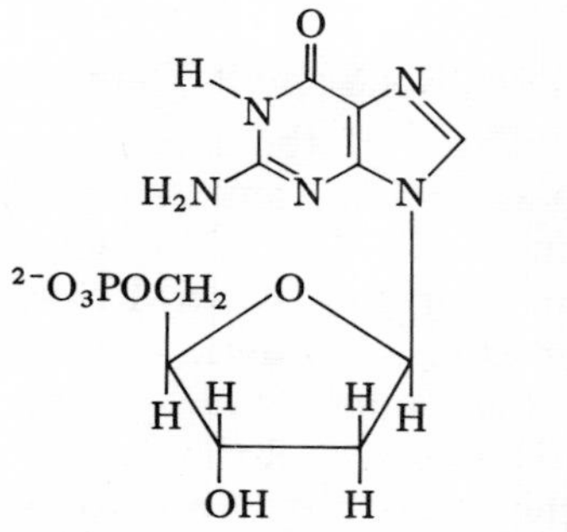

2'-Deoxyguanosine-5'-monophosphate
(deoxyguanylate; dGMP)

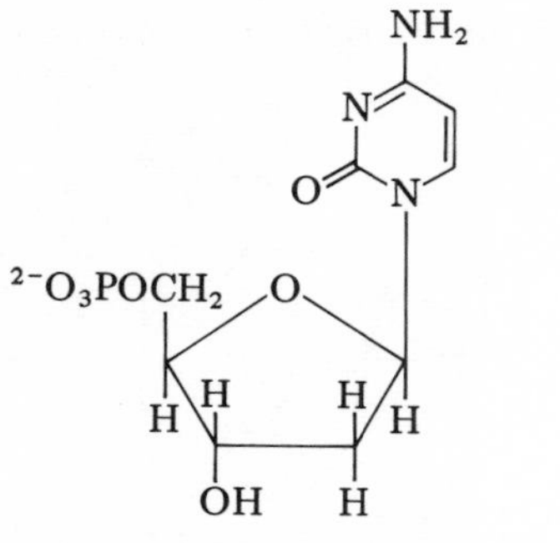

2'-Deoxycytidine-5'-monophosphate
(deoxycytidylate; dCMP)

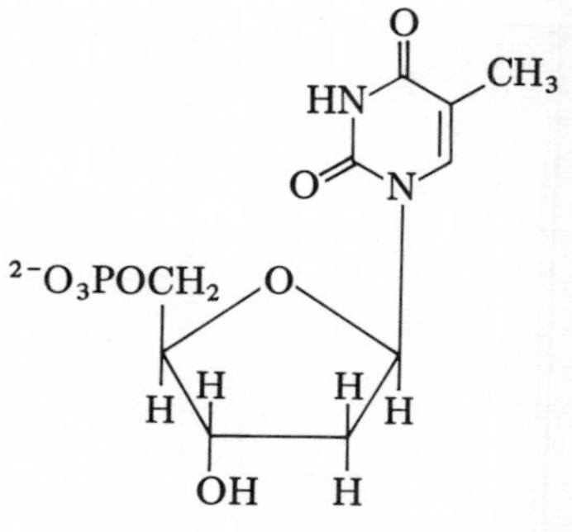

2'-Deoxythymidine-5'-monophosphate
(deoxythymidylate; dTMP)

DNAs are polymers of these deoxyribonucleotides linked by phosphodiester bonds the 3'-0 and 5'-0 of the adjacent residues:

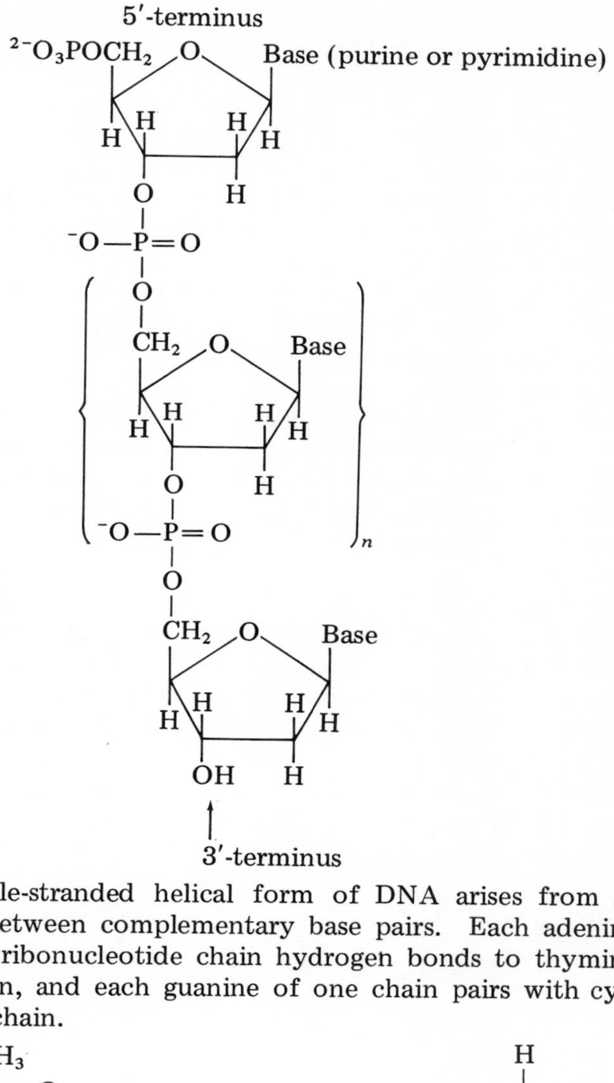

5'-terminus

$^{2-}O_3POCH_2$ — Base (purine or pyrimidine)

H H H H

O H

^-O—P$=$O

O

CH_2 — Base

H H H H

O H

^-O—P$=$O $\Big]_n$

O

CH_2 — Base

H H H H

OH H

3'-terminus

The double-stranded helical form of DNA arises from hydrogen bonding between complementary base pairs. Each adenine of one polydeoxyribonucleotide chain hydrogen bonds to thymine of the other chain, and each guanine of one chain pairs with cytosine of the other chain.

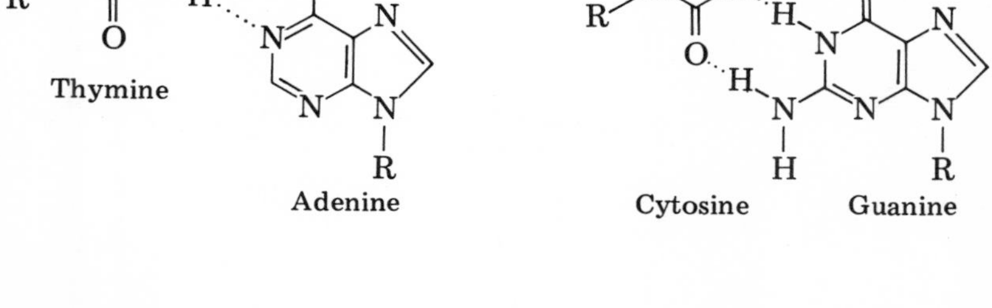

Thymine   Adenine

Cytosine   Guanine

The ratios of adenine:thymine and of guanine:cytosine in double helical DNA are thus one. This 1:1 ratio is a consequence of the complementary base pairing.

The DNA double helix thus consists of two polydeoxyribonucleotide strands coiled around a central axis. The strands are of opposite polarity, i.e., one strand has its 5'-terminus hydrogen bonded to the other strand's 3'-terminus, and vice versa. There are 10 nucleotide pairs per turn of the right-handed helix with a translation of approximately 34Å, giving 3.4Å per base pair. The bases are arranged in a stacked fashion such that their planes are perpendicular to the axis of the DNA helix. The helix has 2 grooves, 1 shallow (minor) and 1 deep (major) as shown in Fig. 6.3.

DNA Replication.—The most notable feature of the DNA molecule is represented by the ability of each strand of the double helix to serve as a template for replication of the complementary strand. This ability, correctly referred to as semiconservative replication, can be represented as shown in Fig. 6.4. This molecular property uniquely provides the chemical basis for the genetic continuity of biological systems.

The two strands of a "parent" DNA molecule separate and are duplicated, producing two double-stranded molecules, each identical to the original molecule. Thus, each daughter cell contains the same quantity and quality of genetic material as did the parent cell. These molecules can in turn replicate by the same mechanism for subsequent cell division.

Polymerization of nucleotides to form DNA is catalyzed by an enzyme called DNA polymerase. This enzyme utilizes deoxynucleoside 5'-triphosphates, i.e., dATP, dGTP, dCTP and dTTP.

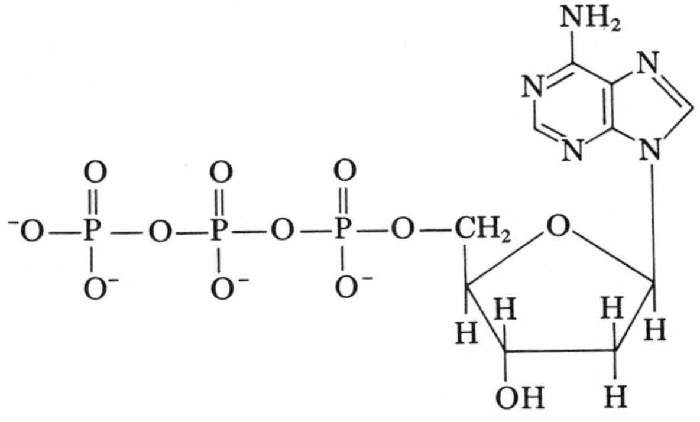

2'-Deoxyadenosine-5'-triphosphate
(dATP)

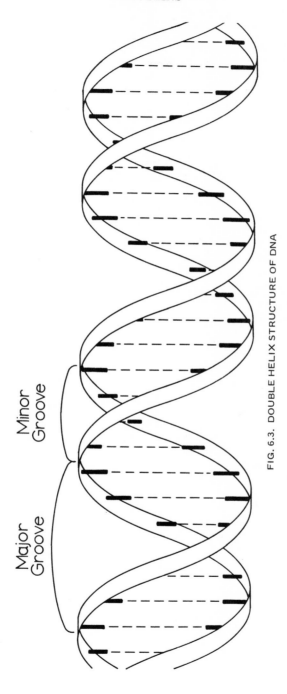

FIG. 6.3. DOUBLE HELIX STRUCTURE OF DNA

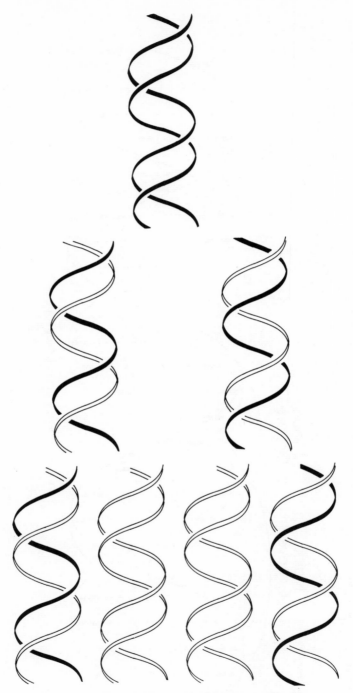

FIG. 6.4. DUPLICATION OF DOUBLE HELIX OF DNA

Parent DNA is shown as dark lines.

As in the case of virtually all nucleoside triphosphate metabolic reactions, Mg^{2+} is required. The enzyme also requires an existing polynucleotide which serves as a "template." The reaction can be represented as:

n(deoxynucleoside triphosphates) + DNA template strand from

parent molecule $\overset{Mg^{2+}}{\rightleftharpoons}$ (deoxynucleoside monophosphate)$_n$-DNA template strand + nPP$_i$

It should be pointed out that Fig. 6.4 is an oversimplification. Both strands of the double helix appear to be duplicated simultaneously rather than splitting, then duplicating. DNA polymerase which builds a chain in the $5' \rightarrow 3'$ direction is augmented by another enzyme, polynucleotide ligase, which completes the chain by catalyzing covalent bond formation between segments of DNA polymerase-synthesized chains. The partially completed duplication is shown in Fig. 6.5. The double strand of the parent molecule (dark lines) are of opposite polarity as indicated by the arrows. Duplication begins at the $3'$ end of the parent chain and proceeds along this chain adding deoxynucleoside monophosphate units having $5'$-$3'$ phosphodiester linkages (light line). Ultimately, the duplicating chain "crosses" over to the other parent strand and moves along this chain from the $3'$ to the $5'$ end as in the case of the previous parent chain. It should be noted that the direction is the same in duplication of both parent strands, thus the final daughter molecules have the same polarity as the original parent molecules.

RNA Structure.—Ribonucleic acids are generally considered to be found mainly in the cytoplasm. However, most RNA appears to be formed in nuclei of eucaryotic cells, e.g., liver. There are three major classes of RNA, viz., messenger RNA (mRNA), transfer RNA (tRNA), and ribosomal RNA (rRNA).

The most salient features of RNA that distinguish it from DNA are:

(1) RNA had D-ribofuranose as the component sugar rather than 2-deoxy-D-ribofuranose as found in DNA.

(2) RNA contains primarily the bases adenine, guanine, cytosine, and uracil.
This is in contrast to DNA which contains adenine, guanine, cytosine, and thymine.

(3) The RNA strands do not appear to associate to form the double helix as does DNA, except in certain viruses which contain double-stranded RNA. However, intrachain base pairing does occur.

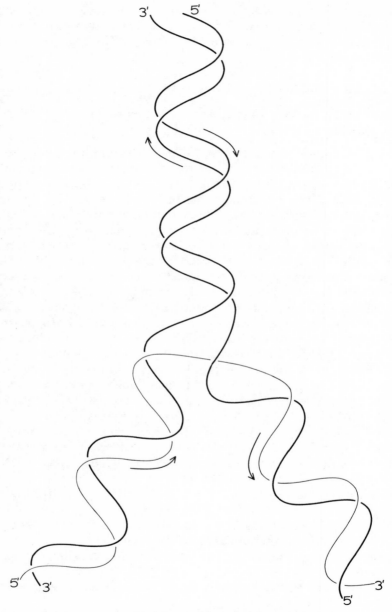

FIG. 6.5. DUPLICATING SEQUENCE OF DNA MOLECULE

Arrows indicate polarities.

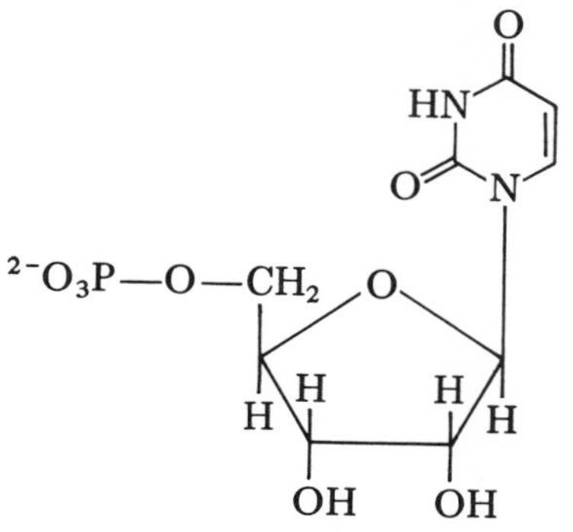

uridine-5'-monophosphate
(uridylate; UMP)

Messenger RNA.—Messenger RNA is synthesized by enzymatic reactions in a process referred to as *transcription*. The transcription process is dictated by a strand of DNA which, through hydrogen bonding of complementary bases, determines the sequence of the ribonucleotides in the mRNA strand that is being formed. The sequence of the mRNA chain determines, ultimately, the order in which amino acids are linked when a polypeptide chain is synthesized. Each sequence of three adjacent nucleotide residues in the mRNA chain beginning at or near its 5'-terminus is called a codon. These units of three residues (i.e., triplet codons) determine which of the tRNA species (carrying activated amino acids) will attach to the mRNA. Three complementary bases in each tRNA species are called anticodons. The interrelationship of the codon-anticondon and their role in protein synthesis will be discussed later in this chapter. A list of the codons for each of the 20 activated amino acids used for protein biosynthesis is presented in Table 6.4.

Transfer RNA.—Transfer RNAs play the important role of mobilizing activated amino acids and mediating their transfer to the proper positions along the mRNA. Each of the 20 amino acids used in the synthesis of proteins has a corresponding tRNA, and some of the amino acids have more than 1 species of tRNA. These tRNAs are named for the amino acid with which they react. For example, the first tRNA whose complete covalent structure was determined was alanyl tRNA isolated from yeast. The covalent structure of alanyl tRNA (tRNA$_{Ala}$) is shown in Fig. 6.6. The amino acid, alanine, is esterified through its carboxyl group to the 2' and 3'-terminal hydroxyl groups of the specific tRNA chain to form what is commonly indicated as alanyl-tRNA$_{Ala}$ (i.e., tRNA$_{Ala}$ "charged"

TABLE 6.4

GENETIC CODE: CODONS OF mRNA (5' TO 3')[1]

	U	C	A	G
U	UUU Phe UUC Phe	UCU Ser UCC Ser	UAU Tyr UAC Tyr	UGU Cys UGC Cys
	UUA Leu UUG Leu	UCA Ser UCG Ser	UAA Ochre UAG Amber	UGA Umber UGG trp
C	CUU Leu CUC Leu	CCU Pro CCC Pro	CAU His CAC His	CGU Arg CGC Arg
	CUA Leu CUG Leu	CCA Pro CCG Pro	CAA Gln CAG Gln	CGA Arg CGG Arg
A	AUU Ile AUC Ile	ACU Thr ACC Thr	AAU Asn AAC Asn	AGU Ser AGC Ser
	AUA Ile AUG Met	ACA Thr ACG Thr	AAA Lys AAG Lys	AGA Arg AGG Arg
G	GUU Val GUC Val	GCU Ala GCC Ala	GAU Asp GAC Asp	GGU Gly GGC Gly
	GUA Val GUG Val	GCA Ala GCG Ala	GAA Glu GAG Glu	GGA Gly GGG Gly

[1] Codons in blocks are termination signals.

with alanine). This ester linkage represents an "activated" form of the carboxyl group, which can thus be "transferred" to the free α-amino group of an adjacent activated amino acid at the site of the mRNA.

Protein Synthesis

Proteins are polymers of amino acids (both essential and non-essential). Thus, it follows that both types of amino acids must be at the protein biosynthetic site at the time of synthesis. Since peptide bonds are not formed spontaneously, biochemical systems must also be present to activate amino acids and to mediate their incorporation into the bond in the proper sequence, as dictated by the cell's genetic material.

The sites of protein biosynthesis are ribonucleoprotein particles called ribosomes. In addition to these intracellular structures, other factors are essential for protein synthesis. These include: transfer RNA (tRNA), messenger RNA (mRNA), aminoacyl-tRNA synthetases, ATP, Mg^{2++}, GTP, initiation factions, K^+, elongation factors, peptide synthetase, transfer factors, and release factors.

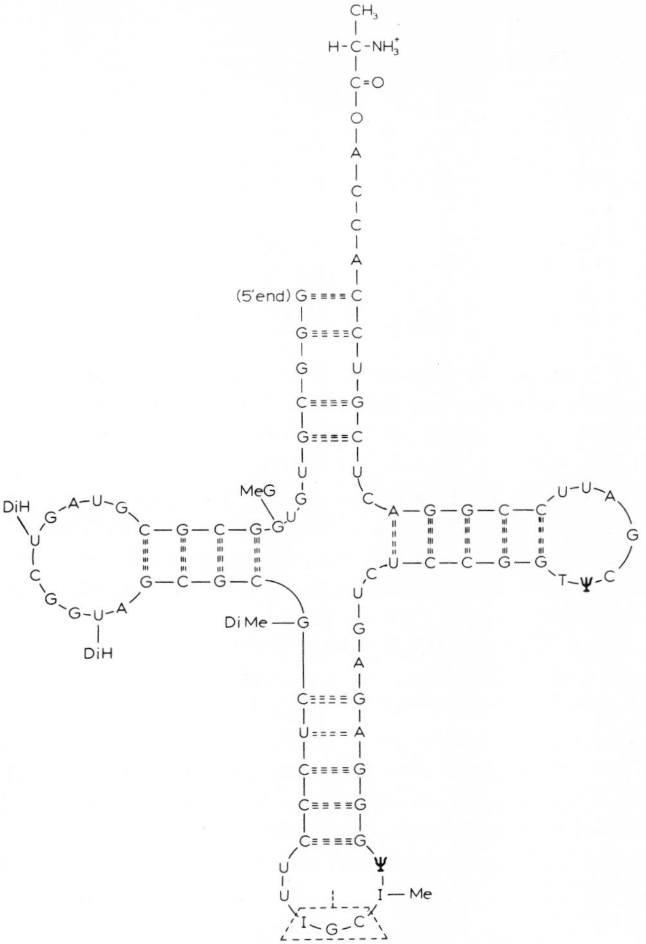

FIG. 6.6. ALANINE TRANSFER RNA

Anticodon is shown inside dotted lined area. MeG = 1-methyl-guanosine, DiHU = 4,5-dihydrouridine, I = inosine, DiMeG = Dimethylguanosine, MeI = 1-methylinosine, ψ = pseudouridine, T = thymidine.

The various stages of protein synthesis can be summarized as follows:

(1) Each amino acid is "activated" by ATP to form an amino-acyl-tRNA. These two-stage reactions are catalyzed by specific aminoacyl-tRNA synthetases (e.g., alanyl-tRNA synthetase, phenylalanyl-tRNA synthetase, etc.).

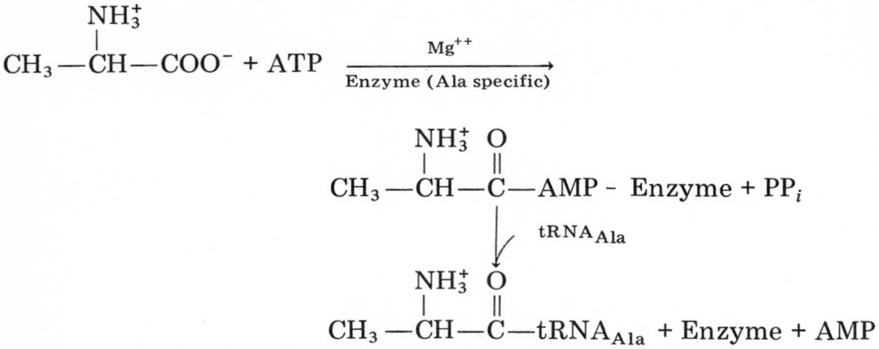

$$\underset{\text{CH}_3\text{—CH—COO}^- + \text{ATP}}{\overset{\text{NH}_3^+}{|}} \xrightarrow[\text{Enzyme (Ala specific)}]{\text{Mg}^{++}}$$

$$\underset{\text{CH}_3\text{—CH—C—AMP}}{\overset{\text{NH}_3^+ \quad \text{O}}{| \quad\quad ||}}\text{ - Enzyme + PP}_i$$

$$\Big\downarrow \text{tRNA}_{\text{Ala}}$$

$$\underset{\text{CH}_3\text{—CH—C—tRNA}_{\text{Ala}}}{\overset{\text{NH}_3^+ \quad \text{O}}{| \quad\quad ||}}\text{ + Enzyme + AMP}$$

(2) As the ribosome attaches to the mRNA chain at or near its 5'-terminus, the aminoacyl-tRNA is attached via the ribosome to the chain according to the first codon (three nucleotide unit) of the mRNA chain and the anticodon of the particular aminoacyl-tRNA (Fig. 6.7). The initiation of this first step in most microorganisms is controlled by the first aminoacyl-tRNA attached to the mRNA. In bacteria N-formylmethionyl-tRNA is the initiating factor, and thus becomes the N-terminus of the growing polypeptide chain.

(3) A second aminoacyl-tRNA (AA_2tRNA_2) enters the ribosome at the codon adjacent to that which binds the first amino-acyl-tRNA (AA_1tRNA_1). This brings the two amino acids into close proximity and the elongation factor, GTP and peptide synthetase promote the formation of a peptide bond with the release of tRNA_1, leaving a dipeptidyl-tRNA$_2$ attached to the second codon of the mRNA chain.

(4) Dipeptidyl-tRNA$_2$ remains attached to its codon and a new AA_3-tRNA$_3$ then attaches to an adjacent codon (in the direction proceeding from the 5' end toward the 3' end of the mRNA). Again GTP, the elongation factor and protein synthetase produce a new peptide bond to yield a tripeptidyl-tRNA$_3$ with release of tRNA$_2$.

(5) This process is repeated until the entire "message" of codons in the mRNA has been "translated"; at that point a terminating codon is reached on the mRNA chain. Thereupon, the release factor catalyzes the dissociation of the completed polypeptide chain from the terminal tRNA. The ribosome is then released from the mRNA.

Other Metabolic Roles of Amino Acids

In addition to their role as constituents of proteins, amino acids are found in a number of nonprotein compounds. For instance,

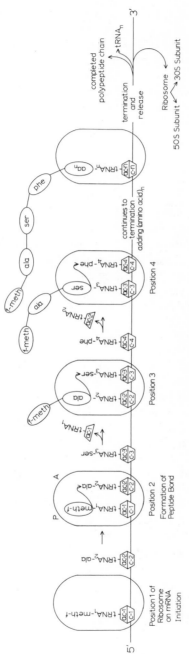

FIG. 6.7. SEQUENCE OF PROTEIN SYNTHESIS

ac = anticodon
c = codon

glycine is incorporated into the porphyrin portion of hemoglobin and the cytochromes; the hormones, adrenaline, and thyroxine are formed from tyrosine; glutathione, an important cellular constituent, is a tripeptide composed of glutamate, cysteine, and glycine; and the posterior pituitary hormones, vasopressin and oxytocin, are oligopeptides each containing nine amino acid residues. The nucleotides, themselves, are synthesized from amino acids such as glycine, aspartate, and glutamine.

Nitrogen Balance

In a healthy adult animal, the breaking down of tissues (catabolism) and the building up of tissues (anabolism) are in dynamic equilibrium. Expressed in another way, the dietary nitrogen intake is equal to the amount of nitrogen excreted (in the urine and feces). During growth and convalescence from disease, increased rates of protein synthesis will depress the excretion of nitrogenous catabolites, and the animal is said to be in a state of positive nitrogen balance. Conversely, during starvation or wasting diseases, the reverse is true; i.e., the rate of catabolism exceeds that of anabolism. Under such circumstances the animal is in a state of negative nitrogen balance.

Metabolic Fate of Nitrogen

Amino acids present at levels in excess of metabolic requirements for the synthesis of body proteins and essential nonprotein-nitrogenous compounds can be catabolized for the production of energy. The amino group is generally removed from the carbon chain early in the catabolic process. Many of the resulting α-keto acids are shunted into the general metabolic pathways to be eventually oxidized to CO_2 and H_2O. In ureotelic animals, including man, the nitrogen appears in the urine in the form of urea, which is synthesized by an energy-requiring process from ammonia and CO_2. The possible metabolic pathways are: (a) Oxidative deamination of amino acids to α-keto acids. In this reaction two hydrogen atoms are probably removed to form an imino acid which in turn is hydrolyzed to ammonia and a keto acid.

$$
\begin{array}{ccccc}
\overset{\displaystyle H \;\;\; H}{\underset{\displaystyle |}{\overset{\displaystyle \diagdown \; \diagup}{N}}} & & NH & & O \\
| & & \| & & \| \\
R-C-COOH & \xrightarrow{-2H} & R-C-COOH & \xrightarrow{+H_2O} & R-C-COOH + NH_3 \\
| \\
H
\end{array}
$$

The reaction is catalyzed by specific enzymes (L-amino acid oxidases), some of which have flavin adenine dinucleotide (FAD) as a prosthetic group to serve as the hydrogen acceptor. (b) Transamination to α-keto acids. This reaction, which is possibly the most important general pathway for elimination of nitrogen, involves the transfer of an amino group from the amino acid to α-ketoglutaric acid, giving the corresponding α-keto acid and L-glutamic acid. The transfer of the amino group is catalyzed by specific enzymes (transaminases) via the prosthetic group, pyridoxal-5-phosphate. The α-ketoglutaric acid required for this reaction is readily available as one of the intermediaries of the tricarboxylic acid cycle.

Most transamination reactions are metabolically reversible. Therefore, certain amino acids can be formed from the corresponding α-keto acids and L-glutamate. For example, L-alanine can by synthesized from pyruvate. However, each transaminase is highly specific with regard to amino acid substrates, and several amino acids (lysine, threonine, and others) are not transaminated. In addition, there are a number of amino acids for which the α-keto precursors or other suitable intermediates are not synthesized by an organism. As a consequence, these amino acids must be supplied to the organism; these are the essential amino acids (See Table 6.3).

The amino group of glutamic acid is subsequently removed through the action of glutamic acid dehydrogenase, which uses nicotinamide adenine dinucleotide (NAD^+) as the hydrogen acceptor. The products of reaction are reduced NAD^+ (NADH), ammonia, and α-ketoglutarate:

$$\text{Glutamate} + NAD^+ + H_2O \longrightarrow NH_4^+ + \text{α-ketoglutarate} + NADH$$

The reduced pyridine coenzyme, NADH, then transfers its hydrogen and pair of electrons to other systems. The ammonia that is formed can be detoxified by biosynthesis of urea. The net reaction can be written as follows:

$$CO_2 + 2NH_4^+ \longrightarrow H_2N - \overset{\overset{\displaystyle O}{\|}}{C} - NH_2 + H_2O$$

It should be recognized that the above reaction is a gross oversimplication of fact. Four amino acids, ornithine, citrulline, aspartic acid and arginine, play important roles in the cyclic process. and ATP is hydrolyzed to provide energy required in the process.

$$\text{H}_2\text{N}-\overset{\displaystyle \text{O}}{\overset{\|}{\text{C}}}-\text{NH}_2$$

L-ornithine

$\text{NH}_4^+ + \text{CO}_2 + \text{ATP}$

Urea

arginase

Citrulline + ADP + P_i

H_2O

NH_4^+ (L-aspartic acid) + ATP

L-arginine
+ AMP + PP_i

fumarate

(c) Decarboxylation of amino acids. This type of reaction is quite common in bacteria. Decarboxylation reactions are catalyzed by specific enzymes (amino acid decarboxylases), which require pyridoxal phosphate, and the net result is the production of CO_2 and a primary amine. Some of the latter compounds produced by mammalian decarboxylases have important pharmacological effects (e.g., histamine, tyramine, γ-aminobutyric acid) and some may serve as precursors of hormones, as components of coenzymes and in other metabolic roles. For example, the decarboxylation of serine gives rise to ethanolamine which is found in phosphatides (it is also the parent substance of choline), and the decarboxylation of cysteine gives β-mercaptoethylamine which is a constituent of coenzyme A.

Nutritive Value of Proteins

It is well-known that proteins differ in their nutritive values. Such differences in the nutritive value of proteins are due to the variability of amino acid compositions. Accordingly, it is possible to rate proteins on the basis of their constituent amino acids and to assign numbers to these ratings. One useful rating system is based on the biological values (BV) of proteins. Actually, a number of nutritional characteristics are included in this expression: the digestibility, the availability of the digested product to the organism, and the presence and amounts of the various essential amino acids. The values are useful for comparing proteins from a variety of sources and for judging the nutritional adequacy of a combination of proteins such as might be found in a normal diet.

In a sense, evaluation of the biological value of proteins is unrealistic since one does not normally consume pure protein from a single source. Protein score, based on the amino acid composition of a protein mixture (or protein), permits one to predict the "performance" of a dietary mixture. This method is based on the concept that the limiting factor in the quality of a protein is the concentration of an essential amino acid which falls below the requirement. The standard of reference, the amino acid pattern of the nutrient that is used in calculating the score, is still a matter of debate. Some of the proposed reference standards are: whole egg, cow's milk, human milk, and a pattern based on human amino acid requirements (FAO).

Several other methods have been developed for evaluating protein quality. Two of the more widely used methods are the protein efficiency ratio (PER) which is equal to the gain in body weight per gram of protein ingested and net protein utilization (NPU) which characterizes the relationship between the nitrogen (protein) ingested and the increase in carcass nitrogen.

The problem of improving protein quality is one of major importance in the world today. A knowledge of the quality of individual proteins permits one to improve the nutritional adequacy of a given protein of low biological value by supplementing it with one or more amino acids (such as lysine) or with another protein which provides the limiting or missing essential amino acids (mutual supplementation).

Effect of Heat on the Nutritive Value of Protein.—Proteins are generally affected by heat; the changes they undergo may be beneficial in some respects and harmful in other respects.

The beneficial effects relate to some change in the structure of the protein molecule. These transformations, commonly involving partial denaturation, render the proteins more susceptible to enzymatic digestion, reduce their solubility, and destroy (or lower) the biological activity of toxic proteins. The effect of heat in inactivating a trypsin inhibitor present in soybeans is well-known. Raw fish contains an enzyme (thiaminase) that catalyzes the destruction of vitamin B_1; heat inactivates the enzyme, thereby preventing the destruction of thiamine in diets rich in fish. The effect of heat on the curd of calcium caseinate of milk has been used to advantage in child feeding. Raw eggs contain a protein, avidin, which combines with and inactivates another B-vitamin, biotin. Heat denatures avidin and, as a consequence, the protein cannot function as a vitamin inhibitor.

However, excessive heating of proteins may result in the destruction of certain amino acids or render them unavailable for digestion. One of the most important changes which results from heating is the interaction of certain amino acid residues of the protein with reducing sugars such as glucose. The amino acid, lysine, is most frequently involved in this type of reaction, but tryptophan, arginine, and histidine may also be involved. In the early stages (melanoidin condensation) a bond is formed between the sugar and the amino group which interferes with the action of proteolytic enzymes but which may be broken by boiling with acid. Thus, the reactions are in a sense reversible. If the reaction is continued, a discoloration (brownish-color) begins to appear. In the last stages, i.e., when browning has become extensive, amino acids are destroyed.

Moisture content plays a very important part in the "browning" reaction. Experiments with simple systems of amino acids and sugars have shown that a moisture content of 30% is most favorable for this reaction. Moisture contents above or below this value are less favorable for the reaction. The browning reaction is peculiar to dried and dehydrated food products for in these circumstances the moisture content is reduced from a high value to a low value, usually passing through the range conducive to protein damage. Similarly, baking should promote protein damage as a result of the browning reaction. In contrast, cooking and toasting should have no adverse effect on the nutritive value of cereal protein.

BIBLIOGRAPHY

ACKERS, G. K. 1970. Analytical gel chromatography of proteins. *In* Advances in Protein Chemistry, Vol. 24, C. B. Anfinson, Jr., J. T. Edsall, and F. M. Richards (Editors). Academic Press, New York.

ALBANESE, A. A. (Editor). 1959. Protein and Amino Acid Nutrition. Academic Press, New York.

ALTSCHUL, A. M. 1958. Processed Plant Protein Foodstuffs. Academic Press, New York.

ALTSCHUL, A. M. 1966. World Protein Resources, Advances in Chemistry Series 57, American Chemical Society, Washington, D.C.

AMERICAN MEAT INSTITUTE FOUNDATION. 1960. The Science of Meat and Meat Products. W. H. Freeman and Co., San Francisco, Calif.

ANON. 1958. Exchange of Genetic Material: Mechanisms and Consequences, Vol. 23. Given at Cold Spring Harbor Symposium on Quantitative Biology, Cold Spring Harbor Laboratory, Long Island, N.Y.

ANON. 1966. The Genetic Code, Vol. 31. Given at Cold Spring Harbor Symposium on Quantitative Biology, Cold Spring Harbor Laboratory, Long Island, N.Y.

ANON. 1968. Replication of DNA in Microorganisms, Vol. 33. Given at Cold Spring Harbor Symposium on Quantitative Biology, Cold Spring Harbor Laboratory, Long Island, N.Y.

ANON. 1969. The Mechanism of Protein Synthesis, Vol. 34. Given at Cold Spring Harbor Symposium on Quantitative Biology. Cold Spring Harbor Laboratory, Long Island, N.Y.

BAILEY, J. L. 1967. Techniques in Protein Chemistry, 2nd Edition. Elsevier Publishing Co., Amsterdam.

BLACKBURN, S. 1968. Amino Acid Determination. Marcel Dekker, New York.

GEIDUSCHEK, E. P., and HASELKORN, R. 1969. Messenger RNA. Ann. Rev. Biochem. *38*, 647–676.

HAUROWITZ, F. 1963. The Chemistry and Function of Proteins, 2nd Edition. Academic Press, New York.

KLOTZ, I. M. 1967. Protein subunits: a table. Science *155*, 697–698.

KLOTZ, I. M., and DARNELL, D. W. 1969. Protein subunits: a table (2nd Edition). Sci. *166*, 126–127.

KOPPLE, K. D. 1966. Peptides and Amino Acids. W. A. Benjamin, New York.

LEHNINGER, A. L. 1970. Biochemistry. Worth Publishers, New York.

LEHNINGER, A. L. 1971. Bioenergetics, 2nd Edition. W. A. Benjamin, Menlo Park, Calif.

LIPMAN, F. 1969. Polypeptide chain elongation in protein biosynthesis. Science *164*, 1024–1031.

MAHLER, H. R., and CORDES, E. H. 1971. Biological Chemistry, 2nd Edition. Harper and Row Publisher, New York.

MEISTER, A. 1965. Biochemistry of Amino Acids, 2nd Edition. Academic Press, New York.

MOLDAVE, K. 1965. Nucleic acids and protein biosynthesis. Ann. Rev. Biochem. *34*, 419–448.

NATIONAL RESEARCH COUNCIL. 1963. Evaluation of Protein Quality. Publication *1100*, National Academy of Sciences, Washington, D.C.

NATIONAL RESEARCH COUNCIL. 1950. The Problem of Heat Injury to Dietary Protein. Reprint and Circular Series No. 131, National Academy of Sciences, Washington, D.C.

NESELSON, M., and STAHL, F. W. 1958. The replication of DNA. Cold Spring Harbor Symposium on Quantitative Biology *23*, 9–12.

NOVELLI, G. D. 1967. Amino acid activation for protein synthesis. Ann. Rev. Biochem. *36*, 449–484.

PLATT, B. S., and MILLER, D. S. 1959. The net dietary protein value—its definition and application. Proc. Nutr. Soc. *18*, vii–viii.

SCHULTZ, H. W. (Editor). 1964. Symposium on Foods, Proteins and Their Reactions. Avi Publishing Co., Westport, Conn.

SCHWEET, R., and HEINTZ, R. 1965. Protein synthesis. Ann. Rev. Biochem. *34*, 723–758.

SOBER, H. A. (Editor). 1970. Handbook of Biochemistry, 2nd Edition. Chemical Rubber Co., Cleveland, Ohio.

STEIN, S., and MOORE, W. 1961. The structure of proteins. Sci. Am., Feb., 81–92.

TANFORD, C. 1970. Protein denaturation. *In* Advances in Protein Chemistry, Vol. 24, C. B. Anfinson, Jr., J. T. Edsall, and F. M. Richards (Editors). Academic Press, New York.

VOGEL, H. J., and VOGEL, R. H. 1967. Regulation of protein synthesis. Ann. Rev. Biochem. *36*, 519–538.

WATSON, J. D. 1970. Molecular Biology of the Gene, 2nd Edition. W. A. Benjamin, New York.

CHAPTER 7

Enzymes

One of the characteristics of normal living cells is that most of the chemical reactions taking place within the cell are controlled and regulated by enzymes. These chemical reactions, if performed *in vitro*, would proceed at a very slow rate or would require more drastic conditions to reach a velocity equivalent to those observed in the cell. Enzyme catalyzed reactions take place very readily under the mild conditions of the environment of the cell. Similarly, the food eaten by an animal undergoes a series of controlled hydrolytic reactions within the gastrointestinal tract.

Enzymes are unique biochemical catalysts which always contain protein and which may also have an organic moiety called the prosthetic group or coenzyme. The prosthetic group is tightly bound to the protein and remains attached throughout the course of the catalytic reaction, e.g., the flavin adenine dinucleotide (FAD) enzymes such as dehydrogenases (succinic and fatty acyl). However, organic molecules such as nicotinamide adenine dinucleotide (NAD^+) may also bind to enzymes but to a lesser degree and thus will dissociate from the enzyme during or at the termination of the catalytic reaction. Such organic molecules are called coenzymes. Additionally, enzymes often have an obligatory requirement for metal ions. Some metal ions and other cations or anions act only as activators since their presence only increases the catalytic activity of the enzyme, but the enzyme functions without these activating ions.

Since enzymes are proteins, any agent such as heat, strong acids or bases, organic solvents or other materials which will denature protein will also destroy the activity of an enzyme. Thus, one of the important characteristics of enzymes is heat inactivation. A temperature of 80°C for a few minutes is sufficient to inactivate most enzymes.

With the probable exception of some lipases from plant seeds (e.g., castor bean), enzymes are soluble in water, glycerol, dilute acetone, and alcohol. Enzymes are nondialyzable because of their colloidal nature and they can be precipitated from solution by agents such as ammonium sulfate, trichloroacetic acid, and concentrated alcohol.

Enzymes as Catalysts

A catalyst is a substance which accelerates a chemical reaction. As in the case of conventional catalysts, enzymes function quite efficiently and require only small concentrations to be present and can repeat their action almost indefinitely. The protein nature of the enzyme gives the property of specificity. Thus, different enzymes are required to catalyze different reactions. As in ordinary equilibrium reactions an enzyme catalyzed reaction has no effect on the equilibrium constant. Increasing the concentration of an enzyme will only decrease the time needed to attain equilibrium. Since the reaction is reversible, the same enzyme catalyzes the reaction in both directions. There are some reactions in which one enzyme is required for the reaction to occur in one direction and another enzyme is required for the reaction to take place in a reverse manner. An example of such a reaction is:

$$\text{glucose} + \text{ATP} \underset{\text{phosphatase}}{\overset{\text{hexokinase}}{\rightleftharpoons}} \text{glucose-6-phosphate} + \text{ADP}$$

Reactions of this type have an equilibrium constant that favors the formation of the product to such a degree that the reaction can be considered essentially irreversible. Pyruvate kinase, which converts phosphoenolpyruvate to pyruvate, is another example of an enzyme which is functionally irreversible.

Properties of an Enzyme—Catalyzed Reaction

A. **Enzyme Concentration.**—The rate of an enzyme-catalyzed reaction is proportional to the concentration of enzyme. This relationship is the basis for methods used to determine enzyme concentrations in samples of unknowns. Figure 7.1, Curve a, shows a linear

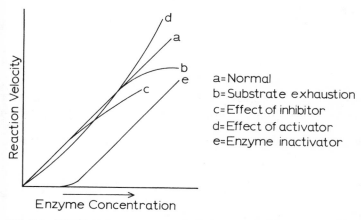

a=Normal
b=Substrate exhaustion
c=Effect of inhibitor
d=Effect of activator
e=Enzyme inactivator

FIG. 7.1. EFFECTS OF VARIOUS FACTORS ON THE RELATIONSHIP BETWEEN THE REACTION VELOCITY AND THE CONCENTRATION OF AN ENZYME

relationship between the rate of the reaction and increasing enzyme concentration in the presence of an excess of substrate. Deviations from this curve indicate some limiting factor. For example, if the concentration of an enzyme is increased a considerable amount, the rate of the reaction will decrease due to substrate exhaustion as indicated on line b, Fig. 7.1.

Deviations from linearity also occur when an enzyme preparation contains either an activator or an inhibitor. In the presence of an activator, the response curve shows an upward curvature (Curve d, Fig. 7.1). As one increases the concentration of both the enzyme and inhibitor, a greater proportion of both will be combined in an inactive enzyme-inhibitor complex. The response curve will then show a downward curvature (Curve c, Fig. 7.1).

If a toxic substance, such as a trace of heavy metal (Pb or Hg), is present the first portions of the enzyme are inactivated but with increasing amounts of the enzyme a normal response curve will be produced (Curve e, Fig. 7.1).

B. Substrate Concentration.—The rate of an enzyme reaction depends on the concentration of the substrate. It will be noted that at a low substrate concentration the relation of reaction rate to substrate is almost linear and complies with first-order kinetics. The latter may be expressed as:

$$\frac{d[S]}{dt} = k'([S] - [P])$$

where k' is the first-order reaction constant, and $([S] - [P])$ is the concentration of substrate remaining at any given time. The amount of remaining substrate is proportional to the rate of reaction. For purposes of graphical presentation, the equation may be integrated to give:

$$k' \times t = 2.3 \log \frac{[S]}{[S] - [P]}$$

where $[S]$ = initial concentration of substrate, $[P]$ = concentration of substrate converted to product after the lapse of time, t. If the time, t, is plotted against the log of $\frac{[S]}{[S] - [P]}$ a straight line results, the slope of the line is constant.

At high substrate concentration, however, the velocity of the reaction is maximum and is independent of substrate; hence, the course of reaction follows zero-order kinetics:

$$\frac{d[S]}{dt} = k^0$$

where k^0 is the zero-order reaction constant. For such a reaction the amount of end-product formed is proportional to time.

The velocity (μ moles of substrate changed per minute) of an enzyme reaction is much greater than that of other chemically catalyzed organic reactions. The effectiveness of this kind of reaction is described by its molecular activity (turnover number). The latter is defined as the number of molecules of substrate transformed per minute per molecule of enzyme. The usual values range from several hundred to several thousand molecules of substrate per molecule of enzyme per minute. However, for some enzymes, e.g., catalase, the molecular activity is as high as one million or more. However, with increasing concentration, the rate of reaction begins to decrease until a certain substrate concentration is reached beyond which no further change in rate is observed. This effect is easily explained if we assume the formation of an enzyme-substrate complex. As the enzyme molecules combine with substrate molecules, the rate of reaction will increase with the addition of more substrate. When sufficient substrate is present so that all enzyme molecules have combined with the substrate, an increase in substrate will no longer increase the rate of reaction. Such observations suggest that the enzyme binds the substrate to form an unstable enzyme-substrate complex. The formation of the enzyme-substrate complex from its components and its breakdown to the free enzyme and product is indicated by the following equation:

$$E + S \; \underset{k_{-1}}{\overset{k_1}{\rightleftharpoons}} \; ES \; \underset{k_{-2}}{\overset{k_2}{\rightleftharpoons}} \; P + E$$

where E = enzyme, S = substrate, ES = enzyme-substrate complex, P = end products and k_1, k_{-1}, k_2, and k_{-2} are the velocity constants of the reaction. The formation of ES from $P + E$ is negligible for initial velocity measurements and is eliminated from the equation. The initial velocity being defined as the velocity measured before an appreciable quantity of product is formed. If $[E]$ = total molecular concentration of the enzyme, $[S]$ = molecular concentration of the substrate, $[ES]$ = concentration of the enzyme-substrate complex and $([E] - [ES])$ = concentration of free enzyme, one obtains the following expression:

$$\frac{[S]\,([E] - [ES])}{[ES]} = \frac{k_{-1} + k_2}{k_1} = K_m$$

where K_m is the Michaelis-Menten constant. The K_m is determined solely from the reaction velocities.

$$v = \frac{V[S]}{K_m + [S]}$$

Michaelis-Menten Equation

where v = the observed reaction velocity and V is maximum velocity of the reaction at saturating substrate concentration. When the actual velocity of the reaction, v, is equal to half the maximum velocity, V, K_m is equal to the substrate concentration. This is illustrated graphically in Fig. 7.2. The K_m can therefore be deter-

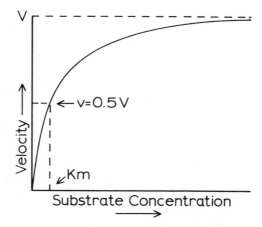

FIG. 7.2. MICHAELIS-MENTEN PLOT OF REACTION VELOC-ITY VERSUS SUBSTRATE CONCENTRATION

mined experimentally by plotting the reaction rates for varying substrate concentrations. Alternatively, a useful modification of the Michaelis-Menten equation, by Lineweaver and Burk, is obtained by taking the reciprocal of the Michaelis-Menten equation:

$$\frac{1}{v} = \frac{K_m}{V} \frac{1}{[S]} + \frac{1}{V}$$

Lineweaver-Burk

yielding an equation for a straight line whose intercept on the y axis is equal to $1/V$ and whose slope is equal to K_m/V (Fig. 7.3).

The Michaelis-Menten constant is an important constant for characterizing enzymes, e.g., a small K_m value indicates a high affinity of the enzyme for its substrate while a large K_m value indicates that a high substrate concentration is necessary to reach half-saturation. Michaelis-Menten constants are usually expressed in moles per liter,

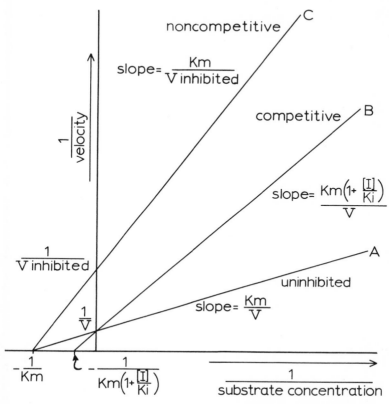

FIG. 7.3. LINEWEAVER-BURK PLOT OF MICHAELIS-MENTEN EQUATION

Normal, competitively inhibited and noncompetitively inhibited reactions are shown.

but if the molecular weight of the substrate is unknown, percentage strengths may be used. These constants usually range from 10^{-2} to 10^{-5} moles per liter.

Effect of Temperature.—An increase in temperature increases the velocity of an enzyme catalyzed reaction only within definite limits. Initially the reaction velocity increases with increasing temperature to an optimum, but at higher temperatures it decreases eventually to zero. The optimum temperature is dependent upon time; i.e., lengthening of time of exposure at elevated temperatures will cause a fall in the apparent optimum (Fig. 7.4). This is due to two opposing effects: (a) the temperature dependent increase in velocity of the catalyzed reaction due to a greater molecular activity, and (b) an increase in the rate of destruction of the enzyme by heat denaturation. As a

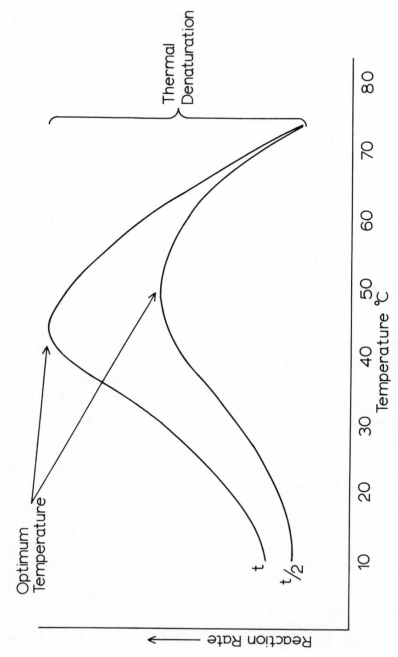

FIG. 7.4. EFFECT OF TEMPERATURE ON ENZYME REACTION RATE

result of effect (b), the activity of the enzyme gradually falls to zero and, in consequence, the catalysis ceases. It is generally found that an increase in temperature to about 45°C will produce an increase in the reaction rate (effect a). About 45°C, effect (b) will become increasingly important due to the thermal denaturation of protein. Most enzymes are almost instantly inactivated by exposure to temperatures near 100°C while heating at 80°C requires a longer exposure time. This fact is utilized in the preparation of vegetables for canning and freezing. The vegetables are blanched by immersion in hot water or by treating with steam in order to inactivate enzymes that would otherwise adversely affect nutritive values, colors, and flavors.

One should recognize that the optimum temperature for an enzyme changes not only in relation to time but also may change in relation to hydrogen ion concentration (pH), the effect of activators or inhibitors, the presence of protective proteins, etc.

In some instances heat inactivation is reversible. For example, the peroxidase of peas can be completely inactivated by blanching for 60 sec, but regeneration occurs on standing.

The effect of temperature changes on the kinetics of the enzyme reaction itself is highly complicated and will not be considered in detail here. It is generally found that the temperature coefficient (Q_{10}), which is an expression of the increase in reaction rate for a 10°C increase in temperature of enzyme reactions vary from about 1.1 to 5.3. A study of such effects permits one to determine the energy of activation ($E_{activation}$) of enzyme reactions. This value (cal/mole) represents the amount of energy required to activate the molecules of a reactant sufficiently for them to collide and react. Table 7.1 lists the values of $E_{activation}$ for a number of reactions showing the effect of catalysts of various kinds.

It is apparent that enzyme catalyzed reactions have lower energies of activation than the same reactions catalyzed by inorganic cata-

TABLE 7.1

EXAMPLES OF ACTIVATION ENERGIES WITH VARIOUS CATALYSTS

Reaction	Catalyst	$E_{activation}$
Sucrose inversion	H^+ (nonenzymatic)	26,000
	Yeast invertase	11,500
Casein hydrolysis	H^+ (nonenzymatic)	20,600
	Trypsin	12,000
Ethyl butyrate hydrolysis	H^+ (nonenzymatic)	13,200
	Pancreatic lipase	4,200

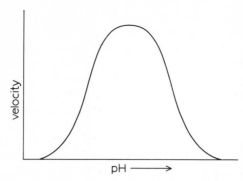

FIG. 7.5. ENZYME REACTION VELOCITY AS AFFECTED BY
pH

lysts. In other words, the presence of an enzyme mediates a chemical reaction at a lower energy level and at a lower temperature.

Effect of pH.—The activity of an enzyme is greatly affected by the hydrogen ion concentration of its medium. It is likely that this change in activity with varying pH is due to the changes in ionization of either the enzyme, the substrate, or the enzyme-substrate complex. In addition to the ionic effects, low or high pH values can cause inactivation due to the denaturation of the enzyme protein.

If the rate of an enzymatic reaction, for a given enzyme and substrate concentration is plotted against different pH values, the resulting curve usually is bell-shaped (Fig. 7.5). It will be noted the curve has a relatively small plateau of optimum activity with sharply decreasing rates on either side of the optimal pH point.

The optimal pH is not a fixed point for all conditions but may vary with the source of the enzyme, the kind of substrate, and the temperature. This is illustrated in Table 7.2.

TABLE 7.2

OPTIMUM pH OF SOME ENZYMES AS AFFECTED
BY SOURCE, SUBSTRATE AND TEMPERATURE

Factors	Enzyme	Optimum pH
Source		
Green bean	Pectin methylesterase	8.2
Fungae	Pectin methylesterase	5.5
Substrate		
Ovalbumin	Pepsin	1.5
Casein	Pepsin	1.8
Gelatin	Pepsin	2.0
Temperature		
25°C	Malt diastase	4.3
45°C	Malt diastase	5.0
60°C	Malt diastase	5.7

Activation.—Some enzymes show an absolute requirement for a particular inorganic ion for their catalytic activity, while other enzymes show increased activity when certain cations are included in the reaction medium. Examples of absolute requirement are the Fe^{2+} in cytochrome oxidase and Mg^{2+} or Mn^{2+} in enolase. On the other hand, pyruvate kinase is activated by K^+, NH_4^+, and others. Among the more important cation activators are: K^+, Mg^{2+}, Zn^{2+}, Fe^{2+}, Ca^{2+}, and Co^{2+}.

Some of the divalent cations can replace each other but occasionally they compete with one another. For example, Mn^{2+} can replace Mg^{2+} in activating some of the phosphate transferring enzymes, but pyruvate kinase normally activated by Mg^{2+} is inhibited by Ca^{2+}.

Relatively few enzymes are affected by the presence or absence of anions. Salivary and pancreatic amylases which are activated by chlorides are notable exceptions.

Cells sometimes produce proteins which are inactive forms of enzymes. This precursor is called a zymogen or proenzyme. An example of a zymogen is trypsinogen, which is produced by the pancreas. When the pancreatic juice containing trypsinogen reaches the small intestine, it is converted to trypsin by an enzyme (enterokinase). In converting the inactive form to the active form, an inhibitory peptide is removed and there is an alteration in the conformation of the protein molecule.

Another type of activator involves the use of reducing agents to maintain the integrity of sulfhydryl groups in the enzyme protein. These groups are essential parts of the active center of the enzyme and when oxidized to the disulfide form the enzyme is inactivated. The plant proteolytic enzymes papain, ficin, and bromelin are inactivated by exposure to oxygen; when a suitable reductant is added (cysteine, glutathione, or bisulfite), the enzyme remains in an active state.

Inhibition.—Inhibitors lower the catalytic activity of enzymes. These substances may be divided into two categories, competitive and noncompetitive inhibitors.

Competitive Inhibition.—This type of inhibition occurs when the compound competes with a substrate (or coenzyme) for the binding site of the enzyme. It implies a similarity in the structure of the inhibitor and the substrate. The amount of inhibition is related to (a) the concentration of substrate, (b) the concentration of inhibitor, and (c) the relative affinities (K_m) for the enzyme-substrate and enzyme-inhibitor complex. The inhibitory effect is reversible; that is, activity can be restored by increasing substrate concentration. A comparison of the kinetic behavior of a competitively inhibited system is shown in Fig. 7.3. It may be noted that in the competitive inhibited system, the maximal velocity remains unchanged since the effect of the inhibitor is overcome at higher substrate concentrations. The slope is increased due to decreased velocities up to this point. The K_m is increased by the factor $(1 + [I]/K_i)$ where K_i is the dissociation constant of the enzyme-inhibitor complex.

Noncompetitive Inhibition.—This type of inhibition cannot be reversed by increasing the substrate concentration. The amount of inhibition is dependent upon inhibitor concentration and the affinity of the inhibitor for the enzyme. Noncompetitive inhibition as presented in Fig. 7.3 shows a decrease in maximal velocity which is due to decreased active enzyme concentration. The K_m is unchanged since noncompetitive inhibitors appear kinetically only to remove active enzymes from the reaction. The slope is increased due to decreased velocity throughout the reaction. Some of the inhibitors are specific in their action: iron-containing enzymes are inhibited by cyanide; enzymes containing sulfhydryl groups are inhibited by Cu^{2+}, Hg^{2+}, and p-hydroxymercuribenzoate. Certain organic phosphates are inhibitors of enzymes which have esterase activity, e.g., parathion and tetraethyl pyrophosphate.

The use of chemical enzyme inhibitors in foods is for the most part rather limited because of the toxic nature of the substances. However, living organisms produce substances that inhibit enzyme action. For example, a trypsin inhibitor occurs naturally in soybeans which inhibits the digestion of the protein in raw soybean meal. Antipepsin and antitrypsin protect the stomach and intestines from the action of proteolytic enzymes which are active in these organs.

Active Sites of Enzymes.—The active site(s) of an enzyme is the position or area at which the catalysis of the substrate occurs. Since a large number of enzymes contain only protein it follows that in such cases the active site must in fact be one or more amino acid residues. Additionally, coenzymes and metals are frequently involved in the catalytic process as an integral part of the enzyme-substrate complex. Thus, there must also be binding sites for these obligatory components of the reaction. Kinetically, the coenzymes and metal ions frequently follow the same type of Michaelis kinetics as is shown by the substrate. These observations present an even more complicated situation since many enzymes are known to undergo conformational changes when placed in contact with the substrate, cofactor, or metal ion, thus indicating a modification of the tertiary structure during reaction. Although some enzymes contain only amino acids, not all of the amino acids are involved as a part of the active site. Large portions of the protein of some enzymes can be removed with little change in activity. This would indicate that the portion removed played no special role in the catalytic process. Amino acids that are frequently found at the active site are serine, histidine, glutamic acid, aspartic acid, arginine, and tyrosine. Serine is especially ubiquitous as an active site amino acid. It is known to be the active site of chymotrypsin, trypsin, phosphoglucomutase, phosphorylase, and alkaline phosphatase. A classic example of the role of serine in enzymatic catalysis is phosphoglucomutase. The intermediate (glucose-1, 6-diphosphate) and the phosphorylated enzyme are sufficiently stable to allow isolation.

Serine phosphate may be isolated from the phosphorylated enzyme, while the amino acid residue on the N-terminal side of serine is alanine or glycine and histidine on the C-terminal side.

Active serine residues may be located in other enzymes by reaction with diisopropylfluorophosphate.

Enzymes which contain more than one serine residue appear to react with diisopropylfluorophosphate more rapidly at the active site hydroxyl.

Nomenclature and Classification

Enzymes are frequently named after the substrate upon which they act united with the suffix "-ase." Thus, the term "amylase" indicates an enzyme which acts upon starch, and lipase is an enzyme acting upon lipids. Further definition has proven necessary in order to indicate narrower substrate specificates, e.g., acid phosphatase and alkaline phosphatase. It is clear that a nomenclature which is based partly on trivial names, partly on names of substrates, etc., is not very satisfactory.

The International Union of Biochemistry has adopted the recommendations of its Commission on Enzymes for naming and classifying enzymes. The classification of enzymes is based on the type of reaction catalyzed by the enzyme. Six main divisions were employed in the classification:

(1) Oxidoreductases
(2) Transferases
(3) Hydrolases
(4) Lyases
(5) Isomerases
(6) Ligases

Oxidoreductases are enzymes which catalyze oxidation-reduction reactions. Dehydrogenases, oxygenases, and peroxidases are typical enzymes of this group. Transferases are enzymes catalyzing group transfers. Transaminases and kinases are typical enzymes of this group. Hydrolases have as their primary function the hydrolysis of a variety of compounds by water. Lipases and peptidases are well known enzymes in this group. Lyases form a group of enzymes that split substrates or remove groups within a substrate molecule. This group of enzymes is divided into racemases, epimerases, *cis-trans* isomerases, intramolecular ketol isomerases, and mutases. Finally, ligases catalyze the linking together of two substrate molecules with the breaking of a pyrophosphate bond.

In the systematic nomenclature the enzymes are given a number which consists of four parts and are separated by decimals and preceded by "EC" which denotes the Enzyme Commission. An enzyme designated EC 1.1.1.1 would be deciphered as follows:

1. Oxidoreductase
1.1 Acting on $-CH_2-OH$
1.1.1 NAD^+ or $NADP^+$ as hydrogen acceptor
1.1.1.1 Specific enzyme—Alcohol: NAD^+ oxidoreductase

In general, the systematic name of an enzyme consists of two parts: the first part denotes the substrate and the second part indicates the nature of the reaction. To illustrate, the well-known β-amylase (trivial name) has the systematic name α-1,4-glucan maltohydrolase (EC 3.2.1.2). The name indicates the substrate is a glucan, a glucose polymer, in which the molecules are joined by α-1,4-glucosidic linkages. The reaction is hydrolytic and it results in the splitting off of maltose. Systematic names are recommended for the enzymes but in food technology the trivial name is most frequently used.

Food Enzymes

The enzymes, present in most fresh food materials, have the capability of causing both undesirable and desirable changes in foods. Therefore, the management of these naturally occurring enzymes is an important consideration in food technology.

Amylases are among the most widely distributed of all enzymes, being found in plants, animals, and some microorganisms. These enzymes hydrolyze polysaccharides to disaccharides and some monosaccharides. These enzymes find wide usage in the brewing and baking industries.

Most living cells contain proteolytic enzymes that can act on proteins under appropriate conditions. In living tissue these enzymes are inactive due to unfavorable hydrogen ion concentration. Tissue becomes more acid following death, the proteolytic enzymes are activated resulting in protein hydrolysis. Meat tenderization is accomplished by the action of such enzymes. The aging of beef at temperatures of approximately 40°F for 1–4 weeks has been in commercial practice.

Enzymes are often highly specific for bringing about the changes whereby a flavor precursor is synthesized and then converted into the flavor itself. For example, in materials such as celery, onions, tomatoes, bananas, oranges, and pineapples the development of flavor has been attributed to one enzyme activity or another.

Enzymes have been associated with changes in color. There are instances where color components of foods are broken down, such as in the artificial ripening of fruits where the green color is caused to disappear and the previously masked orange and yellow colors allowed to appear. Another example is the blanching of spinach at 180°F (77°C) which preserves the green color. This is probably related to the maximum temperature (77°C) for chlorophyllase activity and the enzyme converts chlorophyll into chlorophyllin which possesses a green color.

Increasing production of frozen and dehydrated foods have made it clear that naturally occurring enzymes are active in these foods and may affect their quality. A variety of enzymes are involved in these changes, e.g., enzymatic browning catalyzed by phenolases, lipolysis catalyzed by lipases, and oxidations catalyzed lipoxidase. Phenolases are especially important in the development of brown coloration on fruits and vegetables after exposure of the interior to oxygen. Both monohydric and dihydric phenols act as substrates producing quinones. Polymerization of these quinones is the well-known browning reaction. These enzymatic reactions can be controlled by blanching prior to processing and, in some cases, by inhibition of the enzyme through the use of chemicals such as sulfite as SO_2 gas or $NaHSO_3$.

Rapid and extensive enzymatic changes may take place when the tissues of fruits and vegetables are damaged by bruising, cutting and crushing, during harvesting and transport, freeze injury during storage, insect and microbial attack, or during packing, pitting, halving and slicing in food processing operations. These changes include darkening of peeled and cut fruits and vegetables, the development of off-flavors in bruised vegetables, etc.

Milk and Milk Products.—A considerable number of enzymes occur in milk. Many of these undoubtedly find their way into the milk from the blood during the process of milk synthesis in the mammary gland. Most of the enzymes present in milk exert little effect on the milk components and, in some instances, have no substrate present to act upon. The presence of certain enzymes are used to indicate milk quality and proper pasteurizaiton.

Lipases must be taken into account in the processing of dairy products, since they may lead to undesirable rancidity. Lipolytic activity varies with increasing pH of milk, homogenization, and the stage of lactation (greatest near the end of the period). Lipases are inactivated by pasteurization temperatures.

The presence of phosphatase in milk is useful as a test for proper pasteurization. When milk is properly pasteurized, phosphatase inactivation is 99.9% complete. The fact that conditions of inactivation are practically identical with those of pasteurization of milk has allowed the phosphatase test to become the common test for determining adequate pasteurization of milk and milk products.

Cereal Products.—Cereals are grown for their edible seeds and include wheat, rye, barley, corn, oats, and rice.

The cereals are, in general, the cheapest sources of food energy and normally constitute about one-third or more of the caloric intake of humans. The cereals as harvested and stored are living materials and as such continue to undergo enzymatic metabolism. Hence, the cereal grains contain a number of enzymes and a few of these play an important role in cereal technology. Chief of these are the α (alpha) and β (beta) amylases which convert starch to sugar. These enzymes are of great importance in flour for breadmaking. Flour normally contains only a very small amount of α-amylase but ample quantities of β-amylase. Maltose is necessary for yeast leavened products in order to ensure adequate gas production. Therefore, it is essential to have sufficient amounts of α-amylase present in flours and this is accomplished by use of malt flour (0.3%) in the formulation.

Protease activity is very important in cracker production for it is necessary to hydrolyze some of the gluten for proper structure and texture in the finished cracker. Small amounts of proteases are introduced into the flour when the miller adds the malted flour to increase α-amylase activity. The dough can also be supplemented with added fungal proteases to improve its properties.

A lipoxidase enzyme also occurs in flour. Carotenoid pigments are oxidized during oxidation of polyunsaturated fatty acids. Lipoxidase may be responsible for the bleaching of flour during natural aging, as well as for oxidative rancidity in cereals and cereal products.

Vegetables and Fruits.—Changes that occur in fruit and vegetables as a result of enzymatic activity are usually disadvantageous. Therefore, special precautions such as proper temperature, humidity, ventilation, and maturity are essential in harvesting, packing, storage, keeping quality, and processing of vegetables and fruits.

In addition to the respiratory activity, other enzymatic changes may occur in fruits and vegetables in storage. Sweet corn, when freshly picked, contains appreciable sugar in the kernels. In a matter of a few hours, the sugar has disappeared with a resulting loss of sweetness and toughening of textures. Potatoes held in storage will have a higher sugar content at low temperatures than at higher temperatures. Potatoes to be used for chip manufacture are placed at a higher temperature for a period of time previous to chipping to reduce the sugar content to a minimum. A high sugar content in potatoes produces a dark colored chip. In ripening, enzymatic conversion of pectic substances occur, resulting in general softening and change in texture.

Enzymes do not accelerate reactions unless they are in direct contact with their substrate(s). For instance, fruits do not show browning unless they are bruised or cut, which permits contact of the enzyme polyphenol oxidase with oxygen and the polyphenols of the fruit. The proteases of fresh pineapple do not exert a proteolytic function because pineapple contains little protein. However, if fresh pineapple is added to a gelatin dessert, liquefaction takes place.

Meats.—The metabolism (glycolytic enzymes) of postmortem muscle results in the development of rigor mortis. If we were to eat meat which is in the state of rigor, the meat would be tough; however, if the meat is allowed to age for a few days in a cooler, it will gradually begin to soften. This is presumed to be due to the presence of proteolytic enzymes which were inactive in the living animal.

Rigor mortis also occurs in fish and seafood products. However, proteolysis is undesirable in this case because this kind of change is usually associated with microbial action. As a consequence, processes such as freezing, canning, smoking, salting, and drying are used to prevent proteolysis in these food products.

Enzyme Applications

Enzymes were used in a variety of ways long before they were recognized as definite chemical substances. For example, their application in fermentation precedes our knowledge of the existence of enzymes in living cells. Processes such as breadmaking, winemaking, brewing, alcohol and vinegar manufacture, and foods such as sauerkraut and pickles have been known from antiquity.

Enzymes have several desirable characteristics for use in industrial processes: (1) they accomplish a reaction more efficiently than other catalysts; (2) their rates of reaction can be readily controlled by adjusting temperature, pH, and reaction time; (3) activity may be destroyed by heating to a temperature sufficient to inactivate the enzyme; (4) enzymes are natural in origin and are nontoxic, therefore in most cases the enzyme may remain in the finished product; and (5) since enzymes act more specifically than other catalysts, their activity can be readily standardized.

Carbohydrases.—This group of enzymes hydrolyzes polysaccharides or oligosaccharides. In Table 7.3 are tabulated representative commercial applications of carbohydrases in foods.

Amylases.—There are three types of amylases: alpha-amylases which hydrolyze $\alpha (1 \rightarrow 4)$ linkages in large starch molecules, in a random fashion, to form dextrins; beta-amylases which convert starch into maltose by splitting the disaccharide units progressively from the nonreducing end of the chain polymer, and finally, amyloglucosidases which produce glucose by the progressive hydrolysis from the nonreducing end of the starch molecule. The latter enzyme is capable of converting starch to glucose without the formation of dextrins and maltose.

Alpha-amylase may be obtained from animals, higher plants, fungi, and bacteria while beta-amylase is produced only by higher plants, particularly cereals. These enzymes vary widely in sugar forming ability, in thermal stability, and in the rate and extent of hydrolysis. For example, alpha-amylase is often referred to as the liquefying

TABLE 7.3

ENZYME APPLICATIONS

Enzyme Type	Typical Commercial Use
Carbohydrases	
Amylases	Production of high conversion syrups and dextrose. Conversion of cereal starches into fermentable sugars in brewing and distilling. Modification of cereal starches in precooked cereals. Viscosity control of chocolate syrups. Removal of starch from fruit juices, fruit extracts, and pectin.
Pectinases	Production and clarification of fruit juices and wine, production of low methoxyl pectins, treating orange, grape, and prune pulps prior to drying.
Glucose oxidase-catalase	Removal of glucose in egg solids production, removal of oxygen in foods and beverages.
Invertase	Preparing soft cream candy centers.
Proteases	Tenderizing meat, modification of dough for bread and cracker baking, production of protein hydrolyzates, chill-proofing of beer, cheesemaking.
Lipases	Flavor production in cheese, enhance flavor of chocolate products and margarines by use of lipase modified butterfat-containing products.

enzyme, whereas beta-amylase is often referred to as the sugar-producing enzyme.

Pectic Enzymes.—Pectins are polymers made up of chains of galacturonic acid units linked by $\alpha(1 \to 4)$ glycosidic linkages. Three pectic substances are known; namely, protopectin, pectin, and pectic acid. Protopectin occurs in the cell wall of plants and it is the mother substance of this class of compounds. During the ripening of fruits, there is a decrease in protopectin and a proportional increase in pectin. Thus, a transformation occurs during the ripening of fruits. Pectin contains more than 10% of methanol combined as methyl ester groups and it is these esterified substances which form semisolid gels with sugar and acid of the kind found in jellies. Acid hydrolysis of the methyl groups yields a pectic acid while partial hydrolysis yields substances known as low-methoxyl pectins. The latter substances will form gels with small amounts of calcium ions.

The enzymes which catalyze the breakdown of the pectic substances may be classified into two groups: the pectases or pectin methylesterases, and the pectinases or polygalacturonases. The latter enzymes may be further divided into endo and exo enzymes. The endo polygalacturonases act within the molecule, on $\alpha(1 \to 4)$ linkages, while the exo enzymes catalyze the progressive removal of galacturonic acid molecules from the nonreducing end of the chain. A group of enzymes which catalyze a nonhydrolytic type of cleavages of the $\alpha(1 \to 4)$ linkage, are referred to as transeliminases. These enzymes show the same effect as the polygalacturonases; i.e., a lowering in viscosity of pectin and the production of one mole of reducing sugar for each $\alpha(1 \to 4)$ linkage hydrolyzed.

Glucose Oxidases.—A number of fungi produce glucose oxidases which catalyze the breakdown of β-D-glucose to gluconic acid. Commercial preparations of glucose oxidase usually contain catalase and this has proven to be advantageous in most of the food applications of this enzyme. This system is used extensively for the removal of glucose from egg whites and whole eggs prior to drying to retard darkening and for reducing dissolved and head space oxygen in packaged foods containing glucose.

Invertases.—Invertases may be isolated from yeast (*S. cerevisiae* or *S. carlsbergensis*) and from fungi (*A. oryzae, A. niger,* and *M. verrucaria*). They are primarily β-fructosidases and hydrolyze sucrose to glucose and fructose. These enzymes are used in the manufacture of invert sugar which is more soluble than sucrose. Invert sugar is used in confections, candies, frozen desserts, and liqueurs.

Proteases.—A protease is an enzyme that catalyzes the hydrolysis of proteins to yield proteoses, peptones, polypeptides, and small amounts of amino acids. There are two types of proteases: exopeptidases and endopeptidases. The use of the prefix "exo" and "endo" is analogous to their use with carbohydrases. Therefore, exopeptidases split off terminal amino acids by hydrolyzing the peptide linkage. These enzymes may be further divided into two types: carboxypeptidase and aminopeptidases. The former enzymes act on the C-terminal peptide linkage while the latter enzymes act on the N-terminal peptide bond. The exopeptidases find little use in the food processing industry. The important proteases are the endopeptidases which hydrolyze internal peptide linkages to yield peptides.

A large number of commercial plant, animal, and microbial proteases are available for use in food processing. The commercial preparations are generally used on the basis of their specificity; however, factors such as heat stability, pH optimum, the presence of activators or inhibitors, availability and price may influence the choice of an enzyme preparation. For example, in cheesemaking rennin is used for the formation of milk curds even though most known proteases will clot milk. This is due to the fact that rennin splits only a specific bond or bonds, whereas the other proteases catalyze a more extensive hydrolysis of the casein. In contrast, the production of protein hydrolyzates requires proteases which lead to extensive hydrolysis of the protein yielding peptides and amino acids.

The heat stability of papain is one of the main reasons for its extensive use in meat tenderizing. The heat stability permits the enzyme catalyzed reaction to continue for a time during the cooking, frying, or roasting of meat and as a consequence more extensive hydrolysis can be obtained.

The optimum pH of a protease affects its use in foods. For example, in the chillproofing of beer, a protease is used to prevent the formation of "chill haze" which contains protein, tannin, and carbohydrates. The normal pH of beer is pH 4.5, therefore, an enzyme is required which will be active at this pH. Papain alone or in combination with pepsin, bromelin, or fungal protease is used in the application.

Lipases.—Lipases hydrolyze insoluble fats and fatty acid esters. Enzyme catalysis takes place at the oil-water interface of the emulsion and as a consequence enzyme reaction velocity is dependent on the surface area. The lipases show considerable specificity with respect to chain length of the fatty acids, the degree of saturation, position of the fatty acids, and physical state of the substrate. In general, lipases hydrolyze triglycerides of fatty acids with 4–10 carbon atoms more rapidly than the longer chained fatty acids. Lipases remove the long chain fatty acids (C_{12} to C_{18}) and the most frequent unsaturated fatty acids (C_{18}) at about the same rate. The diglycerides formed on hydrolysis are largely 1,2-diglycerides and monoglycerides which are of the 2 configuration. For a fixed amount of enzyme, lipase activity increases with an increase in the surface area of the emulsified fat.

The action of lipolytic enzymes is important in the dairy industry. A high degree of lipolysis is necessary in the manufacture of certain Italian cheeses (e.g., Romano and Provolone). Traditionally, rennin paste is used in the manufacture of these cheeses because the paste contains lipases as well as proteolytic enzymes.

Pregastric lipase is used in treating butterfat-containing products to produce a wide variety of food flavors. For example, in the chocolate industry, cultured butter or pregastric lipase-modified butter products are used to enhance the flavor of milk chocolate, butter creams, and caramels. At low levels of free fatty acids, the flavor of the confection is enhanced without the formation of a new flavor. At intermediate levels a buttery flavor will be created and at high levels a cheesy flavor will be produced. Lipase-modified butter products are also used to enhance the flavors of food products such as margarines, shortenings, popcorn oils, bakery products, and vegetable oils.

Enzymatic Browning

Browning of fruits such as apples, pears, peaches, and apricots, and vegetables such as potatoes occurs when the tissue is exposed to oxygen. This exposure is commonly due to bruises, cuts, and other injury to the peel. The browning reaction occurs when the enzyme catalyzed reaction of oxygen with certain phenolic compounds produces quinone structures and their polymerization products which are responsible for the brown color. The enzyme that catalyzes these reactions is more frequently called polyphenol oxidase (o-diphenol: oxygen oxidoreductase; EC 1.10.3.1). This enzyme has also been referred to as phenolase, tryosinase, catechol oxidase, and potato oxidase. These names are taken from the varied substrate activity of the enzyme or its source.

Polyphenol oxidase is a copper-containing enzyme which can undergo reversible oxidation and reduction in the process of hydroxylation and oxidation. In hydroxylation, Cu^+ is oxidized to Cu^{2+} and in oxidation, Cu^{2+} is reduced to Cu^+. Since mushroom polyphenol oxidase can exist in multiple molecular form, it can exhibit variable hydroxylation and oxidation activity depending on the multiple form present.

Polyphenol oxidase catalyzes two basic types of reactions, hydroxylation and oxidation. Hydroxylation occurs on phenols containing only one hydroxyl group.

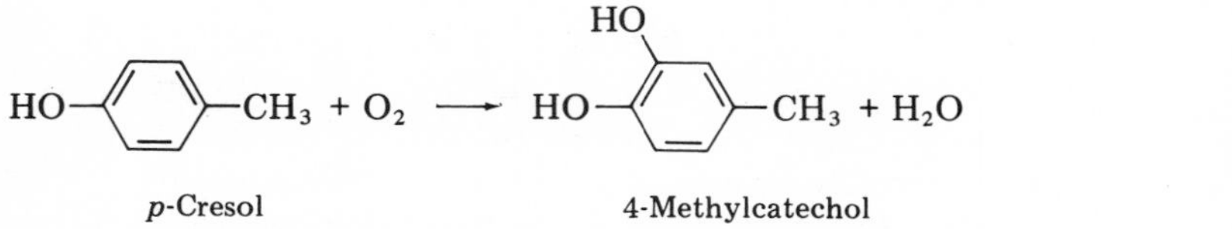

Tyrosine → 3,4-Dihydroxyphenylalanine (DOPA)

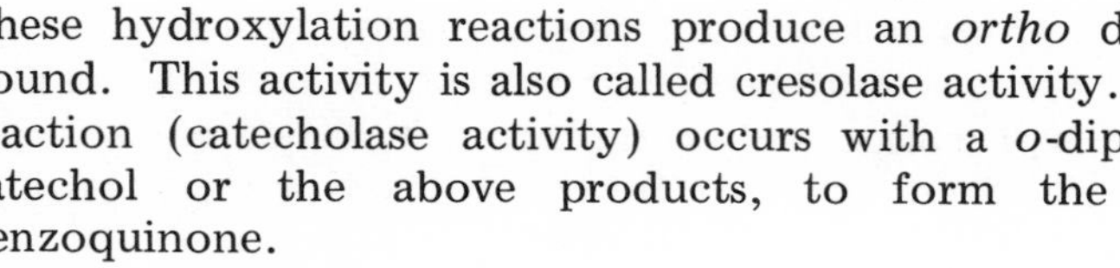

p-Cresol → 4-Methylcatechol

These hydroxylation reactions produce an *ortho* diphenolic compound. This activity is also called cresolase activity. The oxidation reaction (catecholase activity) occurs with a o-diphenol, such as catechol or the above products, to form the corresponding benzoquinone.

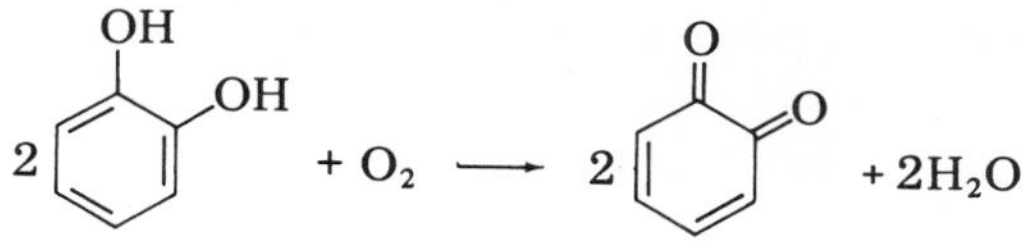

Substrate specificity varies considerably for polyphenol oxidase from various sources. Potato polyphenol oxidase utilizes chlorogenic acid, caffeic acid, catechol and 3,4-dihydroxy-L-phenylalanine (DOPA) and p-cresol. Chlorogenic acid is especially ubiquitous as a substrate for polyphenol oxidase in vegetables such as potatoes and fruits such as apples and pears.

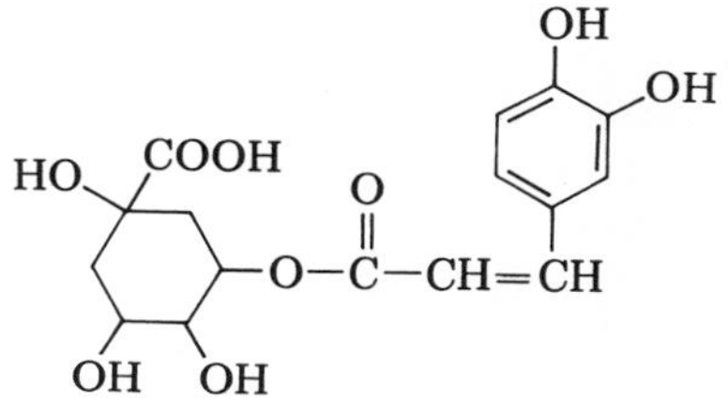

Chlorogenic acid

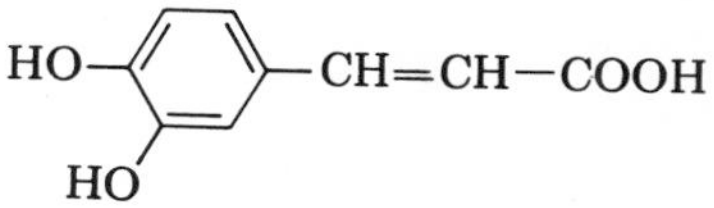

Caffeic Acid

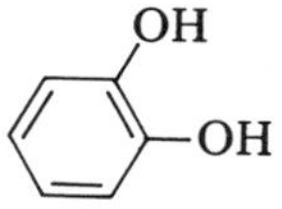

Catechol

4-Methylcatechol, gallic acid, protocatechuic acid, and dopamine are utilized by peach polyphenol oxidase in addition to the above named phonolic compound, with the exception of p-cresol.

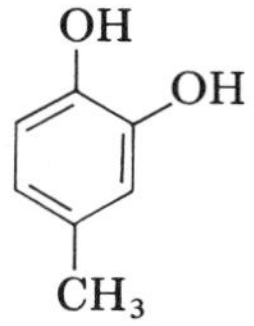

4-Methylcatechol 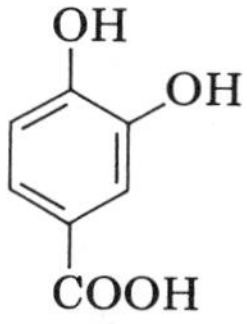   Protocatechuic acid 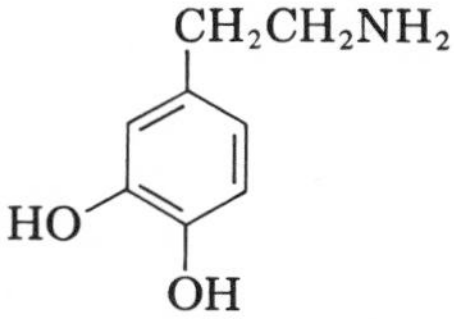   Dopamine

Prevention of Enzymatic Browning.—Several methods have been used to control enzymatic browning. These include inhibitors, heat, exclusion of oxygen, and antioxidants.

Heating is one of the most convenient methods for prevention of browning. Polyphenol oxidases from various sources differ somewhat in their susceptibility to heat inactivation. However, most are inactivated almost completely upon heating to 90–95°C for approximately 7 sec. This type of inactivation is complicated by the pH dependence which also varies considerably for polyphenol oxidases from different fruits and vegetables.

Sodium chloride, sulfur dioxide, sodium sulfite, and sodium hydrogen sulfite are used to inhibit polyphenol oxidase activity. The browning reaction may be significantly inhibited by 1000 ppm NaCl or by 1 ppm SO_2. Ascorbic acid has been used to prevent polyphenol oxidase-induced browning. Ascorbic acid acts by reducing the o-diphenol and by lowering the pH.

The pH may be adjusted to prevent enzymatic browning, since the optimum pH for polyphenol oxidases is in the range of 6–7. Citric acid, malic acid, ascorbic acid, and other organic acids have been used to lower the pH of fruits which prevents enzymatic browning by inhibiting polyphenol oxidase. If the pH of the media is lowered to pH 3 or below, negligible polyphenol oxidase activity is observed.

Insolublized Enzymes

Enzymes in their native state are water soluble and when used in commercial continuous or batch processes present some problems; e.g., inhibitors may be necessary to terminate the reaction. It may also be necessary to precipitate the protein-containing enzyme for removal. Purification of the product is often a problem when the enzyme is soluble. For these reasons the insolubilization of enzymes afford several advantages; the ease of separation of the enzyme from the reaction product(s); the reuse of the insolubilized enzyme; modification of properties such as specificity, Michaelis constant and pH optimum, and generally increased stability to both heat and pH.

Insolublization can be achieved by attaching an enzyme to an insoluble carrier. Numerous types of carriers have been used for the purpose of insolublization. Earlier attempts to insolublize enzymes were made using adsorption on charcoal and similar adsorbants. Entrapment of enzymes in a copolyacrylamide matrix has also been investigated. These methods proved unsatisfactory due to desorption of the enzyme from the adsorbant or loss of enzyme protein from the matrix of the polyacrylamide gel. These problems have been resolved through the development of techniques whereby the enzyme can be covalently attached to the insoluble carrier.

Miles Laboratories, Inc. (Kankakee, Ill.) offers insolubilized chymotrypsin, trypsin, papain, and subtilisin which are attached to a polyanionic carrier, ethylene-maleic anhydride copolymer, to a water-insoluble diazonium salt of p-amino-DL-phenylalanine-L-leucine copolymer or to a neutral synthetic resin, starch (dialdehyde) methylene-dianiline. Aldrich Chemical Co. (Milwaukee, Wis.) distributes a number of carriers which may be used for enzyme insolubilization. These are hydrophillic carriers of cross-linked polyacrylamides marketed an Enzacryl[1] and fall into five main categories: (1) Enzacryl AA has been used to insolubilize alpha-amylase, beta-amylase, gamma-amylase, and carboxypeptidase, (2) Enzacryl AH has been found to insolublize alpha-amylase, (3) Enzacryl Polyacetal will insolublize trypsin, papain, alpha-amylase, dextranase, and urease, (4) Enzacryl Polythiol couples with compounds which contain disulfide bridges (e.g., lipoic acid and insulin). (5) Enzacryl Polythiolactone binds proteins which contain side chain amino groups (lysine) and hydroxyl groups (serine and tyrosine). The Pharmacia Fine Chemicals Company (Piscataway, N.J.) has immobilized a number of enzymes by coupling the enzyme with cyanogen bromide-activated Sepharose.[2] Sepharose is a beaded form of agarose, a polysaccharide polymer. Among the enzymes reported to be immobilized by Sepharose are chymotrypsin, rennin, trypsin, trypsinogen, protease, ribonuclease, and others. Sepharose insolublized enzymes offered by various companies include bromelins, ficin, glucose oxidase, peroxidase, alcohol dehydrogenase, asparaginase, hexokinase, glucose-6-phosphate dehydrogenase, and others.

Insolublized enzymes have been used primarily in batch processes. Continuous methods however would be preferable. Fluidized bed reactors have shown some promise as an alternative to batch processes or less desirable continuous methods such as fixed reactor bed. In the fluidized bed reactor the insolublized enzyme is suspended, the substrate solution flows in the bottom of the reactor and the product flows out of the top. The suspended insoluble enzyme is kept in suspension by agitation by the substrate flow which is counteracted by gravity. This procedure has been used to convert corn starch to glucose using insolublized alpha-amylase. Papain in the insolublized form has been used to hydrolyze protein in beer which in turn prevents the hazing of beer when chilled. This process shortens the process from days to minutes. Undoubtedly many other processes have been automated using insolublized enzymes. The

---

[1] Trademark of Koch-Light Ltd, Colnbrook Bucks, England.
[2] Trademark of Pharmacia Fine Chemicals.

insolublization of more than one enzyme on the same carrier offers exciting possibilities for coupled reactions.

BIBLIOGRAPHY

AMERICAN MEAT INSTITUTE FOUNDATION. 1960. The Science of Meat and Meat Products. W. H. Freeman and Co., San Francisco.

AYLWARD, F., and HAISMAN, D. R. 1969. Oxidation systems in fruits and vegetables—their relation to the quality of preserved products. In Advances in Food Research, C. O. Chichester et al. (Editors). Academic Press, New York.

BECKHORN, C. J., LABBEE, M. D., and UNDERKOFLER, L. A. 1965. Production and use of microbial enzymes for food processing. J. Agr. Food Chem. 13, 30-34.

BERNHARD, S. A. 1968. The Structure and Function of Enzymes. W. A. Benjamin, New York.

DESNUELLE, P., and SAVARY, P. 1963. Specificities of lipases. J. Lipid Res. 4, 369-384.

DIXON, M., and WEBB, E. C. 1964. Enzymes, 2nd Edition. Academic Press, New York.

EPTON, R., and THOMAS, T. H. 1971. Improving nature's catalysts. Aldrichimica Acta. 4, 61-65.

EPTON, R., and THOMAS, T. H. 1971. An Introduction to Water-Insoluble Enzymes. Koch-Light Labs. Ltd., Colnbrook, Bucks, England.

FURIA, T. E. (Editor). 1968. Handbook of Food Additives. Chemical Rubber Co., Cleveland, Ohio.

HEWITT, E. J. et al. 1956. The role of enzymes in food flavors, Food Technol. 10, 487-489.

INTERNATIONAL UNION OF BIOCHEMISTRY. 1965. Enzyme Nomenclature. Elsevier Publishing Co., New York.

JOSLYN, M. A., and HEID, J. L. 1964. Food Processing Operations, Vol. 2. Avi Publishing Co., Westport, Conn.

JOSLYN, M. A., and PONTING, J. D. 1951. Enzyme-catalyzed oxidative browning of fruit products. In Advances in Food Research, Vol. III, E. M. Mrak, and G. F. Stewart (Editors). Academic Press, New York.

MAHLER, H. R., and CORDES, E. H. 1971. Biological Chemistry, 2nd Edition. Harper and Row, New York.

REED, G. 1966. Enzymes in Food Processing. Academic Press, New York.

SCHULTZ, H. W. (Editor). 1960. Food Enzymes. Avi Publishing Co., Westport, Conn.

SCHWEIGERT, B. S. 1960. Food aspects of enzymes affecting proteins. In Food Enzymes, H. W. Schultz (Editor). Avi Publishing Co., Westport, Conn.

UNDERKOFLER, L. A. 1961. Production and application of plant and microbial proteinases. Soc. Chem. Ind. (London), Monograph 11, 48-70.

VAN BUREN, J. P., MOYER, J. C., and ROBINSON, W. B. 1962. Pecti eth-ylesterase in snapbeans. J. Food Sci. 27, 291-294.

WHITAKER, J. R. 1972. Principles of Enzymology for the Food S   es. Marcel Dekker, New York.

WOLD, F. 1971. Macromolecules Structure and Function. Prentice-Hall, Englewood Cliffs, N.J.

CHAPTER 8

The Vitamins

An early landmark leading to the recognition of vitamins as a dietary essential dates back to 1881, when Lunin demonstrated that mice could not survive on purified diets consisting of proteins, carbohydrates, fats, and inorganic salts but would develop normally when milk was added. Lunin concluded that milk contained a substance essential for life and growth.

An important discovery indicating specificity of the dietary essentials was Eijkman's production of beriberi in chickens in 1897 by feeding them polished rice. This disease was prevented or cured by feeding either a diet of unpolished rice or a diet to which alcoholic extract of rice bran was added.

In 1906, Hopkins confirmed the findings of Lunin and suggested that these essential nutrients be designated as "accessory food factors."

The work of Eijkman was confirmed by Funk in 1911, who isolated from rice polishings, a crystalline fraction that cured beriberi. This fraction was amine-like in chemical properties; hence, he suggested the substance be called "vitamine." The terminal "e" was deleted in the early 1920s when it was realized that some substances effective in curing deficiency diseases were not amines.

As research progressed, findings indicated that many types of nutrients were necessary for growth and reproduction. Osborne and Mendel and McCollum and Davis discovered that growing rats require a fat-soluble factor for normal growth. This factor, found in certain animal fats, such as butter, was designated as fat-soluble A. The water-soluble factor, which cured beriberi, was designated as water-soluble B. Holst and Frolich, working in Norway, showed that guinea pigs restricted to a diet of cereals and hay developed scurvy while those fed fresh foods did not. The scurvy-preventing factor is now known as vitamin C.

Similarly, the value of fish-liver oils in curing or preventing rickets in children was explained by the isolation and identification of vitamin D.

The obvious difference in solubility between the antiberiberi and antiscorbutic vitamins on the one hand and antirachitic vitamin on the other led to the classification of vitamins as water-soluble and fat-soluble. Subsequent identification of the structures and metabolic functions of the accessory food factors have added much to our understanding of these dietary essentials. However, a biochemical explanation has not been discovered in all cases for the observed deficiency diseases caused by a lack of these essential nutrients.

Vitamins may be defined as complex organic compounds required in catalytic amounts for the proper functioning of living cells and not synthesized in amounts to meet physiological needs. The quantities required may range from micrograms per day (e.g., vitamin B_{12}) to milligrams per day (e.g., vitamin C).

Although it is convenient to list specific symptoms resulting from an inadequate intake of an individual vitamin, deficiencies due to a single vitamin are seldom encountered in practice. A diet that is deficient in one vitamin is usually deficient in several vitamins. As a result, the vitamin that is lowest in amount relative to its dietary requirements will probably determine the major signs of a deficiency but the symptoms of other deficiencies will also be present. Deficiency diseases, therefore, are most frequently clinical manifestations of several vitamin deficiencies.

WATER-SOLUBLE VITAMINS

The water-soluble vitamins have many properties in common. They have a similar distribution in foods, which explains why a deficiency of several factors is observed more frequently than a deficiency of a single vitamin. This group of vitamins must be supplied every day for there is minimal storage of dietary excesses. These accessory food factors are excreted in urine. The most significant fact about this group is that they have been found to function as coenzymes for specific enzyme systems essential for various metabolic processes of the cell.

Thiamine (Vitamin B_1)

General Properties.—Thiamine is a crystalline compound which is relatively heat stable in dry form but heat labile in solution, particularly when it is alkaline. It is oxidized in the presence of mild oxidizing agents to form thiochrome, a fluorescent pigment. This reaction is the basis for the chemical assay of thiamine.

Thiamine has a molecular weight of 337 and a chemical structure as follows:

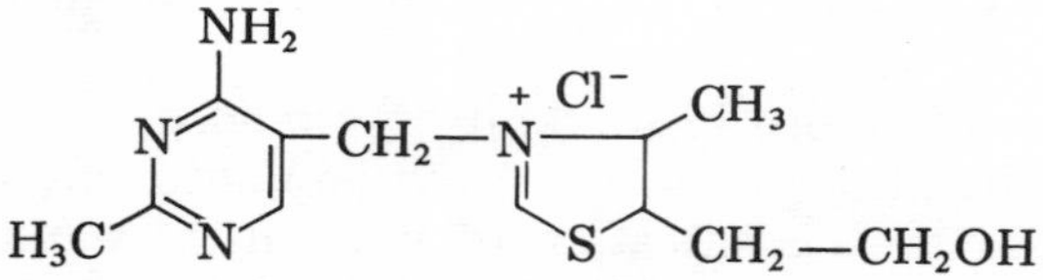

Thiamine chloride

This molecule is composed of a pyrimidine nucleus and a thiazole nucleus connected by a methylene bridge. The pyrimidine moiety has a relatively high stability; whereas the thiazole moiety opens readily in alkaline solutions. Thiamine contains an amino group on the pyrimidine ring, and a quaternary nitrogen, which is very active chemically, on the thiazole ring. The thiazole ring also contains an ethoxy group, which is reactive in much the same way as other hydroxyl groups and is essential for vitamin activity.

Thiamine is absorbed from the small intestine and is phosphorylated in the intestinal mucosa. Though salts of the vitamin are not completely absorbed from the intestinal tract, modified derivatives (e.g., thiamine propyl disulfide, benzoylthiamine disulfide, and others), which are biologically active are absorbed to a greater degree in weak alkaline solution. The latter compounds are relatively insoluble and are stable to heat; therefore, they may be of value in the enrichment of foods.

Biosynthesis.—The details of biosynthetic pathways for the pyrimidine and the thiazole moieties are unknown. There are enzymes in certain plant materials that are able to effect the condensation of preformed thiazole and pyrimidine moieties of thiamine. The following scheme illustrates the reactions for which evidence is available (Fig. 8.1).

Thiamine pyrophosphate, the coenzyme form of thiamine, is synthesized by the direct transfer of the pyrophosphate group from ATP.

Thiamine + ATP $\longrightarrow$ Thiamine pyrophosphate (TPP) + AMP

Function and Effects of Deficiency.—Thiamine functions in carbohydrate metabolism as the coenzyme, thiamine pyrophosphate or cocarboxylase, in the decarboxylation of α-keto acids, and in the utilization of pentose in the hexose monophosphate shunt. A mechanism by which thiamine pyrophosphate exerts its action is shown by the following:

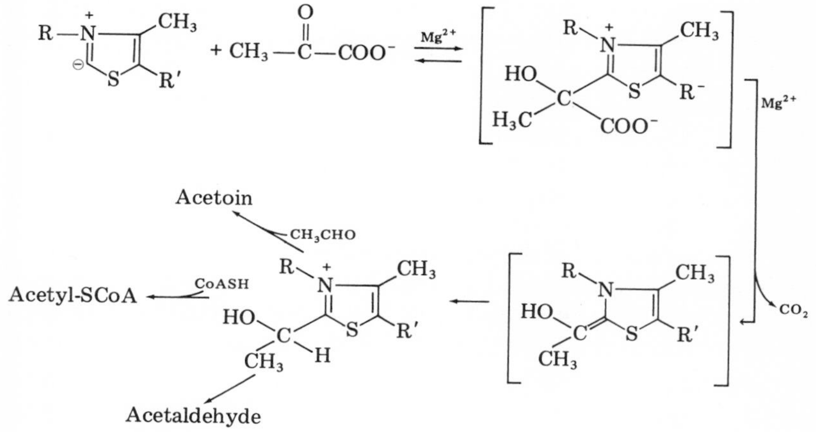

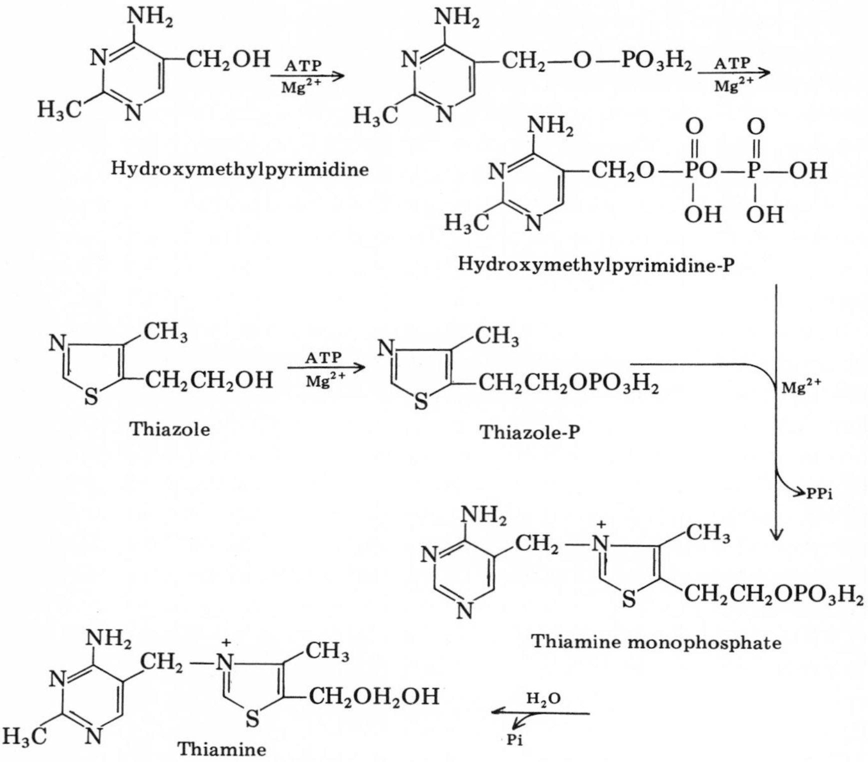

FIG. 8.1. BIOSYNTHESIS OF THIAMINE

Active aldehyde complex can give rise to acetaldehyde, acetoin, or acetyl-SCoA. Thiamine and lipoic acid are essential components of the multienzyme pyruvate dehydrogenase complex and the glutamic dehydrogenase complex. This is needed to achieve oxidative decarboxylation of α-keto acids and their subsequent conversion to acyl-SCoA derivatives.

In view of the function of thiamine in carbohydrate metabolism, it generally has been assumed that the needs are related to caloric intake, particularly to those calories derived from carbohydrate. When protein and fat serve as a source of energy, they exert a sparing action on thiamine needs. Thiamine requirements are dependent on body size, physical activity, environmental temperature, and the physiological state of an individual. The most striking symptom of a thiamine deficiency is a disease of the nervous system, polyneuritis in lower animals and beriberi in man. Experimental deficiency symptoms can be produced by use of an analogue of thiamine, such as pyrithiamine or oxythiamine.

Recommended Dietary Allowances.—All animals except ruminants require an exogenous source of thiamine. For the average man and woman, the recommended daily dietary allowance is 1.0 to 1.4 mg (See Table 8.1). Thiamine needs are increased when there is greatly increased metabolism such as occurs in febrile conditions, hyperthyroidism, or muscular activity. Additional recommended allowances are 0.1 mg per day during pregnancy and 0.5 mg per day during lactation.

Distribution in Foods.—Thiamine is distributed widely in nature. Among the richer sources, none of which is highly potent, are the whole cereal grains, nuts, pork, and eggs. Pork contains several times as much as beef (0.193 mg/100 gm to 0.009 mg/100 gm). Butter and cheese contain only negligible amounts, while milk is a better source. Potatoes furnish significant quantities of thiamine when used extensively in the diet (1 medium, 2.5-in. diameter, 0.10 mg B_1). Legumes are a good source of this vitamin, but the usual methods of cooking them cause a considerable loss in the amount available for ingestion. Wheat flour is a poor source of thiamine, inasmuch as most of the vitamin is removed in the milling process.

Thiamine, one of the more labile of the vitamins, undergoes considerable loss during the preparation of food for human consumption. In aqueous solutions at pH 3.5 thiamine can be heated to 120°C for 20 min without deterioration, but if the pH of the solution is above pH 5.5, losses are marked. Thiamine is leached out of foods during wet processing, such as the blanching of vegetables. Cooking by boiling in an excessive amount of water and discarding the cooking water results in loss of thiamine. Washing before cooking also can cause a thiamine loss. For example, washing whole rice once can result in a thiamine loss of 25%.

Baking has an adverse effect on the thiamine content of cereal products. The losses vary with the product, the duration of heating, the temperature, the amount of surface area exposed and the amount of alkaline baking powder present. Baking of bread can result in a loss of 15–25%, while baking rolls to the usual degree of brownness causes losses of only about 15% of thiamine.

Thiamine losses from meat are related to cooking conditions, the size of the cut, and the fat content. Fluids from the thawing of frozen meats, from cooking of meats, and from slicing of meats contain significant amounts of the water-soluble vitamin. Canned meats undergo loss of thiamine during storage. For example, canned

TABLE 8.1

FOOD AND NUTRITION BOARD, NATIONAL ACADEMY OF SCIENCES—NATIONAL RESEARCH COUNCIL RECOMMENDED DAILY DIETARY ALLOWANCES,[1] REVISED 1968

Designed for the maintenance of most normal people as they live in the U.S.A.

AGE[2]					FAT-SOLUBLE VITAMINS		
From-Up to	WEIGHT	HEIGHT	KCALORIES	PROTEIN	Vitamin A Activity	Vitamin D	Vitamin E Activity
Years	Kg (Lb)	Cm (In.)	Gm		IU	IU	IU
Infants							
Birth–1/6	4(9)	55(22)	kg × 120[5]	kg × 2.2	1,500	400	5
1/6–1/2	7(15)	63(25)	kg × 110[5]	kg × 2.0	1,500	400	5
1/2–1	9(20)	72(28)	kg × 100[5]	kg × 1.8	1,500	400	5
Children							
1–2	12(26)	81(32)	1,100	25	2,000	400	10
2–3	14(31)	91(36)	1,250	25	2,000	400	10
3–4	16(35)	100(39)	1,400	30	2,500	400	10
4–6	19(42)	110(43)	1,600	30	2,500	400	10
6–8	23(51)	121(48)	2,000	35	3,500	400	15
8–10	28(62)	131(52)	2,200	40	3,500	400	15
Males							
10–12	35(77)	140(55)	2,500	45	4,500	400	20
12–14	43(95)	151(59)	2,700	50	5,000	400	20
14–18	59(130)	170(67)	3,000	60	5,000	400	25
18–22	67(147)	175(69)	2,800	60	5,000	400	30
22–35	70(154)	175(69)	2,800	65	5,000	—	30
35–55	70(154)	173(68)	2,600	65	5,000	—	30
55–75+	70(154)	171(67)	2,400	65	5,000	—	30
Females							
10–12	35(77)	142(56)	2,250	50	4,500	400	20
12–14	44(97)	154(61)	2,300	50	5,000	400	20
14–16	52(114)	157(62)	2,400	55	5,000	400	25
16–18	54(119)	160(63)	2,300	55	5,000	400	25
18–22	58(128)	163(64)	2,000	55	5,000	400	25
22–35	58(128)	163(64)	2,000	55	5,000	—	25
35–55	58(128)	160(63)	1,850	55	5,000	—	25
55–75+	58(128)	157(62)	1,700	55	5,000	—	25
Pregnancy			+ 200	65	6,000	400	30
Lactation			+1,000	75	8,000	400	30

[1] The allowance levels are intended to cover individual variations among most normal persons as they live in the United States under usual environmental stresses. The recommended allowances can be attained with a variety of common foods providing other nutrients for which human requirements have been less well-defined. See text for more detailed discussion of allowances and of nutrients not tabulated.

[2] Entries on lines for age range 22–35 yr represent the reference man and woman at age 22. All other entries represent allowances for the midpoint of the specified age range.

[3] The folacin allowances refer to dietary sources as determined by *Lactobacillus casei* assay. Pure forms of folacin may be effective in doses less than 1/4 of the RDA.

	WATER-SOLUBLE VITAMINS						MINERALS				
Ascorbic Acid	Folacin[3]	Niacin	Riboflavin	Thiamine	Vitamin B_6	Vitamin B_{12}	Calcium	Phosphorus	Iodine	Iron	Magnesium
						Infants					
Mg	Mg	Mg Equiv.[4]	Mg	Mg	Mg	Mcg	Gm	Gm	Mcg	Mg	Mg
35	0.05	5	0.4	0.2	0.2	1.0	0.4	0.2	25	6	40
35	0.05	7	0.5	0.4	0.3	1.5	0.5	0.4	40	10	60
35	0.1	8	0.6	0.5	0.4	2.0	0.6	0.5	45	15	70
						Children					
40	0.1	8	0.6	0.6	0.5	2.0	0.7	0.7	55	15	100
40	0.2	8	0.7	0.6	0.6	2.5	0.8	0.8	60	15	150
40	0.2	9	0.8	0.7	0.7	3	0.8	0.8	70	10	200
40	0.2	11	0.9	0.8	0.9	4	0.8	0.8	80	10	200
40	0.2	13	1.1	1.0	1.0	4	0.9	0.9	100	10	250
40	0.3	15	1.2	1.1	1.2	5	1.0	1.0	110	10	250
						Males					
40	0.4	17	1.3	1.3	1.4	5	1.2	1.2	125	10	300
45	0.4	18	1.4	1.4	1.6	5	1.4	1.4	135	18	350
55	0.4	20	1.5	1.5	1.8	5	1.4	1.4	150	18	400
60	0.4	18	1.6	1.4	2.0	5	0.8	0.8	140	10	400
60	0.4	18	1.7	1.4	2.0	5	0.8	0.8	140	10	350
60	0.4	17	1.7	1.3	2.0	5	0.8	0.8	125	10	350
60	0.4	14	1.7	1.2	2.0	6	0.8	0.8	110	10	350
						Females					
40	0.4	15	1.3	1.1	1.4	5	1.2	1.2	110	18	300
45	0.4	15	1.4	1.2	1.6	5	1.3	1.3	115	18	350
50	0.4	16	1.4'	1.2	1.8	5	1.3	1.3	120	18	350
50	0.4	15	1.5	1.2	2.0	5	1.3	1.3	115	18	350
55	0.4	13	1.5	1.0	2.0	5	0.8	0.8	100	18	350
55	0.4	13	1.5	1.0	2.0	5	0.8	0.8	100	18	350
55	0.4	13	1.5	1.0	2.0	5	0.8	0.8	90	18	300
55	0.4	13	1.5	1.0	2.0	6	0.8	0.8	80	10	300
60	0.8	15	1.8	+0.1	2.5	8	+0.4	+0.4	125	18	450
60	0.5	20	2.0	+0.5	2.5	6	+0.5	+0.5	150	18	450

[4] Niacin equivalents include dietary sources of the vitamin itself plus 1 mg equivalent for each 60 mg of dietary tryptophan.

[5] Assumes protein equivalent to human milk. For proteins not 100% utilized, factors should be increased proportionately.

NOTE: The "Recommended Daily Dietary Allowances" should not be confused with "Minimum Daily Requirements." The latter values have been established by the U.S. Food and Drug Administration as standards for labeling purposes of foods and pharmaceutical preparations for special dietary uses. The "Minimum Daily Requirements" are set forth in the Federal Register, Vol. 22, No. 106, p. 3841 (June 1, 1957), and Federal Register, Vol. 22, No. 134, p. 4910 (July 12, 1957).

pork luncheon meat may lose as much as 30% of its thiamine content by the end of 6 months storage at 70° F.

Cereals stored as whole grain can undergo losses, the extent of which depend on the moisture content. Similary, fortified white flour loses thiamine even under favorable storage conditions.

Riboflavin (Vitamin B_2)

General Properties.—Riboflavin was first isolated from milk in 1879 as lactochrome, a natural yellow fluorescent pigment in milk whey. Not until 1933 was it shown that this essential dietary factor of milk whey was similar to the yellow fluorescent pigments isolated from eggs and liver. In the meantime, Warburg and Christian had isolated from yeast a flavin-protein complex, "yellow enzyme," necessary for cell respiration.

Chemical studies soon demonstrated that the fluorescent pigment associated with the "yellow enzyme" was the same as that of milk, eggs, and liver. Degradation studies of the pigment molecule showed that it consisted essentially of a cyclic ring structure, isoalloxazine, and a side chain of a pentose sugar (ribose). The structure of riboflavin, confirmed by total synthesis, is as follows:

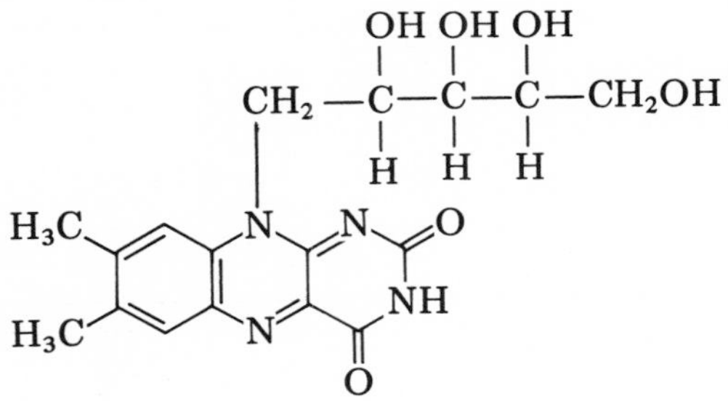

Riboflavin
6,7-Dimethyl-9-(1'-D-ribityl)-isoalloxazine

Riboflavin is sparingly soluble in water. It is stable to heat, air, and oxygen, but is photolabile. Exposure of the vitamin to either ultraviolet irradiation or to visible light results in irreversible decomposition. It is sensitive to alkalies, but it is quite stable in strong acid solutions.

Biosynthesis.—Riboflavin is synthesized by all green plants and by most bacteria, molds, fungi, and yeast. The initial stages of biosynthesis are the same as with those of purine biosynthesis. The first established intermediate precursor is 6,7-dimethyl-8-ribityllumazine.

Riboflavin synthesis is completed by the catalytic action of riboflavin synthetase involving two molecules of the substituted lumazine.

In this reaction the diazine ring of one molecule is ruptured and a 4 carbon unit is added to the second lumazine molecule to form riboflavin and 4-ribitylamino-5-amino-2,6-dihydroxypyrimidine. The conversion of lumazine to riboflavin is shown in the following diagram:

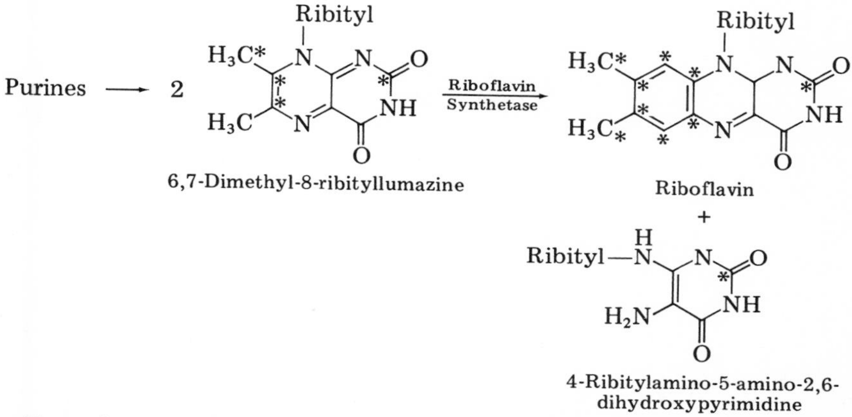

Purines ⟶ 2

6,7-Dimethyl-8-ribityllumazine

Riboflavin Synthetase

Riboflavin

+

4-Ribitylamino-5-amino-2,6-dihydroxypyrimidine

Function.—Riboflavin, an essential dietary constituent for mammals, is part of the structure of two flavin coenzymes, flavin mononucleotide (FMN) and flavin adenine dinucleotide (FAD). Flavin mononucleotide (riboflavin 5'-phosphate) is formed from riboflavin and ATP in a reaction catalyzed by flavokinase.

$$\text{Riboflavin} + \text{ATP} \longrightarrow \text{FMN} + \text{ADP}$$

FAD is formed from FMN by reaction with ATP and an enzyme, flavin nucleotide pyrophosphorylase.

$$\text{FMN} + \text{ATP} \xrightarrow{\text{Mg}^{2+}} \text{FAD} + \text{PP}$$

The foregoing coenzymes undergo reversible oxidation-reduction when participating in enzyme catalyzed reactions such as succinic dehydrogenase.

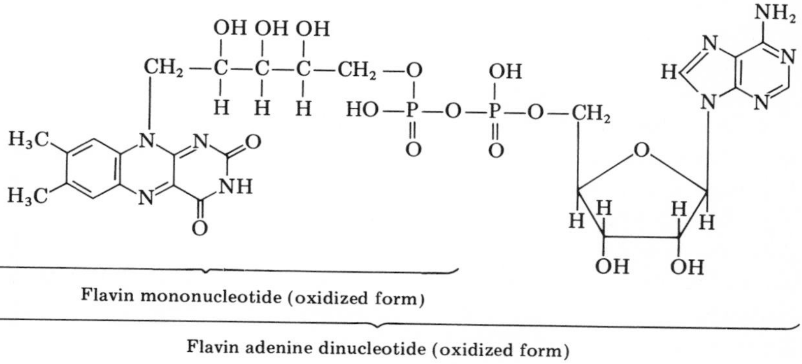

Flavin mononucleotide (oxidized form)

Flavin adenine dinucleotide (oxidized form)

FMN or FAD (reduced form)

It is a common observation that humans with one vitamin deficiency are likely to have other associated vitamin deficiencies. This is manifested especially with respect to thiamine, riboflavin, and niacin since these water-soluble vitamins often occur together in foods. Consequently, humans having the deficiency syndromes of either beriberi or pellagra generally are deficient in riboflavin.

Riboflavin deficiency in man is characterized by fissuring in the angles of the mouth (cheilosis), a localized seborrheic dermatitis of the face, a magenta-colored tongue, and organic disorders of the eye (corneal vascularization). Despite the fact that riboflavin functions as the prosthetic group of flavoproteins concerned with oxidative processes, the clinical changes attributed to its deficiency are minor. In general, both FMN and FAD decrease in concentration, both of which decrease more rapidly in organs such as liver and kidney than in heart and brain. Inasmuch as riboflavin is essential for growth, there is a relationship between protein metabolism and riboflavin retention and excretion; animals on low-protein diets excrete increased amounts of riboflavin. The amount of riboflavin excreted in the urine tends to reflect dietary supply and body stores.

Recommended Dietary Allowances.—Riboflavin requirements are related closely to energy expenditure. The Food and Nutrition Board of the National Research Council recommended, in 1968, an intake of 0.6 mg/1000 kcal. Thus, the daily allowance falls between 1.3 and 1.7 mg for men and 1.2 and 1.3 mg for women. The daily allowance is increased 0.3 mg during pregnancy and an additional 0.5 mg during lactation. The requirements for children are approximately the same as for adults, 0.6 mg/1000 kcal (See Table 8.1).

Yeast is possibly the best source of riboflavin. Other good sources are milk, cheese, eggs, whole-grain and enriched cereals, green leafy vegetables, peas, lima beans, and most meats. Fish, as compared to beef, pork, and chicken is a poor source of the vitamin. Fruits contain insignificant amounts.

Milk is an important source of this vitamin. Since riboflavin is stable to heat, pasteurization and spray drying of milk have very little effect on riboflavin content. The ease with which riboflavin is destroyed by light can result in an extensive loss of riboflavin if milk is exposed to direct sunlight.

Riboflavin is one of the nutrients used in enrichment of bread, alimentary paste products (macaroni, spaghetti, noodles and vermicelli), corn meal and corn grits, rice, and farina. Enrichment standards, which set minimum and maximum levels, include not only riboflavin but also niacin, thiamine, and iron.

Niacin (Nicotinic Acid)

General Properites.—Niacin is one of the most stable of the vitamins. It is stable to acids, bases, mild oxidizing agents, heat, and light. It is sparingly soluble in cold water but soluble in hot water and alcohol. Nicotinic acid and niacinamide are active biologically, but the amide is the form that exists in nature.

Biosynthesis.—Tryptophan can be converted into niacin in the body. The pathways for the conversion of tryptophan into niacin involve several intermediary steps. One pathway involves the oxidation of tryptophan to kynurenine which is converted by way of a number of intermediates to nicotinic acid mononucleotide. This substance is utilized in the synthesis of nicotinamide adenine dinucleotide (NAD$^+$), Fig. 8.2.

Function and Effects of Deficiency.—The function of niacin in the body, in the form of NAD$^+$, is a coenzyme which functions as an acceptor of electrons from a substrate. The protein moiety gives substrate specificity to the system. It will be noted that in addition to a hydride ion being transferred from the substrate to the nicotinamide moiety, a proton is liberated into the medium:

$$NAD^+ \text{ (or } NADP^+) + MH_2 \longrightarrow M + NADH \text{ (or } NADPH) + H^+$$

Less frequently, the coenzyme may be the phosphorylated derivative of NAD$^+$, nicotinamide adenine dinucleotide phosphate (NADP$^+$). This coenzyme functions in the same way as NAD$^+$. These coenzymes participate in many biochemical reactions such as: pyruvate metabolism, citric acid cycle, lipid metabolism, and synthesis of high energy bonds. Reduction and oxidation of NAD$^+$ occurs at the C-4 position. The oxidation and reduction process is sterospecific to yield either the α-isomer or the β-isomer.

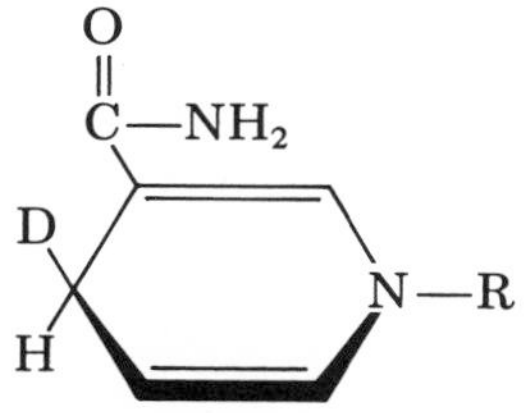

α-isomer   β-isomer

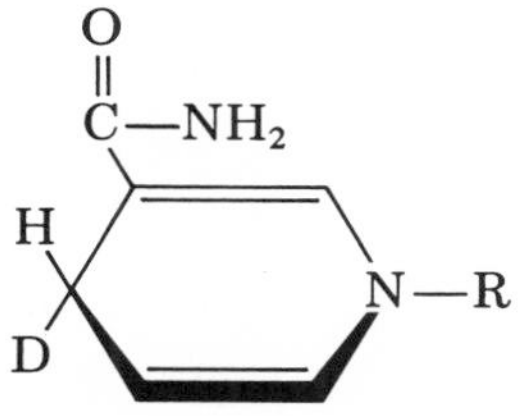

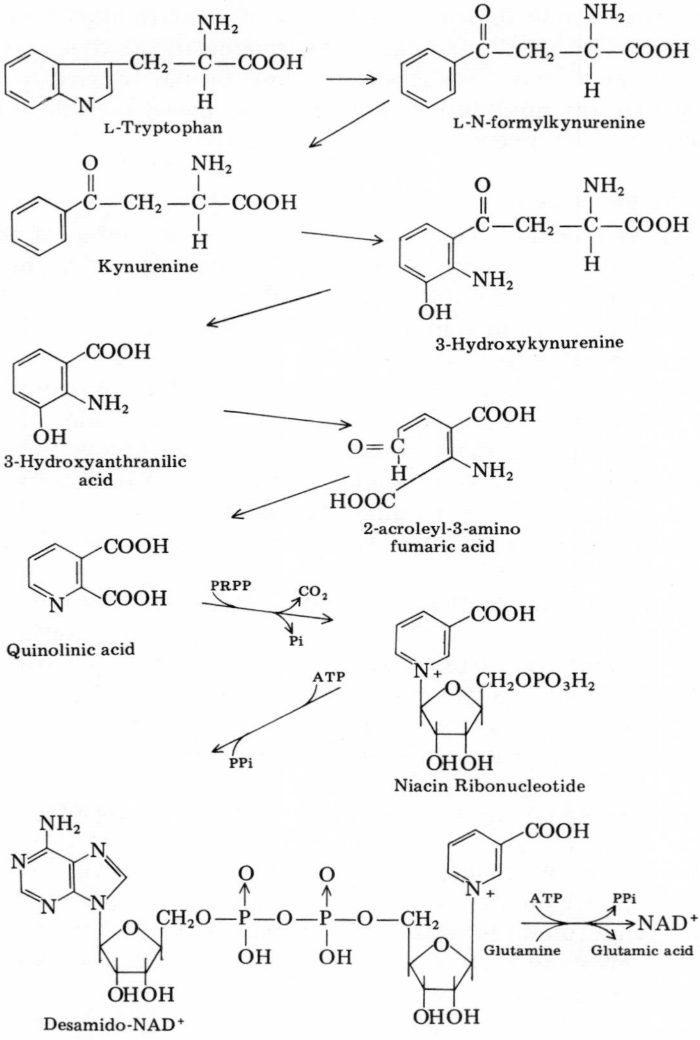

FIG. 8.2. TRYPTOPHAN METABOLISM AND NAD⁺ SYNTHESIS

These isomers are based on the configuration of the monodeuterated reduced NAD$^+$ derivatives i.e., above or below the plane of the ring. Alcohol dehydrogenase and lactic dehydrogenase utilize the α-isomer while α-glycerophosphate dehydrogenase and L-glutamic dehydrogenase utilize the β-isomer.

A deficiency of niacin leads to the disease known as pellagra. Inasmuch as tryptophan is a precursor of niacin in man, pellagra must be considered from deficiencies of both the vitamin and the amount and the kinds of dietary protein available. In human dietaries, 60 mg of dietary tryptophan is equivalent to 1 mg of niacin. The characteristic glossitis and stomatitis usually appear early in pellagra. A dermatitis may appear on any part of the body, but generally it is confined to areas exposed to sunlight. Nonspecific mental symptoms include irritability, confusion, mental anxiety, and depression which can develop to delirium and dementia. Severe persistent diarrhea occurs only in advanced cases.

Recommended Dietary Allowances.—The term "niacin equivalent" is used to express the combined values of dietary sources of this vitamin and that converted from dietary tryptophan (1 mg niacin/60 mg tryptophan). The values recommended for men are 14 to 20 mg per day. For women the range is 13 to 15 mg. For children up to 10 yr, the allowance varies from 8 to 15 mg per day (see Table 19).

Distribution in Foods.—The richest sources are yeast, liver, lean meats, poultry, beans, peas, nuts, whole-grain, and enriched cereal products. Milk and eggs are low in this vitamin but they are effective in preventing or curing pellagra, probably because of their high quality protein.

Pyridoxine Group (Vitamin B₆)

Vitamin B_6 does not denote a single substance but consists of a group of three related substances; namely, pyridoxine, pyridoxal, and pyridoxamine:

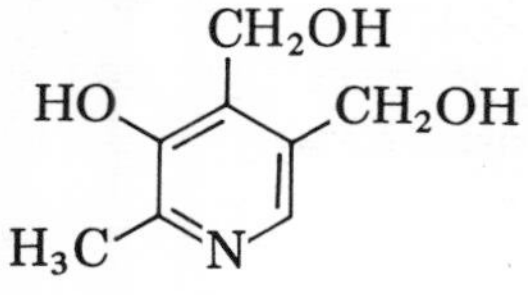

Pyridoxine 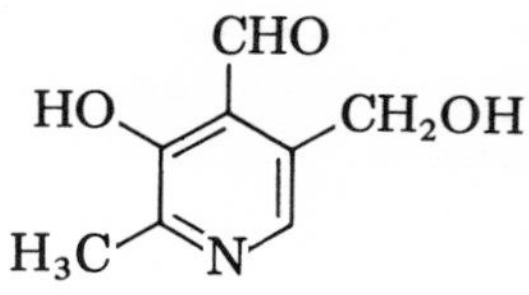   Pyridoxal 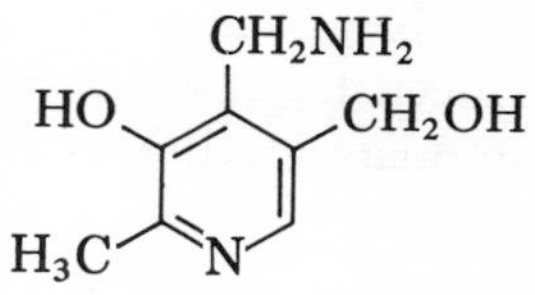   Pyridoxamine

Pyridoxine is found in plant products while pyridoxal and pyridoxamine are found primarily in animal products. These substances are present in either the free or bound forms.

General Properties.—Pyridoxine is readily soluble in water, acetone, and alcohol, and slightly soluble in ether and chloroform. It is stable to heat in either acidic or basic solution. Pyridoxal and pyridoxamine decompose rapidly at high temperatures. Pyridoxine is destroyed on irradiation in neutral or alkaline solutions, but is stable in acid solution. All three substances are destroyed by oxidizing agents such as nitric acid, permanganate, and hydrogen peroxide.

Biosynthesis.—Pyridoxine is synthesized by green plants and microorganisms but the biosynthetic pathway is not completely elucidated. Serine, glycine, glycolaldehyde, and tryptophan have been implicated as possible precursors of pyridoxine synthesis in *E. coli*.

Function and Effects of Deficiency.—Vitamin B_6 occurs in tissues predominantly as the phosphates of pyridoxal and pyridoxamine. Pyridoxine is phosphorylated in the liver by a specific kinase and oxidized to pyridoxal phosphate (coenzyme form) by a specific flavoprotein. The latter form functions as a coenzyme in a number of chemical reactions involving amino acids.

The interrelationships are as follows:

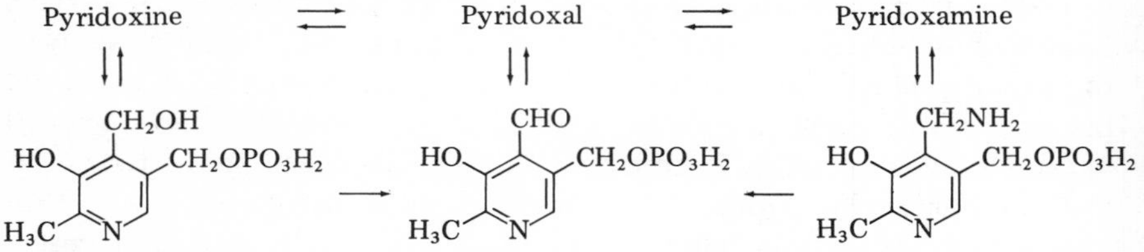

$$\text{Pyridoxine} \quad \rightleftarrows \quad \text{Pyridoxal} \quad \rightleftarrows \quad \text{Pyridoxamine}$$

| Pyridoxine phosphate | Pyridoxal phosphate | Pyridoxamine phosphate |

Some of these enzymes are amino acid decarboxylases, transaminases, enzymes involved in tryptophan metabolism (tryptophan to niacin), racemases (formation of equilibrium mixture of DL-alanine from D or L-alanine) and cystathionase (conversion of cystathionine to serine and homocysteine). This explains the increased need of the vitamin when diets are high in protein.

The occurrence of vitamin B_6 is so widespread that a deficiency rarely occurs in humans. However, a vitamin deficiency can be induced by the administration of antagonists such as deoxypyridoxine and isonicotinic acid hydrazide, used in tuberculosis therapy.

4-Deoxypyridoxine   Isoniazid

The symptoms observed following use of these compounds are skin lesions, anemia, and convulsive seizures.

The effect of pyridoxine deficiency is more dramatic in infants than in adults. A deficiency of this nutrient was the cause of an outbreak of convulsive seizures and nervous irritability in infants, less than 6 months old, fed a commercial canned liquid-milk formula. It is now known that the deficiency was caused by the destruction of vitamin B₆ during heat processing.

Recommended Dietary Allowances.—The human requirement for vitamin B_6 is not known, but 1.4 to 2.0 mg daily is recommended as a reasonable allowance for the adult (See Table 8.1). It is believed that the need for the vitamin increases during pregnancy, during lactation, with aging and in such special situations as radiation exposure, cardiac failure, and isoniazid therapy for tuberculosis. Since the B_6 group is widely distributed in both plant and animal foods, an average mixed diet will provide an adequate intake.

Distribution in Foods.—The vitamin B_6 group is widely distributed in foods and occurs in both free and bound form. The best sources of this vitamin are liver, muscle meats, fish, whole-grain cereals, brewers' yeast, milk, egg yolk, lettuce, vegetables, bananas, lemons, oatmeal, and nuts. Generally, foods rich in the other members of the B-complex are also good sources of the pyridoxine group.

Pantothenic Acid

Pantothenic acid was partially purified from a variety of sources, but it was not recognized as the same factor in each case. Thus, it was referred to as the chick antidermatitis factor, the liver filtrate factor, the chick antipellagra factor, and the yeast factor. Finally, it was isolated from yeast by Williams and his colleagues. The significance of this nutrient in animal nutrition was established by Jukes, Woolley, and their associates. Its chemical structure is:

$$HOCH_2 - \underset{\underset{CH_3}{|}}{\overset{\overset{CH_3}{|}}{C}} - \overset{\overset{OH}{|}}{CH} - \overset{\overset{O}{\|}}{C} - NH - CH_2CH_2OH$$

Pantothenic acid
D(+)-N-(2,4-Dihydroxy-3,3-dimethylbutyryl)-β-alanine

General Properties.—Chemically, pantothenic acid is an unstable, viscous oil. It is customary to use the vitamin in the form of the calcium salt, which is a white solid. It dissolves freely in water, is bitter to the taste, and is readily hydrolyzed by acid or alkali. The vitamin is relatively stable to heat in neutral solution and long storage in foods.

Biosynthesis.—Pantothenic acid can be synthesized by green plants and most microorganisms but not by mammalian tissues. The biosynthetic pathway in yeast, neurospora and bacteria (*e.g.*, *Escherichia coli*, *Neurospora crassa*) is shown in Fig. 8.3. Pantoic acid is formed

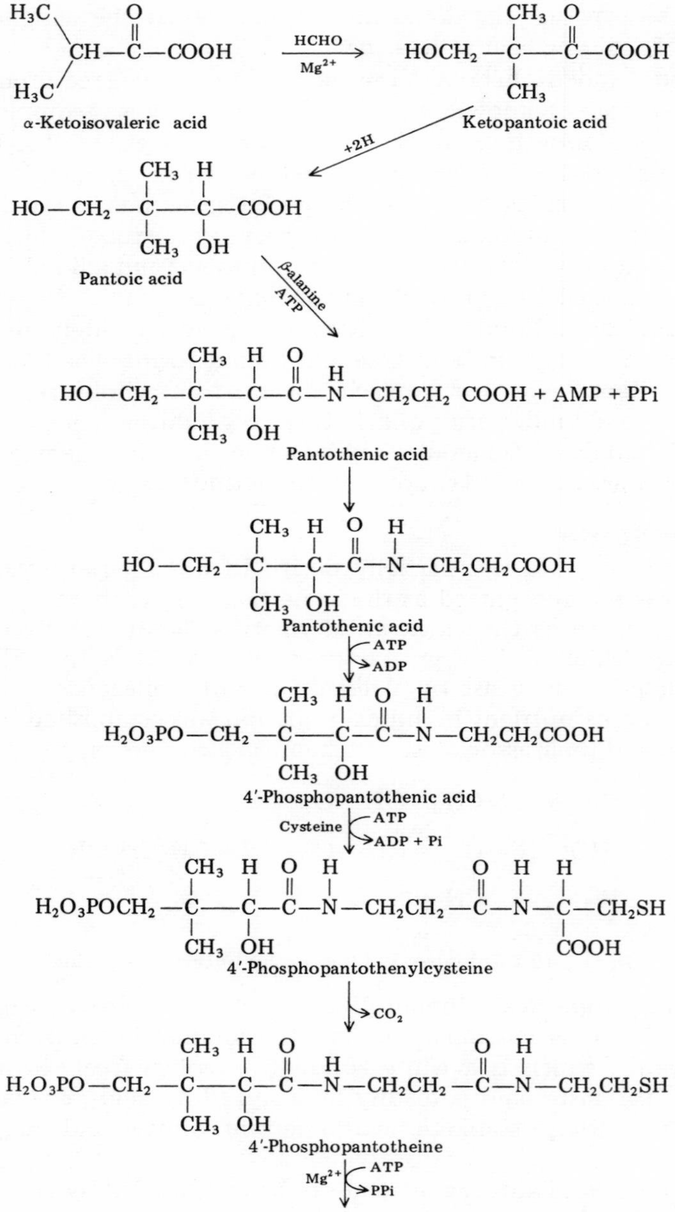

α-Ketoisovaleric acid $\xrightarrow[\text{Mg}^{2+}]{\text{HCHO}}$ Ketopantoic acid

$+2H$

Pantoic acid

β-alanine, ATP

Pantothenic acid $+ AMP + PPi$

Pantothenic acid

$\begin{array}{c}\text{ATP}\\\downarrow\text{ADP}\end{array}$

4'-Phosphopantothenic acid

Cysteine $\begin{array}{c}\text{ATP}\\\downarrow\text{ADP} + \text{Pi}\end{array}$

4'-Phosphopantothenylcysteine

$\downarrow CO_2$

4'-Phosphopantotheine

$\text{Mg}^{2+} \begin{array}{c}\text{ATP}\\\downarrow\text{PPi}\end{array}$

FIG. 8.3 (Continued)

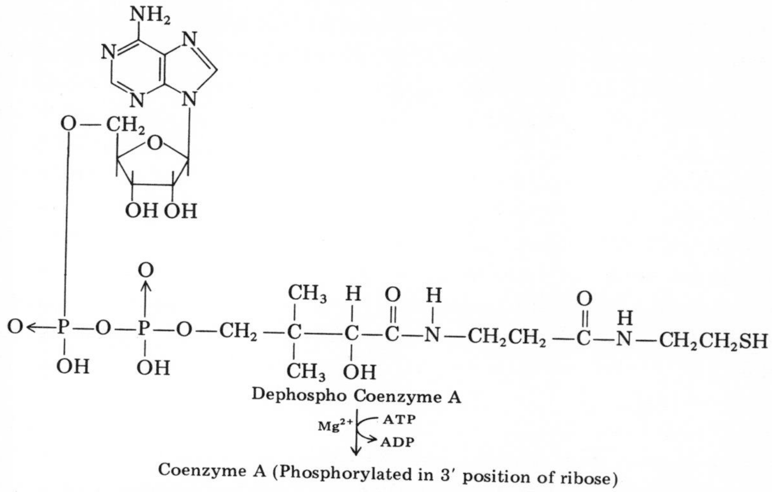

FIG. 8.3. BIOSYNTHESIS OF PANTOTHENIC ACID AND COENZYME A

from α-ketoisovaleric acid by the addition of a C-1 unit to give ketopantoic acid, which is reduced to pantoic acid. The formation of pantothenic acid from pantoic acid and β-alanine is catalyzed by an ATP-dependent enzyme system. Pantothenic acid is then incorporated into coenzyme A (CoA) both in animals and microorganisms. The proposed pathway for biosynthesis of the coenzyme is also shown in Fig. 8.3.

Function and Effects of Deficiency.—Pantothenic acid has a vital role in metabolism because it is a component of coenzyme A. This coenzyme is required for the metabolism of two-carbon compounds, notably acetyl groups. In general the CoASH acts as an acyl acceptor:

$$R—\overset{O}{\overset{\|}{C}}—O^- + CoASH \longrightarrow R—\overset{O}{\overset{\|}{C}}—SCoA$$

Coenzyme A is involved in the aerobic utilization of carbohydrates and in the breakdown and synthesis of fatty acids and lipids. Coenzyme A functions in the synthesis of sterols, steroid hormones, porphyrin, and acetylcholine.

Pantothenic acid is so widely distributed in foods that a deficiency disease due to a lack of the vitamin has not been observed in man on a natural diet. If, however, a pantothenic acid antimetabolite (antagonist), omegamethyl pantothenic acid, is given with a deficient diet, an illness closely resembling the deficiency observed in animals develops. The syndrome consists of headaches, fatigue, abdominal distress, sleep disturbances, numbness and tingling of hands and feet, nausea, and malaise. The syndrome is not relieved by administration of pantothenic acid although improvement is noted on a good high protein diet; consequently, it is believed that the deficiency-effects observed are due to the toxicity of the antagonist rather than to a complete lack of pantothenic acid. An increase in susceptibility to infections is associated with pantothenic acid deficiency.

Recommended Dietary Allowances.—The human requirement for pantothenic acid has not been established but is probably not above 5 mg daily. The Food and Nutrition Board, National Research Council, estimate that the average American diet furnishes about 10–15 mg of pantothenic acid daily, which intake apparently is adequate (Table 8.1).

Distribution in Foods.—Pantothenic acid is present in all plant and animal tissues. The greatest amounts of this nutrient occur in egg yolk, liver, kidney, fresh vegetables, and yeast. Skim milk, butter-milk, lean beef, grains, white potatoes, tomatoes, broccoli, cauli-flower, fruits, peanuts, and molasses are good sources. Egg white, beets, turnips, corn, rice, and apples are poor sources.

Biotin

Three separate lines of research led to the discovery of biotin. In 1916, Bateman showed that rats fed a diet rich in raw or uncooked egg white developed a peculiar skin disorder characterized by extreme losses of body hair and finally death. This condition was known as "egg-white injury." The toxic factor in the egg-white was identified as avidin. Györgi, in 1931, isolated from yeast a protective factor, "vitamin H," which was similar to the anti-egg-white injury factor. In 1933 a factor necessary for the growth and respiration of the nitrogen fixing organism, *Rhizobium*, was discovered and designated as coenzyme R. In 1936, Kögl and Tönnis isolated from egg yolk a crystalline material which they termed biotin. Finally, in 1940, Györgyi showed that vitamin H, coenzyme R, and biotin were identical. The structure of biotin is presented below:

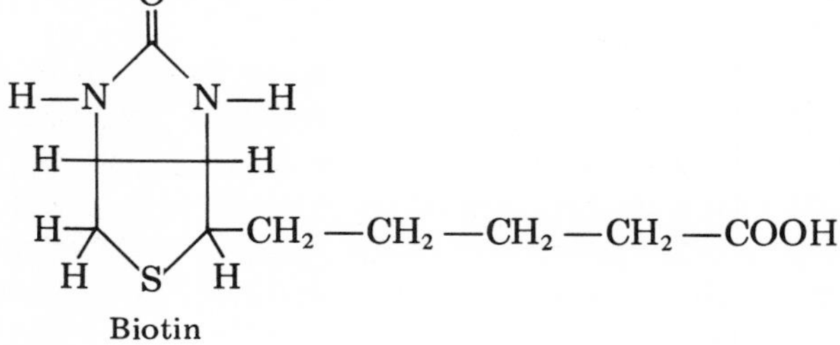

Biotin

General Properties.—Biotin is readily soluble in hot water, sparingly soluble in cold water, stable to heat, and labile to strong acids, alkalies, and oxidizing agents. Biotin combines with avidin, a glycoprotein found in raw egg white, to form an insoluble substance that cannot be absorbed from the intestinal tract. Avidin is readily inactivated by heating.

Biosynthesis.—The pathway of biotin synthesis in plants and microorganisms is not known. The biosynthesis of biotin has been accomplished with *Achromobacter IVS* using isovaleric acid and C^{14}_3 cysteine or $C^{14}O_2$. The postulated pathway is as follows:

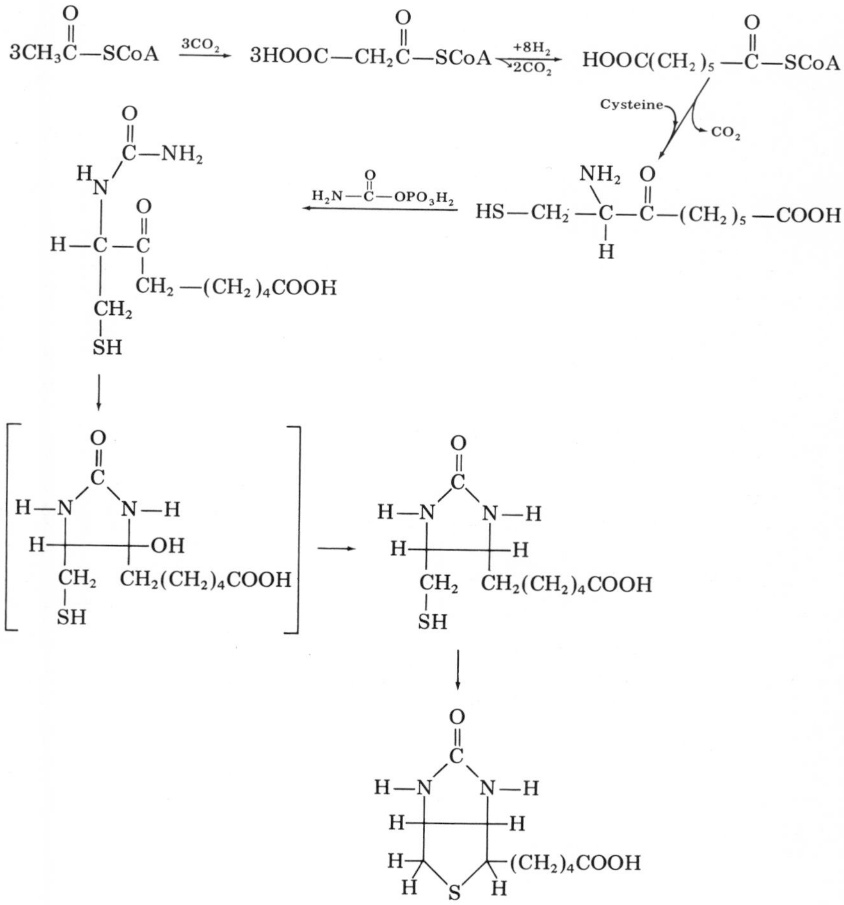

$$3CH_3\overset{O}{\overset{\|}{C}}-SCoA \xrightarrow{3CO_2} 3HOOC-CH_2\overset{O}{\overset{\|}{C}}-SCoA \xrightarrow[-2CO_2]{+8H_2} HOOC(CH_2)_5-\overset{O}{\overset{\|}{C}}-SCoA$$

$$HS-CH_2-\overset{NH_2}{\underset{H}{\overset{|}{C}}}-\overset{O}{\overset{\|}{C}}-(CH_2)_5-COOH \quad \xleftarrow{\text{Cysteine}}\ \searrow_{CO_2}$$

$$\xleftarrow{H_2N-\overset{O}{\overset{\|}{C}}-OPO_3H_2}$$

Structure: C—NH$_2$ / H—C—C / CH$_2$—(CH$_2$)$_4$COOH / CH$_2$ / SH

$$\left[\begin{array}{c} \text{structure with } \text{OH} \\ \text{CH}_2 \quad \text{CH}_2(\text{CH}_2)_4\text{COOH} \\ \text{SH} \end{array} \right] \longrightarrow \begin{array}{c} \text{structure} \\ \text{CH}_2 \quad \text{CH}_2(\text{CH}_2)_4\text{COOH} \\ \text{SH} \end{array}$$

Biotin

Function.—Biotin is essential for the activity of many enzyme systems in plants, microorganisms, and animals. It serves as the prosthetic group of a series of enzymes involved in synthesis and breakdown of fatty acids and amino acids through the addition of CO_2 and its removal from active compounds, and in deamination reactions of amino acids. Acetyl-SCoA carboxylase is a key enzyme in the synthesis of fatty acids in *E. coli*.

$$CH_3-\overset{\overset{\displaystyle O}{\parallel}}{C}-SCoA + C^{14}O_2 + ATP \xrightarrow{Mg^{2+}}$$

$$HOOC^{14}-CH_2-\overset{\overset{\displaystyle O}{\parallel}}{C}-SCoA + ADP + Pi$$

The role of biotin is to form *N*-carboxybiotin-enzyme in which CO_2 attaches to the *N*-1 position of biotin. Labeled ($C^{14}O_2$) appears first in the biotin as N-C^{14} (carboxy) then later in malonyl-SCoA indicating that biotin is, in fact, mediating the transfer of CO_2.

Biotin deficiency in man does not occur naturally through a dietary shortage. Experimental deficiency, induced by a low biotin diet containing large quantities of dried, uncooked egg white, results in scaly dermatitis, muscle pains, lassitude, anorexia, insomnia, and a slight anemia. All of these symptoms clear after feeding biotin. Spontaneous biotin deficiency in man seems unlikely because of intestinal bacterial synthesis of this compound. The total urinary and fecal excretions of biotin by man exceeds his dietary intake.

Recommended Dietary Allowances.—Dietary requirements for biotin have not been established. The Food and Nutrition Board, National Research Council suggested that diets providing a daily intake of 0.15 to 0.30 mg per day are adequate for adults.

Distribution in Foods.—Good sources of biotin are peanuts, chocolate, egg yolk, milk, organ meats (liver, kidney), most vegetables (peas and cauliflower), and some fruits (bananas, grapefruit, and strawberries). Foods having moderate or low concentrations are meat, milk products, cereals, bread, and flour. For humans and some animals, synthesis by intestinal bacteria is an important source of biotin. Although royal jelly generally is not considered as a human food, it is the richest source of biotin, having approximately 410 μg/100 gm.

Folacin

The term folic acid includes a number of derivatives of folacin (or pteroylmonoglutamic acid), all of which are interconvertible. The structure is:

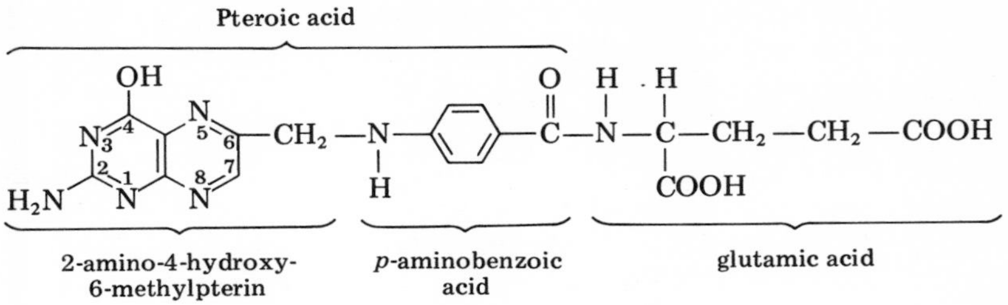

Pteroic acid

2-amino-4-hydroxy-   p-aminobenzoic   glutamic acid
6-methylpterin   acid

Pteroylmonoglutamic Acid

General Properties.—Folacin is a yellow crystalline compound, slightly soluble in cold water and moderately soluble in hot water. It is stable to heat in neutral or alkaline solutions but is inactivated when heated in acidic solutions. Either partial or complete inactivation is caused by sunlight, oxidation, reduction, esterification, and methylation. It is readily absorbed from the gastrointestinal tract and is stored primarily in the liver.

Biosynthesis.—Guanosine is utilized directly for pteridine synthesis; 2-amino-4-hydroxy-6-hydroxymethyldehydropteridine can be converted to dihydrofolic acid via dihydropteroic acid with partially purified enzymes (Fig. 8.4). The physiologically active form is the reduced tetrahydrofolic acid, which is formed by the action of folacin reductase.

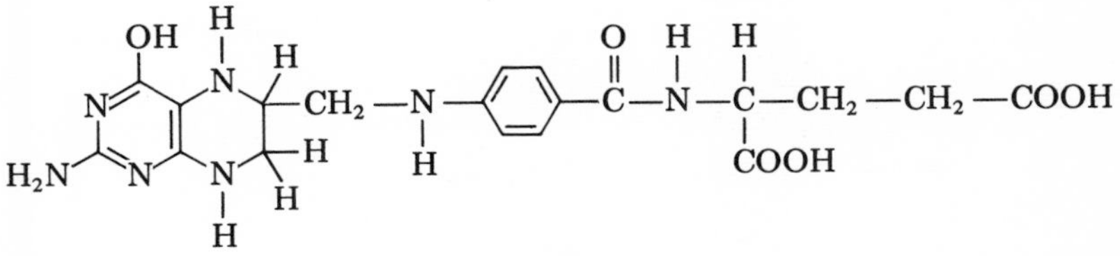

Tetrahydrofolic acid

Function and Effects of Deficiency.—Folacin coenzymes function in the transfer and the utilization of single carbon groups, such as formyl, hydroxymethyl and methyl, particularly in the synthesis of purine and pyrimidine ribotides and deoxyribotides, and in amino acid interconversions. The oxidized folacin derivatives are enzymatically reduced to tetrahydrofolic acid (FH_4), which functions as the active coenzyme. FH_4 functions specifically in transferring one-carbon fragments, e.g., serine → glycine + 1-C. These transfers can be mediated either by the attachment of the one-carbon unit to either the N^5 or N^{10} position of pteroic acid or by forming a methylene bridge between N^5 and N^{10}. Examples of these are shown on page 229.

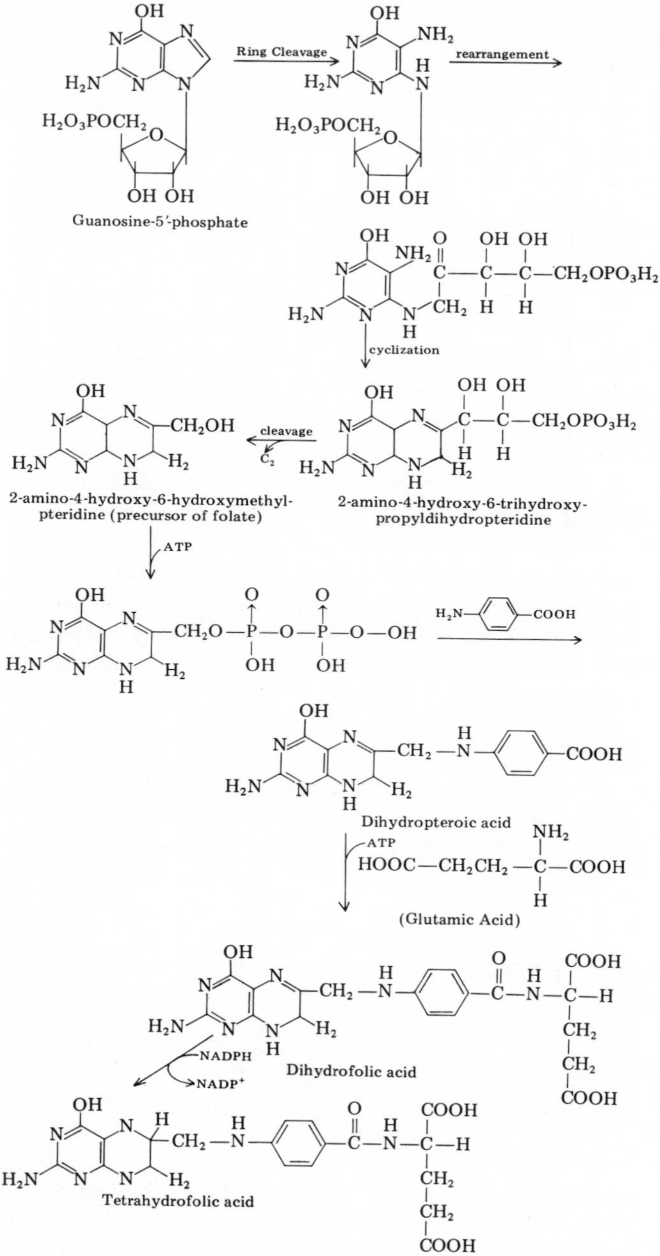

FIG. 8.4. BIOSYNTHESIS OF TETRAHYDROFOLIC ACID

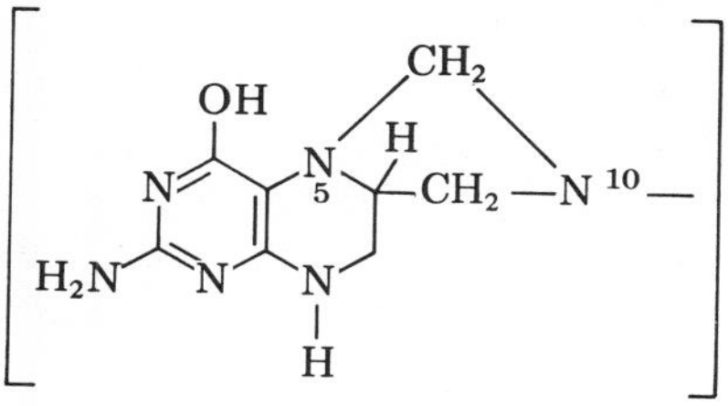

FH₄—N⁵,N¹⁰-Methylene

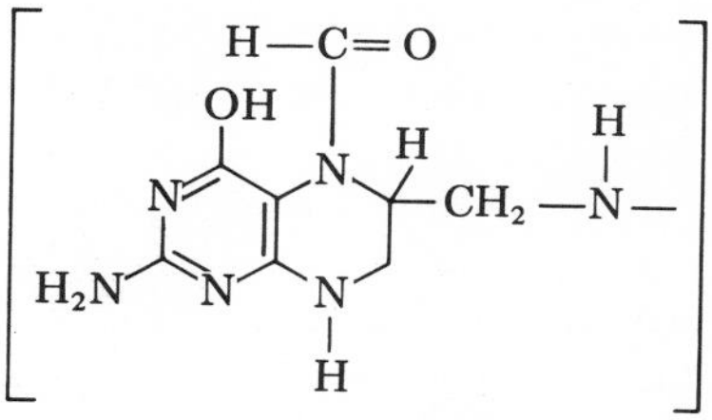

FH₄—N⁵-Formyl

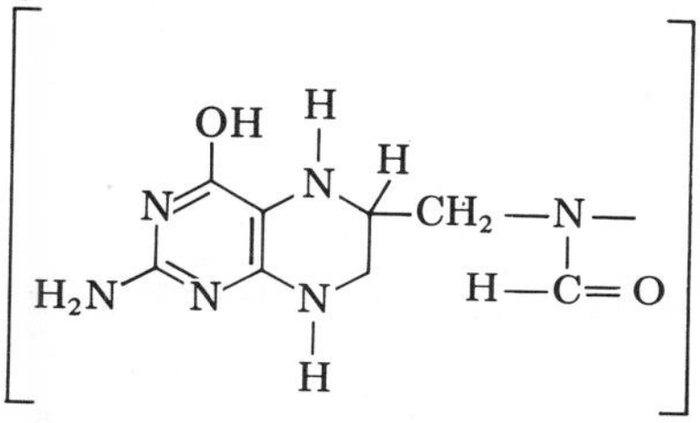

FH₄—N¹⁰-Formyl

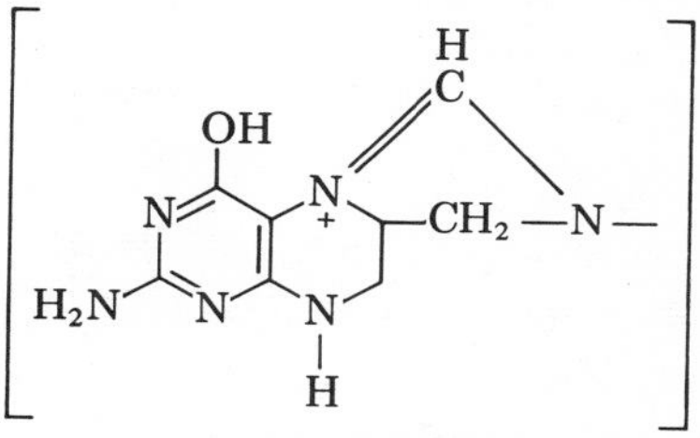

FH₄—N⁵,N¹⁰-Methenyl

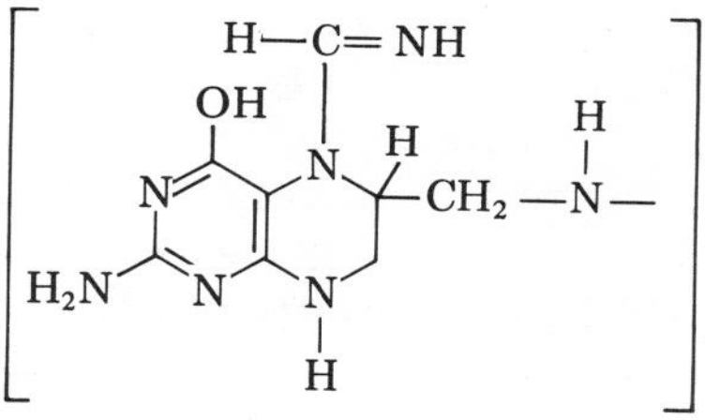

FH₄—N⁵-Formimino

An example of the removal of a one-carbon unit is shown in the degradation of serine to glycine. FH_4 + serine → glycine + FH_4 - N^5, N^{10} methylene.

A deficiency of folacin causes certain anemias, which are characterized by large erythrocytes in the peripheral blood and the accumulation in the bone marrow of immature red blood cells (megaloblasts). Dietary deficiencies of folacin are difficult to produce, since intestinal bacteria synthesize folacin. A deficiency can be induced experimentally through use of inhibitory analogs such as aminopterin and amethopterin. These analogs interfere with the biosynthesis of many tissue constituents; thus, this activity is utilized in the treatment of some leukemias.

Folacin deficiency may arise from inadequate dietary intake, malabsorption, excessive demands by the tissues of the body (pregnancy and lactation), and metabolic derangements. Manifestations of a deficiency include glossitis (a sore, red, smooth tongue), diarrhea, gastrointestinal disturbances, and anemia. In man the anemias of pellagra, sprue, and pregnancy often improve when folacin is administered.

Recommended Dietary Allowances.—The dietary allowances for the normal adult is 0.4 mg daily. A daily allowance of 0.8 mg is recommended during pregnancy and 0.5 mg during lactation (Table 8.1).

Distribution in Foods.—Excellent sources include liver, dark green leafy vegetables, asparagus, broccoli, dry beans, lentils, soybeans, and yeast; good sources are kidney, lima beans, cabbage, sweet corn, beet greens, bananas, strawberries, and whole wheat products. Meat, tubers, and cereals are fair sources.

Vitamin B_{12} (Cyanocobalamin)

Pernicious anemia was first treated successfully in 1926 by Minot and Murphy through ingestion of large quantities of liver or by taking a specially prepared liver extract. In 1929, Castle suggested that two factors were necessary to restore normal cell count in a pernicious-anemia patient. He designated the factor in normal gastric juice as the intrinsic factor (a mucoprotein secreted in the stomach) and that in food as an extrinsic factor. Purification procedures of the extrinsic factor were restricted because of the minute amounts in foods and the necessity of using humans as a method of assay. Shorb observed that a growth factor for *Lactobacillus lactis* in purified liver extracts could be correlated with antipernicious anemia activity. This observation led to the isolation of this factor (B_{12}) from liver extract.

General Properties.—Vitamin B_{12} is a slightly water-soluble, dark red crystalline compound that is labile to strong acids, and alkalies, and to light. This vitamin contains a porphyrin nucleus and the heavy metal, cobalt (Fig. 8.5). Cyanide is an artifact of isolation. The coenzyme form of B_{12} has a 5-deoxyandenosyl group attached to the cobalt through the 5'-methylene group. This replaces the cyanide of the well-known cyanocobalamin. Vitamin B_{12} is not a single substance but consists of several closely related compounds with similar activity. In contrast to most of the B vitamins, vitamin B_{12} is not generally synthesized by higher plants; some microorganisms require it for growth.

Function.—One specific reaction of the B_{12} coenzyme is the isomerization of methylmalonyl CoA to succinyl CoA. This reaction is important in the utilization of odd-number fatty acids that ultimately yield propionyl-SCoA via β-oxidation. The synthesis of methionine from homocysteine is catalyzed by another of the coenzyme forms

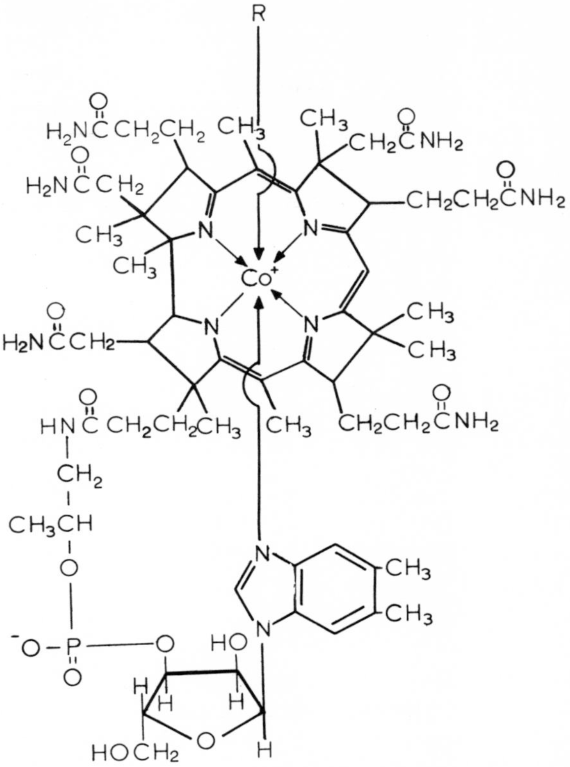

FIG. 8.5. VITAMIN B_{12}

R = cyanide; cyanocobalamin.   R = 5'-deoxyadenosyl (via
5' methylene); coenzyme form of cobalamin.

of B_{12}. It is essential also for the normal functioning of all cells but particularly those of the bone marrow, the nervous system, and the gastrointestinal tract.

The symptoms of a vitamin B_{12} deficiency are the same as those for pernicious anemia. It is characterized by macrocytic anemia, glossitis, degenerative lesions in the spinal cord and peripheral nerves, and achlorhydria (no HCl in gastric juice).

A deficiency is due primarily to a failure of absorption of the vitamin from the intestinal tract in the absence of intrinsic factor in the gastric juice rather than a dietary inadequacy. Persons who subsist on a strict vegetarian diet may show low blood serum levels of the vitamin but anemia is uncommon. Pernicious anemia may occur in persons who have had surgical removal of the stomach, who are infected with the fish tape worm, and who are suffering from malabsorption syndromes, such as sprue.

Recommended Dietary Allowances.—The daily allowance recommended by the Food and Nutrition Board, National Research Council is 5 μg/day. Average American diets are believed to meet these allowances (Table 8.1).

Distribution in Foods.—Vitamin B_{12} occurs in animal protein foods. The best sources are liver and kidney. Other sources include muscle meat, fish, oysters, milk, cheese, and eggs. Plant tissues are devoid of this vitamin.

Choline

There is some question as to whether or not choline should be classified as a vitamin because a deficiency cannot be produced in animals receiving a diet adequate in protein. It is synthesized in the body by transmethylation involving methionine, folic acid, vitamin B_{12}, betaine, and certain other compounds.

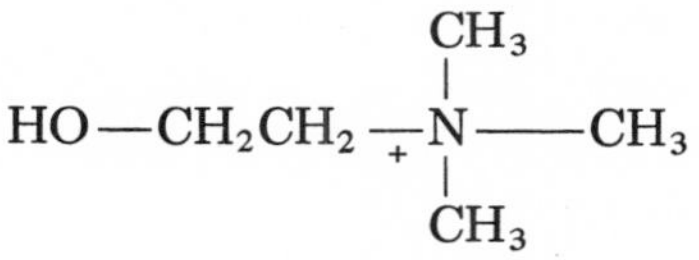

$$HO—CH_2CH_2 \overset{+}{—N} \overset{\displaystyle CH_3}{\underset{\displaystyle CH_3}{|}} —CH_3$$

Choline
(trimethylaminoethanol)

Choline functions in the body as a source of labile methyl groups and in the formation of phospholipids. Choline is an important constituent of acetylcholine, which functions in the transmission of nerve impulses.

Though choline deficiency has not been demonstrated in man, some evidence suggests that it may prevent fatty infiltration of the liver.

The richest known source of choline is egg yolk. Other good sources are liver, kidney, lean meat, yeast, skim milk, soybeans, beans, peas, and wheat germ. The average diet contains 250 to 600 mg/day, an amount known to be adequate when compared to animal requirements.

Ascorbic Acid (Vitamin C)

Scurvy is a disease that has been known and described for several centuries. At one time it was prevalent during famines and wars. Sailors on a long voyage were commonly affected with this disease. It is now known that insufficient fresh fruits and vegetables, which supply vitamin C, was the causal factor. Even with the modern knowledge of dietary essentials, there is evidence that subclinical scurvy is fairly prevalent in our society.

General Properties.—Ascorbic acid is a white, water-soluble, crystalline compound. It is reasonably stable in acid solution but sensitive to oxidation, which is accelerated by alkalies, iron and copper salts, heat, oxidative enzymes, air, and light. L-Ascorbic is the physiologically active compound. It readily loses two of its hydrogen atoms to form L-dehydroascorbic acid. Reactions between these two forms are reversible but further oxidation of the latter to L-ketogulonic acid results in an irreversible physiological activity.

Biosynthesis.—Plants and all mammals except man, monkey, and the guinea pig have the ability to synthesize ascorbic acid. Experiments have shown that the administration of uniformly labelled glucose will result in a uniformly labelled ascorbic acid. On the basis of these studies, the major steps in the synthesis of L-ascorbic acid in animals appear to be those indicated in Fig. 8.6. D-Galactose can also serve as a precursor in the synthesis of ascorbic acid. Interestingly, the L-hexose sugars, which closely resemble L-ascorbic acid, do not serve as precursors. Animals that do not have the enzyme necessary to convert L-gulonolactone to 3-keto-L-gulonolactone, need L-ascorbic as an essential dietary constituent.

Function and Effects of Deficiency.—All of the biochemical functions of vitamin C are not well-established; although its reversible oxidation of L-ascorbic acid to L-dehydroascorbic acid suggests that it plays some part in oxidation-reduction reactions in the body. This vitamin participates in the oxidative degradation of tyrosine (*p*-hydroxyphenylpyruvic acid to homogentisic acid) and in the conversion of folacin to the biologically active folinic acid. Ascorbic acid does not appear to be required as a specific cofactor in either process. However, a copper-containing enzyme, dopamine hydroxylase, which converts 3,4-dihydroxyphenylethylamine to norepinephrine, requires ascorbate as a necessary co-substrate.

Ascorbic acid enhances the absorption of iron from the intestinal tract, participates in the mobilization of iron reserves and in electron transport, and promotes wound healing, which involves the formation of new connective tissue by conversion of proline to hydroxyproline in the synthesis of collagen and elastin.

Ascorbic acid is essential for the formation and maintenance of the intercellular substance that binds together the cells of bone, teeth, blood capillary walls, and cartilage.

The disease which results from a deficiency of vitamin C in the diet is known as scurvy. In human beings the development of the disease is slow. In the early stages, the individual becomes lazy, loses

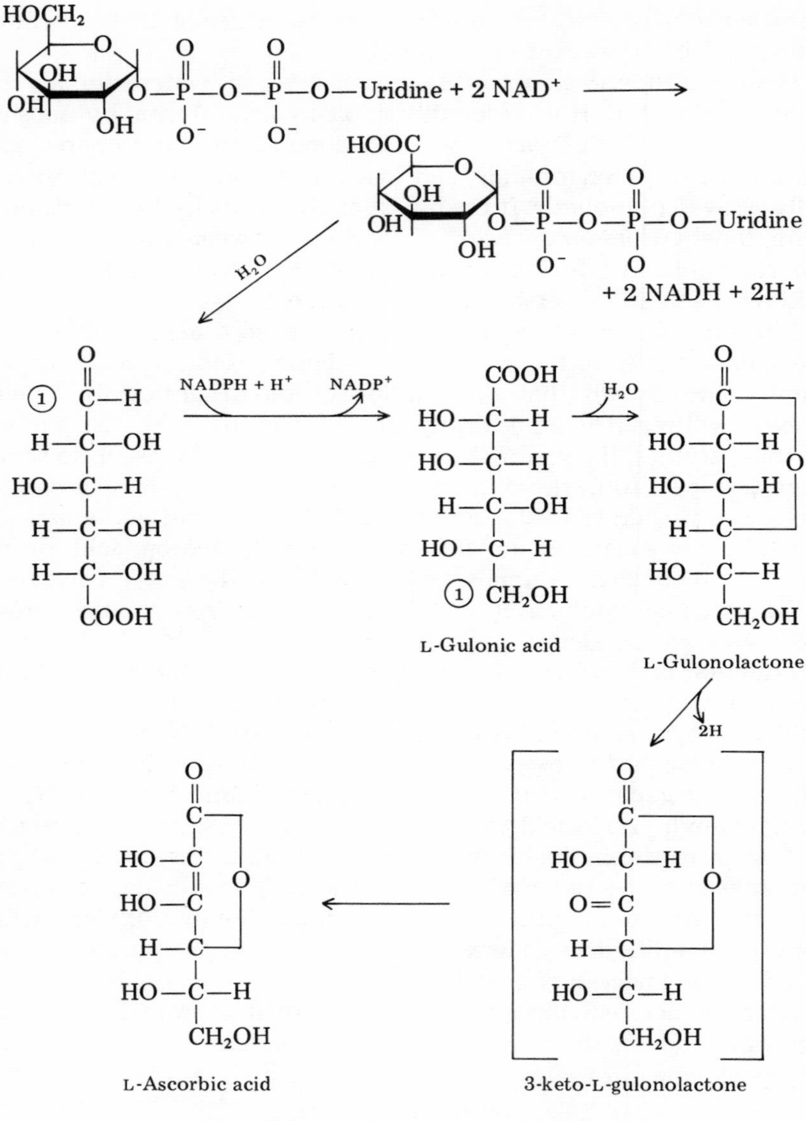

FIG. 8.6. BIOSYNTHESIS OF L-ASCORBIC ACID

appetite, and develops anemia. Later the gums become sore, bleed, and the teeth loosen. There may be pain in the muscles and joints. Subcutaneous hemorrhages are characteristic of the disease and death is sometimes due to internal bleeding.

Recommended Dietary Allowances.—Recommendations for daily dietary allowances are: 60 mg for the adult male; 55 mg for the adult female, except during pregnancy and lactation, when allowances are 60 mg; 40 mg for children, and 35 mg for infants (see Table 8.1).

Distribution in Foods.—The outstanding sources of vitamin C are citrus fruits (oranges, lemons, limes, and grapefruit), fresh fruits, and green leafy vegetables. Tomatoes, cabbage, cauliflower, broccoli, and Brussels sprouts provide liberal quantities of ascorbic acid. Potatoes, green beans, peas, and apples are important sources of the vitamin because of the quantities consumed.

The vitamin content of fruits and vegetables varies with the conditions under which they are grown, stored, and processed. For example, the amount of sunlight available during ripening will affect the ascorbic acid content. During processing there is considerable loss in the vitamin content due to cutting, bruising, and prolonged storage at room temperatures. Freezing and frozen storage results in little loss of the vitamin; whereas washing, blanching, and canning causes loss of the vitamin. Because the ascorbic acid is readily oxidized when exposed to air and is easily leached in water, further losses during the cooking of food can be reduced by cooking in a minimum amount of water in a covered container.

FAT-SOLUBLE VITAMINS

Members of this group of dietary essentials are characterized as being soluble in fat and fat solvents. They are found in nature closely associated with tissues that store fat. Therefore, intakes in excess of daily requirements are stored in the body and it is not necessary to have these accessory food factors in the diet every day. Deficiencies due to inadequate intake of these accessory food factors are slow to develop.

Vitamin A

Vitamin A was the first fat-soluble vitamin to be recognized. In 1913 Osborne and Mendel and McCollum and Davis discovered that rats grew normally on diets containing either butterfat or ether extract of egg yolk but failed to grow when lard was the only source of fat. By 1916, McCollum and his associates established that vitamin A was the growth-promoting factor, which is found only in certain animal tissues. The ultimate source of all vitamin A are carotenoids (alpha, beta, and gamma carotenes), which are converted by animals into vitamin A. It occurs naturally in several different forms.

Structurally, vitamin A consists of a beta-ionone ring carrying two isoprene units. Note that vitamin A has a *trans* configuration.

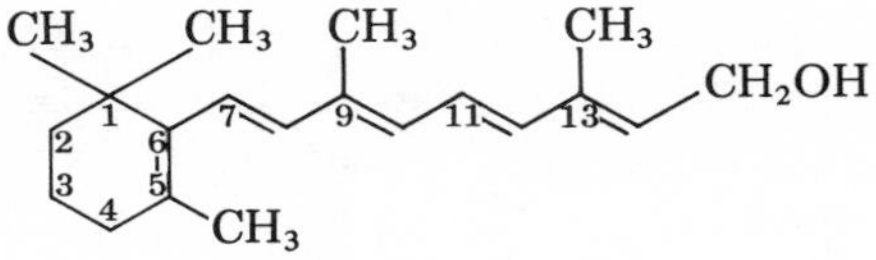

Retinol (vitamin A₁)
All-*trans* configuration

A precursor, therefore, must include this structure and the β-ionone ring.

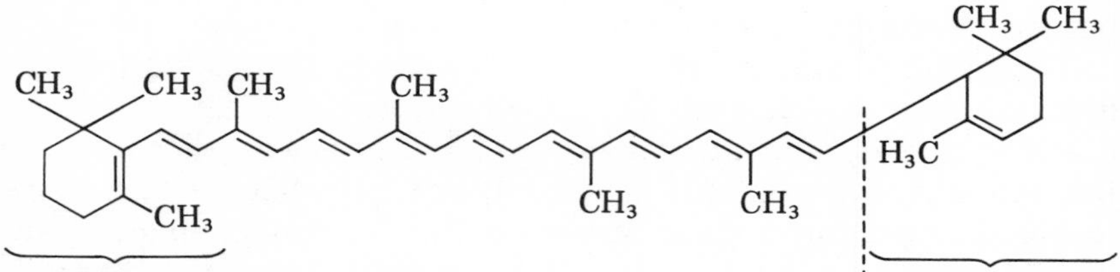

β-Ionone ring   α-Carotene   α-Ionone ring

R

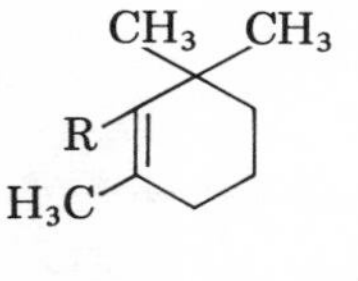

β-Carotene 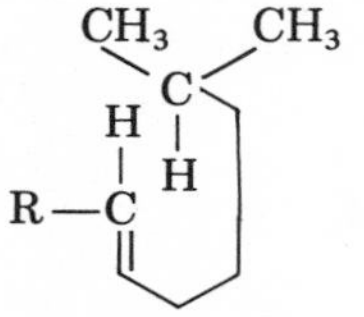   γ-Carotene 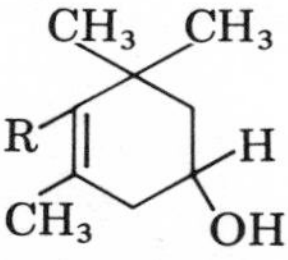   Cryptoxanthin

Beta-carotene is structurally a double molecule of vitamin A but this symmetrical molecule is only one-half as active as vitamin A. Thus, it is degraded *in vivo* with the formation of only one molecule of vitamin A.

General Properties.—Vitamin A crystals form pale yellow prisms that are alcohol and fat soluble. Vitamin A is susceptible to oxidation and autoxidizes very readily. It is heat stable in an inert atmosphere and readily stabilized by the addition of antioxidants such as alpha-tocopherol (vitamin E) and hydroquinone. The vitamin is destroyed by exposure to ultraviolet light.

Biosynthesis.—The distribution of carbon atoms in vitamin A and carotene suggests that the synthesis of those molecules involves the polymerization of isoprenoid units. In plants the biosynthesis of carotene begins with mevalonic acid to form isopentenyl pyrophosphate, which in turn serves as the building units for the carotenes (Fig. 8.7). In the human, conversion of ingested carotene to vitamin

A takes place primarily in the cells of the intestinal mucosa. The scheme is as follows:

$$\beta\text{-carotene} \xrightarrow{\text{oxidation}} \text{retinal} \xrightarrow{\text{reduction}} \text{retinol (vitamin A)}$$

Ingested vitamin A is usually in the form of retenyl esters, which are hydrolyzed in the intestine, reesterified to palmitate, transported with the chylomicra and stored in the liver.

Function and Effects of Deficiency.—The complete biochemical role of vitamin A in the body has not been elucidated. Its role as a precursor of visual pigments is best understood. The ultimate fate of this vitamin and its derivatives is not known.

Vitamin A plays an important part in vision. A specific vitamin A aldehyde (11-*cis*-retinal) in combination with a specific protein (opsin) forms the visual pigment rhodopsin. The retinal forms a Schiff base with the ε-amino of lysine residue of opsin. On exposure to light, rhodopsin is converted to *trans* retinal and opsin, which is accompanied by bleaching. *Trans* retinal is converted to 11-*cis* retinal by a specific isomerase. In the dark, the enzyme equilibrium favors the *trans* form and, thus, some mechanism exists for the accumulation of 11-*cis* isomer. Rhodopsin is regenerated by the reaction of 11-*cis* retinal with opsin. The sequence of events in the visual cycle is summarized as follows:

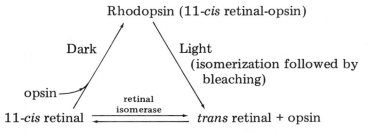

A vitamin A deficient diet leads to an impairment of adaptation to subdued light following exposure to bright light. This condition is known as night blindness, a measurement of which is a common method for evaluating vitamin A requirements in man. In later stages of a vitamin A deficiency the mucous membranes lose their power of secreting moisture, the eyelids become inflamed, and secondary infection usually follows. Finally blindness results. This is commonly referred to as xerophthalmia which means "dry eyes."

Vitamin A is essential for the integrity of the epithelial tissues of the body. Deficiency of the vitamin results in a stratified, keratinized epithelium; i.e., the epithelial cells become hard and scaly.

These changes may occur in the alimentary, respiratory, and genito-urinary tracts, as well as in the epidermis.

Vitamin A is necessary for normal growth and development. The vitamin functions in the maintenance of bone growth, in particular the activity of the osteoblasts. Bones fail to grow in length. An inadequate intake of the vitamin also causes defective formation of the enamel of the teeth, with consequent degeneration of the teeth.

This vitamin functions in the maintenance of spermatogenesis in the male and fetal resorption in the female.

It is involved in the synthesis of corticosterone from cholesterol in the adrenal cortex. Thus, it is required for the synthesis of glycogen.

Recommended Dietary Allowances.—The recommended daily allowances range from 1500 International Units (IU) for infants to

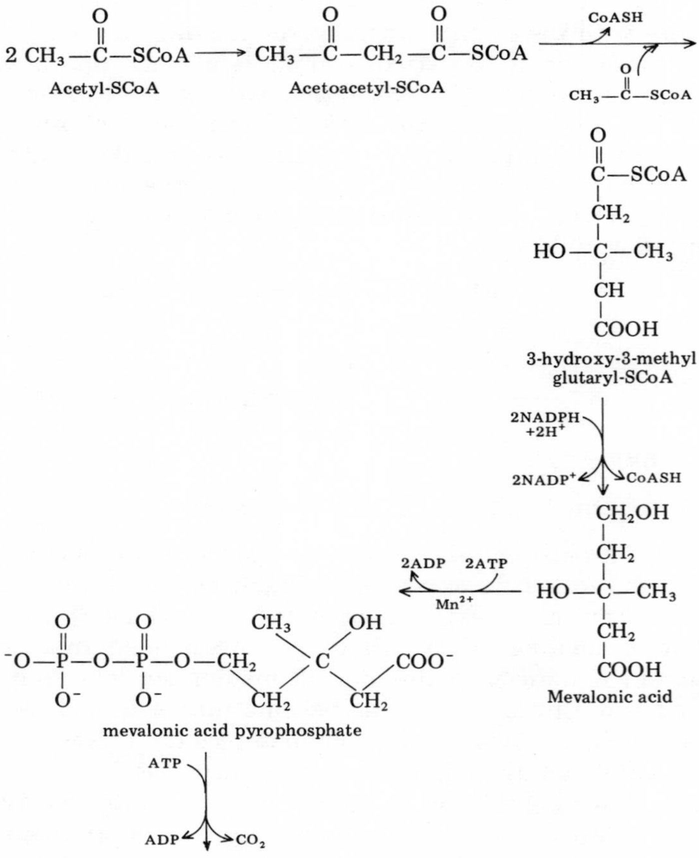

FIG. 8.7 (Continued)

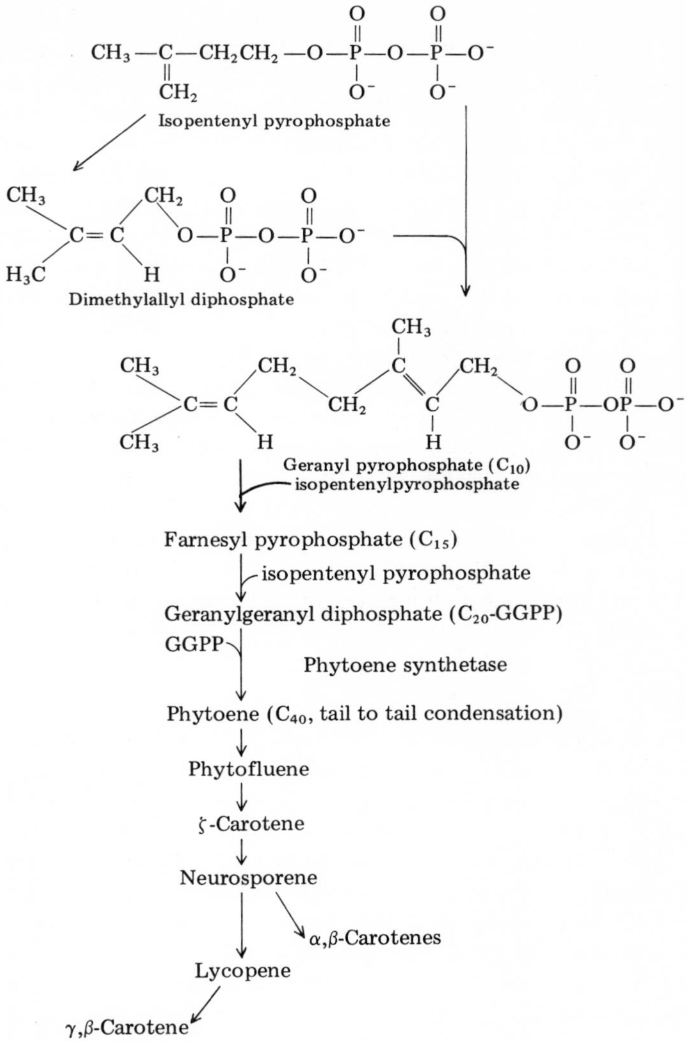

$$CH_3-\overset{\underset{\displaystyle \|}{\displaystyle CH_2}}{C}-CH_2CH_2-O-\overset{\overset{\displaystyle O}{\displaystyle \|}}{\underset{\underset{\displaystyle O^-}{\displaystyle |}}{P}}-O-\overset{\overset{\displaystyle O}{\displaystyle \|}}{\underset{\underset{\displaystyle O^-}{\displaystyle |}}{P}}-O^-$$

Isopentenyl pyrophosphate

$$\underset{H_3C}{\overset{CH_3}{\diagdown}}C=\underset{H}{\overset{CH_2}{C}} \quad O-\overset{\overset{O}{\|}}{\underset{\underset{O^-}{|}}{P}}-O-\overset{\overset{O}{\|}}{\underset{\underset{O^-}{|}}{P}}-O^-$$

Dimethylallyl diphosphate

$$\underset{CH_3}{\overset{CH_3}{\diagdown}}C=\underset{H}{\overset{CH_2}{C}}\cdots\underset{CH_2}{\overset{CH_3}{\underset{C}{|}}}\cdots\underset{H}{\overset{CH_2}{C}}\cdots O-\overset{\overset{O}{\|}}{\underset{\underset{O^-}{|}}{P}}-O\overset{\overset{O}{\|}}{P}-O^-$$

Geranyl pyrophosphate (C_{10})
— isopentenylpyrophosphate

Farnesyl pyrophosphate (C_{15})

— isopentenyl pyrophosphate

Geranylgeranyl diphosphate (C_{20}-GGPP)

GGPP —

Phytoene synthetase

Phytoene (C_{40}, tail to tail condensation)

Phytofluene

ζ-Carotene

Neurosporene

α,β-Carotenes

Lycopene

γ,β-Carotene

FIG. 8.7. BIOSYNTHESIS OF CAROTENES

5000 IU for adults. (One IU is equivalent to 0.3 μg retinol, or 0.6 μg of pure beta-carotene). Recommendations for pregnancy are 6000 IU, and for lactation are 8000 IU (see Table 8.1).

Excessive intakes (50,000 to 100,000 IU) of vitamin A, over time, are likely to result in vitamin A toxicity. Resulting symptoms include bone decalcification, skeletal pain in infants, loss of hair, nausea, headache, and hyperirritability. The availability of vitamin A supplements often results in the use of excessive amounts of the vitamin in the diet. This, coupled with the increasing practice of adding the vitamin to various food products, increases the possibility of a person receiving excessive dietary amounts. The possibility of hypervitaminosis (excessive amounts) occurring in a normal diet is remote.

Among factors affecting amounts of the vitamin needed in the diet are dietary fat, which is needed for absorption of vitamin A; vitamin E, which protects carotene and vitamin A against oxidation; adequate bile secretion, which is essential for the absorption of the vitamin; consumption of laxatives, especially mineral oils, which reduce the absorption of the vitamin; and protein malnutrition, which decreases intestinal absorption of vitamin A.

Distribution in Foods.—Plants do not contain the vitamin. Foods of plant origin contain carotene, the precursor of vitamin A. Excellent sources of carotene include carrots, sweet potatoes, dark green leafy vegetables, winter squash, broccoli, apricots, and pumpkin. Yellow corn is the only cereal grain that makes significant contribution of carotene to the diet. Foods that are excellent sources of vitamin A include whole milk, cheese made of whole milk, butter, enriched margarine, eggs, liver, glandular organs, and fish-liver oils (cod and halibut).

Vitamin D

General Properties.—Vitamin D is a term used to describe a group of similar compounds. Chemically there are 11 sterols having vitamin D activity, but the 2 of greatest importance are vitamin D_2 (calciferol) and vitamin D_3 (activated cholesterol). Ergosterol (provitamin D_2 and 7-dehydrocholesterol (provitamin D_3), upon irradiation with ultraviolet light, give rise to antirachitic vitamins. In plants, ergosterol is the predominant provitamin. Vitamin D_3, the form of vitamin contained in most fish liver oils, is the form produced by the action of sunlight on the 7-dehydrocholesterol in the skin. The transformation of the provitamins to vitamins when irradiated are as follows:

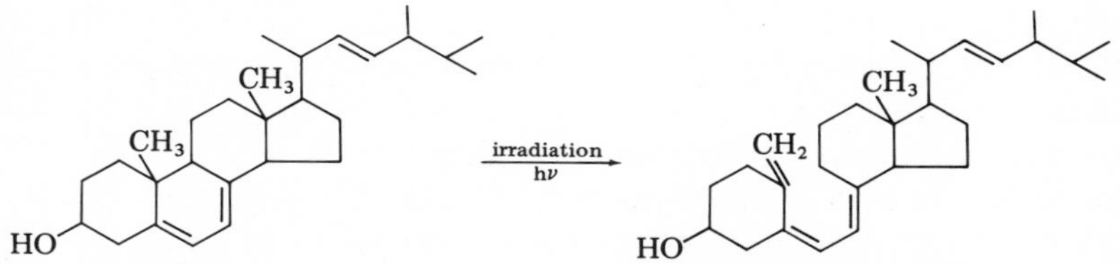

Ergosterol $\xrightarrow[h\nu]{\text{irradiation}}$ Ergo-calciferol (Vitamin D_3)

7-Dehydrocholesterol   irradiation $h\nu$ Cholecalciferol (Vitamin D_3)

The vitamin, being fat-soluble, is absorbed from the intestines along with the lipids. Consequently, conditions interfering with the absorption of fats will also reduce the absorption of vitamin D.

Vitamin D is relatively stable to heat and air oxidation, although prolonged exposure to light may cause some destruction.

Biosynthesis.—The biosynthesis of vitamin D is quite similar to the biosynthesis of vitamin A; i.e., isopentenyl pyrophosphate serves as the building units for both vitamins (see vitamin A). Farnesyl pyrophosphate (C_{15}) condenses (head-to-head) to form squalene (C_{30}). The final steps of the biosynthetic process involves cyclization of squalene to form lanosterol (C_{30}) (Fig. 8.8). Lanosterol is then converted to 7-dehydrocholesterol.

Functions and Effects of Deficiency.—Vitamin D is essential at all ages to maintain calcium homeostasis and skeletal integrity. It is necessary for the absorption and utilization of calcium and phosphorous. A deficiency of this vitamin causes decreased intestinal absorption of calcium and phosphate; increased excretion of phosphate by the kidney; reduced blood calcium levels (hypocalcemia) and a failure to mobilize bone calcium; increases in the level of alkaline phosphatase in the blood; and decreased concentrations of citrate and other Krebs' cycle components in body fluids.

The fact that there is a delay between the administration of vitamin D and a reversal of the physiologic changes which occur in a vitamin D deficiency led to research that suggested the vitamin was metabolically converted to more active forms. Recent research has led to the isolation and identification of a biologically active metabolite, 25-hydrocholecalciferol (De Luca 1969).

The principal manifestation of vitamin D deficiency in the young is rickets. In adults, manifested especially in pregnant and lactating women, the disease is known as osteomalacia.

Rickets is essentially a disturbance of calcium-phosphorus metabolism which results in a deficient calcification of bones. Dental structures are also affected, but to a lesser degree than bone. The disease may be manifested by bowed legs, knock-knees, or enlarged joints. Malformation of the rib cage is another clinical symptom of

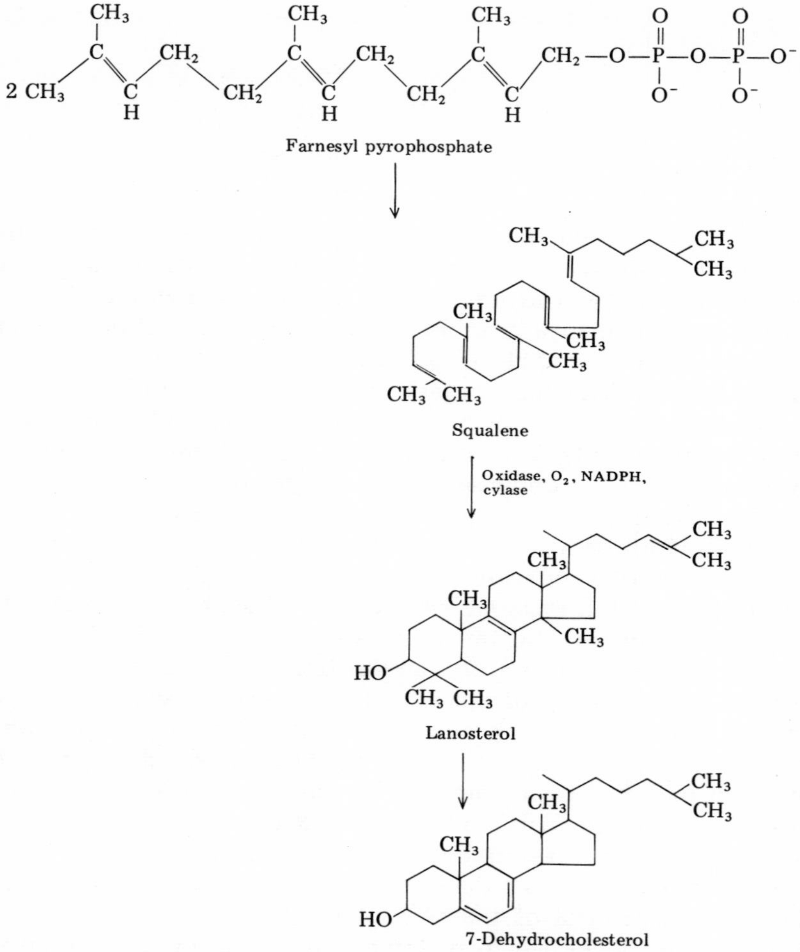

FIG. 8.8. BIOSYNTHESIS OF 7-DEHYDROCHOLESTEROL

the disease. The amounts of calcium and phosphorus in the diet, the availability of these elements, and their ratio to each other are additional factors involved in the incidence and severity of the disease. Inasmuch as ultraviolet rays of the sun are involved in the production of vitamin D activity in the skin, environmental factors such as climate, season, mode of living, smoke, and fog may be correlated with the incidence of rickets.

Recommended Dietary Allowances.—Although vitamin D can be synthesized in the body, it is a dietary essential and must be supplied in the diet. The recommended daily allowance for the vitamin is 400

IU per day. One IU of vitamin D is equivalent to 0.025 µg of ergocalciferol.

Excessive amounts of vitamin D (1000–2000 IU/kg/day) are usually toxic to children and adults, and may lead to the development of hypercalcemia. Adults receiving 50,000 IU per day will show symptoms of toxicity. These symptoms include anorexia, vomiting, diarrhea, and loss of weight. Serum calcium and phosphorus levels are raised and various organs of the body are susceptible to calcium deposits.

Distribution in Foods.—Most natural foods contain either little or negligible amounts of vitamin D. The best food sources are salt water fishes (sardines, herring, mackerel, and tuna) which are high in body oils. Fish-liver oils are rich sources, but they are used primarily in medicinal preparations. Egg yolk, vitamin D fortified foods such as milk, and some breads and breakfast cereals are good sources of vitamin D.

Vitamin E (α-Tocopherol)

Vitamin E, established as a dietary essential in 1922 by Evans and Bishop, was found to be necessary for reproduction in rats. Thus, the vitamin became known as the "antisterility factor." There is, however, no evidence that vitamin E has any effect on human reproduction.

General Properties.—The tocopherols occur as light-yellow viscous oily liquids. The naturally occurring isomers are the α-forms while the synthetic product is a racemic mixture. They are insoluble in water, but soluble in fats and fat solvents. Vitamin E is not destroyed by acid, alkali, the process of hydrogenation, or by high temperatures, but is oxidized slowly by air and rapidly in the presence of rancid fats or iron salts. Decomposition occurs in the presence of ultraviolet light.

Vitamin E exists in several forms, α-, β-, γ-, and δ-tocopherols, all of which have been isolated from natural sources. The α-form is the most active and the only one shown to be essential in the human diet.

Chemically, the tocopherols are derivatives of chromane.

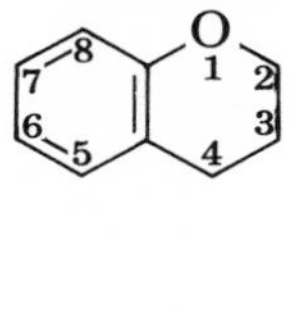

Their general formula is:

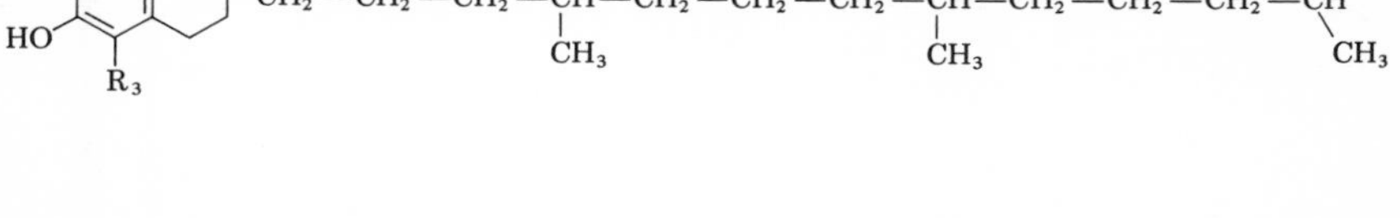

The distinction of the different forms is indicated by the following:

α-tocopherol R_1, R_2, R_3 = CH_3
β-tocopherol R_1, R_3 = CH_3 and R_2 = H
γ-tocopherol R_1, R_2 = CH_3 and R_3 = H
δ-tocopherol R_1 = CH_3 and R_2, R_3 = H

α-Tocopherol, with three methyl groups on the chroman ring, exhibits considerably greater biological activity as compared with its β, γ, and δ homologs. The relative biological activity of β- and γ-tocopherols is 25 and 19, respectively. δ-Tocopherol has little biological activity. Thus, it appears that for optimal activity three methyl groups on the ring are essential; however, it is the hydroxyl group on the chroman ring which is essential for vitamin E activity.

Function and Effects of Deficiency.—A specific function of vitamin E in human metabolism has not been clearly established. The most important recognized role of vitamin E is its antioxidant effect on dietary unsaturated fat and vitamin A. Tests with oxidizing agents such as hydrogen peroxide have indicated that vitamin E protects red blood cells against hemolysis. Vitamin E appears to have a definite correlation with polyunsaturated fatty acid (PUFA) metabolism, especially linoleic acid, in the body. One study indicated that the vitamin E requirement could be directly correlated with the amount of polyunsaturated fatty acids in the diet (Horwit 1960). Consequently, as the intake of polyunsaturated fats increase in the diet, the need for vitamin E may increase. Selenium, chromenols, and certain antioxidants function as a partial substitute for the vitamin. Additional research is needed to determine whether or not vitamin E requirements be increased.

Recommended Dietary Allowances.—Although the biological role of vitamin E in animals is still unsolved, it is clearly an essential dietary nutrient. The Food and Nutrition Board recommended in 1968 daily dietary allowances ranging from 5 IU for infants to 30 IU for adult males and for pregnant and lactating females (see Table 8.1). These allowances are based on size, i.e., the recommended allowance is the body weight in kilograms times 1.25. Hence, there is a gradual increase in requirement throughout the period of growth to maturity.

Toxicity symptoms have not been reported for high intakes of the vitamin.

Distribution in Foods.—Tocopherols occur in greatest concentrations in vegetable oils of which soybean oil is the richest. Dark green leaves, nuts, and the oil found in the germs of cereal grains, especially wheat germ oil, are excellent sources. Eggs, margarine, liver, and dry navy beans are good sources.

Vitamin K

Vitamin K is known as the antihemorrhagic vitamin because it promotes blood coagulation. In 1929, Dam observed that newly hatched chicks developed a fatal hemorrhagic disease when raised on a ration adequate in all known vitamins and dietary essentials. The factor missing from the diet was present in the unsaponifiable non-sterol fraction of hog liver and of alfalfa. In 1935, the same investigator showed that the antihemorrhagic factor was associated with a decrease in the prothrombin concentration in the blood.

Subsequent research led to the isolation and identification of vitamin K in 1939. There are at least two naturally occurring substances, vitamin K_1 and K_2, which are capable of preventing hemorrhagic diathesis due to lowered prothrombin levels. Vitamin K_1 was isolated from alfalfa and K_2 was isolated from fish meal. Both substances are naphthoquinone derivatives:

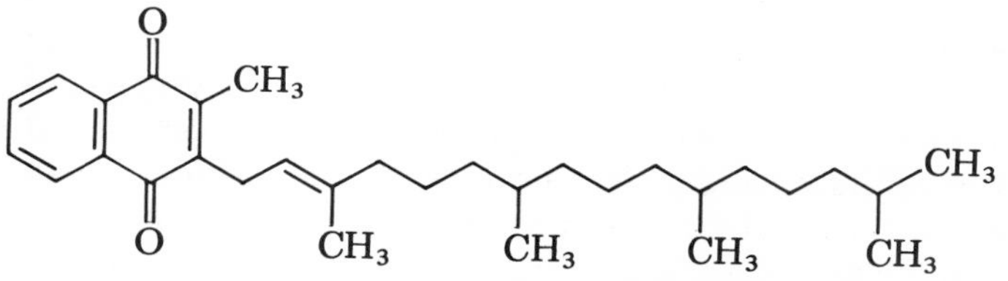

Vitamin K_1 (2-methyl-3-phytyl-1,4-naphthoquinone)

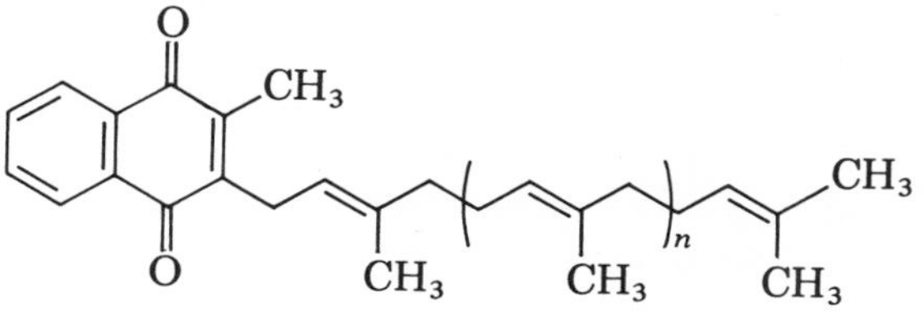

Vitamin K_2 (n = 4, 6, 7 or 8)

Many related compounds also have vitamin K activity. A synthetic compound, 2-methyl-1,4-naphthoquinone (menadione), is more potent than the natural vitamin K. Menadione, the principal form of the vitamin used for clinical purposes, is used as the reference standard for measurement of vitamin K activity.

General Properties.—Vitamin K is fat soluble, relatively stable to heat, oxygen, and moisture, but is destroyed by sunlight and alkalies. There is little or no destruction of the vitamin during food processing.

Biosynthesis.—The metabolic pathways for the synthesis of the vitamin is not known. However, it appears the vitamin is synthesized in a manner similar to vitamins A and E, i.e., mevalonic acid → isopentenyl pyrophosphate → C_{20} unit.

Function and Effects of Deficiency.—The exact biochemical function of vitamin K is not known. However, a well-established symptom of vitamin K deficiency is defective blood coagulation; more specifically, vitamin K is required to maintain normal plasma levels of prothrombin and three other clotting factors (VII, IX, and X). A reduction of any of these four factors, presumably all proteins, may be used to measure the action of vitamin K.

Recent findings indicate that vitamin K may participate in oxidative phosphorylation and in mitochondrial electron transport.

Absorption of vitamin K is dependent upon the presence of bile salts in the upper intestinal tract. After absorption, it is transported to the liver where it catalyzes the synthesis of prothrombin (factor II). Consequently, any disease or injury that obstructs the flow of bile, or damages the liver in such a manner that synthesis of prothrombin is inhibited will cause a reduction in prothrombin. Since the blood clotting process depends on the conversion of fibrinogen to fibrin by the action of thrombin, the active form of prothrombin, decreased prothrombin formation will increase clotting time.

Recommended Dietary Allowances.—The average balanced diet apparently contains adequate amounts of the vitamin. Therefore, no requirement is stated because a deficiency of vitamin K is unlikely. Therapeutic dosages of 2 mg of menadione injected intravenously will correct a vitamin K deficiency. Microgram amounts are required to prevent a decrease in blood clotting factors that usually take place in the blood of the newborn infant; this can be accomplished by administering a prophylactic dose of vitamin K to the infant soon after delivery. Excessive doses of the synthetic vitamin, menadione, causes toxic symptoms (kernicterus) in the infant.

Vitamin K and discoumarol are antagonistic. The latter substance, therefore, is used as an anticoagulant which finds application in the treatment of thrombosis.

Distribution in Foods.—Vitamin K is widely distributed in nature. It is found in green, leafy vegetables such as kale, spinach, cabbage, and collards. Pork liver is a very rich source, while eggs and milk contain smaller amounts.

Intestinal bacteria are able to synthesize vitamin K_2, and this is likely the most important source of the vitamin.

BIBLIOGRAPHY

BROCK, J. F. 1961. Recent Advances in Human Nutrition. Little, Brown and Co., Boston.

BURTON, B. T. (Editor). 1965. Heinz Handbook of Nutrition, 2nd Edition. McGraw-Hill Book Co., New York.

COURSIN, D. B. 1954. Convulsive seizures in infants with pyridoxine-deficient diets. J. Am. Med. Assoc. *1954*, 406-408.

DeLUCA, H. F. 1969. Metabolism and function of vitamin D. *In* The Fat-Soluble Vitamins, H. F. DeLuca, and J. W. Suttie (Editors). University of Wisconsin Press, Madison, Wisc.

FOOD AND NUTRITION BOARD. 1968. Recommended Dietary Allowances. National Research Council, National Academy of Sciences Publ. *1694*, Washington, D.C.

GLOVER, J. 1970. Biosynthesis of the fat-soluble vitamins. *In* Fat-Soluble Vitamins, R. A. Morton (Editor). Pergamon Press, London.

GOODWIN, T. W. 1963. The Biosynthesis of Vitamins and Related Compounds. Academic Press, New York.

GYÖRGY, P., and BERNHARDT, W. L., JR. 1968. Biotin: V and VI. *In* The Vitamins, 2nd Edition, Vol. II. W. H. Sebrell, Jr., and R. S. Harris (Editors). Academic Press, New York.

GYÖRGY, P., and PEARSON, W. N. (Editors). 1967. The Vitamins, Vols. VI and VII. Academic Press, New York.

HARDINGE, M. G., and CROOKS, H. 1961. Lesser known vitamins in foods. J. Am. Dietet. Assoc. *38*, 240-245.

HORWIT, M. K. 1960. Vitamin E and lipid metabolism in man. Am. J. Clin. Nutr. *8*, 451-461.

KRAUSE, M. V. 1969. Food, Nutrition and Diet Therapy, 4th Edition. W. B. Saunders Co., Philadelphia.

MEDER, H., and WISS, O. 1968. Vitamin B_6 groups: V. Occurrence in foods. *In* The Vitamins, 2nd Edition, Vol. II. W. H. Sebrell, Jr., and R. S. Harris (Editors). Academic Press, New York.

ROBINSON, F. A. 1966. The Vitamin Co-Factors of Enzyme Systems. Pergamon Press, New York.

ROSENTHAL, H. L. 1968. Vitamin B_{12} groups: V. Occurrence in foods. *In* The Vitamins, 2nd Edition, Vol. II. W. H. Sebrell, Jr., and R. S. Harris (Editors). Academic Press, New York.

SAUBERLICH, H. E. 1968. Vitamin B_6 group: VII. Biosynthesis of vitamin B_6. *In* The Vitamins, 2nd Edition, Vol. II. W. H. Sebrell, Jr., and R. S. Harris (Editors). Academic Press, New York.

SEBRELL, W. H., JR., and HARRIS, R. S. (Editors). 1967. 1968. 1971. The Vitamins, Vols. I, II, and III. Academic Press, New York.

SELBY, M. A., and GREEN, J. 1970. The fortification of human and animal foods with fat soluble vitamins. *In* Fat-Soluble Vitamins, R. A. Morton (Editor). Pergamon Press, London.

U.S. DEPT. OF AGR. Agriculture Handbook *97*, U.S. Department of Agriculture, Government Printing Office, Washington, D.C.

WALD, G., and HUBBARD, R. 1970. The chemistry of vision. *In* Fat-Soluble Vitamins. R. A. Morton (Editor). Pergamon Press, London.

WHITE, A., HANDLER, P., and SMITH, E. L. 1968. Principles of Biochemistry, 4th Edition. McGraw-Hill Book Co., New York.

WINESTOCK, C. H., and PLANT, G. W. E. 1965. The biosynthesis of coenzymes. *In* Plant Biochemistry, J. Bonner, and J. E. Varner (Editors). Academic Press, New York.

WOHL, M. G., and GOODHART, R. S. (Editors). 1960. Modern Nutrition in Health and Disease. Lea & Febiger, Philadelphia.

CHAPTER 9

Minerals in Foods

Although mineral nutrition has been recognized for over 100 yr, intense study on the specific role that minerals occupy in plants and animals (including humans) has taken place only in the last 50 yr. Originally the major elements considered to be of nutritional significance were C, H, O, N, S, P, Ca, K, Na, Cl, Fe, and Mg. Additionally Cu, Mn, Zn, I, Co, No, Ni, Al, Cr, Sn, Ti, Si, Pb, Rb, Li, F, Br, Se, B, Ba, Sr, V, Ag, Au, and Ce were found in variable quantities in tissues and fluids of animals and plants. Recently, metals such as mercury have been found in plants and animals. There are no known biochemical functions for a large number of the so-called trace elements, but if the history of other trace elements can be taken to predict the role of those with unknown functions, one would expect biochemical functions to be attributed to larger numbers of the trace elements. Literature of only a few years ago considered elements such as Cu, Zn, Mn, and Co to be contaminants with no known physiological function.

One of the limiting factors in studying the trace elements has been the lack of suitable analytical techniques to detect the elements, reliably, and even more importantly determining significantly different levels of these elements in tissues and fluids. Techniques such as spark-emission spectroscopy, flame photometry, neutron activation analysis, and especially atomic absorption spectroscopy have greatly facilitated the study of trace elements.

One of the most useful tools to the nutritional physiologist is the tracer isotope. With the radioisotope, specific location and distribution of the element can be determined.

Foodstuffs are the major sources of both major and trace elements for animals. As an example, a detailed analysis of cow's milk has shown that it contains Ca, Mg, K, Na, P, Cl, Fe, Cu, Mn, I, and minute concentrations of Si, B, Ti, V, Rb, Li, Se, Ba, Sr, Cr, Mo, Pb, Ag, Zn, Co, Ni, Al, Sn, As, Br, F, and possibly others. These examples serve to point out that even the simplest of foodstuffs serve as a ready source of both major and minor mineral elements.

A detailed account of the physiological function of each of the elements is of course beyond the scope of this chapter. However, it is hoped that the examples presented will stimulate the reader to examine more closely scholarly works on mineral nutrition, physiology, and metabolism.

METALS

Metal Ion-Ligand Interactions and Their Role in Biochemical Nutrition

The major role that metal ions play in biochemical nutrition is largely ascribable to their associations with molecules, both large and small. These molecules that associate with metals are called ligands. Ligands such as proteins, nucleic acids, amino acids, and others can associate both reversible and irreversibly with the metal. An example of a reversible complex is Mg^{2+} and ATP, and an example of an irreversible complex is heme or the cytochromes and Fe^{2+} or Fe^{3+}. These complexes between the metal and ligand may be divided into three major classes, depending on the number of ligands complexed with metal ion. If the metal binds two ligands, linear or angular geometry would be observed:

angular

L—M—L

linear

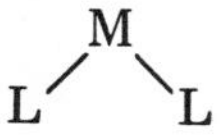

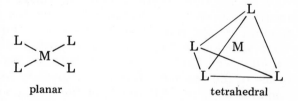

However, if four ligands are bound by a single metal ion, a planar or tetrahedral structure is observed:

planar

tetrahedral

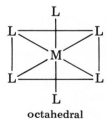

And, if six ligands associate with a metal ion generally an octahedral structure forms:

octahedral

The ability of a metal ion to form a complex is generally in the order:

$$Ca < Mg < Mn < Fe < Co < Cu > Zn$$

The trace elements are observed to have greater abilities to form complexes.

During recent years, investigations on the role of metals in bio-chemical systems have shifted from the gross electrolyte properties to the metal's function in specific biochemical and/or physiological reactions. Typical of such specific functions of cations is the role that magnesium plays in phosphorylation reactions involving adenosine triphosphate. Phosphorylation of glucose by the enzyme glucokinase is an example. This reaction is quite important in the utilization of glucose in intermediary carbohydrate metabolism. Mg^{2+} forms a Mg-ATP complex which functions in the reaction.

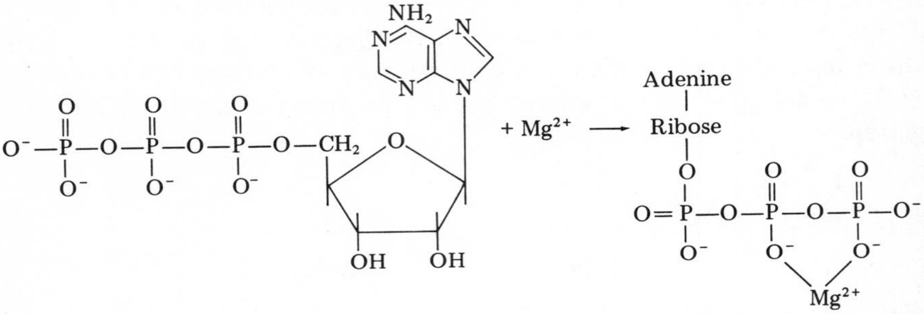

Other important reactions in which magnesium is specifically involved include the enolase reaction where 2-phosphoglycerate and phosphoenol pyruvate are reversibly interconverted, and the essentially irreversible reaction of phosphoenol pyruvate (PEP) conversion to pyruvate by pyruvate kinase. Pyruvate kinase will function quite well with both Mg^{2+} and Mn^{2+}. A complex between the metal ion and the active site of the enzyme is formed. Ultimately a quaternary complex between the enzyme, PEP, ADP, and the metal ion functions in the catalytic conversion. Interestingly, pyruvate kinase is activated by K^+ and NH_4^+ but neither are obligatory. These ions appear to activate the enzyme by combining at a site other than the active site, altering the conformation to yield a protein structure that is catalytically more active.

Calcium ions are antagonistic for the action of Mg^{2+} or Mn^{2+} in the obligatory reaction and Na^+ and Li^+ ions are antagonistic for the activating effect of K^+ or NH_4^+ in the nonobligatory reaction. Quite commonly, antagonistic properties are observed of metal ions of the same charge as the required or activating ion.

The nonequilibrium distribution of alkali cations Na^+ and K^+ with a K^+ concentration inside the plasma membrane greater than that outside, and the reverse for Na^+ is commonly referred to as the K^+/Na^+ pump system. This pump is localized in the plasma membrane of cells and found universally. An enzyme, ATPase, involved in the reaction is sensitive to Na^+ and K^+. The "pump" operates by energy furnished by ATP (which is complexed with Mg^{2+}). Sodium and potassium appear to attach to the membrane protein. This protein undergoes phosphorylation-dephosphorylation, the former requiring Na^+ while the latter requires K^+.

Metalloproteins containing trace metals as well as the more common metals are quite ubiquitous. Dopamine hydroxylase, tyrosinase, laccase, ascorbic acid oxidase, cytochrome oxidase, uricase, δ-aminolevulinic acid dehydrase and mono- and diphenol oxidases require the presence of Cu^{2+} in their function. The Cu^{2+}-protein interaction is typical of transition metals.

Additional examples of metal ion-ligand interactions are vitamin B_{12} (cyanocobalamin) which contains cobalt (Co^+) as an integral part of its structure (the porphyrin-like *corrin* ring) (Fig. 8.5) and the metallo-porphyrin compound, chlorophyll. The metal in chlorophyll is Mg^{2+} (Fig. 10.1).

Other abundant metallo-porphyrin compounds are the iron-porphyrin structures, e.g., ferroprotoporphyrin IX (Fig. 9.1). Hemoglo-

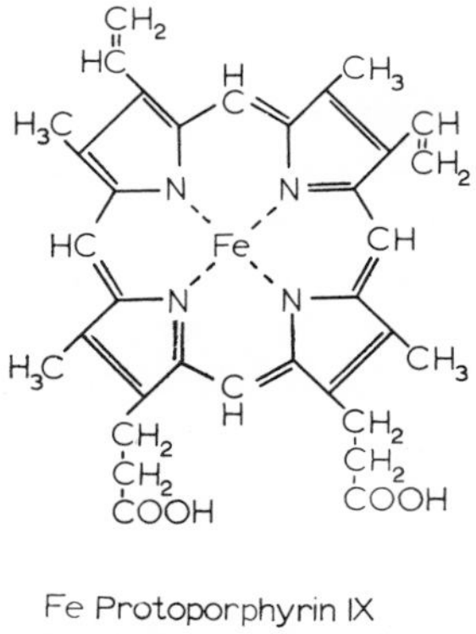

Fe Protoporphyrin IX

FIG. 9.1. Fe PROTOPORPHYRIN IX STRUCTURE

bin of red blood cells, myoglobin of muscle, and the cytochromes of cell mitochondria are typical examples of such compounds. The well-known role of hemoglobin and myoglobin in oxygen transport and the reversible oxidation and reduction of the cytochromes in the oxidation of metabolites in the electron transport system point out their importance.

Zinc has been found to function in the enzyme carboxypeptidase A, which contains one atom of zinc per molecule of enzyme. This enzyme catalyzes the hydrolysis of a peptide bond adjacent to the terminal free carboxyl group. In this reaction, zinc has a specific role in the catalytic process.

Molybdenum is a part of the xanthine dehydrogenase structure (these are also called oxidases when O_2 is used as the electron acceptor). These enzymes can utilize NADH, aldehydes, hypoxanthine, and pteridines as substrates while their electron acceptors can be NAD^+, O_2, dyes, quinones, ferricyanide, nitrate, and cytochrome C. The Mo^{6+} appears to function as both a hydroxyl donor and as an electron acceptor. Hepatic aldehyde oxidase (xanthine oxidase) reaction is an example of an important function of the enzyme. Catabolism of purines ultimately lead to the purine hypoxanthine or xanthine, both of which can be utilized by xanthine oxidase to form uric acid.

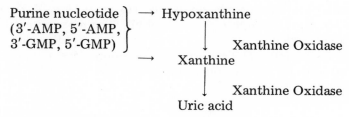

Nutritional Aspects of Metals

Unlike the metabolism of proteins, carbohydrates, and lipids, the intake and metabolism of food minerals does not involve radical changes in their molecular form. In general, metal cations such as Ca^{2+}, Mg^{2+}, K^+ and Na^+ as well as other metals in lesser concentrations are found in foods as salts of either organic acids, e.g., acetic, citric, etc., or inorganic acids, e.g., hydrochloric, phosphoric, etc., or complexed with protein, lipids, or other ligands such as heme, imidazole. After ingestion of the food, the metal ions are frequently associated with the same anions or ligands.

Calcium.—Calcium deficiencies are observed where the diet is generally considered to below standards in protein and/or other major nutrients. Calcium is most needed during growth periods, pregnancy, and lactation. The intake of calcium for most individuals varies from 200–1500 mg/day. In the United States, boys and girls up to age 18 take in considerably more calcium than do adult men and women. In Japan, the average intake of calcium averages only about 400 mg/day. A survey of 35 countries, but excluding USSR and Mainland China, showed that milk and dairy products contribute generally in excess of 75% of the calcium in the diet of these countries. The other major calcium source was cereals which of course would be a major item in the diet of certain eastern countries including Japan, Philippines, etc.

The full extent of a severe calcium deficiency (and only calcium) in humans is not known; however, in rats the deficiency symptoms include (a) retardation of growth, (b) decreased food consumption, (c) high basal metabolic rate, (d) reduced activity and sensitivity, (e) osteoporosis or low calcium rickets, (f) abnormal posture and gait, (g) susceptibility to internal hemorrhage, (h) large increase in the volume of urine, and (i) reduced life span.

Physiological functions such as clotting of blood and muscle excitation and contraction are known to involve calcium. Thus, its role in physiology is quite important.

Various compounds are known to either promote or interfere with the absorption of calcium, vitamin D being one of these. The mechanism whereby vitamin D affects calcium absorption is not fully elucidated.

Another factor that affects calcium metabolism is lactose. When lactose is included in a normal and adequate diet, test animals (rats) will retain larger quantities of calcium than in the absence of lactose.

Sodium phytate (hexaphosphoinositol) is known to interfere with the absorption of calcium.

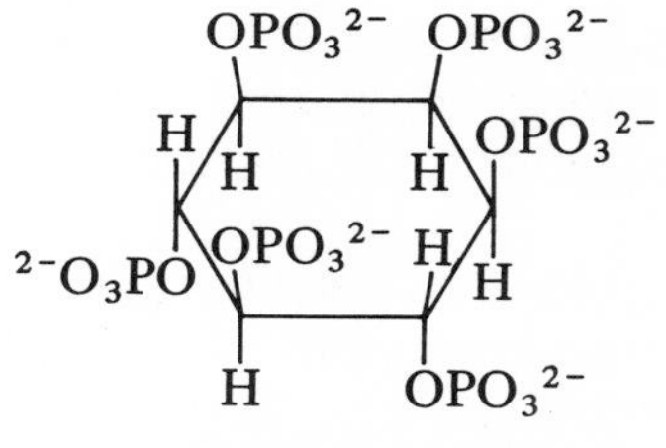

Hexaphosphoinositol

This compound commonly found in cereals has been shown to form insoluble salts with calcium in the intestine, thus making calcium unavailable for absorption.

Some animals, but not humans, are able to overcome the effects of phytate by breaking the insoluble calcium phytate down via enzymes referred to as phytases.

Oxalates play a role in interfering with calcium absorption. Consequently foodstuffs high in oxalates can produce an imbalance in Ca^{2+} due to the formation of insoluble calcium oxalate.

Magnesium.—All plants and animals investigated thus far have been shown to require magnesium. Outstanding examples of the nutritional importance of magnesium are its incorporation into chlorophyll and its role in phosphorylation reactions such as oxidative phosphorylation, glucokinase, and enolase. Undoubtedly these and numerous other biochemical reactions account for the indispensability of magnesium in all living systems. In fact, a large portion of the information concerning magnesium has come from investigation of specific biochemical reactions.

Magnesium deficiencies are not usually observed in adults except in cases of pathological disorders such as cirrhosis, renal diseases, viral hepatitis, and others. Magnesium deficiencies are usually characterized by enhancement of muscle contraction (tetany), muscular weakness, vertigo, tremors, seizures, hypertension, and others.

Magnesium is known to be important in cardiovascular function. Specifically, magnesium is concerned with blood pressure, myocardial conduction and rhythm, and myocardial contraction. Magnesium is thought to decrease the loss of potassium from the cells of myocardial tissue by affecting the membrane permeability or by activating ATPase which is involved in the active transport of potassium into the intracellular space.

The major source of magnesium in the adult diet is chlorophyll. An average adult will take in approximately 300 mg of magnesium per day. Supplements of magnesium to the diet are necessary only under abnormal dietary or physiological conditions. Children, especially infants, having a limited vegetable diet and subsisting mainly on milk should be given supplemental magnesium since cow's milk contains only about 120 mg/liter and human breast milk only approximately 40 mg/liter.

Sodium.—The importance of salt in the diet has been recognized for centuries. Numerous accounts throughout history have mentioned salt as a necessary nutrient. Sodium and chloride are usually considered to be synonymous, in fact conclusions have been made in the literature about sodium when only chloride was determined. This should be avoided since Na:Cl ratios can change during various physiological disorders.

Sodium is primarily involved in maintenance of body fluid pH, osmolality, and body fluid volume. Sodium and potassium and their role in the Na^+/K^+ pump (discussed previously) are also associated with impulse transmission in nerves.

Foods of both vegetable and animal origin are our main sources of sodium. Additionally, water supplies also contain appreciable amounts of sodium but generally not chloride. Vegetables contain only small amounts of Na^+ whereas meats and milk are quite high. Human milk has been reported to contain approximately 7 meq/liter while cow's milk contains significantly higher quantities, 14–40 meq/liter.

During processing various sodium salts are added to foods such as tenderizers, preservatives, or flavor promoters.

Water supplies generally have a Na^+ content in a range of 0.09–15 meq/liter but have been shown to contain as much as 70 meq/liter.

Excess depletion of Na^+ can occur from vomiting, diarrhea, urinary losses (renal insufficiency), excessive sweating, and a host of metabolic diseases such as cystic fibrosis, tuberculosis, meningitis and others.

The effects of the depletion of Na^+ which have been studied more carefully in animals are: failure to grow, softening of bones, decreased food utilization, water retention and ultimate water intoxication (depending on water balance), cardiovascular imbalance, and finally a state of shock and death occurs.

Excessive amounts of sodium are usually the result of excessive intake. Pathological conditions contributing to Na^+ excesses are cardiac failure, liver diseases, renal disease, and pregnancy toxemia. Hormonal imbalances can also lead to increased sodium retention.

Since foodstuffs are our main source of sodium (as added NaCl) close attention should be given to the amounts added to foods during processing. Some reports have indicated that the salt intake in the United States might in fact be excessive.

Potassium.—Discussions on the functions of potassium both on a molecular level and as a contributory electrolyte are generally included with sodium. However potassium has sufficiently unique functions as to warrant separate consideration. Potassium functions mainly in water and electrolyte balance and maintenance of pH of body fluids. Studies on test animals show that the growth of rats is stunted when fed a K^+ deficient diet. These functions are in addition to the previously discussed role of K^+ in enzyme systems. Mammalian cells contain K^+ as the principal intracellular cation whereas sodium is primarily extracellular and found in plasma. The ionic composition of tissues is maintained by Na^+ concentration in blood which in turn helps maintain the concentration of K^+ within the cells. Cell fluid K^+ averages about 140 meq/liter and Na^+ about 20 meq/liter while in plasma the situation is essentially reversed, i.e., Na^+ is 155 meq/liter and K^+ is 5 meq/liter. These data would indicate that Na^+ and K^+ are not freely diffusible; otherwise the intra- and extracellular concentration would not have these marked variances.

Although it is unlikely that a K^+ deficiency would develop due to a low intake in the diet, certain physiological malfunctions can lead to potassium deficiency (referred to as hypokalemia). Hypokalemia has been observed after surgery or severe trauma. This is preceded by an increase in plasma K^+ due to the epinephrine (adrenalin) released during the illness. This results in the release of potassium from the liver into the plasma. The symptoms of the induced hypokalemia include muscle weakness, cardiac weakness, and poor intestinal tone.

Other nutritional factors which can affect K^+ levels are known. An example of such a diet-induced condition is found in infant protein malnutrition, commonly called kwashiorkor. Low intakes of protein or of protein of low biological value lead to obvious deficiencies of dietary amino acids. The children become edematous due to disturbances in the overall water and electrolyte balance. A marked loss of potassium from the cells occurs. This loss in K^+ is aggravated by diarrhea that accompanies kwashiorkor leading to even greater losses of potassium.

Plants in general have a higher potassium content compared to sodium. Ingestion of large quantities of plants containing K^+ leads to excessive Na^+ excretion. This is more serious in the case of herbivorous animals than with humans and other nonherbivorous animals. Cattle and sheep must be supplied with additional NaCl to compensate for the higher intake of potassium.

Iron.—The beneficial effects of iron salts in the diet of humans has been recognized since the 17th century. Later in the 19th century when hemoglobin was measured, a more specific function of iron was assigned. It is now known that iron is an indispensable element for the normal function of hemoglobin of red cells, myoglobin of heart muscle, and the cytochromes of respiration. Additionally, other biochemical functions of iron are manifested in enzymes such as catalase and peroxidase. Most of the above examples involve the complexation of iron by the porphyrin nucleus. However transferrin, a glycopeptide, functions to transport iron by acting as an iron carrier. Transferrin constitutes the major part of the acid soluble iron in plasma. Transferrin also participates in the regulation and control of iron absorption and also protects against iron intoxication. Ferritin is another iron-containing compound in mammals. Ferritin is an iron-protein complex which is found primarily in the liver, spleen, and bone marrow. The ferritin molecule contains 20% iron as ferric hydroxide micelles attached to a protein of approximately 465,000 molecular weight. The primary role of ferritin is to store iron for the purpose of synthesis of porphyrin compounds. Another iron containing compound closely related to ferritin is hemosiderin. Work indicates that hemosiderin is available for porphyrin synthesis, as is ferritin.

Iron is usually ingested in a complex compound form, e.g., iron-porphyrin or iron-protein complexes. Since iron must be released from these complexes, gastric acidity is considered an important part of iron absorption. Interferences to iron absorption can occur when phytic acid (phytate) or phosphate form insoluble iron salts. Diets low in phosphate or high in ascorbic acid promote increased assimilation of iron.

Much of the information concerning the absorption of iron in humans has come from radioisotopic (Fe^{59}) iron in foods obtained by growing vegetables in solutions to which the isotope is added or by injecting iron into hens or rabbits so that eggs, liver, and muscle contain the radioisotope. Milk, bread, and other foods have also been enriched with Fe^{59} in similar experiments. These absorption studies indicate that individuals vary markedly in their ability to absorb iron. Generally, iron-deficient subjects absorb more iron than normal subjects. Iron absorption from bread, liver, muscle, and hemoglobin was more efficient than absorption from eggs or vegetables. The low uptake of iron from eggs may be due to the iron complexing with the phosphate of the yolk phosphoproteins.

Children appear to assimilate iron better than adults. The increased absorption by deficient children is observed as in adults. Children absorb iron more efficiently from milk (9.1%) than do adults (2.1%). Iron retention in normal humans will average 5–10% while in iron-deficient subjects iron retention will average 10–20%.

Iron deficiencies are more common in young mammals during the suckling period due to low concentration in the mother's milk or other milks and low stores of iron in the infant. Iron in milks (human, cow, and goat) generally are close to 0.5 mg/liter. Colostrum has an iron content of 1.5–2.5 mg/liter. Iron occurs in milk as an iron-protein (ferrilactin) which has been isolated from human and cow's milk. Interestingly, addition of iron to the diets of lactating women, cows, or sows does not raise the iron content of the milk to any appreciable level above what appears normally.

It is evident that infants should receive supplemental iron such as iron-fortified foods or medicinal iron. This is recommended even though the mother has received sufficient iron during pregnancy. Adults can show iron deficiencies due to loss of blood. Iron deficiency anemia in women of childbearing age is common due to iron losses during menstruation, pregnancy, and lactation. Thus, these and other adults on low iron diets (e.g., vegetable diet) should have the diet supplemented with additional iron.

Foods rich in iron are meats (especially liver, kidney, and heart), egg yolk, shellfish, cocoa, molasses, and parsley. Muscle meats, fish, poultry, nuts, green vegetables, wholemeal flour, and bread have lesser amounts of iron. Iron-poor foodstuffs are milk and milk products, white sugar, white flour, unenriched bread, polished rice, and most fresh fruit.

Copper.—Although copper has been recognized as a normal constituent of plant and animal tissue for over 150 yr, only during the last few years have a significant number of functions in nutrition been elucidated. Most of the data concerning copper have been gathered from animal studies, but increasing reports are appearing in which copper is implicated with both normal and abnormal physiological function in humans.

As previously pointed out, a number of enzyme systems involve copper as a necessary component, thus copper deficiencies can be traced to decreased copper-enzyme concentrations in the tissue. As is the case for numerous metal ions in metabolism, copper retention and metabolism are dependent upon other metal ions and anions, e.g., molybdenum, zinc, iron, calcium, and sulfate. A dietary balance of minerals thus is quite important not only for copper but for other minerals.

The human body contains approximately 100 mg of copper which is distributed throughout various tissues, but is concentrated in the liver, brain, kidneys, heart, and hair. Also the pigmented parts of the eye and the enamel of teeth are high in copper.

Copper in the blood of humans is found associated with protein. In erythrocytes, copper is found in a colorless copper-protein, erythrocuprein. This compound has a molecular weight of 31,000 and accounts for 60% of the red cell copper. The remainder of the erythrocyte copper is loosely bound to other proteins.

Plasma copper is made up of two basic types. One of these, ceruloplasmin, is a blue copper protein (the protein is an α_2-globulin) with a molecular weight of 151,000 and contains 8 atoms of copper in each molecule of enzyme. Copper loosely bound to proteins such as serum albumin accounts for the second type of copper in plasma. However, this loosely bound type of plasma copper is believed to be in the transportable form.

Diets can affect the copper concentration of blood. High or low intakes of copper give corresponding levels in blood. This should not be oversimplified since other components of the diet affect the levels of copper. These include molybdenum, inorganic sulfate, zinc, and iron. Zinc, cadmium, and molybdenum depress copper absorption; also, ascorbic acid has been shown to have a significant depressing effect on copper. Zinc and cadmium are thought to displace copper from intestinal mucosal protein, while molybdenum is thought to form a copper-molybdenum complex which has low availability.

Copper deficiency in the diet leads to a number of symptoms that can be alleviated by adding copper to the diet. Among these are anemia, depressed growth, bone disorders, impaired reproduction, heart failure, cardiovascular malfunction, and disturbances in the gastrointestinal tract. All of these have not been observed in humans as a direct result of copper deficiency. Copper deficiency causes the aorta of chicks, pigs, and guinea pigs to be susceptible to aortic aneurism.

The requirements for copper in the diets of humans depend on a number of other factors in the diet. Hypocupremia is usually the result of a disease and not dietary intake. Diseases that are known to involve hypocupremia are nephrosis, Wilson's disease, kwashiorkor, and cystic fibrosis. These diseases are the result of several defects; namely, lack of ceruloplasmin synthesis, excretion of excessive amounts of copper, or poor absorption.

Copper deficiencies due to diet appear to be more likely in infants. Human milk during the first week of lactation has been found to contain a mean copper concentration of 0.62 μg/ml. Copper levels decline to near 0.16 μg/ml later in the lactation. Cow's milk contains about 0.6 μg/ml. These low concentrations of copper in milk make it improbable that infants will obtain sufficient copper from an all milk diet although hypocupremia may not necessarily develop.

Severe malnutrition, such as in kwashiorkor, most commonly produces dietary hypocupremia. Low copper intakes can be overcome by supplemental copper in the diet. Estimates of daily dietary copper requirements range from 1.0 mg for 3-yr olds to 2.0 mg/day for adults. Infants with poor body stores require between 42 and 135 μg/kg body weight/day.

Shellfish (e.g., oysters), and crustaceans, liver, kidney, brain, nuts, cocoa, and fruits (grapes and peaches) are good sources of copper and range in concentration from 20 μg/gm to 400 μg/gm. Milk and milk products, white sugar, and honey are poor sources of copper. Nonleafy vegetables, fresh fruits, and refined cereals contain approximately 2 μg/gm Cu. White flour contains only about 1.7 μg/gm whereas the original wheat contains a mean copper content of 5.3 μg/gm.

Manganese.—Manganese is required for proper growth and reproduction in plants and animals. Symptoms of such a deficiency are: imparied growth, skeletal abnormalities, malfunctioning reproductive system, and atoxia in newborn. A deficiency of manganese has not been conclusively demonstrated in humans but its role in essential enzyme reactions is quite well-established.

Enzymes known to require Mg^{2+} will also generally function with Mn^{2+}. Pyruvate kinase is a typical example of an enzyme that will function quite well with either of the two metal ions. Pyruvate carboxylase is an enzyme that contains Mn^{2+} as an integral part of the structure. The latter enzyme contains 4 molecules of biotin and 4 Mn^{2+} per unit of molecular weight 655,000. Manganese has also been shown to occupy a significant role in the synthesis of mucopolysaccharides of cartilage. Liver arginase apparently contains manganese.

Manganese concentrates in mitochondria, thus tissues rich in mitochondria would be expected to contain larger quantities of manganese. Heart, kidney, liver, and pancreas contain relatively high concentrations of manganese.

Cow's milk ranges from 10–40 μg Mn/liter. Colostrum is about ten times more concentrated in manganese. Eggs contain approximately 10–15 μgm of manganese.

Nuts and cereals are the highest in manganese averaging near 20 μg/gm. Poultry, milk products, and seafoods have the lowest mananese concentration (average near 0.37 μg/gm). A cup of tea can contain as much as 1.3 mg of Mn while only 0.15 mg are found in a cup of coffee.

The average diet apparently supplies sufficient manganese in view of the lack of manganese deficiency exhibited by humans.

Zinc.—Zinc occurs in relatively large quantities in humans. It is estimated that a 70 kg man will contain 1.4–2.3 gm of zinc.

One of the physiological functions of zinc in humans is in wound healing. Levels of zinc in the hair have shown to correlate with the rate of wound closure. Normal diets do not furnish sufficient zinc during the wound healing process because of the increased requirement by this tissue. Zinc also plays a role in bone calcification. Hypogonadism and dwarfism have also been linked to zinc levels. Young males in areas of Egypt and Iran have diminished secondary sexual characteristics due to zinc deficiencies. Deoxyribonucleic acid synthesis is inhibited in the liver of rats deficient in zinc. Evidence also exists showing that zinc is necessary for glycine incorporation into glutathione, of methionine into rat tissue protein, and cysteine metabolism.

Insulin production and action are associated with zinc levels. Apparently zinc is necessary in order for rats to properly control insulin levels and subsequently glucose levels. Rats deficient in zinc were more resistent to insulin shock.

Enzymes known to contain zinc are carbonic anhydrase, carboxypeptidase, alcohol dehydrogenase, alkaline phosphatase, malic dehydrogenase, lactic dehydrogenase, and glutamic dehydrogenase. A number of other enzymes utilize zinc as a cofactor, namely, arginase, peptidases, oxalacetate decarboxylase, enolase, and carnosinase.

Although some of the physiological processes of zinc remain obscure, it is evident that a supply of zinc is necessary for a host of physiological processes.

Cow's milk contains approximately 3–5 μg/ml of zinc. This is a much higher concentration than found for iron, copper, manganese cobalt, and iodine. Colostrum contains a larger amount of zinc

(20 μg/ml), but zinc decreases as the lactation period progresses. Foods rich in zinc are oysters (1000 μg/gm), wheat germ and bran (40–120 μg/gm). Foods of moderate zinc concentrations are white flour and bread, leafy vegetables, meat, fish, eggs, whole cereals, and nuts. White bread averages about 7.8 μg/gm.

The adult intake of zinc is near 13 mg/day. In view of the obvious importance of zinc in the growing processes, care should be taken to ensure infants and children of an adequate supply of zinc.

Cobalt.—The importance of cobalt in the diet of humans and animals centers primarily around vitamin B_{12}. This vitamin contains 4% cobalt. The cobalt is coordinated to the 6 coordination positions by the 4 nitrogen atoms of the corrin ring, a nucleotide (5,6-dimethylbenzimidazole ribonucleotide) and either cyanide (an artifact of isolation) or 5'-deoxyadenosyl (via the methylene 5' carbon). The structure is shown in Fig. 8.5. The cobalamin coenzyme has 5'-deoxyadenosyl attached to the cobalt of the corrin ring via the 5'-methylene carbon. It should be pointed out that vitamin B_{12} is not synthesized by humans or animals but is of microbial origin. Ingestion of foodstuffs such as animal protein containing vitamin B_{12} is the main source of B_{12} in the diet.

Ruminants require greater quantities of cobalt since the organisms of multigastric animals utilize relatively large quantities of cobalt in the synthesis of B_{12} analogs which are not utilized by the animal. Low intakes of cobalt lead to failure of the organisms to synthesize sufficient B_{12} for the animal.

Some indication as to the amount of cobalt required by humans can be surmised from estimates of B_{12} requirements. Adult requirement for B_{12} is in the range of 0.1 μg/day. After cessation of ingestion or absorption of B_{12}, body stores of B_{12} will prevent deficiency for approximately 3 to 6 yr. Normal body stores of B_{12} average approximately 5 mg. If one considers B_{12} to contain approximately 4% cobalt then B_{12} stores would account for approximately 0.2 mg of cobalt. It has been reported that a 70-kg man will contain an average of 1.1 mg of cobalt, thus only about 20% of the cobalt in the body is in the form of B_{12}.

Cow's milk has a low cobalt concentration ranging from 0.4 to 1.1 μg/liter. Colostrum is approximately 4–10 times more concentrated in cobalt than normal milk. Other foodstuffs poor in cobalt are cereals, and white flour. Green leafy vegetables and meat such as liver and kidney are the richest sources.

Molybdenum.—No natural dietary deficiency has been shown for molybdenum. The most outstanding physiological features of molybdenum are: its role in interfering with copper absorption, and its biochemical role as an essential metal ion in the metabolic enzyme xanthine dehydrogenase (xanthine oxidase). This enzyme catalyzes the oxidation of numerous substrates including purines, aldehydes, pterins and NADH, and is found in high concentrations in cow's milk. Xanthine oxidase has a molecular weight of 275,000 and contains 8 atoms of iron, 2 molecules of FAD and approximately 1.5 atoms of molybdenum per molecule of protein. Disruption of the protein is necessary to remove the molybdenum. The role of molybdenum in normal physiology is to maintain proper levels of xanthine oxidase in the tissue.

Molybdenum may have an effect on dental caries. In one study addition of molybdenum (25 and 50 ppm) to 50 ppm fluoride was more effective in preventing caries than 50 ppm fluoride alone.

It has been estimated that dietary intake of molybdenum is near 100 μg/day and molybdenum retention appears to be quite low. However, little work has been carried out on the nutritional aspects of molybdenum.

Molybdenum is widely distributed in foods. Foods high in molybdenum are liver, kidney, cereal grains, leafy vegetables, and legumes. Fruits, root and stem vegetables, muscle meats, and milk and products are the poorest in molybdenum. Leguminous seeds have from 0.2–4.7 μg/gm molybdenum, cereal grains from 0.12–1.14 μg/gm and wheat, bread and flour from 0.30–0.66 μg/gm molybdenum.

Nutritional Aspects of Anionic Minerals

The most abundant of the inorganic anionic minerals are the phosphates, sulfates, and chlorides. While a varied array of organic anions are present, they are not considered minerals and thus will not be considered in this discussion. Phosphates, sulfates, and chlorides as well as the lesser of the anions are ingested as the various cation salts.

The sugar phosphates, e.g., glucose-6-phosphate, glucose-1-phosphate, fructose-6-phosphate, and other major members of the glycolytic scheme contribute phosphates as well as the nucleotides such as ATP, ADP, and others.

Sulfur in foods is analyzed as sulfate after ashing or digestion but appears in foodstuffs as both organic and inorganic sulfur. Chondroitin sulfate, glutathione, cystine, cysteine, methionine, and bile salts are the major contributors of organic sulfur.

Chloride.—Chloride has such a wide distribution and is found in such quantities that a discussion of its nutritional importance is unnecessary. It is known to activate certain enzymes, e.g., salivary amylase, but few specific functions on the molecular level are known.

In erythrocytes it appears that Cl^- is freely diffusible since the intracellular fluid of these cells contain approximately 80 meq/liter while the extracellular plasma contains approximately 110 meq/liter. Chloride constitutes approximately 66% of the total anionic content of extracellular plasma of humans. In other cells, phosphates and sulfates are the major intracellular anions and Cl^- and HCO_3^- predominate outside these cells.

In addition to its role in maintaining proper water and electrolyte balance, chloride also plays a major role in maintaining proper pH of extracellular fluids and HCl in gastric juice. Acidosis and alkalosis can occur with changes in the Cl^-/HCO_3^- ratio which is normally about 4.

Alkalosis can develop when excessive sweating or vomiting occurs. The fluid that is expelled has a Cl^-/HCO_3^- ratio greater than 4, thus Cl^- in the remaining extracellular fluid must fall while HCO_3^- rises thereby elevating the pH. In acidosis, the expelled fluid would have to have a Cl^-/HCO_3^- ratio of less than 4. This is true in the case of fluid loss due to prolonged diarrhea.

Meats and animal products contain larger quantities of Cl^- than do vegetables and fruits. Since Cl^- as NaCl is added to foods in so many instances, it is more likely that human subjects on normal diets might in fact obtain an excessive amount of Cl^- in the diet. Sodium chloride is generally considered the best source of chloride and other salts should be avoided. This is most vividly pointed out where LiCl was used as a substitute for cardiac patients. The toxicity of Li^+ was even more evident in this instance.

Phosphorus.—Phosphorus is the general term used to denote both organic and inorganic phosphorus compounds. This organic class includes ADP, ATP, glucose-6-phosphate, fructose-6-phosphate, 2-phosphoglycerate, phytate, and a host of other phosphorus-containing organic compounds. Inorganic phosphorus is in the orthophosphate form such as $H_2PO_4^-$, HPO_4^{2-}, or PO_4^{3-} or in bones as apatite. In all of these compounds, both organic and inorganic, the phosphorus atom has an oxidation number of +5.

Recent attention has been focused on the organic forms of phosphorus such as ATP and cyclic 3', 5'-AMP and their roles in physiological processes. However, the role of phosphorus in bone formation, tooth formation, and disorders or phosphorus metabolism, e.g., osteoporosis, should not be underemphasized.

Dietary sources of phosphate are milk products, cereals, meat, and eggs. These foodstuffs occur as caseinogen of milk, phytates of cereals, phosphate esters of meat, and vitellin of eggs. Interestingly, the phosphate in soil is in an insoluble apatite form and generally unavailable.

There is an interrelationship between phosphorus and calcium in phosphorus retention and uptake. Phosphorus retention can be increased by increased phosphorus in the diet when calcium intake is in excess of 940 mg/day. These data would indicate that calcium and phosphorus retention is dependent upon the levels of intake rather than the ratio of intake as has been suggested. Thus, low Ca intakes may be responsible for low phosphorus retention.

Low P intake affects both bones and teeth by interfering with calcification. In general, low phosphorus intake causes deterioration due to malfunction of calcification (or rickets). In animals, phosphorus deficiencies lead to loss of appetite, poor growth, a low blood phosphorus level and a marked increase in thirst and urine production.

Rickets due to either low phosphorus or low calcium may be lessened or cured by additional vitamin D in the diet. Vitamin D probably does not increase intestinal absorption of phosphorus directly but acts primarily on calcium. Vitamin D does, however, appear to cause a shift of phosphorus from soft tissue to bone. In soft tissue and fluids phosphate appears as the soluble anionic or organic phosphate; however, in bone and teeth it appears as hydroxyapatite, $Ca_{10}(PO_4)_6(OH)_2$.

Iodine.—Iodine is quite important as a dietary mineral due to its incorporation into the thyroid hormone thyroxine:

Thyroxine (3,5,3′,5′-tetraiodothyronine)

Other iodinated derivatives of thyronine are found in the thyroid glands as well as iodinated tyrosine derivatives. These include 3-iodotyrosine, 3,5-diiodotyrosine, and 3,5,3′-triiodothyronine. Low dietary intakes of iodine cause the thyroid to enlarge leading to the condition commonly referred to as simple goiter. Thyroid hormone functions in a variety of physiological functions which include: (a) control of energy metabolism; (b) influences physical and mental growth; (c) affects other endocrine glands, particularly the hypophysis and the gonads; (d) influences neuromuscular function; (e) affects circulation; (f) influences metabolism of foods nutrients, minerals, and water. In most underdeveloped countries where crude salt is used (e.g., from evaporation of sea water) the iodide is unstable. It oxidizes and is lost; thus iodine is sometimes added as Ca $(IO_3)_2$.

Reports of domestic surveys in the United States indicate that iodine-deficiency goiter may again be a problem if steps are not taken to ensure the consuming public receives iodine in foods.

Although certain food (seafoods, etc.) and waters contain iodine, dietary intake in excess of these are required for proper iodine levels.

Selenium.—Selenium has been shown to aid in preventing liver necrosis in rats fed on a diet of torula yeast. This condition could be prevented by addition of bakers' yeast, which was found to contain selenium.

Additionally, an interrelationship between selenium and vitamin E was observed. In animals and fowl a selenium deficiency can be alleviated by vitamin E. Likewise, selenium can substitute for a normal intake of vitamin E. However, selenium does not function solely as a substitute for vitamin E.

A selenium deficiency in humans has not been conclusively demonstrated; however, in animals and fowl, selenium deficiency has been linked with a number of disorders which are interrelated to vitamin E. Among these diseases is nutritional muscular dystrophy. Other malfunctions associated with selenium and vitamin E are growth, fertility, and exudative diathesis in chicks. This disease is characterized by edema in the breast, wing and neck and ultimately appears as subcutaneous hemorrhages which give a green-blue discoloration to the skin. These conditions respond to selenium therapy. Young pigs on a low vitamin E or selenium diet develop necrotic liver lesions with some myocardial and skeletal muscle degeneration. This condition is referred to as hepatosis dietetica. Selenium is effective in preventing the liver lesions but vitamin E appears to be more effective in preventing skeletal muscle degeneration.

The role of selenium is not completely elucidated; however, selenium functions as an antioxidant in tissues and membranes. In light of the many functions of selenium and its interrelationship with vitamin E, it is unlikely that a simple role for selenium exists. Elevation of aryl sulfatase and β-glucuronidase, and lowering of levels of lactic dehydrogenase, glutamic oxalacetic transaminase, and peroxidase are observed in the skeletal muscles of selenium deficient lambs. It has also been proposed that selenium is associated with the biosynthesis of coenzyme Q, because reduced levels of tocopherol and selenium result in lower levels of CoQ in tissue.

No selenium requirements have been established for humans. Areas that are low in selenium, as well as high in selenium, are known. Selenium in foods can be related to the soil from which they originated. It has been shown that if a plant contains more than 50 μg/gm selenium, the soil ranges in selenium content from 0.4 to 128 μg/gm. Alkaline soils promote selenium uptake by plants. Since soil selenium levels determine its content in foods, no so-called normal levels can be stated. An example of such a difference in levels of selenium is in milk and eggs from a low and a high selenium area. The eggs from low selenium areas contained approximately 0.056 μg/gm and milk 0.005 μg/gm, while in the high selenium areas milk contained from 0.05–0.07 μg/gm and eggs 0.4–0.5 μg/gm. Liver, kidneys, and fish are relatively high in selenium, ranging approximately from 0.15–0.8 μg/gm.

Processing of food has an effect on the selenium content. The water from cooked vegetables contains the major portion of selenium.

Analytical Methods for Metals and Anions

The classic methods for determining the major metals and anions, which include generally a digestion and/or ashing of the foodstuff followed by a gravimetric, titrimetric, or colorimetric analysis has generally been sufficient for elements in rather large quantities. However, to actually determine small differences in concentration of various metals or even more importantly the presence and concentration of the trace minerals, the classical methods are not usually sufficiently sensitive to yield such information. Two methods commonly in use for metals are flame photometry (flame emission) and atomic absorption. The salient features of each system are shown in Fig. 9.2.

Analytical

In flame emission, the sample solution is aspirated into the flame where the element is excited and thus emits radiation of wavelengths specific for the element being analyzed. The monochromator selects one of these wavelengths as the radiation passes on to the detector (e.g., phototube or photomultiplier). The intensity of the radiation is compared to standard solutions of known concentration.

Atomic absorption might well be described as the inverse of the flame emission method for determining metallic elements. However, in atomic absorption the element is not excited, but rather is dissociated from its chemical bonds and placed in an unexcited, un-ionized state. In this form the element is then capable of absorbing radiation of discrete wavelengths, which are the same wavelengths of radiation emitted when excited by flame as in flame emission analysis.

The dissociation process is usually achieved by burning the sample in a flame; while the radiation source is commonly a hollow cathode lamp. These lamps are filled with argon or neon at low pressure and the cathode is made of the element being analyzed.

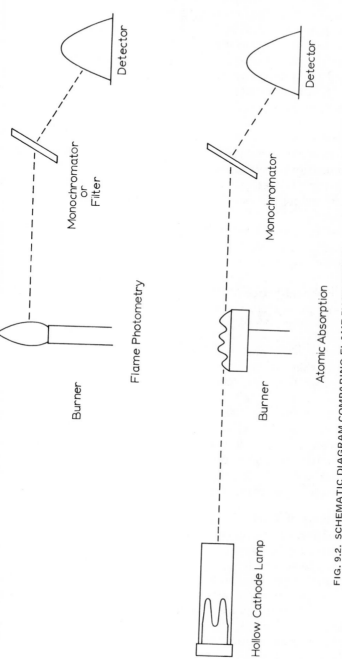

FIG. 9.2. SCHEMATIC DIAGRAM COMPARING FLAME PHOTOMETRY AND ATOMIC ABSORPTION

Nonflame methods have recently received considerable attention, particularly for mercury. In this method the mercury compounds are reduced to free atomic mercury by chemical methods. The mercury is then aspirated into a cell (glass) with quartz windows. The mercury vapor absorbs the radiant energy from the hollow cathode lamp as in the flame process. Using this technique, levels of mercury (0.01 ppm) previously below conventional flame methods may be determined.

Flame photometry (flame emission) has been used quite successfully for a number of metal ions, e.g., Na^+, K^+, etc., but is hampered by the ionization interferences of other elements present in the solution giving erroneous concentrations (either higher or lower). Ionization interferences are usually much lower using atomic absorption analysis.

For most elements, elimination or recognition of spectral interferences and excitation problems are necessary for flame emission analysis while these can be generally ignored in atomic absorption spectroscopy.

Other analytical procedures for metallic elements, especially trace elements, are ark and spark emission, x-ray fluorescence, and neutron activation analysis.

Trace Elements in Submicro Quantities

Ordinarily there is no need to concentrate trace elements in order to analyze for their presence and quantity. However, certain trace elements, e.g., Co, Ni, Pb, and others may normally occur in foodstuffs and water in quantities below the level of detection of various analytical instruments such as atomic absorption. One technique that has been used for Pb, Co, Ni, Cu, Cd, Fe, and Mn is chelation with ammonium pyrrolidine dithiocarbonate followed by extraction with methyl isobutyl ketone. The final analysis is carried out by atomic absorption or other techniques.

Special Aspects of Trace Minerals

Several reports have recently been presented in which mercury as dimethyl mercury (in organic form) has been found in the food chain. This organic form of mercury concentrates as it moves up the food chain (primarily by fish and aquatic life), and ultimately reaching the terminus of the chain when the aquatic foodstuffs are consumed by humans. Mercury poisoning has been observed in Japan (Minamata disease) in humans ingesting large quantities of fish that had concentrated mercury from industrial wastes.

Recently several lakes and reservoirs in the United States have been found to contain appreciable quantities of mercury. Additionally, ocean fish such as swordfish have been found to contain unacceptable levels of methyl mercury.

Lithium has recently received considerable attention as a chemotherapeutic agent for the treatment of manic psychosis. Since its sedating action was first observed by Cade in Australia in 1949, numerous reports have appeared substantiating the usefulness of lithium salts such as Li_2CO_3 in breaking the manic siege of most patients. The actual mechanism for the function of lithium is unknown. Lithium salts are found in appreciable quantities in springwaters, wells, and various plants grown in soils high in lithium. However, the concentration required for therapeutic use (0.5–1.5 meq/liter of serum) is much above any levels so far observed in any human subjects in the United States, Central America, Europe, and Australia.

Another trace mineral that has been shown to have a beneficial effect in nutrition is fluorine. Apparently no essential role in either plants or animals can be ascribed to fluorine. However, fluorine does interact with teeth to produce a mottled enamel (fluorosis) when ingested in large quantities or to prevent dental cavities when used sparingly.

Original objections to fluoridation of water supplies was centered around the toxicity of the fluoride ion; however, these objections have essentially subsided and fluoridation of city water supplies and inclusion of fluoride compounds in commercial tooth pastes are now accepted practices.

BIBLIOGRAPHY

ADELSTEIN, S. J., and VALLEE, B. K. 1962. Copper. *In* Mineral Metabolism, Vol. 2, Part B, C. L. Comar, and Felix Bronner (Editors). Academic Press, New York.

BARTTER, C. 1964. Disturbances of phosphorus metabolism. *In* Mineral Metabolism, Vol. 2, Part A, C. L. Comar, and Felix Bronner (Editors). Academic Press, New York.

BRONNER, F. 1964. Dynamics of function of calcium. *In* Mineral Metabolism, Vol. 2, Part A, C. L. Comar, and Felix Bronner (Editors). Academic Press, New York.

CATLORE, E., and HOGBEN, C. A. M. 1962. Chloride. *In* Mineral Metabolism, Vol. 2, Part B, C. L. Comar, and Felix Bronner (Editors). Academic Press, New York.

CAUSSONS, H. 1969. Magnesium metabolism in infants and children. Postgrad. Med., *12*, 135–139.

COTZIAS, G. C. 1962. Manganese. *In* Mineral Metabolism, Vol. 2, Part B, C. L. Comar, and Felix Bronner (Editors). Academic Press, New York.

DE RENZO, E. C. 1962. Molybdenum. *In* Mineral Metabolism, Vol. 2, Part B, C. L. Comar, and Felix Bronner (Editors). Academic Press, New York.

DZIEWIATKOWSKI, D. C. 1962. Sulfur. *In* Mineral Metabolism, Vol. 2, Part B, C. L. Comar, and Felix Bronner (Editors). Academic Press, New York.

FISHMAN, M. J., and MIDGETT, M. R. 1968. Extraction techniques for the determination of cobalt, nickel, and lead in fresh water by atomic absorption. *In* Trace Inorganics in Water, R. A. Baker (Editor). American Chemical Society, Washington, D.C.

FORBES, G. B. 1962. Sodium. *In* Mineral Metabolism, Vol. 2, Part B, C. L. Comar, and Felix Bronner (Editors). Academic Press, New York.

GILBERT, F. A. 1957. Mineral Nutrition and the Balance of Life. University of Oklahoma Press, Norman, Okla.

GROSS, J. 1962. Iodine and bromine. *In* Mineral Metabolism, Vol. 2, Part B, C. L. Comar, and Felix Bronner (Editors). Academic Press, New York.

HATHAWAY, M. L., and LEVERTON, R. M. 1959. Calcium and phosphorous. *In* Food, The Yearbook of Agriculture, A. Stefferud (Editor). U.S. Department of Agriculture, Washington, D.C.

HODGE, H. C. 1964. Fluoride. *In* Mineral Metabolism, Vol. 2, Part A, C. L. Comar, and Felix Bronner (Editors). Academic Press, New York.

IRVING, J. T. 1964. Dynamics and function of phosphorus. *In* Mineral Metabolism, Vol. 2, Part A, C. L. Comar, and Felix Bronner (Editors). Academic Press, New York.

KAHN, H. L. 1968. Principle and practice of atomic absorption. *In* Trace Inorganics in Water, R. A. Baker (Editor). American Chemical Society, Washington, D.C.

LEHNINGER, A. L. 1970. Biochemistry. Worth Publishers, New York.

LEVERTON, R. M. 1959. Sodium, potassium and magnesium. *In* Food, The Yearbook of Agriculture, A. Stefferud (Editor). U.S. Department of Agriculture, Washington, D.C.

MAHLER, H. R. 1961. Interrelationships with enzymes. *In* Mineral Metabolism, Vol. 1, Part B, C. L. Comar, and Felix Bronner (Editors). Academic Press, New York.

MAHLER, H. R., and CORDES, E. H. 1971. Biological Chemistry, 2nd Edition. Harper & Row Publishers, New York.

MONTY, K. J., and McELROY, W. D. 1959. The trace elements. *In* Food, The Yearbook of Agriculture, A. Stefferud (Editor). U.S. Department of Agriculture, Washington, D.C.

MOORE, C. V., and DUBACH, R. 1962. Iron. *In* Mineral Metabolism, Vol. 2, Part B, C. L. Comar, and Felix Bronner (Editors). Academic Press, New York.

SCOTT, M. L. 1962. Selenium. *In* Mineral Metabolism, Vol. 2, Part B, C. L. Comar, and Felix Bronner (Editors). Academic Press, New York.

SELLER, R. H., RAMIREZ, O., BREST, A. N., and MOYER, J. H. 1966. Serum and erythrocytic magnesium levels in congestive heart failure. Am. J. Cardiol. *17*, 786–791.

SLAVIN, W. 1968. Atomic absorption spectroscopy. *In* Chemical Analysis, Vol. 25, P. J. Elving, and I. M. Kolthoff (Editors). John Wiley & Sons, New York.

CHAPTER 10

Photosynthesis

Photosynthesis is the process whereby plant cells utilize the energy of sunlight for the synthesis of carbohydrates from absorbed carbon dioxide. The overall reaction carried out by photosynthetic organisms is shown below:

$$CO_2 + H_2O \xrightarrow{\text{light}} (CH_2O) + O_2$$

(CH_2O) = carbohydrate

The products of this reaction form the staple food of animals and plants. Consequently, if photosynthesis were to cease, all life on this planet would come to an end.

Chloroplasts

Photosynthesis takes place within highly specialized particles or organelles called plastids. In higher plants, algae and Euglena, the plastids contain chlorophyll and are referred to as chloroplasts. There may be from one to several hundred chloroplasts in the cells of a leaf, depending on the type of plant.

The chloroplasts have morphologically distinct parts: (a) a pigmented lamellar system of proteins (40–50%) and lipids (35–40%) in which the photochemical reactions occur, (b) a background matrix called stroma which contains the enzymes involved in CO_2 fixation and the CO_2 cycles, (c) spherical bodies or globules composed mainly of lipids, (d) starch grains, and (e) a limiting membrane surrounding the chloroplasts.

Chlorophyll

The organic molecule within the chloroplast, which makes photosynthesis possible, is a green-colored molecule called chlorophyll. The molecule is a magnesium-containing derivative of porphyrin, with phytol attached to one of the side chains as an ester of propionic acid. The chemical structure of chlorophyll a and chlorophyll b (Fig. 10.1) are well-known. Both chlorophylls are present in green plant tissue. Green plants which are able to produce O_2 contain chlorophyll a. Higher plants, algae and Euglena also contain chlorophyll b. The biosynthesis of chlorophyll begins with glycine and succinic acid. By a number of steps, which need not be discussed here, a substance identified as protoporphyrin IX is synthesized (Fig. 10.2). Next, a magnesium ion is incorporated into

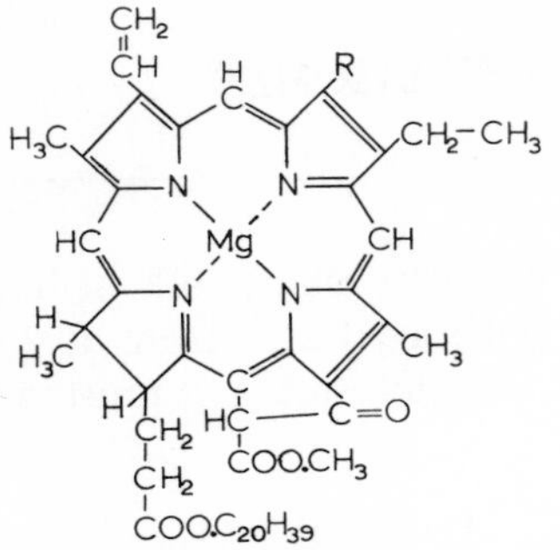

R=CH$_3$; chlorophyll a
R=CHO; chlorophyll b

FIG. 10.1. STRUCTURE OF CHLOROPHYLL a AND CHLORO-
PHYLL b

protoporphyrin a_5 (protochlorophyllide a). The conversion of the latter compound to protochlorophyll a occurs when the protochlorophyllide a is combined with the appropriate protein. Esterification with phytol yields chlorophyll a. The precursor of chlorophyll b appears to be chlorophyll a.

Carotenoids

The carotenoids, which also absorb light for photosynthesis, are found in the chromoplasts of the cell. These compounds may be divided into two main groups, the carotenes and the xanthophylls. The biosynthesis and function of the carotenoids is still under investigation.

Photosynthesis

The purpose of photosynthetic pigments (chlorophyll a and b, carotenoids and phycobilins) is to gather radiant energy for transfer to a reaction center (plastids) where the radiant energy can be transformed into chemical energy. The fundamental mechanisms of photosynthesis still have many gaps; however, it is clear that the important phases in green plants and photosynthetic bacteria are the light reaction and the dark reaction. In the light reaction there is an absorption of red light quantum by chlorophyll, which causes the release of an electron to a higher energy level. The electron is transferred to cofactors and is eventually utilized in an electron transfer chain to form ATP from ADP. This solar energy also produces an evolution of oxygen from water. In photosynthetic bacteria the light reaction is cyclic; i.e., the electrons are transferred from chlorophyll to cofactors and then returned to vacated low energy level of chlorophyll. In green plants there is a flow of electrons from OH$^-$ groups of water to NADP. Since a water molecule provides electrons to replace those used to produce NADPH, the process is

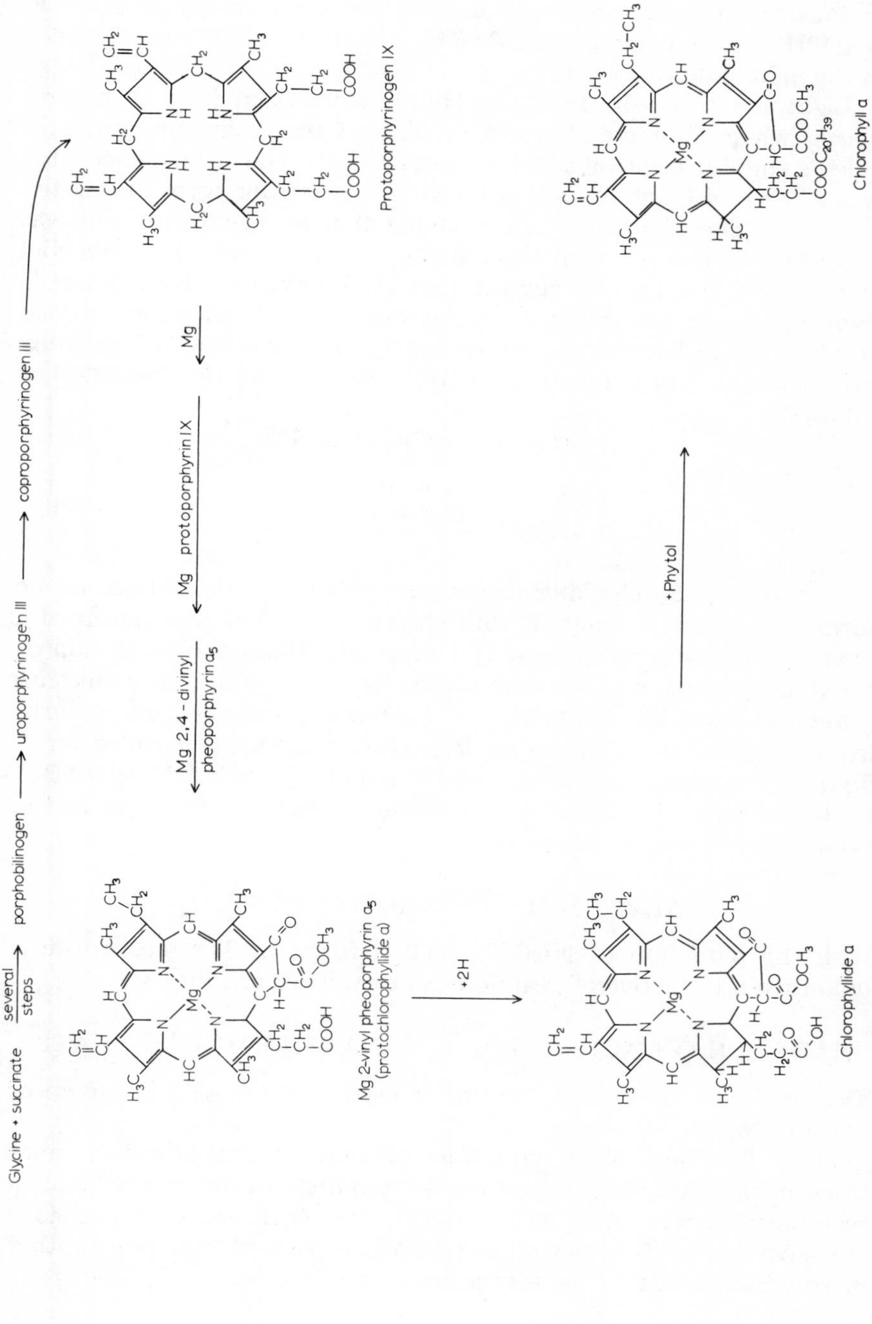

FIG. 10.2. BIOSYNTHESIS OF CHLOROPHYLL a

called noncyclic photophosphorylation. In the dark reaction, there is a fixation of CO_2 into carbohydrates in the absence of light using various biochemical pathways and the chemical energy from ATP, NADPH (green plants), and $FADH_2$ (bacteria) that was produced in the light reaction.

Light Reaction.—In 1937, R. Hill observed that isolated chloroplasts, when illuminated, were capable of producing oxygen, provided a suitable electron acceptor was present. The electron acceptor was a ferric salt which was reduced to the ferrous form during the reaction. Therefore, it was concluded that an electron donor was oxidized to yield O_2 with the reduction of the ferric ion. Van Niel (1941) was the first to suggest that H_2O served as the oxidizable hydrogen donor and that the oxygen was derived from water. Ruben *et al.* (1941) showed the above relationship through O^{18} labeling experiments. Consequently, the Hill reaction can be illustrated as follows:

$$\begin{array}{ccc} 2H_2O & \text{light} & 4Fe^{3+} \\ \downarrow & \downarrow & \downarrow \\ O_2 + 4H^+ & \xrightarrow[4e^-]{\text{chloroplasts}} & 4Fe^{2+} \end{array}$$

A number of years later it was discovered that NADPH could be formed in the Hill reaction with chloroplasts. The absorption of a quantum of light by chlorophyll a brought about the formation of a reducing entity x^-_{red} and an oxidizing entity, y^+_{ox}. The electron generated from the photolysis of H_2O was transferred via a short-lived intermediate x^-_{red} to an iron containing protein called ferredoxin. Ferredoxin can then directly reduce either NAD^+ or $NADP^+$ to form NADPH. Thus, the pyridine nucleotides function in the capacity of hydrogen acceptors.

$$NADP^+ + H_2O \xrightarrow{\text{light}} NADPH + H^+ + \tfrac{1}{2} O_2$$

With the reduction of $NADP^+$, ATP is formed. The mechanism is unknown but the overall reaction can be written as follows:

$$NADP^+ + H_2O + ADP + H_3PO_4 \xrightarrow{\text{light}} NADPH + H^+ + \tfrac{1}{2}O_2 + ATP$$

The process whereby light energy is used to form ATP is known as photophosphorylation.

Dark Reaction.—The reduction of CO_2 to carbohydrate takes place in the dark, but it requires the products of the photochemical reactions; namely, ATP and NADPH. The light and dark reactions are separable in time as well as spatially separated from one another in the chloroplast. The formation of glucose from CO_2 involves a cyclic process in which 6 molecules of CO_2 and 6 molecules of H_2O are utilized to form 1 molecule of a hexose. The cyclic nature of the dark reaction is shown in Fig. 10.3.

The immediate acceptor of CO_2 is a phosphorylated pentose, ribulose-1, 5-diphosphate and the reaction is catalyzed by the enzyme carboxydismutase.

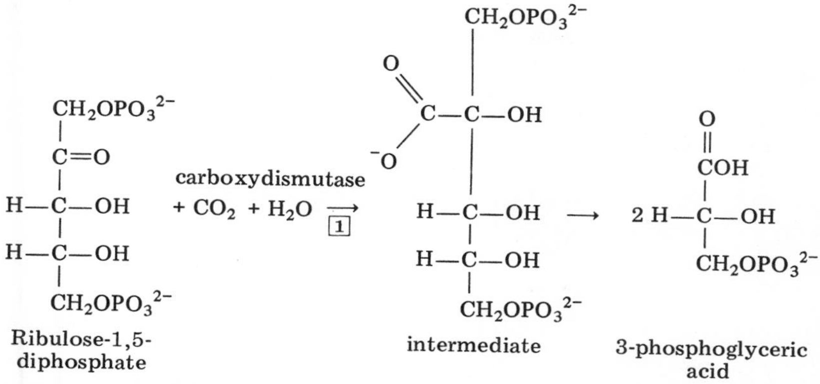

Ribulose-1,5-diphosphate   intermediate   3-phosphoglyceric acid

The postulated intermediate is formed as a result of CO_2 addition to the enol form of ribulose diphosphate followed by symmetrical cleavage to give two molecules of 3-phosphoglyceric acid (Reaction 1). The transformation of 3-phosphoglyceric acid to 1,3-diphosphoglyceric acid requires ATP (Reaction 2) and thence to glyceraldehyde-3-phosphate by utilization of NADPH (Reaction 3). Thus, the dark reaction requires six molecules of CO_2 and equivalent number of ATP and NADPH molecules to produce 12 molecules of glyceraldehyde-3-phosphate.

The 12 molecules of glyceraldehyde-3-phosphate are converted to 6 molecules of ribulose-5-phosphate and 1 molecule of fructose-6-phosphate by a series of complex reactions involving the intermediate of 4,5, and 7-carbon sugars. The fructose-6-phosphate (Reaction 6) may be changed into glucose by the following reaction:

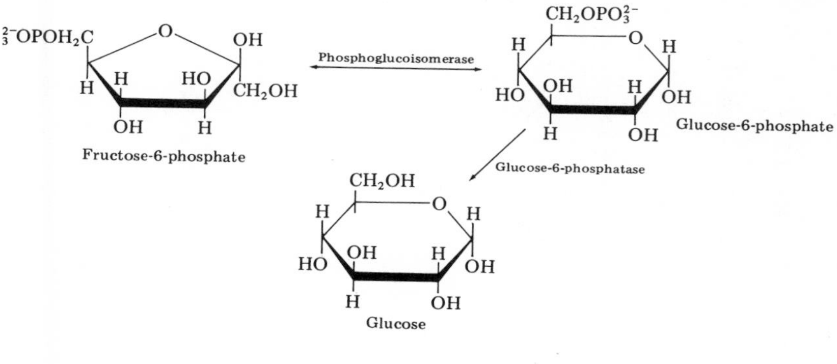

Fructose-6-phosphate   Glucose-6-phosphate

Glucose

1. (6) Ribulose-1, 5-diP + (6) CO_2 + (6) H_2O $\xrightarrow{\boxed{\text{carboxydismutase}}}$ (12) 3-P-glyceric acid (3-PGA)

2. (12) 3-PGA + (12) ATP $\xrightarrow{\text{3-PGA kinase}}$ (12) 1, 3-diP glyceric acid (1, 3-diPGA) + (12) ADP

3. (12) 1, 3-diPGA + (12) NADPH $\xrightarrow{\boxed{\text{glyceraldehyde phosphate dehydrogenase}}}$ (12) glyceraldehyde-3-P (G-3-P) + (12) NADP⁺ + (12) P_i

4. (5) G-3-P $\xrightarrow{\text{triosephosphate isomerase}}$ (5) dihydroxyacetone phosphate (DHAP)

5. (3) G-3-P + (3) DHAP $\xrightarrow{\text{aldolase}}$ (3) Fructose-1, 6-diP (F-1, 6-diP)

6. (3) F-1, 6-diP $\xrightarrow{\boxed{\text{phosphatase}}}$ (3) fructose-6-P (F-6-P) + (3) P_i

7. (2) F-6-P + (2) G-3-P $\xrightarrow{\text{transketolase}}$ (2) erythrose-4-P + (2) xylulose-5-P

8. (2) Erythrose-4-P + (2) DHAP $\xrightarrow{\text{aldolase}}$ (2) sedoheptulose-1, 7-diP

9. (2) Sedoheptulose-1, 7-diP + (2) H_2O $\xrightarrow{\boxed{\text{phosphatase}}}$ (2) sedoheptulose-7-P + (2) P_i

10. (2) Sedoheptulose-7-P + (2) G-3-P $\xrightarrow{\text{transketolase}}$ (2) ribose-5-P + (2) xylulose-5-P

11. (2) Ribose-5-P $\xrightarrow{\text{phosphopentose isomerase}}$ (2) ribulose-5-P

12. (4) Xylulose-5-P $\xrightarrow{\text{phosphoketopentose epimerase}}$ (4) ribulose-5-P

13. (6) Ribulose-5-P + (6) ATP $\xrightarrow{\text{phosphopentokinase}}$ (6) ribulose-1, 5-diP + (6) ADP

Sum:

(6) Ribulose-1, 5-diP + (6) CO_2 + (18) ATP + (12) NADPH ⟶ (6) ribulose-1, 5-diP + fructose-6-P + (18) ADP + (17) P_i + (12) NADP⁺

[1] Numbers in parentheses indicate the number of molecules participating in one turn of the cycle. Enzymes enclosed in boxes are specific. Reactions 6, 9 and 13 are thermodynamically irreversible.

FIG. 10.3. STOICHIOMETRY OF CYCLIC PHOTOPHOSPHORYLATION

Phosphorylation of ribulose-5-phosphate by ATP (Reaction 13) produces ribulose-1,5-diphosphate, the acceptor of CO_2. Thus, 1 turn of the cycle serves to convert 6 molecules of CO_2 and 6 molecules of water into 1 molecule of glucose. It will be noted that 12 molecules each of ATP and NADPH are required to synthesize 1 molecule of glucose with an additional 6 molecules of ATP to convert 6 molecules of ribulose-5-phosphate to 6 molecules of ribulose-1,6-diphosphate.

It is evident that the light reactions of photosynthesis must lead to the formation of high levels of ATP and NADPH in order to support the synthesis of carbohydrate during the dark reactions. If a plant is placed in the dark for a prolonged period of time, ATP and NADPH will be depleted. The plants then reverse the process, breaking down the stored carbohydrate with oxygen (respiration) to release the energy with CO_2 and H_2O as by-products.

BIBLIOGRAPHY

ARNON, D. I. 1967. Photosynthetic phosphorylation: facts and concepts. *In* Biochemistry of Chloroplasts, T. W. Goodwin (Editor). Academic Press, New York.

BAILEY, J. L. 1963. Photosynthesis: Lecture Series, No. 5. Royal Institute of Chemistry, London.

BOARDMAN, N. K. 1968. The photochemical systems of photosynthesis. *In* Advances in Enzymology, Vol. 30, F. F. Nord (Editor), John Wiley & Sons, New York.

BOGORAD, L. 1965. Chlorophyll biosynthesis. *In* Chemistry and Biochemistry of Plant Pigments, T. W. Goodwin (Editor). Academic Press, New York.

CALVIN, M. 1962. Photosynthesis. Science *135*, 879–889.

DOBY, G. 1965. Plant Biochemistry. John Wiley & Sons, London.

FULLER, R. C., and CONTI, S. F. 1963. The microbial photosynthetic apparatus. *In* Studies on Micro-algae and Photosynthetic Bacteria. Special issue of Plant and Cell Physiology, 49–63.

GIBBS, M. 1967. Photosynthesis. Ann. Rev. Biochem. *36*, 757–784.

HILL, R. 1939. Oxygen produced by isolated chloroplasts. Proc. Roy. Soc. (London), Ser. B, *127*, 192–210.

LASCELLES, J. 1965. The biosynthesis of chlorophyll. *In* Biosynthetic Pathways in Higher Plants, J. B. Pridham, and T. Swain (Editors). Academic Press, New York.

PARK, R. B. 1965. The chloroplast. *In* Plant Biochemistry, J. Bonner, and J. E. Varner (Editors). Academic Press, New York.

PARK, R. B. 1966. Subunits of chloroplasts structure and quantum conversion in photosynthesis. Intern. Rev. Cytol. *20*, 67–95.

RUBEN, S., RANDALL, M., KAMEN, M., and HYDE, J. H. 1941. Heavy oxygen (O^{18}) as a trace in the study of photosynthesis. J. Am. Chem. Soc. *63*, 877–879.

VAN NEIL, C. B. 1941. The bacterial photosynthesis and their importance for the general problem of photosynthesis. *In* Advances in Enzymology, Vol. 1, F. F. Nord, and C. H. Werkman (Editors). John Wiley & Sons, New York.

CHAPTER 11

Fermentation and Glycolysis

Knowledge of alcoholic fermentation has been known for 4000 to 5000 yr or perhaps longer. But the nature of the process did not become established until the 19th century. As a consequence, the history of the investigation of alcoholic fermentation parallels that of biochemistry from its inception to the present. Lavoisier undertook the first quantitative study of the products of fermentation. His results showed that alcohol, CO_2, and acid were produced during wine fermentations. Gay-Lussac formulated the correct overall equation for the fermentation reaction. Schwann postulated that fermentation of beer involved the participation of living yeast cells. He believed that the fermentation process was linked with the life of the yeast cell. Pasteur, who had made many discoveries about the chemical activity of microorganisms, boldly declared, "no fermentation without life." Thus the stage was set for a dramatic discussion regarding the role of enzymes (ferments) in the conversion of sugar to CO_2 and ethanol.

Years later the arguments centering around the vitalistic theory of fermentation were settled when Buchner demonstrated that enzymes could be separated from the yeast cells, and in the absence of living cells, the enzymes were able to ferment sugar to alcohol and CO_2. These discoveries opened a new era in the field of fermentation and biochemistry.

Pathways of Anaerobic Glycolysis and Fermentation

It is now well-established that there are several pathways by which sugars can be broken down. Pyruvate occupies a key position in these catabolic processes. The glycolytic pathway is an important metabolic pathway in plants and animals. One of the characteristics of the glycolytic pathway is that the formation of pyruvate from a glucose unit proceeds anaerobically and still provides energy sufficient to convert 2 moles of inorganic phosphate into energy rich ATP. The overall reaction can be represented by the following equation:

$$C_6H_{12}O_6 + 2NAD^+ + 2ADP + 2Pi \rightarrow$$

$$2CH_3CO\ COOH + 2NADH + H^+ + 2ATP$$

The reactions and intermediates of glycolysis are summarized in Fig. 11.1.

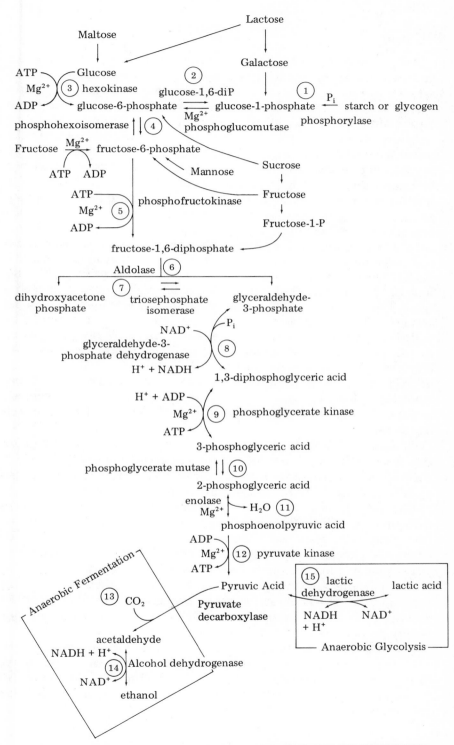

FIG. 11.1. REACTION PATHWAYS FOR GLYCOLYSIS AND FERMENTATION

All of these intermediates have been isolated and characterized; the reactions are catalyzed by enzymes located in the soluble (supernatant) portion of cells. No structural organization, e.g., mitochondria, is required for these reactions to proceed. Since numerous carbohydrates may be utilized as substrates for glycolysis, depending on the particular organism, preliminary reactions must precede the actual glycolytic pathway. Substrates such as starch, glycogen, lactose, sucrose, maltose, fructose, and others must first be converted to intermediates which are usable by the glycolytic pathway. Glucose-1-phosphate, fructose-6-phosphate, and fructose 1,6-diphosphate are the key sugar phosphates that must be formed in order for an organism (macro or micro) to carry out glycolysis.

In order to be utilized, ingested carbohydrates (oligosaccharides and polysaccharides) must be hydrolyzed to the monosaccharide.

Glycogen in animals and starch in plants can be utilized by splitting of the nonreducing terminal glucose residue by the phosphorylase reaction (Fig. 4.6). Glucose-1-phosphate is formed in these reactions. This sugar is then readily metabolized in the glycolytic pathway. Similarly individual monosaccharides are phosphorylated to either glucose-1-phosphate, glucose-6-phosphate, or fructose-6-phosphate by a variety of reactions. It should be noted that 1 mole of ATP must be expended for each mole of monosaccharide that undergoes phosphorylation. The pathway for anaerobic glycolysis is shown in Fig. 11.2. The enzymes and cofactors are listed for each of the reactions.

Glucose-6-phosphate may be formed from glucose-1-phosphate by the action of phosphoglucomutase (glucose-1,6-diphosphate is a cofactor in this reaction) or by the direct phosphorylation of glucose by ATP and Mg^{2+} and the enzyme hexokinase (Reactions 2 and 3).

Glucose-6-phosphate undergoes an isomerization to yield fructose-6-phosphate. This reaction is catalyzed by phosphoglucoisomerase (Reaction 4). Mannose-6-phosphate can also be converted to fructose-6-phosphate by a similar enzyme, phosphomannoisomerase.

Phosphorylation of fructose-6-phosphate is catalyzed by ATP, Mg^{2+}, and the enzyme phosphofructokinase (Reaction 5). This reaction is not reversible and requires a specific phosphatase, fructose-1,6-diphosphatase. These enzymes act as metabolic regulators for energy production (ATP) and gluconeogenesis.

Fructose-1,6-diphosphate is cleaved by the enzyme aldolase into two triose phosphates, glycerceraldehyde-3-phosphate and dihydroxyacetone phosphate. Aldolase is specific for dihydroxyacetone phosphate (DHAP) but will utilize other aldehydes for the reverse reaction. The keto group of DHAP forms a Schiff

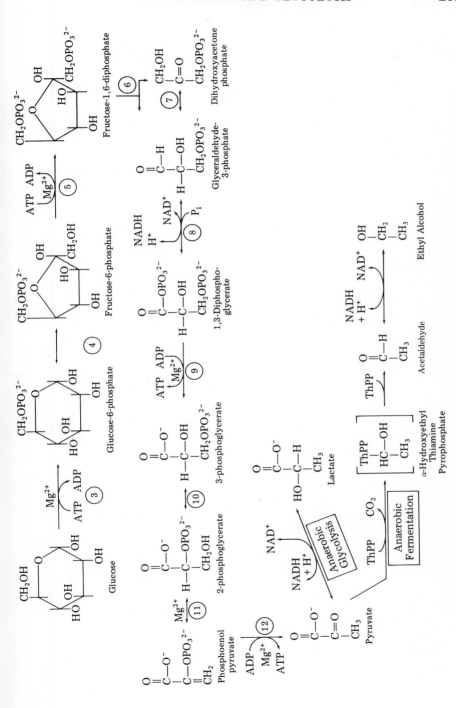

FIG. 11.2. STRUCTURES, ENZYMES, AND COFACTORS FOR GLYCOLYSIS AND FERMENTATION

base $\left(\begin{array}{c} R \\ \diagdown \\ \diagup \\ R \end{array} C = N — Enz \right)$ with an ϵ-amino group of a lysine residue

of the enzyme (Reaction 6).

DHAP and glyceraldehyde-3-phosphate can be interconverted by the enzyme triose phosphate isomerase, although the equilibrium of this reaction favors the formation of DHAP. The latter compound is important for the synthesis of glycerolphosphate. The further metabolism of glyceraldehyde-3-phosphate shifts the reaction toward glyceraldehyde-3-phosphate formation. Thus, two molecules of the latter compound can be formed from fructose-1,6-diphosphate (Reaction 7).

The next step is the first oxidation-reduction of this pathway. 1,3-diphosphoglycerate is formed in the presence of NAD^+, inorganic phosphate and glyceraldehyde-3-phosphate dehydrogenase (Reaction 8). The carboxylic-phosphoric acid anhydride is a high energy compound capable of converting ADP to ATP.

The acid anhydride, 1,3-diphosphoglycerate, is converted to 3-phosphoglycerate by phosphoglycerate kinase in the presence of ADP and forms ATP (Reaction 9). This type of ATP formation is termed substrate-linked phosphorylation, to distinguish it from oxidative production of ATP. The conversion of glycerate-3-phosphate to glycerate-2-phosphate is catalyzed by phosphoglycerate mutase. The cofactor in this reaction is glycerate-2,3-diphosphate (Reaction 10). This reaction is analogous to the conversion of glucose-1-phosphate to glucose-6-phosphate with glucose-1,6-diphosphate as the cofactor (Reaction 2).

Enolase catalyzes a reversible hydration-dehydration of glycerate-2-phosphate to form phosphoenolpyruvate (Reaction 11). This enzyme has an obligatory requirement for Mg^{2+} or Mn^{2+}. The phosphoenolpyruvate formed in this reaction is a high energy compound (approximately-13 Kcal/mole).

The second substrate-linked phosphorylation occurs when the phosphate of phosphenolpyruvate is transferred to ADP by pyruvate kinase with the concurrent formation of pyruvate (Reaction 12). This enzyme has a necessary requirement for divalent metals such as Mg^{2+} or Mn^{2+}, and is activated by ions such as K^+ and NH_4^+. This reaction is essentially irreversible and affords a barrier for gluconeogenesis.

Glycolysis is essentially the same for plants and animals to the point of pyruvate formation. At pyruvate, two divergent reactions can occur which differentiate fermentative processes that occur in yeast and microorganisms from anaerobic glycolysis such as the reactions of mammalian tissue and certain lactic acid producing microorganisms. In fermentation, pyruvate is decarboxylated to acetaldehyde via the enzyme pyruvate decarboxylase and the co-enzyme thiamine pyrophosphate (Reaction 13). The acetaldehyde is reduced to ethanol by NADH and the enzyme alcohol dehydrogenase (Reaction 14). Not only does this reaction produce ethanol but it serves as a ready source of NAD^+ needed for the glyceraldehyde-3-phosphate dehydrogenase reaction (Reaction 8).

The formation of lactate from pyruvate is accomplished by the enzyme lactic dehydrogenase with NADH as the reducing coenzyme. The NAD^+ produced is then available for use in glyceraldehyde-3-phosphate dehydrogenase.

Products of Anaerobic Fermentation

Glycerol.—Small amounts of glycerol are formed during the fermentation of glucose by yeast under acid conditions (pH 5-6). It was found that the production of glycerol could be increased by either the addition of bisulfites or by conducting the fermentation at an alkaline pH. With the scheme presented in Fig. 11.1 as a background, it is possible to return to a consideration of some other end-products of glycolysis. Acetaldehyde, produced by the catalytic action of pyruvate decarboxylase, is trapped by the bisulfite as an addition compound. The acetaldehyde is no longer able to act as a hydrogen acceptor for reduced NADH, thus blocking the regeneration of the NAD^+. Under these conditions dihydroxyacetone phosphate replaces acetaldehyde as the hydrogen acceptor, and is reduced to glyceraldehyde-3-phosphate,

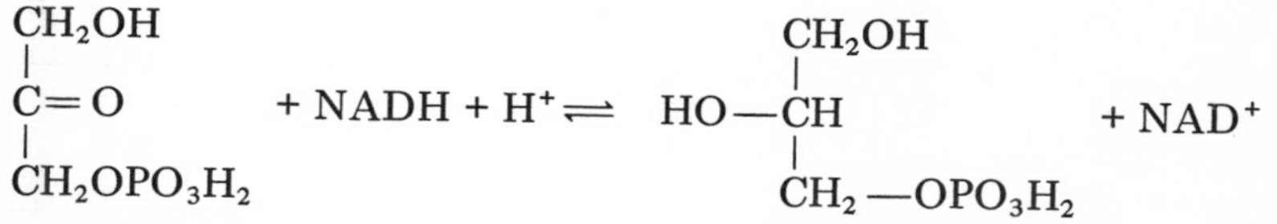

$$
\begin{array}{cc}
\begin{array}{l} CH_2OH \\ | \\ C=O \\ | \\ CH_2OPO_3H_2 \end{array} + NADH + H^+ \rightleftharpoons &
HO-\begin{array}{l} CH_2OH \\ | \\ CH \\ | \\ CH_2-OPO_3H_2 \end{array} + NAD^+
\end{array}
$$

Dihydroxyacetone phosphate · · · · · · · · L-α-glycerophosphate

The latter substance is hydrolyzed by a phosphatase to form glycerol.

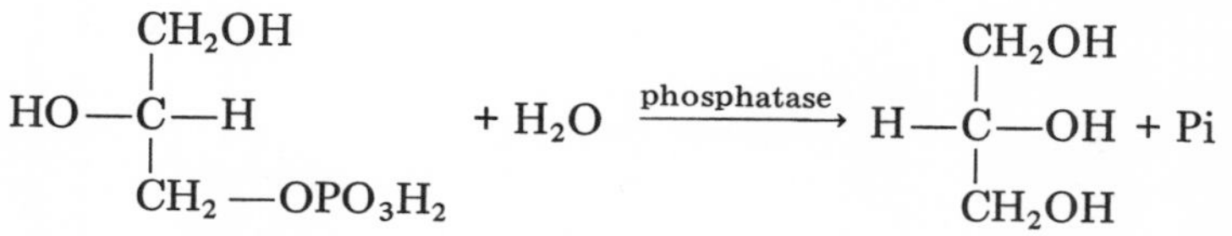

$$
HO-\begin{array}{l} CH_2OH \\ | \\ C-H \\ | \\ CH_2-OPO_3H_2 \end{array} + H_2O \xrightarrow{\text{phosphatase}} H-\begin{array}{l} CH_2OH \\ | \\ C-OH \\ | \\ CH_2OH \end{array} + Pi
$$

The overall fermentation process can be represented as follows:

$$\text{Glucose} + HSO_3^-Na^+ \rightleftharpoons \text{glycerol} + CH_3 - \overset{\displaystyle OH}{\underset{\displaystyle H}{\overset{|}{\underset{|}{C}}}} - SO_3^-Na^+ + CO_2$$

This process has been used industrially for the production of glycerol but it has some limitations due to the fact that the concentration of bisulfite is a critical factor. High concentrations of bisulfite inhibit the fermentation, while insufficient amounts decrease maximum yield.

If the fermentation is conducted in an alkaline medium the dihydroxyacetone phosphate is reduced to glycerol. This results in an insufficient amount of NAD^+ for the reduction of acetaldehyde which, instead of accumulating, undergoes a disproportionation to acetate and ethyl alcohol. This form of fermentation can be represented as follows:

$$2 \text{ glucose} \longrightarrow 2 \text{ glycerol} + 2 \text{ } CO_2 + \text{acetic acid} + \text{ethyl alcohol}$$

Lactic Acid Fermentation (Homolactic).—Lactic acid is produced in small quantities by many species of microorganisms. However, the lactic acid bacteria produce lactic acid as the major end-product of anaerobic glycolysis of sugars. The genera *Streptococcus, Microbacterium, Pediococcus*, a large number of *Lactobacillus* species, and certain *Bacillus* and *Rhizopus* species are homofermenters which ferment glucose to lactic acid.

The mechanism of the glucose breakdown by this group of microorganisms is similar to that of alcoholic fermentation except pyruvic acid is reduced to lactic acid. These organisms contain NAD^+ linked lactic dehydrogenase specific for D-lactic acid in addition to an L-lactic dehydrogenase. The lactic acid produced by most microorganisms is a racemic mixture of D and L forms (but a few organisms (*Rhizopus oryzae*) produce only the L (+) isomer).

Lactic acid has a pleasant sour taste, no odor, and is miscible with water in all proportions. This acid is used for preserving pickles and sauerkraut, acidifying soups and jams, and as an acidulant in the food and beverage industry.

Acetic Acid.—Very little pure acetic acid, as such, is used in foods. However, as the principal component of vinegar, large amounts of acetic acid are used in foods.

The production of vinegar involves two types of biochemical changes: first, a yeast fermentation for the production of alcohol (cf Fig. 11.2) from a carbohydrate source such as cider, grapes, sucrose, and malt, and second, the aerobic oxidation of ethanol to acetic acid by the action of acetic acid bacteria (acetobacter).

Vinegars are extensively employed in preparing salad dressings, mayonnaise, sour pickles, catsups, sauce, in curing of meats and in the canning of certain vegetables.

Additional Products of Fermentation.—In addition to the above fermentations, pyruvate is transformed to a variety of end-products. Some of these products are shown in Fig. 11.3. In all of these fermentations the microorganisms metabolize the carbohydrate to pyruvic acid by means of the glycolytic pathway. The further reactions of pyruvic acid vary according to the species of microorganism and lead to the formation of characteristic fermentation end-products (e.g., propionic acid in the *Propionibacteriaceae*).

Fermentation of Nitrogenous Substances.—Microorganisms require an exogenous source of nitrogen in order to synthesize proteins and nucleic acids. This requirement is met by supplying nitrogenous substances derived from some inexpensive sources or from the raw material undergoing fermentation. It has been shown that certain amino acids can be fermented anaerobically. This kind of fermentation is of secondary importance as compared with carbohydrate fermentation. However, the formation of aliphatic alcohols other than ethanol from fermentation of amino acids has an important bearing on the flavor of alcoholic beverages. For example, the higher alcohols contribute to the flavor of beer, wine, rum, and other alcoholic beverages. In contrast, during the aging of whiskey these alcohols become esterified with organic acids as part of the process by which the flavor is mellowed.

A pathway for the formation of isoamyl alcohol from L-leucine is shown in the scheme below.

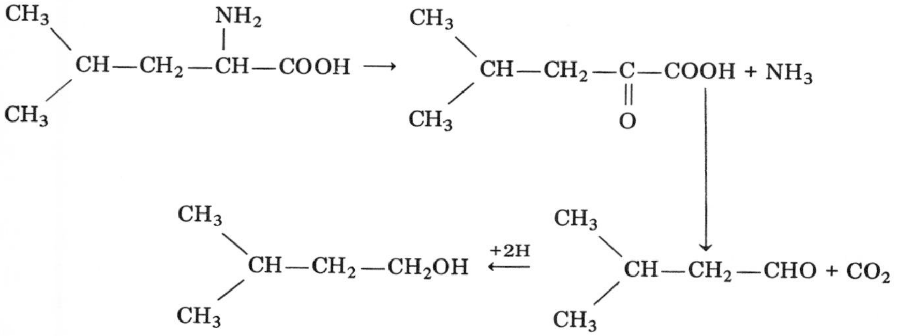

The ammonia set free in the above reaction is utilized by the bacterial cell. During alcoholic fermentation by *S. cerevisiae* small

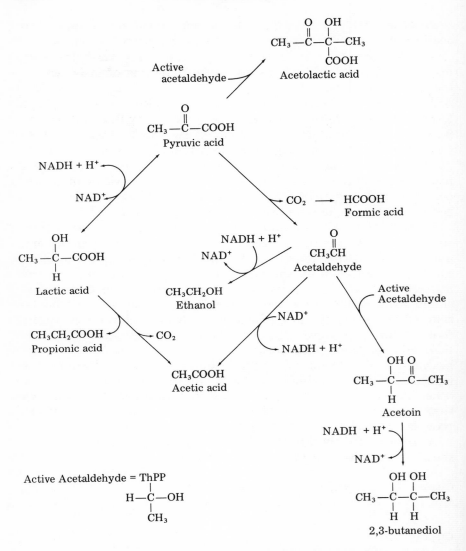

FIG. 11.3. PRODUCTS OF FERMENTATION PRODUCED FROM PYRUVATE

amounts of the higher alcohols are always formed, and this mixture of alcohols is known as "fusel oil." It is composed mostly of isoamyl alcohol followed by isobutyl and active amyl alcohols. Other alcohols are produced from α-amino acids in a similar manner. For example, tyrosol, the alcohol produced from tyrosine, contributes to the bitter flavor of beer.

Pasteur Effect.—Microorganisms that are able to grow with or without oxygen (facultative) behave quite differently metabolically in an aerobic environment as compared to an anaerobic environment. This was first observed by Pasteur during studies on the fermentation of glucose by yeast. He noted that in the presence of air (oxygen) less glucose was broken down and less alcohol was formed, whereas under anaerobic conditions more alcohol was formed and more glucose was fermented. This suppression of glycolysis by oxygen is termed the "Pasteur Effect." It may be explained by the fact that under fully aerobic conditions pyruvate is oxidized to carbon dioxide and water; whereas, under anaerobic conditions the pyruvate is reduced to alcohol (to lactate in other organisms). Thus, the entire potential energy of the glucose molecule is not made available to the cells under anaerobic conditions. As a consequence more rapid utilization of glucose will be needed to meet energy requirements.

This relationship between fermentation (anaerobic) and respiration (aerobic) processes is important in certain areas of food technology (e.g., the baking, brewing and distilling industries).

Baking.—Special strains of *S. cerevisiae* are used in the baking industry because they must have the ability to ferment flour dough vigorously and the ability to reproduce well and in good yield. Shortly after the mixing of flour, water, sugar, and yeast, the conditions within the dough become anaerobic so that the yeast ferments the sugars by the reactions of the fermentative pathway to produce CO_2 and alcohol. The CO_2 entrapped by the gluten (plant protein) enables the dough to rise. Subsequent reactions to fermentation produce flavor products and organic acids that mellow and condition the gluten. The exact proportion of sugars converted to CO_2, as well as overall rate of reaction, are factors which are controlled by the environmental conditions in the dough, by the genetic make-up of the yeast, and pretreatment of the dough.

Brewing.—Brewers yeast may be classified as top fermenting and bottom fermenting. *S. Cerevisiae* is a top fermenting yeast and is used in the manufacture of ale. Bottom fermenting yeast (*S. carlsbergensis*) is used in the production of lager beer. Fermentors are provided with a cooling system which maintains relatively constant temperatures and anaerobic conditions.

Wine.—*S. cerevisiae ellipsoideus* is the yeast used for the fermentation of wines. Once again, a large supply of oxygen is essential for the rapid multiplication of yeast cells during the initial stages of fermentation. However, the latter stage proceeds best under anaerobic conditions; alcohol and CO_2 are the products rather than growth and reproduction.

Deterioration of Fermented Food Products.—Fermented food products may undergo deterioration if not maintained under controlled conditions. Molds, for example, are able to metabolize the acid formed during fermentation and thereby permit the growth of other microorganisms. Spoilage may be controlled by using such food processing procedures as the application of sterilization or refrigeration.

Chemical Prevention of Fermentation.—The food technologist is also faced with the problem of preventing food deterioration by fermentation. In addition to heat treatment and refrigeration, chemical preservatives can be used to prevent deterioration of foods. The use of chemicals must comply with Food and Drug Administration regulations under the Food Additives Amendment to the Food, Drug and Cosmetic Act.

The ideal chemical preservative should: (1) extend the shelf-life of the food, (2) be safe for human consumption when used in effective concentrations in food, (3) not alter color, odor, flavor or texture of the food, (4) be capable of being identified and quantified by accepted methods of food analysis; and (5) provide an economical means of preservation. The following list gives some of the chemical preservatives that meet these requirements and are effective in preventing deterioration of foods.

Benzoic Acid and Benzoates.—The use of these preservatives is permitted in foods provided the quantity added does not exceed the amount permitted by State and Federal laws (most States require that sodium benzoate not exceed 0.1%). Sodium benzoate is more effective in an acid medium than in a neutral medium. Methyl and propyl esters of p-hydroxylbenzoic acid, methyl and ethyl paraben (up to 0.1%), and the sodium and calcium salts are effective in acid, neutral, and alkaline pH ranges. The latter preservatives are effective against yeasts, molds, and bacteria. These compounds have been used to control undesirable fermentations in fruit juices, jams, jellies, preserves, pickles, relishes, olives, salads, and pie fillings.

Boric Acid and Borates, Salicylic Acid and Salicylates.—These preservatives are not permitted in foods in the United States. However, they are permitted in some countries for the preservation of butter, meats, and whole fruits.

Sulfur Dioxide (sulfurous acid) and Sulfites.—These compounds are used in a limited number of foods such as molasses, dried fruit, fruit juices, syrups, and wine, but cannot be used in foods high in thiamine (e.g., meats).

Diethyl Pyrocarbonate (DEPC).—This compound is especially effective against yeasts. It is used to arrest fermentation in fruit juices and in bottled wines (200 ppm). When added to aqueous solutions, it rapidly hydrolyzes to ethanol and CO_2, leaving only trace residues. It decomposes more rapidly in neutral than in alkaline solutions.

BIBLIOGRAPHY

BARKER, H. A. 1961. Fermentation of nitrogenous organic compounds. *In* The Bacteria, Vol. 2, I. C. Gunsalus, and R. Y. Stanier (Editors). Academic Press, New York.

CASIDA, L. E., JR. 1968. Industrial Microbiology. John Wiley & Sons, New York.

CHICHESTER, D. F., and TANNER, JR., F. W. 1968. Antimicrobial food additives. *In* Handbook of Food Additives, T. E. Furia (Editor). Chemical Rubber Co., Cleveland, Ohio.

DESROSIER, N. W. 1970. The Technology of Food Preservation, 3rd Edition. Avi Publishing Co., Westport, Conn.

ELSDEN, S. R. 1952. Bacterial fermentation. *In* The Enzymes, Vol. 2, Part 1, J. B. Sumner, and K. Myrback (Editors). Academic Press, New York.

GUNSALUS, I. C., and SHUSTER, C. W. 1961. Energy-yielding metabolism in bacteria. *In* the Bacteria, Vol. 2, I. C. Gunsalus, and R. Y. Stanier (Editors). Academic Press, New York.

HUANEJ, H. T. 1964. Microbial production of amino acids. *In* Progress in Industrial Microbiology, Vol. 5, D. J. D. Hockenhull (Editor). Gordon & Breach, Science Publishers, London.

KAUFMAN, S., KORKES, S., and DEL CAMPILLO, A. 1951. Biosynthesis of dicarboxylic acids by carbon dioxide fixation V. Further study of the "malic" enzyme of *Lactobacillus arabinosus*. J. Biol. Chem. *192*, 301–312.

MARTH, E. H. 1962. Certain aspects of starter culture metabolism. J. Dairy Sci. *45*, 1271–1277.

PEDERSON, C. S. 1971. Microbiology of Food Fermentations. Avi Publishing Co., Westport, Conn.

PRESCOTT, S. C., and DUNN, C. G. 1959. Industrial Microbiology, 3rd Edition. McGraw-Hill Book Co., New York.

RAINBOW, C., and ROSE, A. H. 1963. Biochemistry of Industrial Microorganisms. Academic Press, New York.

ROSE, A. H. 1961. Industrial Microbiology. Butterworth and Co., Washington, D.C.

WEBB, A. D., KEPNER, R. E., and IKEDA, R. M. 1952. Composition of a typical grape brandy fusel oil. Anal. Chem. *24*, 1944–1949.

WHITE, J. 1954. Yeast Technology. John Wiley & Sons, New York.

WILKINSON, J. F., and ROSE, A. H. 1963. Fermentation processes. *In* Biochemistry of Industrial Micro-organisms. C. Rainbow, and A. H. Rose (Editors). Academic Press, New York.

WOOD, H. G., and STERNHOLM, R. L. 1962. Assimilation of carbon dioxide by heterotropic organisms. *In* The Bacteria, Vol. 3, I. C. Gunsalus, and R. Y. Stanier (Editors). Academic Press, New York.

WOOD, W. A. 1961. Fermentation of carbohydrates and related compounds. *In* The Bacteria, Vol. 2, I. C. Gunsalus, and R. Y. Stanier (Editors). Academic Press, New York.

CHAPTER 12

Respiration

The two main pathways by which energy is derived from foods are anaerobic fermentation-glycolysis and respiration. Anaerobic glycolysis which occurs in cells of most higher plants, animals, and many microorganisms results in the synthesis of two molecules of lactic acid. In anaerobic fermentation, the carbohydrate is broken down into 2 molecules of ethanol and 2 molecules of carbon dioxide. These two processes release only a small fraction of the chemical energy potentially available in sugar. The glycolytic pathway is an obligatory first step for respiration (Fig. 11.2) because it is in this pathway that the different sugars (hexoses) are collected, phosphorylated (at the expense of ATP) and then through a sequence of reactions the carbon skeleton under anaerobic conditions is degraded to pyruvate. Pyruvate is then converted to lactate by anaerobic glycolysis. In alcoholic fermentation, the reactions are identical until pyruvate; at this point pyruvate is decarboxylated to acetaldehyde, which in turn is reduced to ethanol. The storage carbohydrates, glycogen and starch, are introduced into the first stage of glycolysis by several auxiliary enzyme systems.

Respiration occurs in three phases: (1) the mobilization of acetyl-SCoA from pyruvate (or fatty acids and amino acids), (2) the breakdown of acetyl residues by the tricarboxylic acid cycle (TCA) to yield CO_2 and H atoms, and (3) the hydrogen atoms removed during the dehydrogenation are finally combined with molecular oxygen to form water. The latter process (respiratory chain) also occurs in several stages. The sequence of the electron transport chain is presented in Chap. 13.

Citric Acid Cycle

The overall reaction catalyzed by the tricarboxylic acid cycle[1] may be represented as follows:

$$CH_3COOH + 2H_2O \longrightarrow 2CO_2 + 8H$$

It should be noted that neither molecular oxygen, inorganic phosphate, nor ATP take part in the cycle. The primary function is dehydrogenation of acetic acid to form 2 molecules of CO_2 and 4

---

[1] The acids referred to in this chapter exist as the anions at physiological pH rather than the undissociated form used in the following discussions.

pairs of hydrogen atoms. The process is cyclic in nature and takes place in the mitochondria. The various stages of the TCA cycle are illustrated in Fig. 12.1. In each turn of the cycle, 1 mole of acetyl-SCoA enters by condensation with 1 mole of oxaloacetic acid to

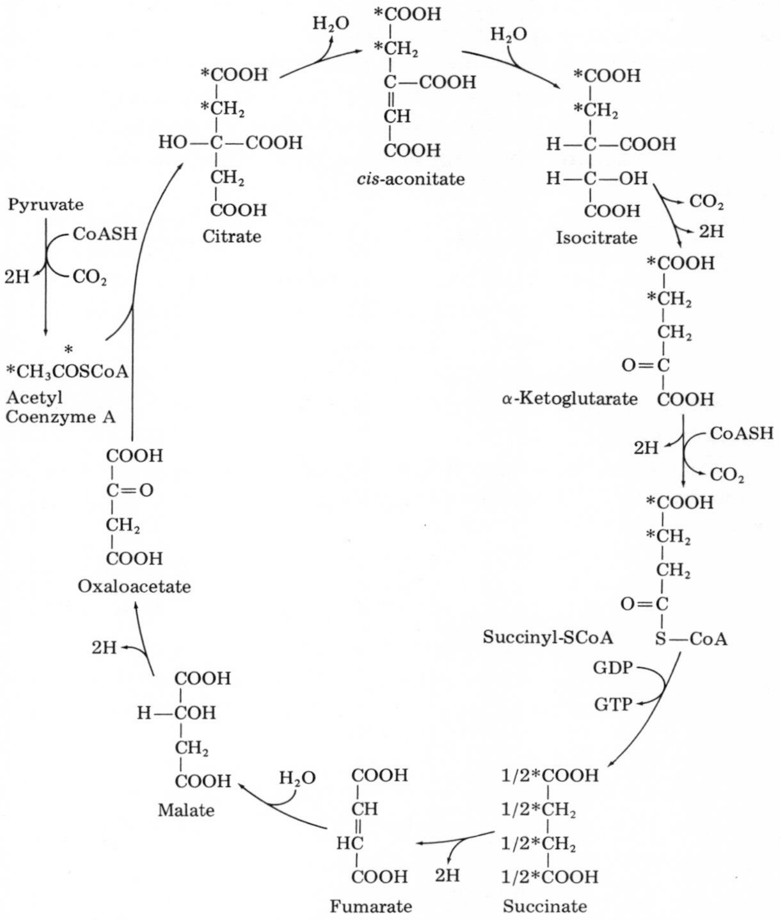

FIG. 12.1. TRICARBOXYLIC ACID CYCLE (CITRIC ACID CYCLE)

form citric acid. By successive loss and addition of water, citric acid is rearranged into isocitric acid. The latter compound is oxidized and decarboxylated to α-ketoglutaric acid. Succinic acid is formed by oxidative decarboxylation from α-ketoglutaric acid.

Succinate[2] is ultimately oxidized to oxaloacetic acid which may then begin another turn of the cycle. Each turn of the cycle uses one mole of oxaloacetate to form citrate but it is regenerated at the end of the cycle. Thus, there is no net loss of oxaloacetate when the cycle operates and one molecule can bring about the oxidation of a large number of acetate molecules.

Pyruvate Dehydrogenase Complex.—The utilization of carbohydrates, lipids, and proteins is dependent upon their transformation into substances that can enter the tricarboxylic acid cycle. The most important of these substances is "active acetyl," the acetyl derivative of coenzyme A. The conversion of pyruvate to acetyl-SCoA is catalyzed by the enzyme complex known as pyruvate dehydrogenase system.

$$CH_3-\underset{\underset{O}{\|}}{C}-COOH + CoA-SH + NAD^+ \xrightarrow[\substack{TPP \\ Lipoic\ Acid}]{Mg^{++}}$$

$$CH_3-\underset{\underset{O}{\|}}{C}-SCoA + NADH + H^+ + CO_2$$

This reaction requires 3 enzymes and 5 cofactors (pyruvate dehydrogenase system).

The initial event is the decarboxylation of pyruvic acid in the presence of Mg^{2+}, thiamine pyrophosphate (TPP), and pyruvic acid decarboxylase.

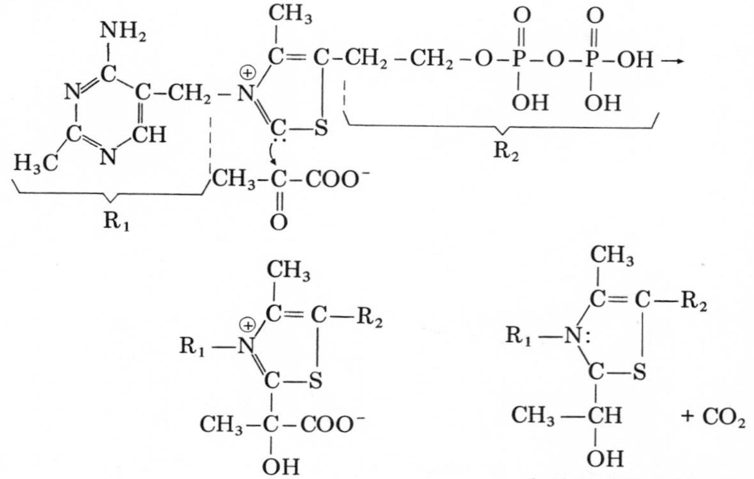

α-hydroxyethyl thiamine pyrophosphate

_____

[2] Since carbon C-1 cannot be distinguished from C-4 and C-2 from C-3 in succinate, the radioactivity of these carbons is designated as one-half of the original (see Fig. 12.1).

Next, the hydroxyethyl group of the latter complex is transferred to one of the sulfhydryl groups of lipoic acid which is covalently bound to the second enzyme of the complex, dihydrolipoyl trans-acetylase. The addition product rearranges and dissociates to re-generate thiamine pyrophosphate and acetyl lipoamide.

Note that as a result of this reaction the hydroxyethyl group

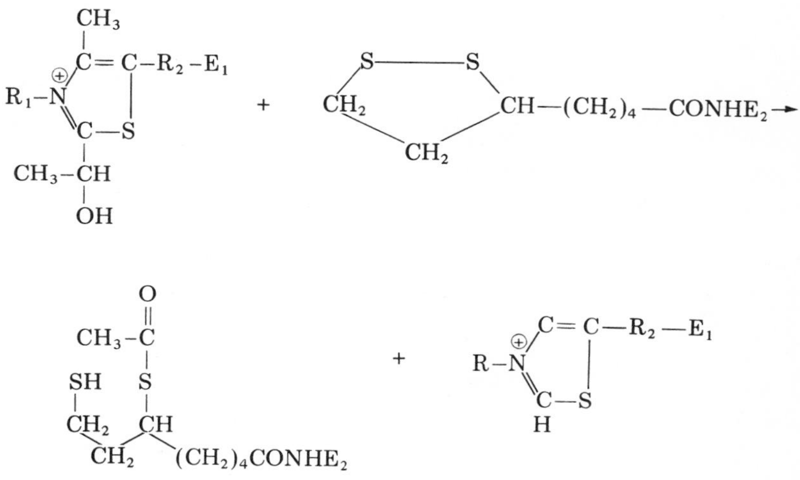

$$
\begin{array}{c}
CH_3 \\
| \\
\overset{\oplus}{R_1-N} \underset{C-S}{\overset{C=C-R_2-E_1}{\big|}} \\
| \\
CH_3-CH \\
| \\
OH
\end{array}
\quad + \quad
\begin{array}{c}
S\text{———}S \\
CH_2 \qquad CH-(CH_2)_4-CONHE_2 \rightarrow \\
CH_2
\end{array}
$$

$$
\begin{array}{c}
\quad\quad O \\
\quad\quad \| \\
CH_3-C \\
| \\
SH \quad S \\
| \quad\quad | \\
CH_2 \quad CH \\
CH_2 \quad (CH_2)_4CONHE_2
\end{array}
\quad + \quad
\begin{array}{c}
\overset{\oplus}{R-N} \underset{C-S}{\overset{C=C-R_2-E_1}{\big|}} \\
\quad\quad H
\end{array}
$$

Acetyl lipoamide

$$
\begin{array}{c}
CH_2 \\
CH_2 \quad CH-(CH_2)_4-CONHE_2 \\
| \quad\quad | \\
SH \quad S \\
\quad\quad | \\
\quad\quad C \\
CH_3 \quad O
\end{array}
+ \; CoASH \rightarrow
\begin{array}{c}
CH_2 \\
CH_2 \quad CH_2-(CH_2)_4-CONHE_2 \; + \\
| \quad\quad | \\
SH \quad SH
\end{array}
$$

$$
\begin{array}{c}
\quad\quad O \\
\quad\quad \| \\
CH_3-C-SCoA
\end{array}
$$

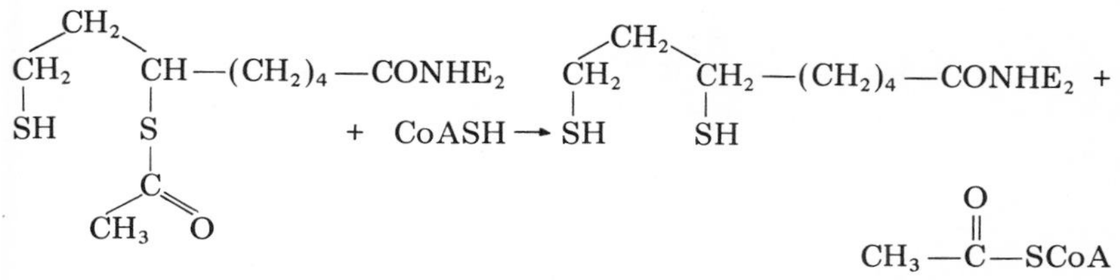

becomes an acetyl group and oxidized lipoic acid has been reduced.

Next the acetyl group is enzymatically transferred from the lipoyl group of dihydrolipoyl transacetylase to the thiol group of coenzyme A to form acetyl-SCoA. At this point the pyruvic acid has been oxidized to acetyl CoA and is ready to enter the tricarboxy-lic acid cycle. The thiamine pyrophosphate is regenerated but the lipoamide which is in the disulfhydryl form must be oxidized to its original disulfide form. This step is catalyzed by a flavoprotein, dihydrolipoyl dehydrogenase (E_3-FAD) as follows:

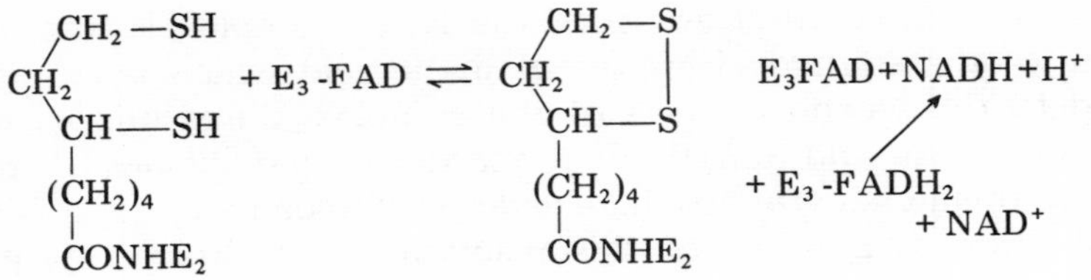

$$\begin{array}{c}
CH_2-SH \\
| \\
CH_2 \\
\backslash \\
CH-SH \\
| \\
(CH_2)_4 \\
| \\
CONHE_2
\end{array}
\quad + E_3\text{-FAD} \rightleftharpoons \quad
\begin{array}{c}
CH_2-S \\
| \qquad | \\
CH_2 \qquad | \\
\backslash \qquad | \\
CH-S \\
| \\
(CH_2)_4 \\
| \\
CONHE_2
\end{array}
\quad
\begin{array}{c}
E_3FAD+NADH+H^+ \\
\nearrow \\
+ E_3\text{-}FADH_2 \\
+ NAD^+
\end{array}$$

The final step is the regeneration of oxidized FAD to perpetuate the reaction.

Citrate Synthase.—Citrate synthase catalyzes the entry of acetyl-SCoA into the cycle via condensation with oxaloacetate to form citrate. In forming the latter acid, the methyl group of acetyl-SCoA condenses with the carbonyl carbon atom of oxaloacetic acid, with subsequent hydrolysis of the thioester and the formation of CoA-SH.

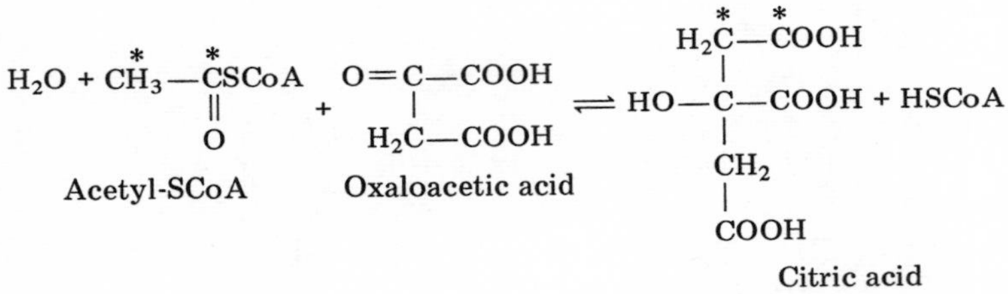

$$H_2O + \overset{*}{C}H_3-\underset{\underset{O}{\|}}{\overset{*}{C}}SCoA \quad + \quad
\begin{array}{c}
O=C-COOH \\
| \\
H_2C-COOH
\end{array}
\rightleftharpoons
\begin{array}{c}
\overset{*}{H_2}\overset{*}{C}-COOH \\
| \\
HO-C-COOH \\
| \\
CH_2 \\
| \\
COOH
\end{array}
+ HSCoA$$

Acetyl-SCoA   Oxaloacetic acid   Citric acid

This reaction proceeds to the right in the production of citrate.

Aconitase.—This reaction, which is catalyzed by the enzyme aconitase, results in the isomerization of citric acid (a symmetric molecule) to isocitric acid (an asymmetric molecule). Note that aconitic acid has a *cis* double bond while citric acid and isocitric acid have a specific stereochemical configuration about their asymmetric carbon atoms. Therefore, the reactions involve the stereo-

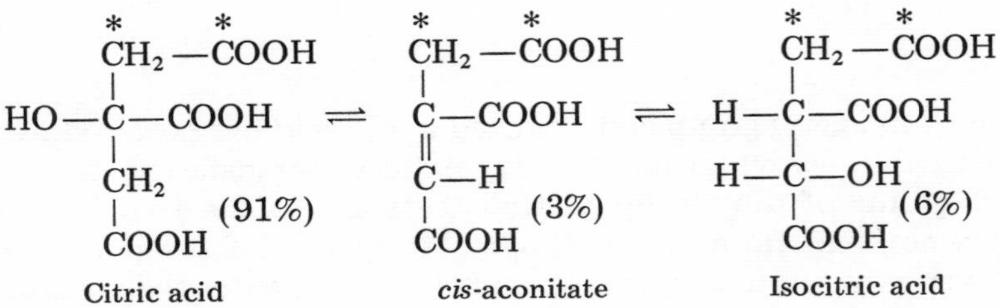

$$\begin{array}{c}
\overset{*}{C}H_2-\overset{*}{C}OOH \\
| \\
HO-C-COOH \\
| \\
CH_2 \\
| \quad (91\%) \\
COOH
\end{array}
\rightleftharpoons
\begin{array}{c}
\overset{*}{C}H_2-\overset{*}{C}OOH \\
| \\
C-COOH \\
\| \\
C-H \\
| \quad (3\%) \\
COOH
\end{array}
\rightleftharpoons
\begin{array}{c}
\overset{*}{C}H_2-\overset{*}{C}OOH \\
| \\
H-C-COOH \\
| \\
H-C-OH \\
| \quad (6\%) \\
COOH
\end{array}$$

Citric acid   *cis*-aconitate   Isocitric acid

specific *trans* addition of water to the α,β double bond of *cis*-aconitate. The enzyme aconitase requires the presence of ferrous iron (Fe^{2+}).

Isocitric Dehydrogenase.—The oxidative decarboxylation of isocitric acid to α-ketoglutaric acid is catalyzed by the enzyme isocitric dehydrogenase. There are 2 types of the enzyme: 1 type requires NAD^+ as the electron acceptor and the presence of Mg^{2+} or Mn^{2+} for activity; the other type requires $NADP^+$ as the electron acceptor. The NAD^+-requiring enzyme is the normal catalyst for isocitric acid oxidation, while the $NADP^+$ type enzyme is involved in auxiliary biosynthetic reactions. In either case the overall reactions are identical and the reaction is usually the rate-limiting reaction of the tricarboxylic acid cycle.

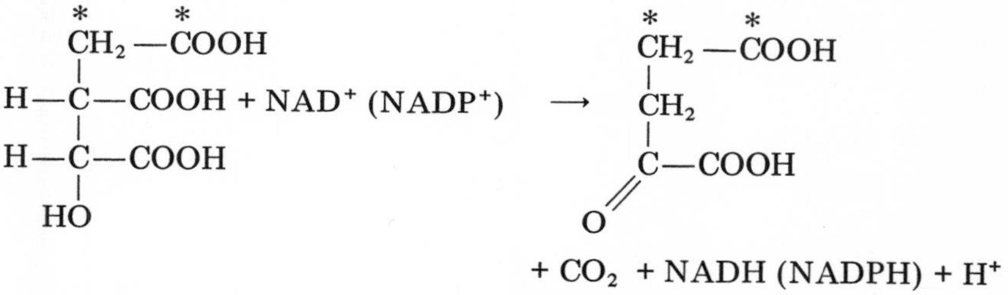

$$
\begin{array}{l}
\overset{*}{C}H_2-\overset{*}{C}OOH \\
H-C-COOH + NAD^+ (NADP^+) \;\longrightarrow\; \\
H-C-COOH \\
HO
\end{array}
\qquad
\begin{array}{l}
\overset{*}{C}H_2-\overset{*}{C}OOH \\
CH_2 \\
C-COOH \\
O
\end{array}
$$

$$+ CO_2 + NADH\ (NADPH) + H^+$$

α-Ketoglutaric Dehydrogenase Complex.—The oxidation of α-ketoglutaric acid to succinate occurs in two stages. The first stage involves the oxidative decarboxylation of α-ketoglutaric acid to form succinyl-SCoA. This reaction, catalyzed by α-ketoglutaric decarboxylase, requires as cofactors TPP, Mg^{2+}, NAD^+, lipoic acid, and CoA-SH. This complex is quite similar to the pyruvate dehydrogenase complex. The reaction is not reversible primarily because of the decarboxylation of the α-keto acid.

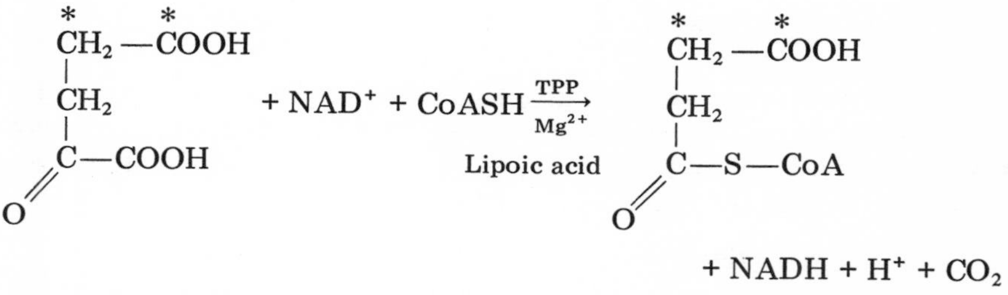

$$
\begin{array}{l}
\overset{*}{C}H_2-\overset{*}{C}OOH \\
CH_2 \\
C-COOH \\
O
\end{array}
+ NAD^+ + CoASH \xrightarrow[\text{Mg}^{2+}]{\text{TPP}}
\begin{array}{l}
\overset{*}{C}H_2-\overset{*}{C}OOH \\
CH_2 \\
C-S-CoA \\
O
\end{array}
$$

Lipoic acid

$$+ NADH + H^+ + CO_2$$

Succinyl Thiokinase.—The end-product of the above reaction undergoes loss of CoASH by reaction with guanosine diphosphate (GDP) and phosphate to yield succinate. Succinyl thiokinase catalyzes the reaction with the formation of GTP which is a high energy compound. This reaction is referred to as a substrate level phosphorylation.

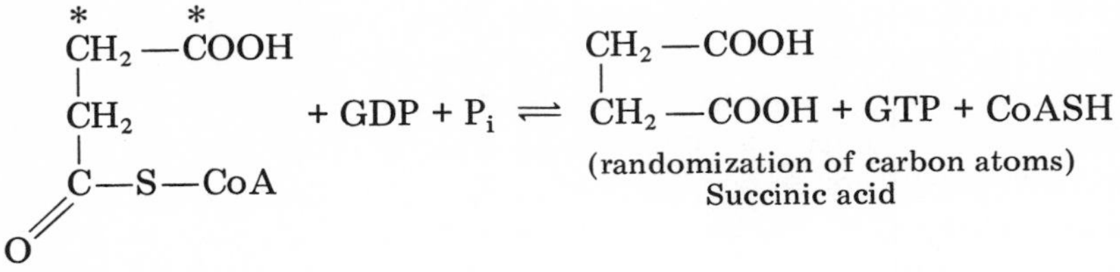

$$\begin{matrix} \overset{*}{CH_2}-COOH \\ | \\ CH_2 \\ | \\ C-S-CoA \\ \diagdown\!\!\diagup \\ O \end{matrix} \quad + GDP + P_i \rightleftharpoons \begin{matrix} \overset{*}{CH_2}-COOH \\ | \\ CH_2-COOH \end{matrix} + GTP + CoASH$$

Succinyl-SCoA

(randomization of carbon atoms)
Succinic acid

Succinic Dehydrogenase.—This enzyme catalyzes the oxidation of succinate to fumarate by splitting off two hydrogen atoms and thereby reducing covalently bound flavine adenine dinucleotide (FAD). The enzyme is competitively inhibited by malonic acid and oxaloacetic acid.

$$\begin{matrix} CH_2-COOH \\ | \\ CH_2-COOH \end{matrix} + E\text{-}FAD \rightleftharpoons \begin{matrix} HC-COOH \\ || \\ HOOC-CH \end{matrix} + E\text{-}FADH_2$$

Succinic acid   Fumaric acid

Fumarase.—Fumarase catalyzes the reversible hydration of fumarate to L-malate. The enzyme acts stereospecifically since it forms only the L-stereoisomer of malate (addition of H_2O is *trans*).

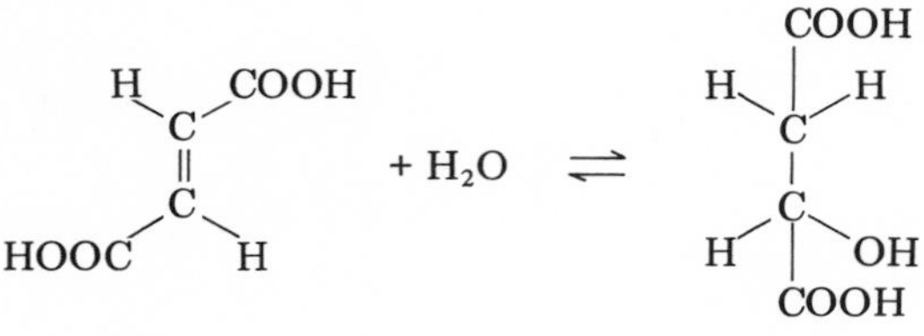

$$\begin{matrix} H \diagdown \quad COOH \\ \quad C \\ \quad || \\ \quad C \\ HOOC \diagup \quad H \end{matrix} \quad + H_2O \rightleftharpoons \begin{matrix} COOH \\ H\diagdown | \diagup H \\ C \\ C \\ H \diagup | \diagdown OH \\ COOH \end{matrix}$$

Fumaric   L-malic

Malic Dehydrogenase.—Finally, L-malate dehydrogenase, an NAD^+-linked enzyme, catalyzes the oxidation of L-malate to oxaloacetate. Oxaloacetate is then ready to accept another molecule of acetyl-SCoA and repeat the cycle.

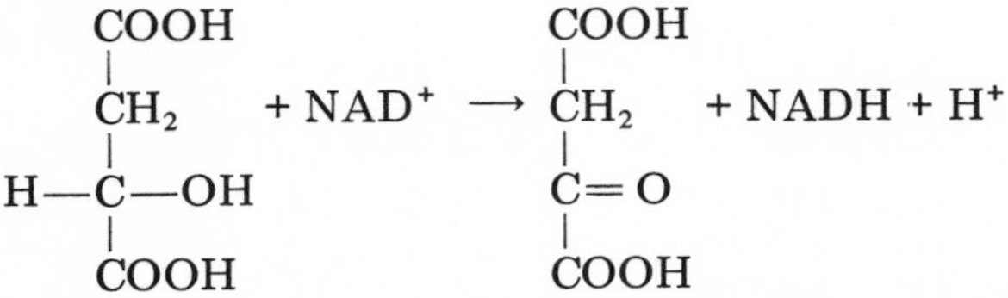

$$\begin{matrix} COOH \\ | \\ CH_2 \\ | \\ H-C-OH \\ | \\ COOH \end{matrix} + NAD^+ \rightarrow \begin{matrix} COOH \\ | \\ CH_2 \\ | \\ C=O \\ | \\ COOH \end{matrix} + NADH + H^+$$

In summary, for each turn of the cycle 1 molecule of acetyl-SCoA is consumed, 2 carbon atoms appear as carbon dioxide (equivalent to, but not identical to, the 2 carbon atoms of the acetyl group), and oxaloacetic acid is regenerated. Four of the individual reactions are dehydrogenation reactions; 3 of which result in the reduction of NAD^+ (reactions 5, 6 and 10) and one results in the reduction of FAD (reaction 8). The oxidation of the reduced pyridine nucleotides by the electron transport chain releases the energy available from respiration. The electrons from the hydrogen combine with oxygen via the electron transport chain to form water.

Regulation of the Citric Acid Cycle

The enzymes of the tricarboxylic acid cycle, together with the associated electron-transfer and oxidase systems are located in the mitochondria. In addition, mitochondria contain other enzymes such as dehydrogenases (glutamic, pyruvic), enzymes for the biosynthesis of compounds (phospholipids), enzymes for activation and elongation of fatty acids, and hydrolytic enzymes (glutaminase). Thus, mitochondria are specialized organelles in cells that if given a supply of either acetyl-SCoA or of any single citric acid cycle intermediate, each cell has the capability of producing any of the TCA acids.

An important aspect of mitochondria is the selective permeability of the mitochondrial membrane. For example, reduced cytoplasmic pyridine nucleotide (NADH) cannot enter the mitochondrion, thus cannot be oxidized directly. A shuttle exists between the mitochondrion and cytoplasm for the oxidation of NADH. This is accomplished by enzyme systems capable of catalyzing reversible oxidation-reduction reactions. Several enzyme systems are known, but β-hydroxybutyrate dehydrogenase, an NAD^+ linked enzyme, will serve to illustrate the action of the shuttle. In the cytoplasm NADH is oxidized to NAD^+ while acetoacetate is reduced to β-hydroxybutyrate. The latter compound is transported across the membrane into the mitochondrion where it is oxidized to acetoacetate with the concomitant reduction of NAD^+ to $NADH + H^+$. The acetoacetate leaves the mitochondrion to complete the cycle.

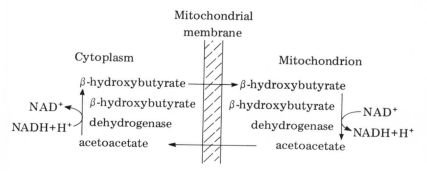

There is evidence to support the theory that ADP and ATP are actively transported into and out of the mitochondrion (Klingenberg and Pfaff 1968). In the scheme proposed, ADP and ATP are transported from the cristae to the matrix by a system called "adenylate translocase" which is highly specific for ADP and ATP but having a low affinity for other nucleotides such as AMP, GTP, and GDP. The system has enzyme characteristics such as temperature dependence, inhibition, kinetics, etc. In the transport into the matrix, ADP is exchanged several times faster than ATP. In the reverse reaction out of the matrix, ADP and ATP are translocated at about equal rates.

A key enzyme for control of the citric acid cycle is isocitric dehydrogenase. This enzyme is specifically inhibited by ATP and NADH, and is activated by ADP and AMP. In any metabolic condition wherein ADP or AMP concentration increases, presumably because of an increase in rate of breakdown of ATP in energy requiring reactions, there is an increase in the rate of isocitrate oxidation and with it an increase in the rate of the citric acid cycle. An increase in the rate of the cycle causes an increased rate of electron transport and, thus, of oxidative phosphorylation of ADP or AMP to ATP. As the concentration of the mitochondrial metabolites increase, the ratio of $\dfrac{\text{ATP}}{\text{ADP} + P_i}$ increases and the respiratory rate drops, the electron flow through the electron transport chain stops, and ATP and NADH + H$^+$ accumulate. As the ATP and NADH accumulate, isocitric dehydrogenase is inhibited. Citric acid begins to accumulate and it also inhibits isocitric dehydrogenase.

Some of the ATP diffuses into cytoplasm for biosynthetic reactions. Citrate also moves into the cytoplasm where it is converted into oxaloacetic acid and acetyl-SCoA. The oxaloacetic acid can be converted to aspartate by transamination which is a precursor for proteins and pyrimidines.

Isocitrate also will begin to pass into the cytoplasm where part of it is oxidized by the NADP$^+$ linked enzyme to generate NADPH + H$^+$ for biosynthetic purposes such as fatty acid metabolism. The remaining portion of isocitrate will be converted to acetyl-SCoA and four-carbon dicarboxylic acids.

The acetyl-SCoA is used for long-chain fatty acid synthesis. As the long-chain fatty acids increase, the citrate synthase will be inhibited with the net effect of having acetyl-SCoA and oxaloacetate diverted to other biosynthetic pathways (e.g., oxaloacetate is utilized in the synthesis of porphyrins). As a result of these reactions, ADP accumulates in the cytoplasm, which then moves into the mitochondria. As ADP increases, this causes the $\dfrac{ADP + P_i}{ATP}$ ratio to increase and, as a consequence, respiration begins. This is accomplished primarily by ADP activation of isocitric dehydrogenase. Conversely, with the accumulation of ATP, isocitric dehydrogenase is inhibited and respiration slows down.

Accumulation of Organic Acids

Each cell can produce any of the acids of the citric acid cycle. Organic acids of the TCA cycle often accumulate in plant tissue in high concentrations. When large quantities of citrate and malate are present in fruits they accumulate in the vacuole. The metabolic enzymes of the mitochondrial citric acid cycle are not then available to act on these compounds. Smaller quantities of other citric acid cycle intermediates may also be found in the vacuoles of fruits. This phenomenon occurs when ATP utilization is low. As previously pointed out, the intramitochondrial accumulation of certain of these acids would be expected to slow down the cycle operation. Thus, it would appear there are other enzymic systems which synthesize the accumulating acids independently of the TCA cycle reactions.

Organic acids in living organisms may arise by CO_2 fixation reactions. Of the several CO_2 reactions that are recognized, three of these result in the production of dicarboxylic acids. The enzymes catalyzing these reactions are widely distributed in nature.

(a) The malic enzyme which is common in fruits, catalyzes the following reaction: CO_2 + pyruvic acid + NADPH + H $\rightleftharpoons$ L-malic acid + $NADP^+$. The high concentration of NADPH relative to $NADP^+$ that is observed under conditions occurring in plant cells would favor the formation of malate even though the reaction is readily reversible.

(b) Phosphoenolpyruvate carboxykinase is common in plants and catalyzes the reaction:

$$CO_2 + \text{phosphoenolpyruvic acid} + IDP \overset{Mg^{2+}}{\rightleftharpoons}$$

$$\text{oxaloacetic acid} + ITP$$

This reaction is readily reversible and can go from right to left to produce phosphoenolpyruvate. PEP can then be converted to sugars via reverse glycolysis.

(c) Another CO_2 fixation enzyme, which is found in spinach leaves, is phosphoenolpyruvate carboxylase. The reaction is as follows:

$$CO_2 + \text{Phosphoenolpyruvic acid} + H_2O \xrightarrow{\text{Mg}^{2+}}$$

$$\text{oxaloacetic acid} + P_i$$

This reaction unlike the preceding two reactions, will only proceed from left to right.

The metabolism of tartaric acid is as yet relatively unknown. However, observations have indicated that TCA cycle organic acids are not precursors because labelled $C^{14}O_2$ is not appreciably incorporated into tartaric acid either in mature grapes or excised leaves, whereas malic acid and other TCA cycle acids are labelled. Similarly, malic acid is not converted to tartaric acid in grapes and labelled tartrate when presented to the grape yields no other radioactive component in the fruit.

Similarly no connection has been found between the production or utilization of oxalic acid and the citric acid cycle.

Other Pathways of Carbohydrate Metabolism

The Glyoxylate Cycle—The glyoxylate pathway does not exist in mammalian species but exists in microorganisms, algae, and plants. The cycle functions when acetate must serve both as a source of energy and as a source of intermediates required to synthesize carbohydrates and other cellular constituents, for example, plant seedlings before photosynthesis begins.

The overall scheme of the cycle is shown in Fig. 12.2. There are two points of entry into the citric acid cycle. One is the reaction catalyzed by citrate synthase:

$$\text{acetyl-SCoA} + \text{oxaloacetate} \longrightarrow \text{citrate} + \text{CoASH}$$

The second point of entry is the reaction catalyzed by malic synthetase:

$$\text{acetyl-SCoA} + \text{glyoxylate} \longrightarrow \text{L-malate} + \text{CoASH}$$

The glyoxylate needed for the latter reaction is supplied by the cleavage of isocitrate to succinate by the enzyme isocitratase. Thus, the key enzymes in the cycle are isocitratase and malate synthetase. One revolution of the cycle results in the use of 2 acetate molecules to form 1 molecule of succinate. Succinate is then converted to oxaloacetate via fumarate and malate. Oxaloacetate may be converted to phosphoenolpyruvate which can form monosaccharides by reverse glycolysis (glycogenesis). Malate formed from malate synthetase can also function in this series of reactions leading to sugar formation.

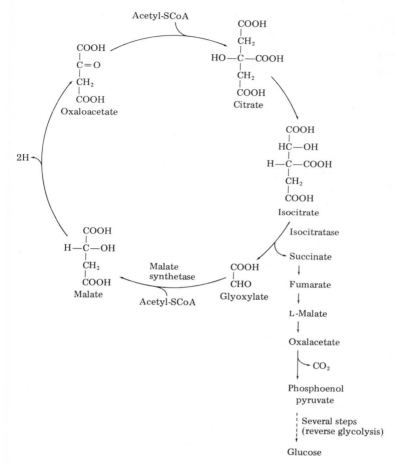

FIG. 12.2. GLYOXYLATE CYCLE

Completion of the cycle requires the participation of the electron transport chain for the removal of electrons and the production of energy.

Isocitratase, in particular, seems to be confined to seeds in which conversion of fat to carbohydrate is occurring, whereas seeds which depend on starch for energy during germination do not have the glyoxylate cycle.

Pentose Phosphate Pathway.—Many cells possess another pathway for glucose degradation, e.g., pentose phosphate pathway (hexose monophosphate pathway). This pathway has two main functions: (a) The first function is to supply NADPH + H^+ which is used for redox reactions such as fatty acid biosynthesis. The NADPH is supplied by dehydrogenase reactions, two of the most important are:

glucose-6-phosphate + NADP$^+$ $\rightleftharpoons$

6-phosphogluconate + NADPH + H$^+$

glucose-6-phosphate + 2NADP$^+$ $\rightleftharpoons$

D-ribose-5-phosphate + CO$_2$ + 2NADPH + 2H$^+$

The NADPH is then used as the reducing agent in biosynthetic reactions such as the reductive synthesis of fatty acids and steroids. (b) A second function is to provide the cell with pentoses that can be converted to D-ribose or 2-deoxy-D-ribose which are used in the synthesis of nucleic acids. This is necessary since pentoses in foods are not easily absorbed from the gastrointestinal tract (intestinal mucosa).

Reactions of the Pentose Phosphate Pathway

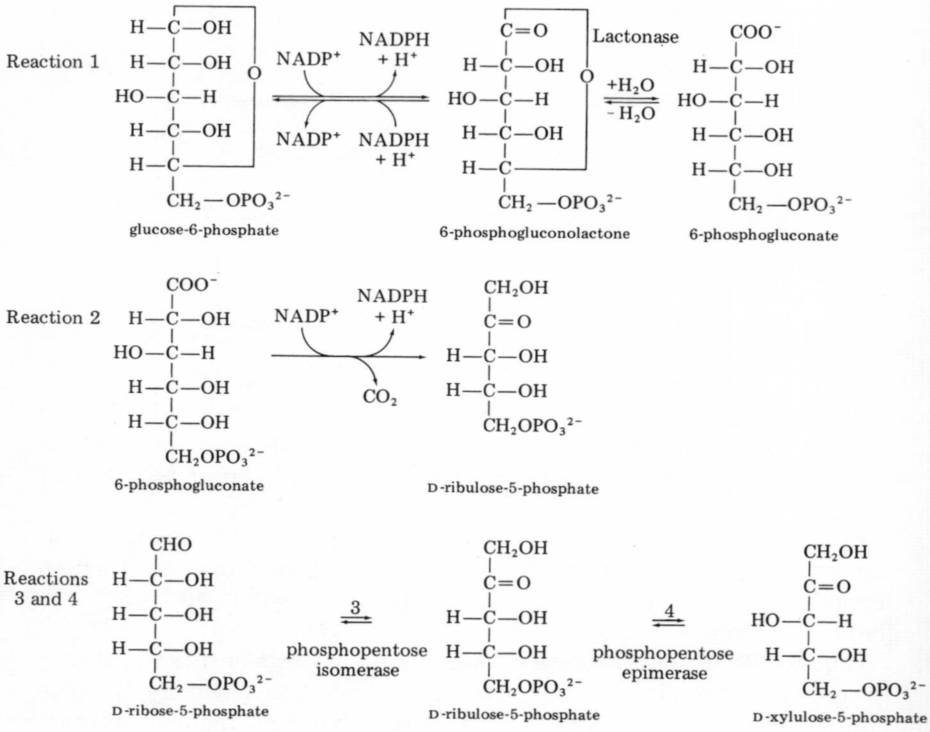

FIG. 12.3 (Continued)

Reaction 5-The Transketolase reaction

D-xylulose-5-phosphate (C₂ donor) + D-ribose-5-phosphate (C₂ acceptor) →(TPP/Mg²⁺) D-sedoheptulose-7-phosphate + D-glyceraldehyde-3-phosphate

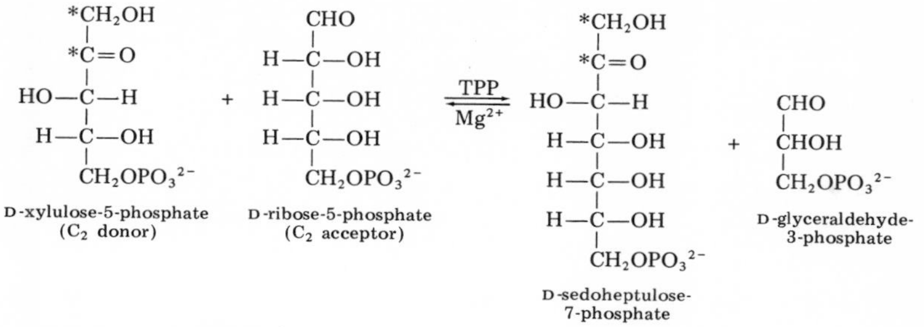

Reaction 6-The transaldolase reaction

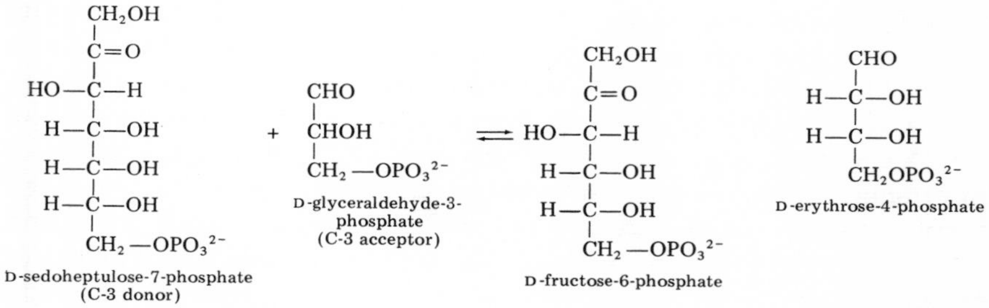

D-sedoheptulose-7-phosphate (C-3 donor) + D-glyceraldehyde-3-phosphate (C-3 acceptor) ⇌ D-fructose-6-phosphate + D-erythrose-4-phosphate

Reaction 7-Second transketolase reaction

D-xylulose-5-phosphate (C₂ donor) + D-erythrose-4-phosphate (C₂ acceptor) ⇌ D-fructose-6-phosphate + D-glyceraldehyde-3-phosphate

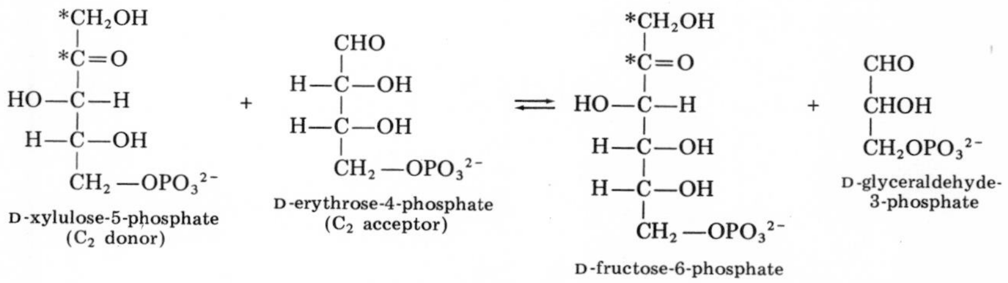

FIG. 12.3. REACTIONS OF THE PENTOSE PHOSPHATE PATHWAY

The various steps of the pentose phosphate pathway are shown in Fig. 12.3. The reactions take place in the soluble portion of the extramitochondrial cytoplasm of cells. The first reaction of the pathway is the oxidation of glucose-6-phosphate to 6-phosphogluconate by the enzyme glucose-6-phosphate dehydrogenase. The intermediate, 6-phosphogluconolactone undergoes hydrolysis to form 6-phosphogluconate. A lactonase has been isolated which is capable of catalyzing the reaction.

The next reaction involves both an oxidation and decarboxylation to yield D-ribulose-5-phosphate and the reaction is catalyzed by the enzyme 6-phosphogluconate dehydrogenase with the formation of a second molecule of NADPH + H$^+$.

Several enzymes exist which bring about isomeric changes in the pentose phosphates. One of these is phosphopentose isomerase, which brings about the conversion of D-ribulose-5-phosphate into its aldo isomer, D-ribose-5-phosphate (reaction 3). In addition, epimeric changes around carbon-3 are brought about by the action of phosphopentose epimerase to form D-xylulose-5-phosphate (reaction 4).

The pentose phosphate pool is a heterogeneous pool. Under some circumstances the pathway terminates with the production of D-ribose which serves as a precursor for nucleotide synthesis. The pentose phosphate pathway carries out rearrangements in which the carbons of the C-5 sugar are recombined to produce hexose and triose units. This series of reactions involves the participation of C-7, C-4, and C-3 phosphorylated sugars and the enzymes. The transketolase catalyzes the cleavage of a C-5 unit. In the presence of thiamine pyrophosphate (TPP) and Mg^{2+} ions, this enzyme carries out the transfer of the glycoaldehyde moiety (carbons 1 and 2) from xylulose-5-phosphate to ribose-5-phosphate. The products are D-sedoheptulose-7-phosphate and D-glyceraldehyde-3-phosphate (reaction 5). The enzyme is specific for a ketose which has the L-configuration at the alpha-carbon and preferably a *trans* configuration for the next hydroxyl group.

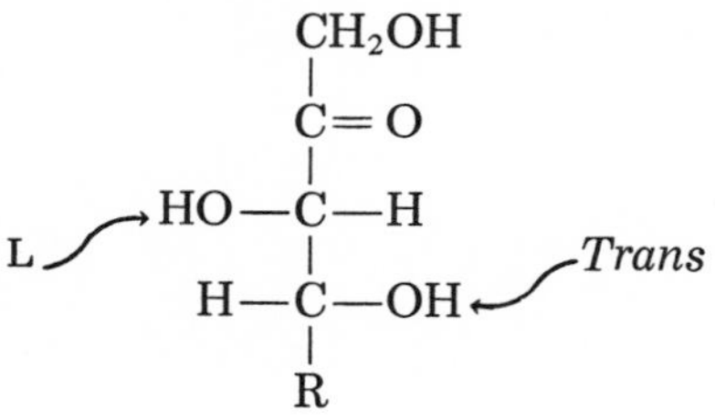

$$
\begin{array}{c}
\text{CH}_2\text{OH} \\
| \\
\text{C} = \text{O} \\
| \\
\text{HO} - \text{C} - \text{H} \\
| \\
\text{H} - \text{C} - \text{OH} \\
| \\
\text{R}
\end{array}
$$

L ↗   — HO—C—H

Trans ↙ — H—C—OH

The action of transketolase is not limited to the transfer indicated in reaction 5, but it can catalyze the transfer of a glycoaldehyde group from a variety of ketoses with the L-configuration at carbon-3 to a variety of acceptor aldoses. D-fructose-6-phosphate and D-sedoheptulose-7-phosphate are examples of other ketol donors and D-glyceraldehyde-3-phosphate and D-erythrose-4-phosphate are other acceptor aldehydes.

D-sedoheptulose-7-phosphate and D-glyceraldehyde-3-phosphate are acted on by the enzyme transaldolase. This enzyme, another TPP-requiring enzyme, transfers a C-3 unit (dihydroxyacetone) from a donor ketone to an acceptor aldose (reaction 6). This reaction, like the transketolase reaction, is not limited to the transfer indicated in reaction 6. Other substances may fill the roles of donor and acceptor.

Transketolase catalyzes another reaction in which erythrose-4-phosphate is the acceptor and xylulose-5-phosphate acts as the C-2 donor to yield fructose-6-phosphate and glyceraldehyde-3-phosphate (reaction 7).

The net result of the above sequence of reactions is that enzymes of the pentose phosphate pathway can carry out the oxidation of glucose-6-phosphate to CO_2 in which 1 molecule of glucose-6-phosphate yields 12 $NADPH + H^+$ and 6 CO_2 and P_i. The net reaction is written as:

$$6 \text{ Glucose-6-P} + 12 \text{ NADP}^+ \longrightarrow 5 \text{ Glucose-6-P} + 6 \text{ CO}_2$$
$$+ 12 \text{ NADPH} + 12\text{H}^+ + \text{P}_i$$
$$\underline{12 \text{ NADPH} + 12 \text{ H}^+ + 3\text{O}_2 \longrightarrow 12 \text{ NADP}^+ + 6 \text{ H}_2\text{O}}$$
$$6 \text{ Glucose-6-P} + 6\text{O}_2 \longrightarrow 5 \text{ glucose-6-P} + 6 \text{ CO}_2 + 6 \text{ H}_2\text{O} + \text{P}_i$$

Thus it may be observed the CO_2 comes solely from the C-1 position of glucose. It should be reemphasized that degradation of glucose-6-phosphate by this pathway is an aerobic process wherein $NADP^+$ is reduced in the initial steps of the cycle.

The pentose phosphate pathway functions in mammals in leucocytes and mammary gland tissue while the glycolytic cycle predominates in mammalian muscle tissue. In plants, the leaves metabolize glucose largely by the pentose phosphate pathway.

Distribution of Organic Acids in Foods

As was shown in the citric acid and other metabolic cycles, numerous organic acids are synthesized which have a pronounced effect on the flavor and texture of foods, especially fruits and berries. The most common and abundant acids in edible plant tissues are citric and malic; however, there are exceptions. Grapes, for example, accumulate relatively large amounts of tartaric acid.

Citric acid is the predominant acid in blueberries, citrus fruits, cranberries, figs, guava, pineapples, pomegranates, raspberries, and strawberries. Malic acid predominates in apples, apricots, bananas, cherries, peaches, pears, and plums.

Vegetables also differ in the proportion of malic acid to citric acid. Vegetables in which citric acid is the major acid include potatoes, leafy vegetables, legumes, and tomatoes. Malic acid abounds in vegetables such as lettuce, broccoli, cauliflower, okra, onion, celery, carrot, turnip, and green beans.

Smaller amounts of numerous other acids are found in plants, but only a few have special significance.

(1) Aliphatic monocarboxylic acids:

Formic acid, $HCOOH$—volatile, widely distributed at low concentrations.

Acetic acid, $CH_3 —COOH$—volatile, widely distributed at low concentrations, as ester in fruit volatiles.

Glycolic acid, $CH_2OH—COOH$—low concentration in unripe fruits as pears and apples.

Glyoxylic acid, $CHO—COOH$ in unripe fruits.

Glyceric acid, $CH_2OH—CHOH—COOH$—as phosphoglyceric acid in green fruits.

Pyruvic acid, $CH_3 —CO—COOH$—common.

(2) Aliphatic di- and tri-carboxylic acids:

Oxalic acid, $HOOC—COOH$—occurs as insoluble calcium oxalate in numerous unripe fruits.

Malonic acid, $HOOC—CH_2 —COOH$—common constituent of mature leaves of certain species of leguminosae.

Succinic acid, $HOOC—(CH_2)_2 —COOH$—present in trace amounts in several fruits.

Fumaric acid (*trans*), $HOOC—CH= CH—COOH$. Found in green apples.

L-malic acid, $HOOC—CH_2 —CHOH—COOH$—widely distributed in plants and found in L-configuration in fruits (apple, apricot, plum, cherry, pear, peach, and banana).

L-tartaric acid, $HOOC—CHOH—CHOH—COOH$—best known as a constituent of the fruit and leaves of grapes.

Citric acid, $HOOC—CH_2 —C(OH)(COOH)—CH_2 —COOH$—major constituent in fruits such as the orange, lemon, lime, strawberry, and currant.

Isocitric acid, $HOOC—CH_2 —CH(COOH)—CH_2 —COOH$—present in relatively small amounts.

cis-aconitic acid, $HOOC—CH_2 —C(COOH)= CH—COOH$—present in relatively small amounts.

Oxaloacetic acid, $HOOC—CH_2 —CO—COOH$—traces.

(3) Acids derived from monosaccharides:

Glucuronic acid, $HOOC—(CHOH)_4 —CHO$—present in apple and plum.

Saccharic acid, $HOOC—(CHOH)_4 —COOH$—pineapple.

Galacturonic acid, $HOOC—(CHOH)_4 —CHO$—present in apricot, apple, pear, and peach.

(4) Aromatic monocarboxylic acids:

Benzoic acid, C_6H_5 —COOH—occurs in free state in cranberries.

Salicylic acid, HO—C_6H_4 —COOH—occurs as a methyl ester in plums.

Coumaric acid (o- and p-), HO—C_6H_4 —CH= CH—COOH— occurs in oil of cinnamon.

Caffeic acid, $(HO)_2$ —C_6H_3 —CH= CH—COOH—present in coffee beans and digitalis.

Chlorogenic acid—occurs in potatoes and many other vegetables, pears, peaches, plums, and cherries.

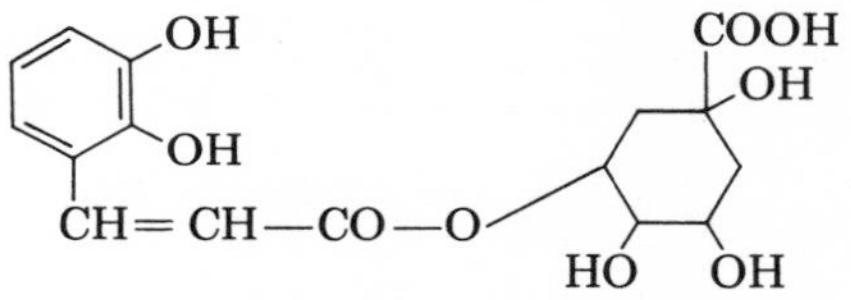

(5) Alicyclic acids:

Quinic acid

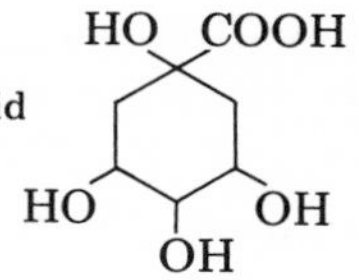

Found in the apple, apricot, peach, pear, and plum.

Shikimic acid

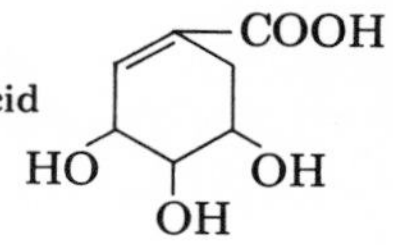

Found in the apple, cherry, pear, strawberry, and quince.

Other Changes Associated with Organic Acids

The life of a plant tissue may be divided into three periods: growth, ripening, and senescence. The first phase involves the synthesis of complex cellular materials from simple precursors; the second phase is one in which the fruit or vegetable becomes edible; the last phase is one of aging in which autolysis sets in and tissue breakdown occurs.

The various acids of the tricarboxylic (TCA) cycle are produced during the respiratory oxidation of carbohydrates, while the aromatic acid, shikimic acid is involved in the synthesis of the aromatic amino acids, phenylalanine, and tryptophan. Some of the acids listed have not been linked to particular metabolic cycles (e.g., oxalic and tartaric acids) but they accumulate in the plant tissues. As a result, fruits and vegetables are normally acid in reaction.

The relative proportions of different acids in plant tissues may vary considerably during growth and ripening. For example, fruits show an increase in organic acids during growth; however, during the ripening process there is a decrease in overall acid content. In many fruits, for example, there is no sharp distinction between peel and pulp, but differences exist in the acid content of the outer layers and the inner layers. In citrus fruits, the peel is poorer in malic acid than the pulp. In other situations the pulp may contain more acid, especially at the time of maturity and during storage.

BIBLIOGRAPHY

AXELROD, B.   1967.   Other pathways of carbohydrate metabolism. *In* Metabolic Pathways, 3rd Edition, Vol. 1, D. M. Greenberg (Editor). Academic Press, New York.

BEEVERS, H.   1961.   Respiratory Metabolism in Plants. Row, Peterson and Company, Evanston, Ill.

BONNER, J., and VARNER, J. E. (Editors).   1965.   Plant Biochemistry. Academic Press, New York.

HULME, A. C. (Editor).   1970.   The Biochemistry of Fruits and Their Products, Vol. I. Academic Press, New York.

KLINGENBERG, M., and PFAFF, E. 1968. Metabolic control in mitochondria by adenine nucleotide translocation.   *In* Metabolic Roles of Citrate, Biochemical Society Symposium No. 27, T. W. Goodwin (Editor). Academic Press, New York.

LARNER, J.   1971.   Intermediary Metabolism and Its Regulation. Prentice-Hall, Englewood Cliffs, N.J.

LEHNINGER, A. L. 1970. Biochemistry. Worth Publishers, New York.

LOWENSTEIN, J. M. (Editor).   1969.   Citric Acid Cycle: Control and Compartmentation. Marcel Dekker, New York.

RUHLAND, W. (Editor).   1960.   Handbook of Plant Physiology. Vol XII/2. Springer, Berlin.

CHAPTER 13

Food and Energy

Carbohydrate, protein, and lipid along with other dietary factors such as vitamins and minerals ultimately function to furnish energy for physical and chemical work in living organisms.

The enzymatic degradation of food releases the energy of the chemical bonds which can, in turn, be transferred to compounds which are commonly referred to as "energy-rich" compounds. Among these types are ATP and other nucleoside triphosphates, enol phosphates, anhydride (acyl) phosphates, creatine and arginine phosphate, and acyl-SCoA.

The energy-rich compounds have $\Delta G°'$ (useful chemical energy) values of 7 kcal/mole to 13 kcal/mole. See Chap. 2 for discussion of $\Delta G°'$. By ordinary standards, however, these energies are not very large since they are scarcely greater than a hydrogen bond. The release of the energy of these compounds is achieved through hydrolysis to yield products that are of lower energy than the original compounds. For example,

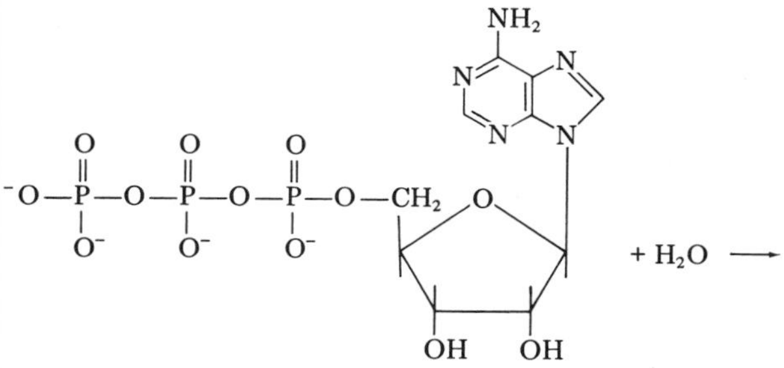

ATP

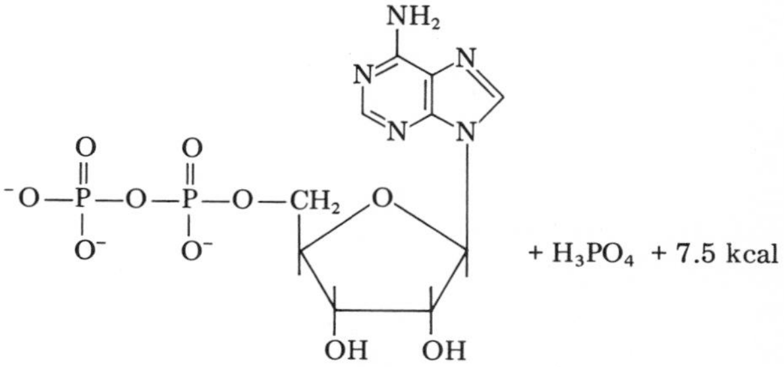

$+ H_2O \longrightarrow$

ADP

$+ H_3PO_4 + 7.5$ kcal

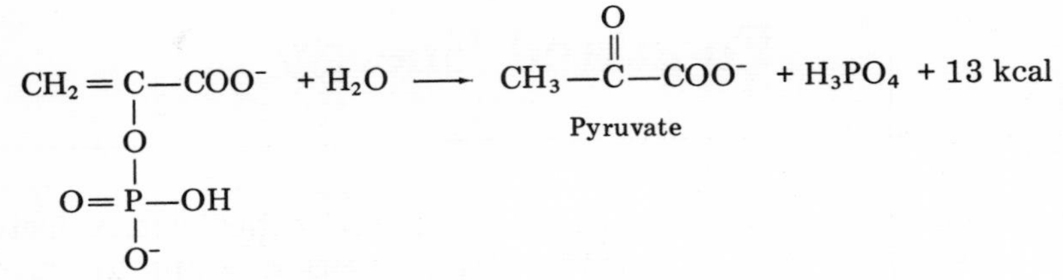

$$CH_2 = C-COO^- \ + H_2O \longrightarrow \ CH_3-\overset{\overset{\textstyle O}{\|}}{C}-COO^- \ + H_3PO_4 + 13 \ kcal$$

$$\underset{\underset{\textstyle O^-}{|}}{\underset{\textstyle O=P-OH}{|}}$$

Pyruvate

Phosphoenolpyruvate

$$\begin{array}{c} \overset{\textstyle O}{\|} \quad \overset{\textstyle O}{\|} \\ C-O-P-O^- \\ | \qquad | \\ \quad\;\; O^- \\ H-C-OH \\ | \\ \quad\;\; \overset{\textstyle O}{\|} \\ CH_2-O-P-O^- \\ | \\ O^- \end{array} \;\; + H_2O \longrightarrow \;\; \begin{array}{c} \overset{\textstyle O}{\|} \\ C-O^- \\ | \\ H-C-OH \\ | \\ \quad\;\; \overset{\textstyle O}{\|} \\ CH_2-O-P-O^- \\ | \\ O^- \end{array} \;\; + H_3PO_4 + 10 \ kcal$$

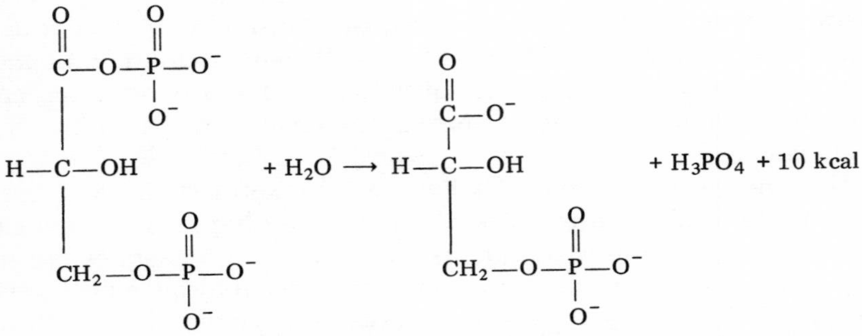

1,3-Diphosphoglycerate   3-Phosphoglycerate

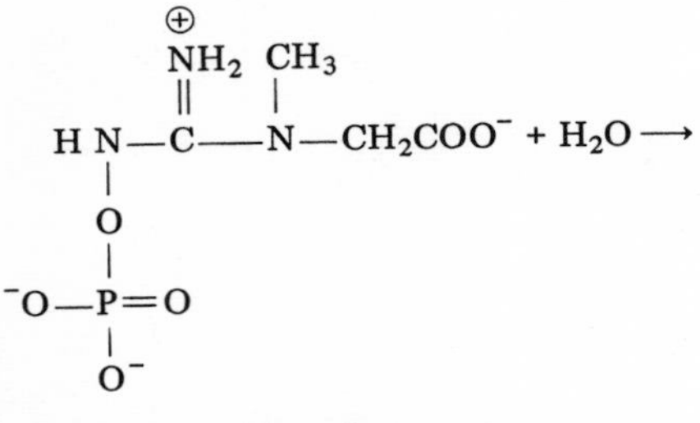

$$\begin{array}{c} \overset{\oplus}{NH_2} \;\; CH_3 \\ \overset{\|}{} \quad | \\ H\,N-C\!-\!-\!N-CH_2COO^- \ + H_2O \longrightarrow \\ | \\ O \\ | \\ ^-O-P=O \\ | \\ O^- \end{array}$$

Creatine Phosphate

$$\begin{array}{c} \overset{\oplus}{NH_2} \;\; CH_3 \\ \overset{\|}{} \quad | \\ H_2N-C\!-\!-\!N-CH_2COO^- \ + H_3PO_4 + \ 10 \ kcal \end{array}$$

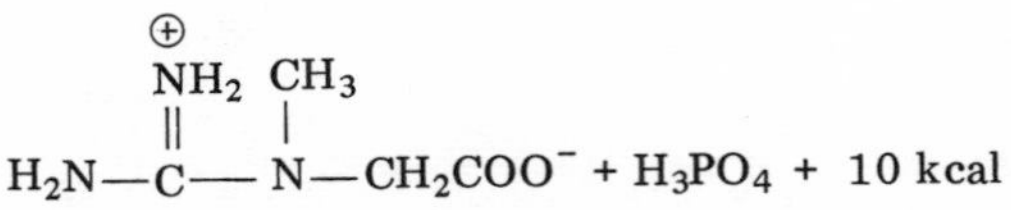

Creatine

These compounds hydrolyze to relieve some type of stress on the high energy compound. When hydrolysis occurs this energy is released. The stresses include repulsion of the electrostatic charges on the phosphate as in ATP and 1,3-diphosphoglycerate, the keto-enol tautomerism of phosphoenolpyruvate, and the resonance of creatine versus creatine phosphate. Additionally, resonance contributes to the stability of the other products of hydrolysis of the above which cause them to be of lower energy than the original compound. Ionization also contributes to the energy of acyl phosphates and ATP.

Logical questions concerning biochemical energetic processes, to list just a few, must include:

(1) What is the origin of the energy?

(2) How is the energy transformed from one form to another?

(3) What mechanisms are operative in the energy transferring reaction?

Solar Energy and Photosynthesis

The origin of all energy is the nuclear fusion on the sun to produce helium and energy.

$$4H_1^1 \longrightarrow He_2^4 + 2e_{-1}^0$$

In this reaction the Σ masses of reactants $> \Sigma$ masses of the products thus a portion of the mass is converted to energy according to the equation:

$$\text{Energy} = \text{mass} \times (\text{velocity of light})^2$$

Solar radiation at the ground has been shown to vary from 220 kcal per cm^2 per yr in desert areas to 70 kcal per cm^2 per yr in polar regions. Between these two extremes would be the solar energy that would be received by a field in the United States on a typical summer day. This has been estimated to be between 500 and 700 cal per cm^2 per day.

Since the main role of solar energy in the food chain is to furnish energy for photosynthesis a few calculations regarding photosynthesis might be appropriate.

Only 25% of the sunlight that ultimately reaches the ground is of the wavelengths that stimulate photosynthesis. And of this 25% only 25% is ultimately utilized by photosynthetic plants.

Using the 500 cal per cm^2 per day as base for daily energy striking the earth, it has been estimated that plant net production is approximately 71 gm per sq m per day during the growing season. If one assumes that carbon compounds yield about 3740 cal per gm this gives 26.6 cal per cm^2 per day. This represents about 5.3% of the total energy (i.e., 5.3% of 500 cal) that ultimately is incorporated into potential foodstuff. The 71 gm per sq m per day production figure took into consideration the gross production minus the amount utilized in respiration by the plant.

It is obvious from these figures that although the percent efficiency for converting solar energy to potential chemical energy is low, relatively large amounts of potential food and energy is conserved.

Photosynthetic and Chemosynthetic Autotrophic Cellular Reactions

The photosynthetic cells from plants and certain photosynthetic bacteria utilize the energy from the sun (Fig. 13.1). Green plants containing chlorophyll absorb the sun's energy. The carbohydrates are then synthesized from this energy, CO_2, and H_2O. The carbohydrates form first as simple sugars and are later stored in the plants as monosaccharides, disaccharides, oligosaccharides, and polysaccharides such as starch and cellulose.

The chemosynthetic autotrophs utilize the energy of redox changes (potential change) to carry out the synthesis of more complex compounds from simpler compounds such as H_2O, CO_2, NH_3, etc. The products of these reactions are protein, carbohydrates, lipids, etc.

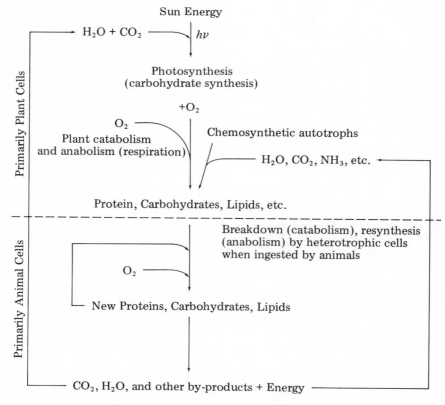

FIG. 13.1. ENERGY PATHWAY IN PLANT AND ANIMAL METABOLISM

The photosynthetic and chemosynthetic cells are of plant origin. Both types, however, are capable of catabolism and anabolism via the respiration process. These reactions are necessary to maintain the integrity of the cells so that they may form the compounds required for their orderly function. As noted previously the respiration process in plants is at the expense of the gross yield of carbohydrate. In these reactions important foodstuffs such as proteins and fats are synthesized in the plants which have considerable nutritive and physiological value for man and animals.

Animal Utilization of Foodstuffs

Animals, including man, carry out life processes principally by breaking down and reassimilating complex compounds. These processes are mediated by heterotrophic cells. These cells, in contrast to autotrophic cells, require rather complex preformed organic molecules. Only in the case of a few reactions such as carboxylation reactions utilizing CO_2 can heterotrophic cells use simple molecules. These cells are able to break down (catabolize) complex molecules or synthesize (anabolize) them. These processes may be anaerobic or aerobic depending on the particular tissue in which the reactions occur. All of these reactions ultimately have a two-fold purpose: (1) produce energy, and (2) synthesize new proteins, carbohydrates, lipids, and other compounds which are necessary for the cells to function. Further, CO_2 and H_2O are released into the atmosphere thereby completing the cycle which began with energy, CO_2, and H_2O.

Conversion of Foods to Energy

Glycolysis.—Carbohydrate catabolism is generally considered to occupy a central role in the overall metabolic processes of all nutrients. This is understandable in light of the large amount of carbohydrate furnished by plants via photosynthesis. Also, the carbon skeleton of the sugars is a key figure in all of the metabolic reactions.

Since polysaccharides or even dissacharides *per se* cannot be utilized directly, reactions are necessary in order to get these to the usable monosaccharide form. As previously pointed out, phosphorylation of the sugar is necessary in order for heterotrophic cells to be able to derive energy from even monosaccharides. In glycogen stores this occurs by the action of phosphorylase giving glucose-1-phosphate. In the case of glucose and a number of other monosaccharides, they are phosphorylated directly at the expense of one mole of ATP. In both instances the glucose phosphate is converted to fructose-6-phosphate which again utilizes one mole of ATP to form fructose-1,6-diphosphate.

During the continued glycolytic catabolism of sugars 2 moles of ATP are formed per triose unit or 4 moles of ATP per hexose unit. Recall that this is possible due to the inconversion of dihydroxyacetone phosphate (DHAP) to glyceraldehyde-3-phosphate. One of the moles of ATP comes from the energy of hydrolysis of the anhydride (acyl) phosphate, 1,3-diphosphoglycerate, while the other ATP is formed from the energy of the enol phosphate (phosphoenolpyruvate) when it is converted to pyruvate by pyruvate kinase.

Anaerobic Glycolysis.—Pyruvate is another central compound in glycolysis. A divergence of reactions can occur at this point. In tissue that is essentially anaerobic, such as muscle tissue undergoing strenuous work, anaerobic glycolysis will be the predominant reaction. In this type of glycolysis only small amounts of energy are produced. When the terminating reaction of pyruvate to lactate occurs we find that only 4 moles of ATP are produced per mole of hexose. If we substract the 2 moles of ATP necessary to initiate glycolysis, then only an overall net gain of 2 moles of ATP is realized (three in the case of glucose formed from glycogen). This makes anaerobic glycolysis a rather inefficient energy converter but it still is an important one since the energy is quickly available for muscle activity.

The enzymes of the anaerobic glycolytic pathway are found in the cytosol of muscle cells and can function without structured bodies such as mitochondria.

Aerobic Glycolysis.—When a tissue has sufficient oxygen the metabolic pathway for the degradation of pyruvate is different from lactate formation in animal tissue or ethanol and other products for organisms such as yeast and bacteria. The reactions commonly called aerobic glycolysis take place primarily in the mitochondria of the cell. These structured cell components are approximately 2 μ in length and 1 μ in diameter. The mitochondrion has an outer membrane which is generally permeable to small molecules and an inner membrane which is folded into inward projections called cristae. This membrane is permeable to $H_2PO_4^-$ or $HPO_4^=$, ADP, ATP, H_2O, and substrates for the enzymes inside the mitochondrion, but will not allow Na^+, K^+, sugars, and other types of polar molecules to pass through freely. These membranes are composed of lipid and protein. The fluid inside the mitochondrion is called the matrix. The enzymes of the citric acid cycle are found in the matrix while the enzymes of electron transport and oxidative phosphorylation are found in the inner membrane.

Pyruvate can form acetyl-SCoA via the pyruvate dehydrogenase system, which enters into the citric acid cycle (tricarboxylic acid cycle) by condensing with oxalacetate to form citrate. One mole of NADH is formed when pyruvate is converted to acetyl-SCoA. NADH is also formed at three other points in the citric acid cycle: (1) isocitrate to oxalsuccinate, (2) α-ketoglutarate to succinyl-SCoA, and (3) malate to oxalacetate. This gives a total of 4 moles of NADH produced by the decarboxylation of pyruvate and 1 revolution of the cycle. NADH in itself is not a high energy compound but, as will be pointed out, it can be utilized by the mitochondrial electron transport system, coupled to oxidative phosphorylation to produce ATP.

One substrate level phosphorylation takes place when succinyl-SCoA reacts with inorganic phosphate and GDP to form GTP and succinate. The energy of the acyl-SCoA is utilized in the synthesis of the high energy GTP which has essentially the same free energy of hydrolysis as ATP. The only other energy yielding reaction of the citric acid cycle is the conversion of succinate to fumarate. In this reaction enzyme-bound FAD is reduced to $FADH_2$. Again as in the case of NADH, $FADH_2$ is not a high energy compound but can be oxidized by the electron transport system to form ATP via oxidative phosphorylation.

Electron Transport and Oxidative Phosphorylation

Before accounting for the energy of the foods such as lipids and proteins, a discussion of the electron transport system and oxidative phosphorylation is necessary. Located in the mitochondrial inner membrane are two systems which supply the major portion of the energy for life processes; namely, electron transport and oxidative phosphorylation. The cytochromes and flavoproteins of the electron transport system are on the outermost side of the inner membrane and the ATP-forming enzymes on the innermost surface of the membrane. The sequence of the electron transport system is shown in Fig. 13.2. Either NADH or $FADH_2$ will serve as the initiator of the respiratory chain. The NADH produced in the aerobic glycolytic process is oxidized to NAD^+ by a flavoprotein which in turn is oxidized by coenzyme Q (ubiquinone). $FADH_2$ produced by the oxidation of succinate can also be oxidized by coenzyme Q. At this point the reaction proceeds sequentially from coenzyme Q to cytochrome b to cytochrome c_1 to cytochrome c then on to cytochrome a and a_3. The redox reactions are terminated when an oxygen atom is reduced to 0^{2-} which reacts with a previously produced H^+ to form H_2O. The oxygen consumed in this reaction is taken in from the atmosphere by the cells.

The structure of coenzyme Q (ubiquinone) is shown as it undergoes reversible oxidation and reduction.

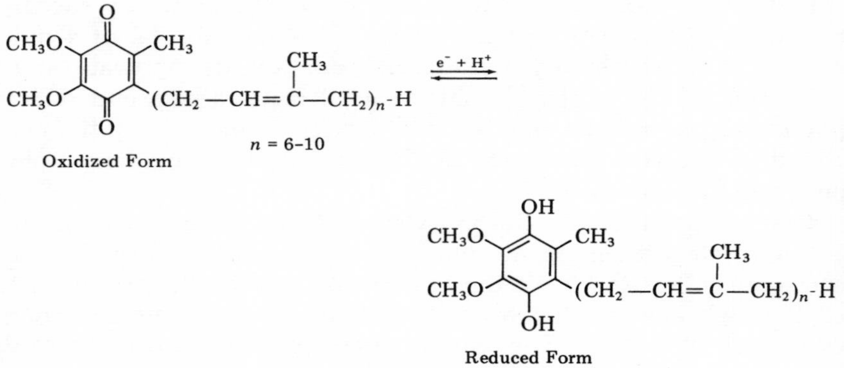

Oxidized Form

$n = 6\text{-}10$

Reduced Form

Coenzyme Q

The cytochromes have the well-known iron-porphyrin structure (see Chap. 9) in which the iron can undergo reversible oxidation-reduction; i.e.,

$$Fe^{2+} \rightleftharpoons Fe^{3+} + e^-$$

As shown in Fig. 13.2 3 moles of ATP can be formed from 1 mole of NADH via electron transport and oxidative phosphorylation. However, only two moles of ATP are formed per mole of $FADH_2$. Thus in all reactions where NADH is formed we can assign an energy value of 3×7.5 kcal or NADH = 3 ATP. Likewise for each mole of $FADH_2$ produced in metabolism we may assign an energy of 2×7.5 kcal or $FADH_2$ = 2 ATP. It should be pointed out that in order for NADH or $FADH_2$ to give these energies they must be formed in or transported into the mitochondria. The electron transport system can be considered to be a redox system in which the overall change in potential ($\Delta E_o'$) would determine the amount of energy that could be produced. Assuming that the system begins with $NAD^+ \rightleftharpoons NADH + H^+$ (-.32 volts) and ends at $O_2 \rightleftharpoons 2O^{2-}$ (+.82 volts) we would get a change in potential of approximately +1.14 volts. The energy may be calculated according to the equation:

$$\Delta G^{\circ\prime} = -n \, \mathcal{F} \, \Delta E_o'$$

$$\Delta G^{\circ\prime} = -2(23,000)\,(1.14)$$

$$= -52.44 \text{ kcal}$$

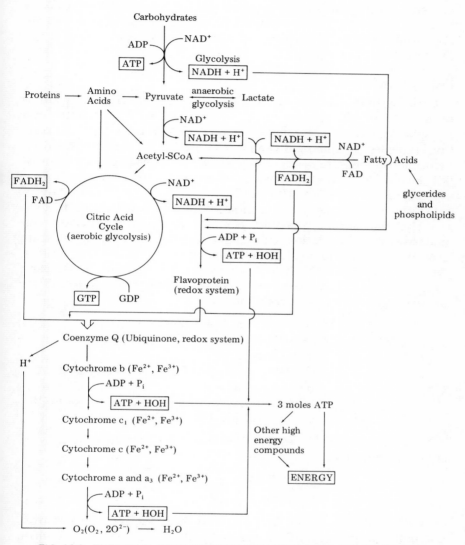

FIG. 13.2. ENERGY FLOW IN METABOLISM LEADING TO ATP FORMATION

This value may be compared to the $\Delta G^{o\prime}$ value of 22.5 kcal for the ATP (3 moles) that is formed in the oxidative phosphorylation process. This gives an efficiency of $(22.5/52.44) \times 100 = 43\%$ for the redox process. These calculations are made assuming unity concentrations of the mitochondrial redox components which is not the actual case for some.

Energy from Foods

Carbohydrate.—It will be recalled that the anaerobic glycolysis of a mole of glucose produced 4 moles of ATP (substrate level phosphorylation) but required 2 moles of ATP to initiate the reaction (glucose → glucose-6-P and fructose-6-P to fructose-1,6-diP). Calorimetric measurements of the energy of glucose gives a value of 686 kcal/mole. The inefficiency of anaerobic muscle glycolysis is evident, $(2 \times 7.5/686) \times 100 = 2.2\%$.

On the other hand when 1 mole of glucose is converted to CO_2 and H_2O via aerobic glycolysis coupled to electron transport and oxidative phosphorylation we can get 6 moles of ATP via substrate level phosphorylations (1,3-diphosphoglycerate → 3-PGA, PEP → pyruvate and succinyl-SCoA → succinate), 10 moles of NADH, and 2 moles of $FADH_2$. Again two moles of ATP are required to initiate the reactions. This then gives a total of:

> 6 ATP (substrate level phosphorylation)
> 10×3 ATP (NADH via electron transport and oxidative
> phosphorylation)
> 2×2 ATP ($FADH_2$ via electron transport and oxidative
> phosphorylation)
> $\underline{-2\ \text{ATP}}$ (phosphorylation of glucose and fructose-6-P)
> 38 ATP per mole of glucose

If each of the ATP gives 7.5 kcal/mole the overall efficiency of aerobic glycolysis is

$$\left(\frac{38 \times 7.5}{686}\right) \times 100 = 41.5\%$$

Lipid.—This value may be compared to the energy derived from one mole of palmityl-SCoA via β-oxidation then on to the citric acid cycle and the respiratory chain.

$$CH_3(CH_2)_{14}\overset{\overset{\text{O}}{\|}}{-C}-SCoA + 7O_2 \longrightarrow 8\ CH_3\overset{\overset{\text{O}}{\|}}{-C}-SCoA$$

The acetyl-SCoA then can be utilized in the citric acid cycle to give 8 revolutions of the cycle to produce 8×12 ATP (TCA produces

12 ATP/revolution of cycle). From β-oxidation 7 moles of NADH and 7 moles of $FADH_2$ are produced which can be utilized by the electron transport and oxidative phosphorylation system to produce 21 moles and 14 moles of ATP, respectively (7 $\times$ 3 for NADH and 7 $\times$ 2 for $FADH_2$). The overall yield of energy per mole of palmityl-SCoA then would be

> 21 ATP from NADH
> 14 ATP from $FADH_2$
> 96 ATP from acetyl-SCoA
> 131 ATP per mole of palmityl-SCoA

From calormetric measurements, palmityl-SCoA gives approximately 2400 kcal/mole thus the efficiency of this reaction would be:

$$\left(\frac{131 \times 7.5}{2400}\right) \times 100 = 41.2\%$$

This is almost identical to the value obtained for the metabolism of 1 mole of glucose; however, on a weight basis 1 mole of glucose weighs 180 gm whereas 1 mole of palmitic acid weighs 256 gm. If palmitic acid is used as the basis for the calculation then the overall yield of ATP is only 130 since 1 mole of ATP would be required to convert palmitic acid to palmityl-SCoA.

Protein.—As in the case of carbohydrates and lipids, proteins must first be broken down into the component amino acids. A number of the amino acids may be transaminated to their corresponding α-keto acids. For example, alanine forms pyruvate which may be metabolized as previously described; glutamic acid can be converted to α-ketoglutaric; whereas aspartic acid will form oxalacetic acid. In these reactions the coenzyme, pyridoxal phosphate mediates the reversible transfer of the amino group of an amino acid to an α-keto acid.

$$R_1-\overset{\overset{\textstyle O}{\|}}{C}-COO^- + R_2-\overset{\overset{\textstyle NH_3^+}{|}}{\underset{\underset{\textstyle H}{|}}{C}}-COO^- \rightleftharpoons R_1-\overset{\overset{\textstyle NH_3^+}{|}}{\underset{\underset{\textstyle H}{|}}{C}}-COO^- + R_2-\overset{\overset{\textstyle O}{\|}}{C}-COO^-$$

Other reactions which are important in amino acid metabolism are: hydrolytic and oxidative deamination to form α-keto acids, racemization, epimerization, and decarboxylation. The most common end-product of all amino acid degradation is an α-keto acid or its acyl-SCoA derivative.

Calculations of the energy yield for proteins must be based on the individual amino acids and the glycolytic intermediate that is formed when the amino acid is degraded.

BIBLIOGRAPHY

BALDWIN, E. 1967. Dynamic Aspects of Biochemistry, 5th Edition. Cambridge University Press, Cambridge, Mass.

GATES, D. M. 1962. Energy Exchange in the Biosphere. Harper & Row, Publishers, New York.

GATES, D. M. 1971. The flow of energy in the biosphere. Sci. Am. *225*, 88–100.

KLOTZ, I. M. 1967. Energy Changes in Biochemical Reactions. Academic Press, New York.

LARNER, J. 1971. Intermediary Metabolism and its Regulation. Prentice-Hall, Englewood Cliffs, N.J.

LEHNINGER, A. L. 1964. The Mitochondrion: Molecular Basis of Structure and Function. W. A. Benjamin, New York.

LEHNINGER, A. L. 1970. Biochemistry. Worth Publishers, New York.

LEHNINGER, A. L. 1971. Bioenergetics, 2nd Edition. W. A. Benjamin, Menlo Park, Calif.

MOROWITZ, H. J. 1968. Energy Flow in Biology. Academic Press, New York.

CHAPTER 14

Food Glycosides

Prior to actually tasting a foodstuff, the consumer is first attracted by essentially two factors; namely, odor (Chap. 15) and exterior physical appearance, which includes the color of the product. Chlorophyll and carotenoids contribute to the color of a large number of fruits, vegetables, and animal products. The redness of a ripe apple or the purple color of a ripe plum gives an aesthetic quality to a rather ordinary flavor. These colors are imparted by a class of compounds generally referred to as glycosides. The glycosides differ from the other plant pigments in that they are water soluble and found in the vacuole sap of the plant cells. They are rarely toxic and their primary importance is the coloring of foodstuffs and in a few instances they impart flavor. The glycosides are composed of two major groups, the anthocyanins and the flavonoids (anthoxanthins).

Anthocyanins

Anthocyanins (Gr. *antho*, flower + Gr. *kyanos*, blue) consist of two major structural features, the sugar moiety and an aglycon (anthocyanidin) which can be separated by acid hydrolysis.

A variety of sugars are found in the glycosides. These include mono-, di-, and trisaccharides. The sugars are generally attached to the anthocyanidin, flavone, flavonol, or flavanones by a β-glycosidic linkage. D-glucose, D-galactose, L-rhamnose, D-arabinose, and D-xylose are the most commonly occurring monosaccharides. Disaccharides include rutinose (L-rhamnosyl (α 1 → 6) D-glucose), gentiobiose (D-glycosyl (β 1 → 6) D-glucose), sophorose (D-glucosyl (β 1 → 2) D-glucose), and sambubiose (D-xylosyl (β 1 → 2) D-glucose).

The carbohydrate moieties are attached most commonly to the 3-hydroxyl position of the anthocyanidin. The sugars in diglycosides are attached to either the 3 and 5 hydroxyl groups or the 3 and 7 hydroxyl groups.

The aglycon of anthocyanidins is made up of two ring structures: benzopyran connected to a phenyl ring.

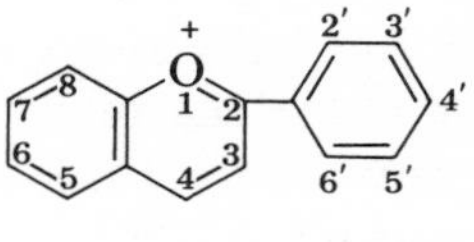

The most common anthocyanidins, shown as the oxonium ions, are cyanidin, pelargonidin, delphinidin, and peonidin.

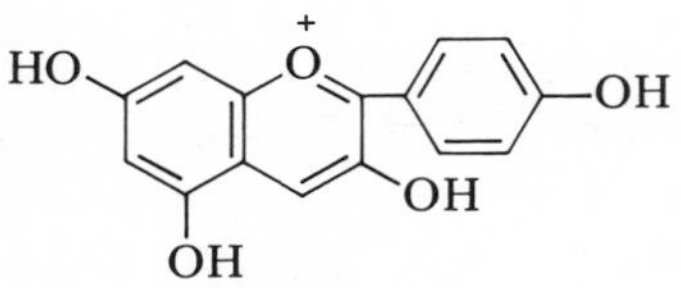

Pelargonidin

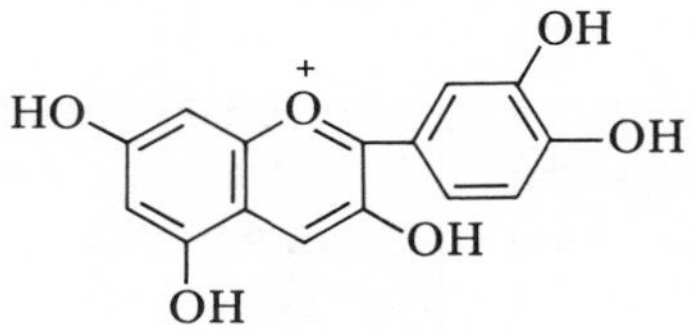

Cyanidin

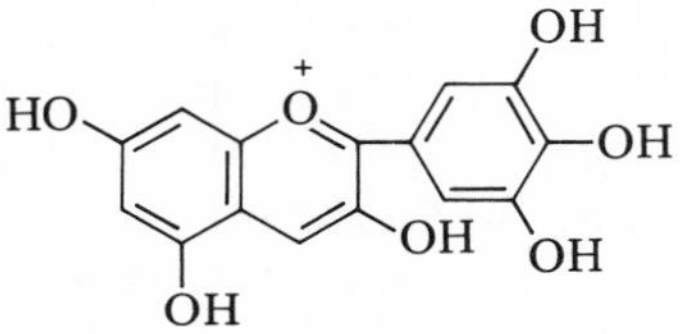

Delphinidin

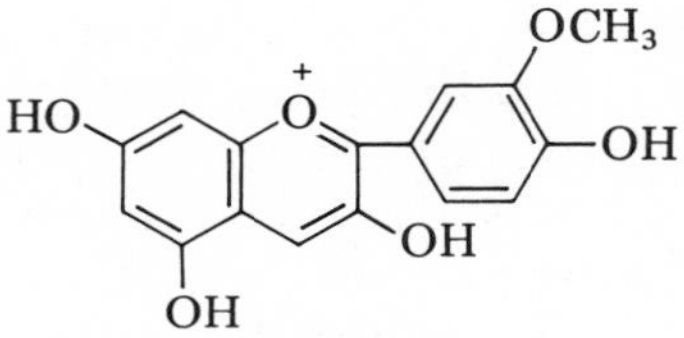

Peonidin

Pelargonidin is the color imparting anthocyanidin in scarlet pelargonidin, orange-red dahlia, and strawberries. Cyanidin is found in the red rose, cranberry, fig, dark cherry, mulberry, elderberry, and almond. The color of eggplant is due to delphinidin. Peonidin (as the arabinoside or galactoside) is found in the cranberry.

The structure of the anthocyanidins always includes the *para*-hydroxy group on the phenyl ring. However, a number of related anthocyanidins have methoxy groups *meta* to the 1′ position (3′ or 5′ positions).

The color of the anthocyanidins is controlled by two major factors: the primary structure and the pH. As the number of hydroxyl groups on the phenyl ring of the anthocyanidins increase so does the shade of blue. Substitution of methoxy groups in the *meta* position (3′ and 5′) increases the shade of red. The anthocyanin's color also depends upon the pH of the media in which it is dissolved. Cyanin, the red pigment in cranberries and dark cherries represents a typical example of the effect of pH on the color. Physiological changes such as the ripening of fruit frequently will result in a change in pH, thereby leading to a change in color of the fruit or berry. An example of the wide range of change in color as affected by pH is shown below for the pigment cyanin (note that the sugar is attached to the cyanidin via a glycosidic linkage at both the 3 and 5 position of the benzopyran ring).

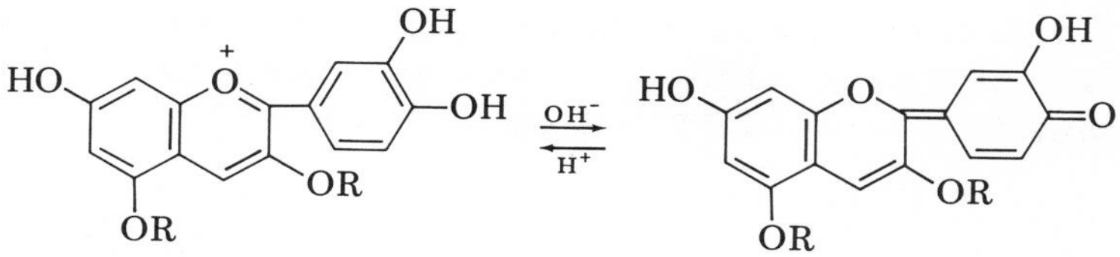

I (pH = 3, red)

II (pH = 8.5, violet)

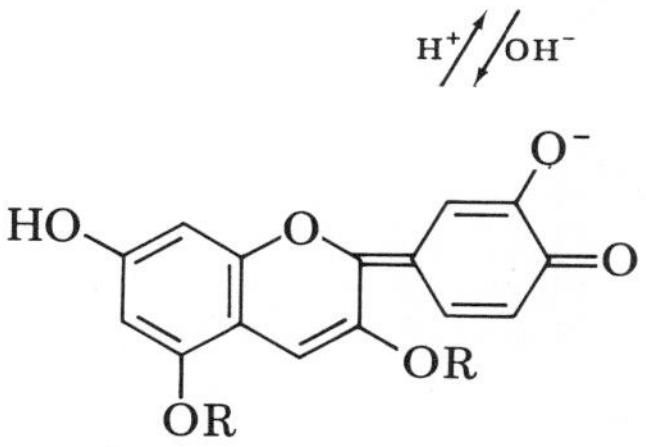

III (pH = 11, blue)

An acidic solution of cyanin is red (Structure I); on neutralization the color changes to violet (II); and finally adjusting to an alkaline pH causes the color to change to blue (III). However, one should be cautious in interpreting color solely on the basis of either primary structure or pH. A typical example can be found in the case of the red rose and the deep blue cornflower. The pigment in both plants is cyanin which is responsible for both the blue color and the red color. The cornflower is blue even though the pH is near 5. The discrepancy for the blue rather than red color has been attributed to the occurrence of K^+, NH_4^+, Na^+, and Ca^{2+} salts of the anthocyanin in the blue cornflower.

Flavonoids (Anthoxanthins)

Another class of plant pigments are the substituted flavones (*L. flavicus*, yellow) or isoflavones. Flavone is a colorless compound with the structure:

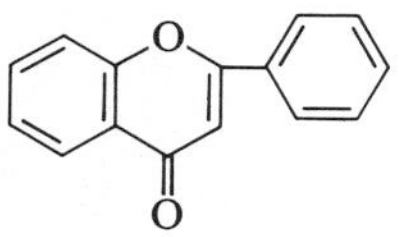

Flavone (2-phenylbenzopyrone)

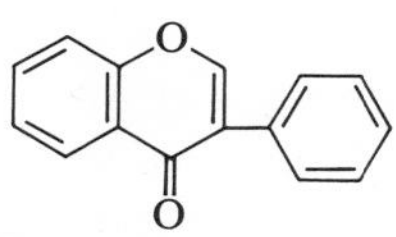

Isoflavone (3-phenylbenzopyrone)

The color of the flavones is due to the substitution of hydroxy or methoxy groups on the phenyl or benzopyrone rings, or both. These substituted flavones and isoflavones occur in plants as glycosides or as esters of tannic acid. The five major classes of anthoxanthins are: flavones, isoflavones, flavonols, flavanones, and flavononols. The basic ring structure for these are as follows: (note: the 2,3 position, encircled, changes with the various classes)

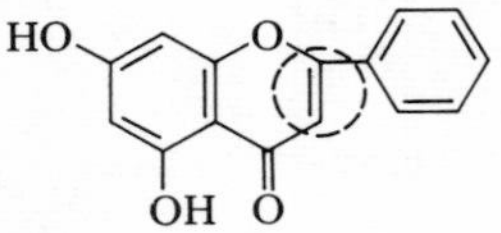

Flavones 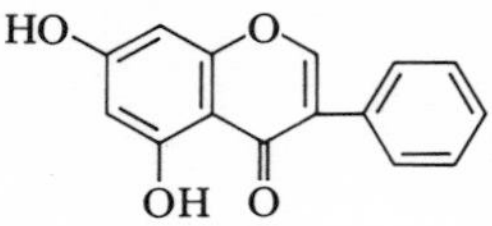   Isoflavones 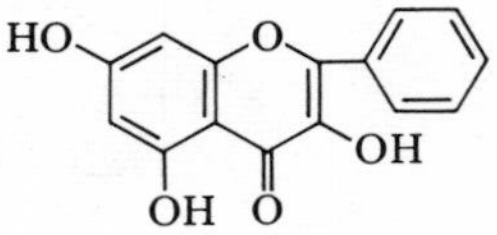   Flavonols

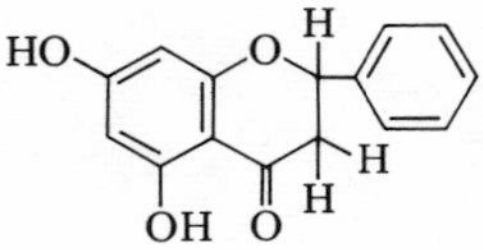

Flavanones 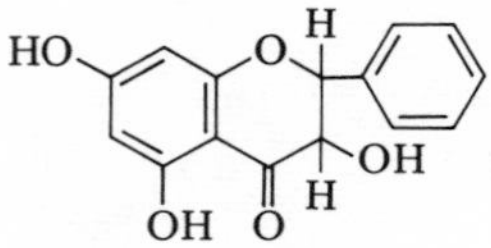   Flavanonols

Most flavones and isoflavones are soluble in alcohol, water, alkali, and dilute mineral acids. The solubility of the flavones in acids is primarily due to the basic properties of the oxygen atom in the γ-pyrone nucleus, forming the oxonium salts. Generally, the salts are more intensely colored than the original compound from which they are formed; however, the oxonium salt is quite unstable in water. This is in contrast to the anthocyanidins, whose oxonium salt is sufficiently stable to occur free in the plant.

Some of the representative flavonoid pigments, both free and glycoside, are given in the following structures:

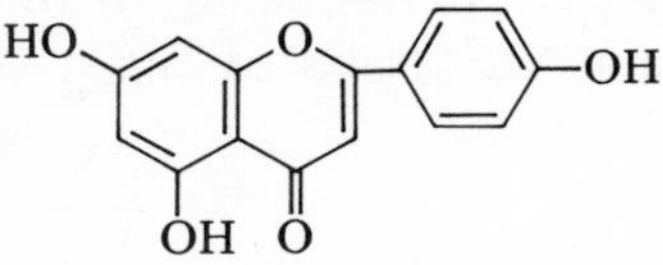

Apigenin (parsley)
a flavone

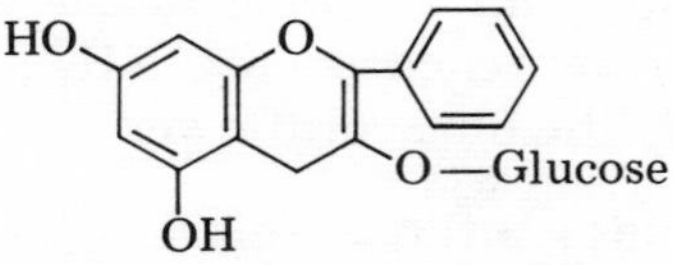

Quercetin (colored onion, strawberry, honey)
a flavonol

Rutin (tea leaves, honey)
a flavonol

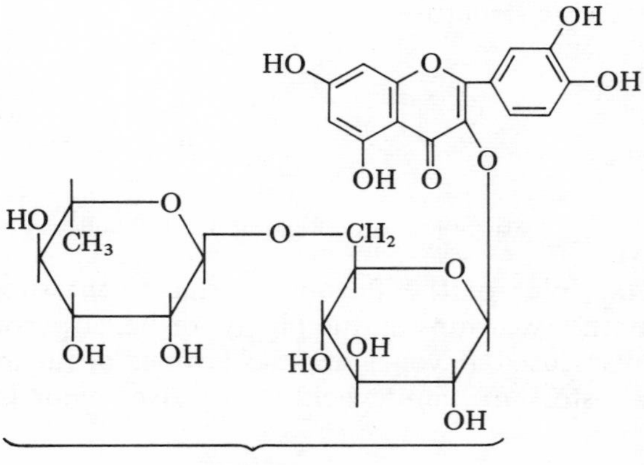

rutinose

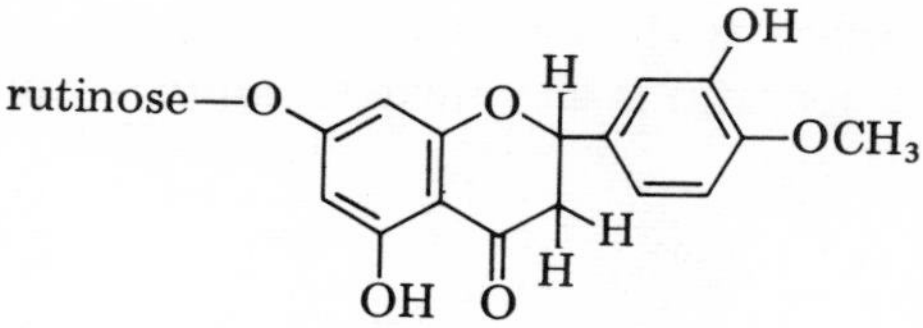

Hesperidin (citrus fruits)
a flavanone

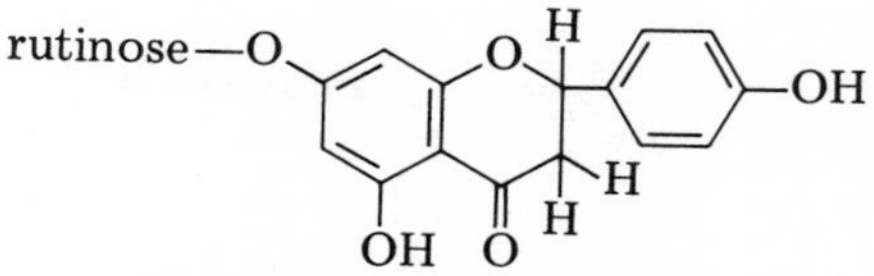

Naringin (citrus peels, e.g., grapefruit)
a flavanone

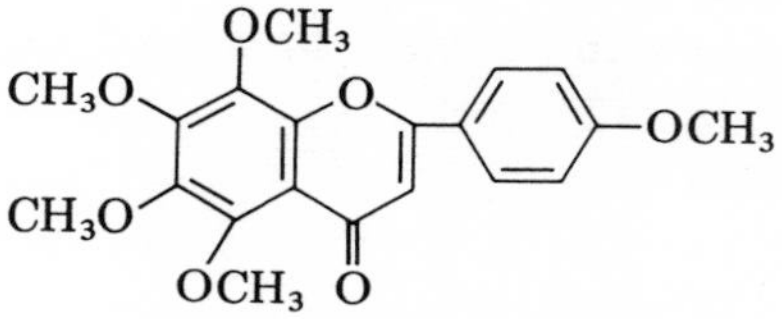

Tangeretin (tangerines)
a flavanone

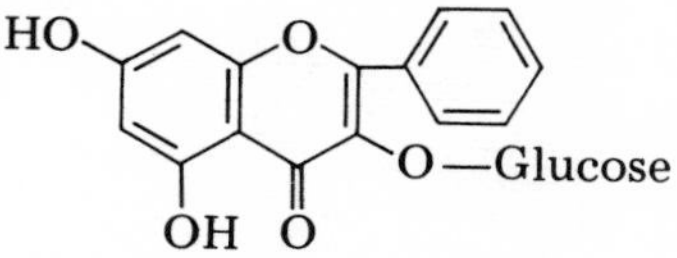

Kaempferin (strawberry)
a flavonol

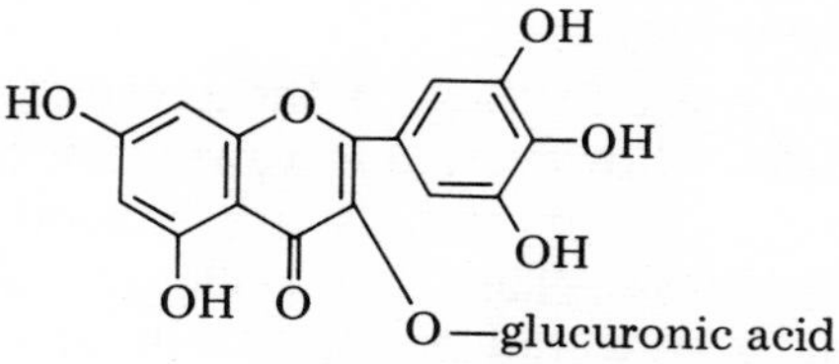

Myricetin (grapes)
a flavonol

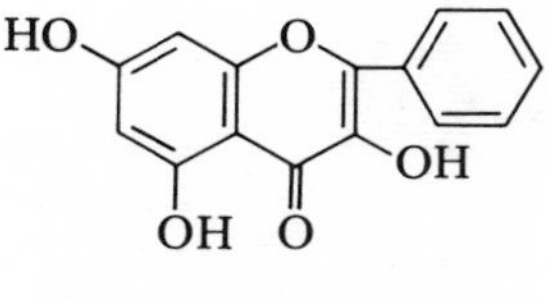

Galangin (galanga root)
a flavonol

The flavanones react with alkali to form an opened benzopyrone ring structure. Hesperidin is a typical example of such a reaction:

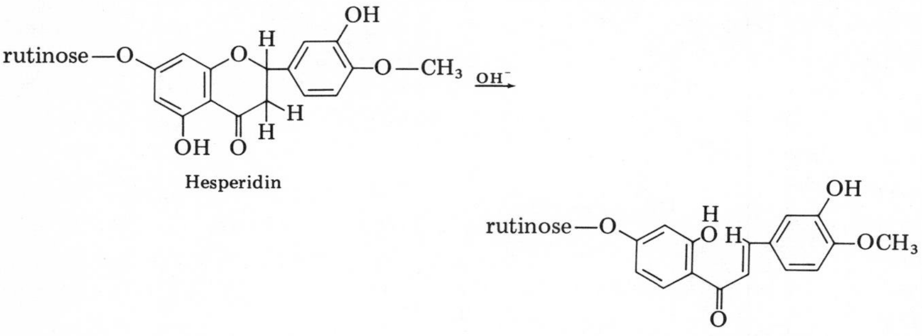

Hesperidin

Hesperidin chalcone

The alkaline degradation of an isoflavone is illustrated for genistein, a pigment of broom (*Genista tinctoria*), clover, and legumes.

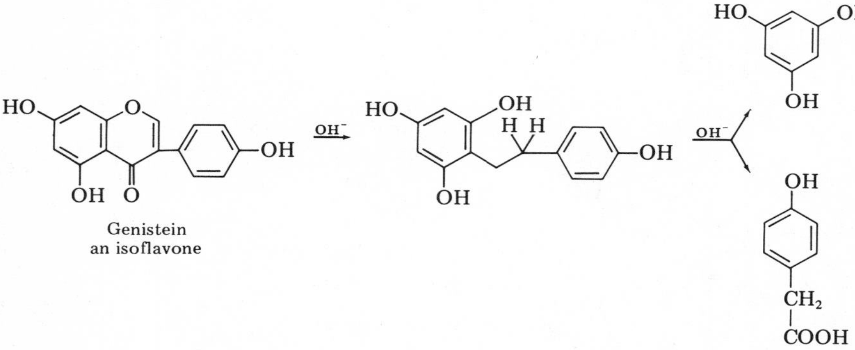

Genistein
an isoflavone

Biosynthesis of Glycosides

The biosynthetic route leading to the glycosides is by no means completely elucidated; however, one can consider two basic steps in their formation: (1) flavonoid biosynthesis, and (2) glycosylation.

Flavonoid Biosynthesis.—The ring skeleton has been found to originate from the head-to-tail condensation of three acetyl units, which form ring A. Ring B and carbons 2, 3, and 4 arise from a phenylpropane unit.

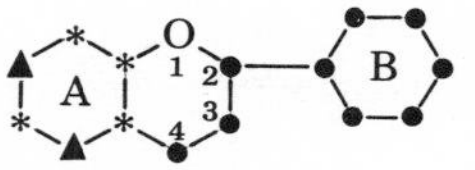

● = phenylpropane
▲ = acetate carboxyl
∗ = methyl from acetate

This biosynthetic pathway has been found in tissues accumulating cyanidin, catechin, and phloretin.

A number of phenylpropane compounds are known to serve as precursors for ring B and carbons 2, 3, and 4. Among these are phenylalanine, cinnamic acid, and *para*-hydroxycinnamic acid.

If the analogy between fatty acid synthesis and flavonoid synthesis is valid then one might assume that malonyl-CoA would be the precursor for ring A.

Glycosylation of Flavonoids.—Probably the glycosylation process is the last step in glycoside biosynthesis. Quercetin-3-glycoside is formed enzymatically from uridine diphospho-D-glucose and quercetin. Rutin is subsequently formed from quercetin-3-glucoside and uridine diphospho-L-rhamnose as shown below:

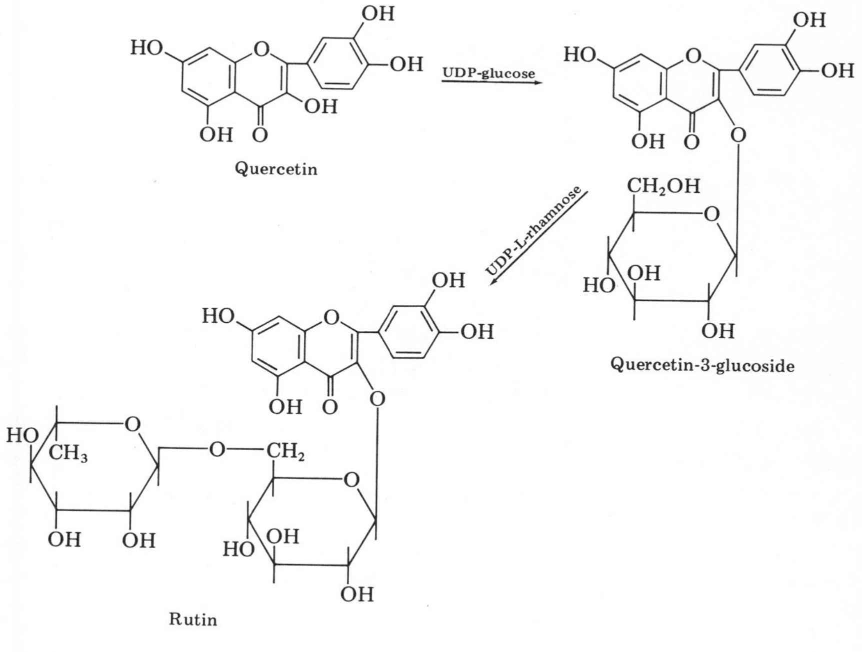

Quercetin

UDP-glucose

Quercetin-3-glucoside

UDP-L-rhamnose

Rutin

Special Characteristics of Certain Glycosides

The glycosides can contribute more than color to foodstuffs. An example of such a glycoside is naringin. This compound is abundant in grapefruit, sour oranges, and the inner white layer of the citrus peels. Naringin is extremely bitter when the disaccharide moiety, rutinose (L-rhamnosyl (α-1,6)-β-D-glucose), is present. An enzyme, Naringinase C, obtained from microorganisms, will rapidly hydrolyze naringin to L-rhamnose and naringenin-7-β-D-glucoside. The narin-genin-7-β-D-glucoside lacks the bitter flavor. This process is used to debitter natural grapefruit juices.

Tangeretin, a glycoside found in tangerines, is one of the special interest glycosides in that it has been shown to be cytotoxic and ultimately leads to neonatal lethality in rats.

Mustard oil glycosides are esters of the isomer of thiocyanic acid which exists in the tautomeric forms.

$$N \equiv C - SH \qquad HN = C = S$$

thiocyanic acid   isothiocyanic acid

The mustard oil ester forms by alkyl or aryl groups replacing the hydrogen atom of the nitrogen of the isothiocyanic acid. Mustard, horseradish, and grape contain these glycosides.

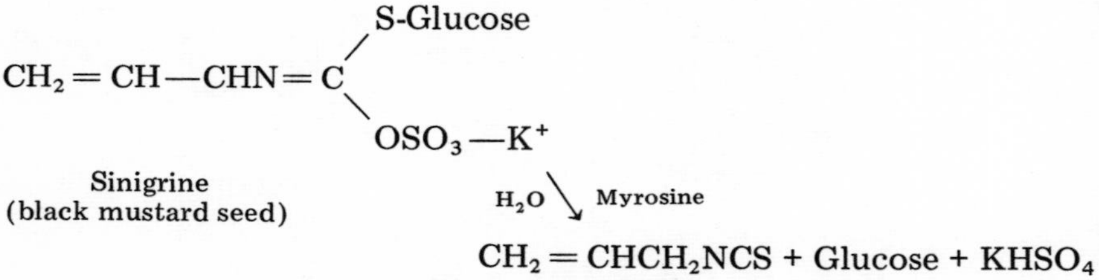

$$CH_2 = CH - CHN = C \begin{array}{l} \diagup \; S\text{-Glucose} \\ \diagdown \; OSO_3 - K^+ \end{array}$$

Sinigrine
(black mustard seed)

$H_2O \diagdown$ Myrosine

$$CH_2 = CHCH_2NCS + Glucose + KHSO_4$$

Mustard oil (allyl isothiocyanate)

Sinigrine is hydrolyzed by the enzyme myrosine which is released from separate cells when the tissue is damaged (e.g., maceration by chewing). Mustard oils are pungent and are lachrymators.

Another type of glycoside occurs in the conifer family of trees, sugar beets, and asparagus.

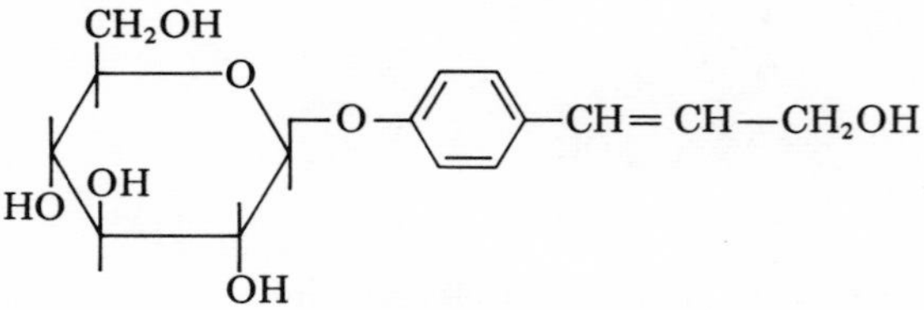

Coniferin

The glucose moiety is attached via a β-glycosidic linkage. Table 14.1 is presented as an indication of the most commonly occurring food glycosides but not as a complete list. It appears that the cyanidin glycosides occur most frequently in foods.

TABLE 14.1

GLYCOSIDES OF FOODSTUFFS

Foodstuff	Glycoside
Cherries	Cyanidin-3-glucoside
	Peonidin-3-glucoside
	Peonidin-3-rutinoside
	Cyanidin-3-gentiobioside
	Cyanidin-3-diglucoside
Cranberries	Cyanidin-3-arabinoside
	Cyanidin-3-galactoside
	Peonidin-3-arabinoside
	Peonidin-3-galactoside
Grapes and Wine	Cyanidin-3-glucoside
	Malvidin-3-glucoside
	Peonidin-3-glucoside
	Petunidin-3-glucoside
	Kaempferol-3-glucoside
	Quercetin-3-glucoside
	Myricetin-3-glucuronoside
	Delphinidin-3-glucoside
	Malvidin-3-glucoside
	Malvidin-3,5-diglucoside
	Peonidin-3,5-diglucoside
	Delphinidin-3,5-diglucoside
Strawberries	Quercetin-3-glycoside
	Kaempferol-3-glucoside
	Pelargonidin-3-glucoside
	Cyanidin-3-glucoside
Eggplant	Delphinidin-3,5-diglucoside
	Delphinidin-3-glucoside
	Delphinidin-3-diglucoside-5-glucoside
	Delphinidin-3-caffeoyldiglucoside-5-glucoside
Currants	Cyanidin-3-glucoside
	Cyanidin-3-rutinoside
	Delphinidin-3-glucoside
	Delphinidin-3-rutinoside
Raspberries	Cyanidin-3-glucoside
	Cyanidin-3,5-diglucoside
	Cyanidin-3-diglucoside
	Cyanidin-3-rhamnoglucoside-5-glucoside
Asparagus	Cyanidin-3,5-diglucoside
	Cyanidin-5-glucoside
Boysenberries	Cyanidin-3-glucoside
	Cyanidin-3-diglucoside
	Cyanidin-3-rhamnoglucoside
	Cyanidin-3-rhamnoglucoside-5-glucoside

Factors Affecting Stability of Anthocyanin Pigments

Anthocyanins and flavonoids are quite susceptible to processing and changes in the environment which can lead to less desirable color. Levels of ascorbic acid and oxygen (as headspace or dissolved oxygen) have been shown to have an effect on the anthocyanin pigments of cranberries and other fruits. Pigment losses in cranberry juice were greatest when both oxygen and ascorbic acid were present in relatively high concentrations. The total red pigments decreased but the percentage of peonidin-3-galactoside and cyanidin-3-galactoside increased, whereas the percentage of peonidin-3-arabinoside decreased.

Enzymes from mushrooms (*Agaricus campestris*), eggplants, potatoes, fungi (*Aspergillus niger*), and other sources apparently have been shown to have the capability of decolorizing anthocyanin pigments. Enzymes from mushrooms, eggplants, and potatoes will decolorize the anthocyanin pigments of oranges, blackberries, and blueberries. The mushroom enzymes decolorized orange and blueberry anthocyanins at an optimum pH of 3.55, while blackberry anthocyanins were decolorized best at pH 3.05. Grape anthocyanins have been reported to be degraded by a polyphenol oxidase from various kinds of grapes.

Analytical Techniques for Anthocyanins and Flavonoids

The most used technique for removing the colored anthocyanins and flavonoids from their natural source has been water extraction. The AOAC method utilizes such a procedure for removing the anthocyanins from grape and various colored fruit juices. Various other techniques have utilized methanol, ethanol, and other alcohols for removing the pigments.

Paper chromatography has been the most popular method for separating and identifying anthocyanins and flavonoids. Commonly, the extracted pigments are applied directly to chromatography paper (Whatman No. 1 and others) followed by development in one or more solvent systems. Butanol, acetic acid, and water of varying ratios is the most used solvent mixture.

Since the anthocyanidins are ionic in nature, paper electrophoresis or other electrophoretic techniques may be used. The advantage of this technique over conventional chromatography is the direct application of the pigmented portion of the plant under investigation. Skins of cherries have been applied directly to electrophoresis paper and the pigments removed by applying an electric potential across the buffered paper strips. In one such study four bands were observed corresponding to cyanidin-3-gentiobioside, cyanidin-3-di-

TABLE 14.2

ABSORPTION MAXIMA FOR FLAVONOIDS

| Compound | Range of Wavelength of Maximum Absorption | |
	Band 1	Band 2
Anthocyanins	475–560	275–280
Flavonols	350–390	250–270
Flavones	330–350	250–270
Flavonones	310–330	275–290
Flavan-3-ols		275–280

Source: Data from Swain (1965A).

glycoside, cyanidin-3-rhamnoglycoside, and cyanidin-3-monoglyc)-side.

Final identification is achieved by a number of procedures. R_f values of the unknown or suspected anthocyanins, anthocyanidins, or flavonoids compared to those of known compounds is the method of choice for chromatographic and electrophoretic techniques.

Further identification of the bands, spots, or zones on the separating media can be achieved by eluting the pigment from the media, dissolving in an appropriate solvent, and determining the absorption spectra. The various classes of flavonoids can absorb characteristically in both the visible and ultraviolet region of the spectra. Table 14.2 gives the wavelength of maximum absorption for some of the flavonoids. The data in this table give only the range of absorption maxima.

The three major anthocyanidins (aglucons) and their glycosides which appear in almost all foodstuffs are usually identified specifically by determining the wavelength of maximum absorption in the visible region of the spectra. Table 14.3 gives these maxima and the color imparted by the compounds. Although numerous other

TABLE 14.3

WAVELENGTH MAXIMA FOR MAJOR ANTHOCYANIDINS AND ANTHOCYANINS

Compound	λ max[1] (nm) (Aglucon)	λ max[2] (nm) (3-Glycoside)	Color Imparted
Cyanidin	535	507	magenta
Delphinidin	545	516	mauve
Pelargonidin	520	492	orange-red

[1] Determined in methanol-HCl.
[2] Determined in aqueous HCl.
Source: Data from Harbourne (1965A).

techniques for positive characterization are available, the data in Table 14.3 represent the most commonly used ones.

Tannins

Tannins play an important role in foodstuffs not only in the acceptance of foods but also in rejection of certain foods. Tea, wines, cocoa, and various other products normally are expected to have an astringency, thus their acceptance is, in part, based on the presence of tannins. However, if one has ever tasted an unripe persimmon, tannins obviously must be considered a key factor in rejection of the product.

These compounds are found in the bark, leaves, and roots of plants such as tea, apple, pear, plums, dates, and other foodstuffs, and cause a bitter flavor or astringency even when present in small concentrations. Additionally, these compounds also impart a tan color to the foodstuff.

Hydrolyzable Tannins.—Tannins are classified as hydrolyzable and nonhydrolyzable. Although hydrolyzable tannins is a general term referring to classes of compounds, these compounds are generally derived from the phenolic compound gallic acid which can form glycosides with glucose.

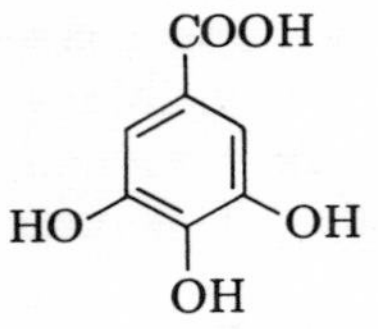

Gallic acid

Gallic acid is found esterified with another molecule of gallic acid to form *meta*-digallic acid, *meta*-Trigallic acid is formed similarly from 3 molecules of gallic acid.

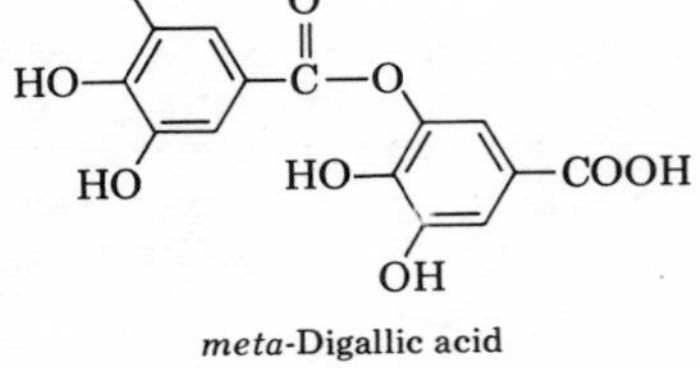

meta-Digallic acid

Interestingly, gallic acid may be formed by the action of hot alkali on anthocyanidins having 3-hydroxyl groups substituted on the phenyl ring.

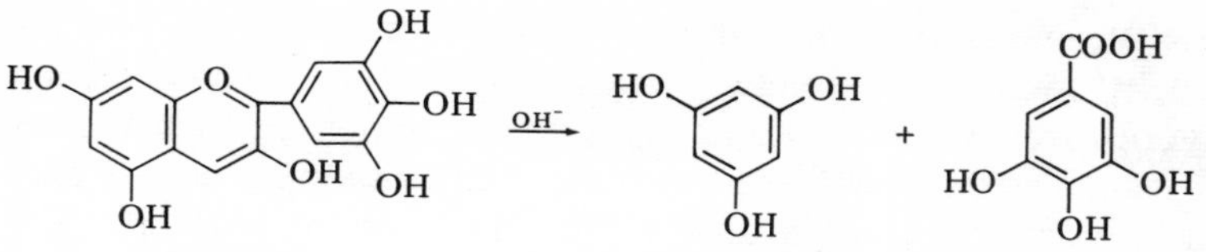

Delphinidin   Phloroglucinol   Gallic acid

Gallic acid also is present in plants as the glucoside. The simplest of this group is β-glucogallin (1-0-galloyl-β-D-glucopyranose) which

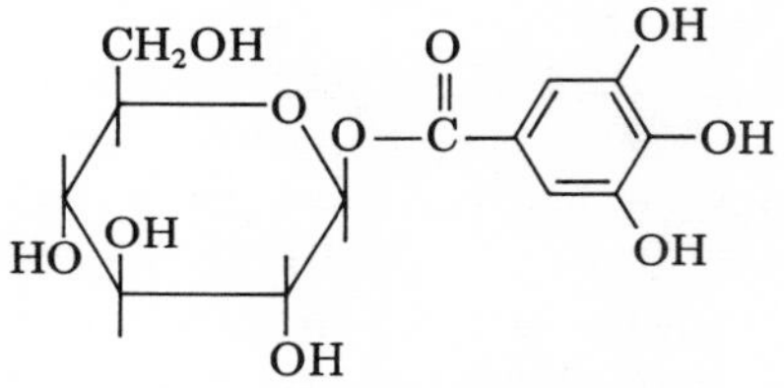

β-glucogallin

is found in Chinese rhubarb. Tannins composed of *meta*-digallic acid are also known in which *meta*-digallic acid is esterified on the 5 available positions of glucopyranose.

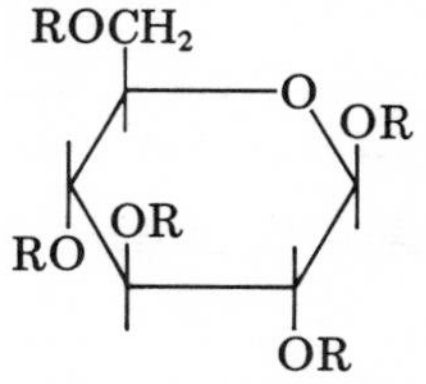

R = *meta*-digallic acid

Penta-*meta*-digalloylglucose

Nonhydrolyzable Tannins.—The nonhydrolyzable tannins are leucoanthocyanins but yield anthocyanidins when treated with hot acid.

Leucoanthocyanins are responsible for the astringency associated with unripe fruits such as grapes, bananas, persimmons, pears, apples, etc. However, the lower molecular weight leucoanthocyanins such as flavan-3,4-diol do not impart the astringency but rather polymeric forms (flavolans) are the astringent compounds.

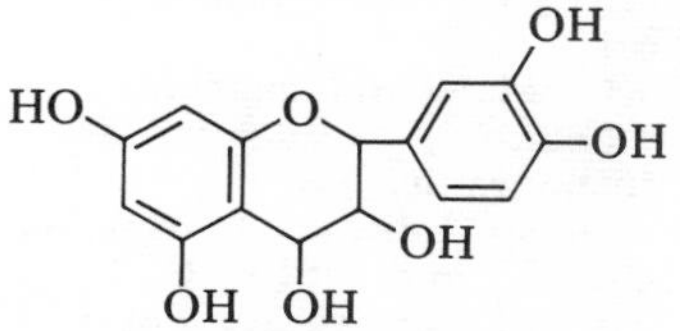

Flavan-3,4-diol

This observation is best explained by examining the mechanism for astringency. The puckery sensation is due to the cross linking of glycoproteins and proteins by tannins which in turn reduce the lubricating action within the mouth. If the tannins are of low molecular weight, such as flavan-3,4-diol, they are too small to facilitate the cross-linking of the glycoproteins and proteins and thus are nonastringent. If the tannins polymerize to such a degree that they are too large to cross-link or too insoluble, they again are ineffective as astringency-producing compounds. Thus, an intermediate size molecule is most astringent.

Fruits contain flavan-3, 4-diols, and flavolans in the oligomeric or polymeric forms. As the fruit matures, the proportion of the polymeric leucoanthocyanins increases to a point that they precipitate as solids, making them unavailable for cross-linking. In this form they produce no astringency. In unripe fruit the more soluble tannins predominate and, therefore, are able to impart their astringent characteristics.

BIBLIOGRAPHY

AKIYOSHI, M., WEBB, A. D., and KEPNER, R. E. 1963. The major anthocyanin pigments of *Vitis vinifera* varieties, Flame Tokay, Emperor, and Red Malaga. J. Food Sci. *28*, 177–178.

ASSOC. OF OFFIC. ANAL. CHEMISTS. 1970. Official Methods of Analysis, W. Horwitz (Editor). Association of Official Analytical Chemists, Washington, D.C.

BARBER, G. A. 1962. Enzymic glycosylation of quercetin of rutin. Biochemistry *1*, 463–468.

BOEHM, H., and VOELCKER, P. E. 1959. Nonvolatile components of orange peel oil. Arch. Pharm. *292*, 529–536.

DARAVINGAS, G. and CAIN, R. F. 1966. The anthocyanin pigments of black raspberries. J. Food Sci. *31*, 927–936.

DOBY, G. 1965. Plant Biochemistry, John Wiley & Sons, London.

FIESER, L. F., and FIESER, M. 1956. Organic Chemistry, 3rd Edition. D. C. Heath & Co., Lexington, Mass.

GOLDSTEIN, J. L., and SWAIN, T. 1963. Changes in tannins in ripening fruits. Phytochemistry *2*, 371–383.

GORIN, P. A. J., and PERLIN, A. S. 1959. Configuration of glycosidic linkages in oligosaccharides. VIII. Synthesis of α-D-mannopyranosyl- and α-L-rhamnopyranosyl-disaccharides by Konigs-Knorr reaction. Can. J. ˑm. *37*, 1930–1933.

HARBORNE, J. B. 1965A. Flavonoids: distribution and contributi   In Chemistry and Biochemistry of Plant Pigments, T. W. Goodwin (Ed   r). Academic Press, New York.

HARBORNE, J. B. 1965B. Flavonoid pigments. In Plant Biochemistry, J. Bonner, and J. E. Varner (Editors). Academic Press, New York.

LINK, K. P. 1943. The anthocyanins and the flavones. In Organic Chemistry, 2nd Edition, Vol. II, H. Gilman (Editor). John Wiley & Sons, New York.

LUH, B. S., STACHOWICZ, K., and HSIA, C. L. 1965. The anthocyanin pigments of boysenberries. J. Food Sci. *30*, 300–306.

LYNN, D. Y. C., and LUH, B. S. 1964. The anthocyanin pigments in bing cherries. J. Food Sci. *29*, 735–743.

SESHARDRI, T. R. 1951. Biochemistry of natural pigments. Annual Reviews of Biochemistry *20*. 487–503.

SMITH, RODNEY M., and LUH, B. S. 1965. Anthocyanin pigments in the hybrid grape variety Rubired. J. Food Sci. *30*, 995–1005.

SOMAATMADJA, D., and POWERS, J. J. 1963. Anthocyanins. IV. Anthocyanin pigments of Cabernet Sauvignon grapes. J. Food Sci. *28*, 617–622.

SOMERS, T. 1966. Grape phenolics; the anthocyanins of *Vitis vinifera* variety Shiraz. J. Food Sci. Agr. *17*, 215–219.

STARR, M. S., and FRANCIS, F. J. 1968. Oxygen and ascorbic acid effect on the relative stability of four anthocyanin pigments in cranberry juice. Food Technol. *22*, 1293–1295.

SWAIN, T. 1965A. Nature and properties of flavonoids. *In* Chemistry and Biochemistry of Plant Pigments, T. W. Goodwin (Editor). Academic Press, New York.

SWAIN, T. 1965B. The tannins. *In* Plant Biochemistry, J. Bonner, and J. E. Varner (Editors). Academic Press, New York.

SWIFT, L. J. 1965. Flavones of the neutral fraction of the benzene extractables of an orange peel juice. J. Agr. Food Chem. *13*, 431–433.

THOMAS, D. W., SMYTHE, C. V., and LABEE, M. 1958. Enzyme hydrolysis of naringin, the bitter principle of grapefruit. Food Res. *23*, 591–598.

TING, S. V. 1958. Enzymic hydrolysis of naringin in grapefruit. J. Agr. Food Chem. *6*, 546–549.

VON ELBE, J. H., BIXBY, D. G., and MOORE, J. D. 1969. Electrophoretic comparison of anthocyanin pigments in eight varieties of sour cherries. J. Food Sci. *34*, 113–115.

WANN, E. V., and THOMPSON, A. E. 1965. The anthocyanin pigments in asparagus. Proc. Am. Soc. Hort. Sci. *87*, 270–273.

CHAPTER 15

Flavoring Compounds

Primitive man existed on a monotonous diet because few foods could be carried from season to season. As a consequence, much of the food that he consumed possessed off-flavors, and in some cases the food was partially spoiled. In short, primitive man used flavor as a means of protecting himself as well as selecting foods that were fit to eat. As time passed man learned to use various flavoring agents to make tasteless food more palatable or to make an objectionable food product acceptable. We still enjoy many of the flavoring agents that were used in years past. The present trend, however, is toward the use of blended flavors to make food more desirable.

Common Spices, Aromatic Seeds and Herbs

These flavoring materials have several things in common: they contain an aromatic flavoring principle; with few exceptions, the particular plant part is used whole or ground to a particular size after being dried; and these dried products have poor flavor strength, normally they must be used at 0.5–1.0% concentration.

There are several advantages associated with the use of these materials; an outstanding one is that the dried ground product maintains flavor identity. They also frequently contain natural antioxidants or they may have antibacterial activity (cloves, cinnamon). Some disadvantages associated with the use of these flavoring materials are the variation among different batches both in color as well as in flavor strength and the length of time it takes for these flavoring agents to reach flavor equilibrium with their usage.

As a consequence of the limitations in use of the natural plant product, it was natural for a flavoring product to be developed which would be more potent and uniform in flavor than the corresponding spice. Natural flavorings consist of volatile and nonvolatile compounds. For the most part essential oils, which are volatile compounds, are the primary flavor components. However, there are some spices wherein the flavor components are wholly or in part nonvolatile compounds. For example, in capsicum the components responsible for the desirable flavor are nonvolatile, while in black pepper a combination of volatiles and nonvolatiles is necessary for a representative flavor. The nonvolatile components are referred to as oleoresins.

Essential Oils

In those spices where the total flavor is found in the volatile portion, essential oils may be used advantageously in place of the spice. They are obtained directly from the leaves, roots, buds, or berries by an extractive process, usually by steam distillation. There are three types of steam distillation in use: water distillation, water and steam distillation, and direct steam distillation. The three methods involve the same general principle, and the differences are in the method of handling the plant material. In water distillation there is direct contact between boiling water and the plant material. In the water and steam distillation, the plant material is supported on a perforated grill some distance from the bottom of the still and saturated wet steam of low pressure flows through the plant material. Direct steam distillation resembles the preceding method except live steam is introduced from an outside boiler. The essential oil, which is carried off with the steam, is passed through water-cooled condensers. The oil being water insoluble will separate on condensation and cooling and can be readily collected.

In addition to steam distillation, some essential oils (notably oils of orange, lemon and lime) are prepared by manual or mechanical expression ("cold press").

Most essential oils are mixtures of hydrocarbons (terpenes and sesquiterpenes), oxygenated compounds, and a small amount of non-volatile residues. The oxygenated compounds are the odoriferous agents while the other compounds contribute little to the odor. The terpenes are unsaturated compounds which oxidize readily under the influence of air, light, and improper storage conditions. These oxidative reactions result in an inferior product. It has, therefore, been the aim of the essential oil industry to produce concentrated terpeneless oil. The process, known as "deterpenation," is based upon two general principles: (a) extraction of the more soluble oxygenated compounds with dilute alcohols, and (b) removal of the terpenes by fractional distillation under reduced pressure. Deterpinated oil has the advantage of being water soluble and does not undergo flavor deterioration as readily as the terpene-containing oil.

Structure.—Examination of the structure of terpenes indicates they are made up of multiples of the hydrocarbon isoprene. Terpenes may be either linear or cyclic in structure and may be regarded as containing 2, 3, 4, 6, and 8 units of isoprene. Terpenes containing 2 isoprene units are called monoterpenes, while those containing 3, 4, 6, and 8 units are called sesquiterpenes, diterpenes, triterpenes, and tetraterpenes, respectively. Examples of linear and cyclic monoterpenes are:

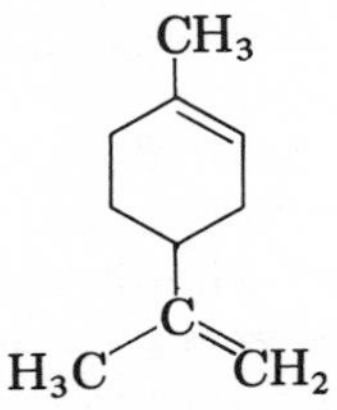

d-Limonene

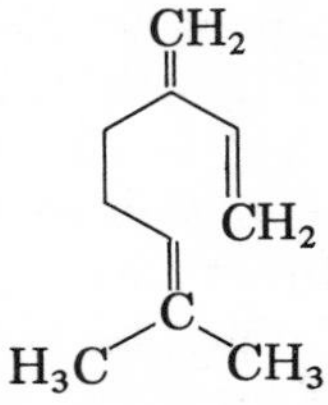

Myrcene

The isoprene units are usually linked in a head-to-tail arrangement, but sometimes the isoprene units are in tail-to-tail or irregular arrangement. The latter can be illustrated by the linkage between two symmetrical halves of carotenoid compounds.

Regular Arrangement (head to tail)

Irregular Arrangement (tail to tail)

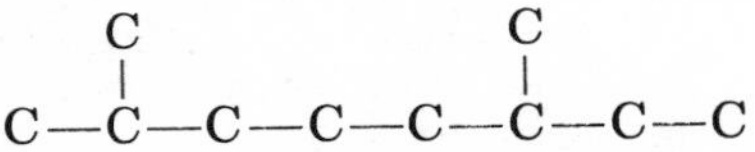

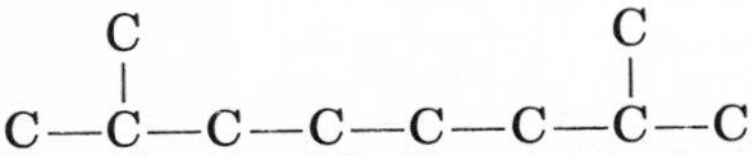

The terpenes and their derivatives are divided into groups as follows: (a) acyclic monoterpenes, (b) monocyclic monoterpenes, and (c) complex cyclic terpenes. Acyclic monoterpenes have the formula $C_{10}H_{16}$ and they include both open chain and acyclic compounds. More than a dozen compounds of this group have been isolated from essential oils. Some of the members of this class of compounds are shown in Fig. 15.1.

The more important of these compounds are not the terpenes themselves, but rather the oxygen-containing compounds. The acyclic alcohols, geraniol and linalool, and the aldehydes, citronellal and citral, represent various stages of oxidation and reduction of this type of terpene compound. Changes in the composition of these compounds alter the odor of the compounds. For example, the removal of two hydrogens from geraniol results in the formation of citral, and the odor changes from rose to lemon. The presence of an asymmetric carbon atom in a compound may have an effect on odor. D-citronellol occurs in lemon oil, the L-isomer occurs in rose oil, while both forms are found in geranium oil.

In vitro the terpenes readily form cyclic derivatives under the influence of acids. For example, geraniol and nerol, which are *trans*

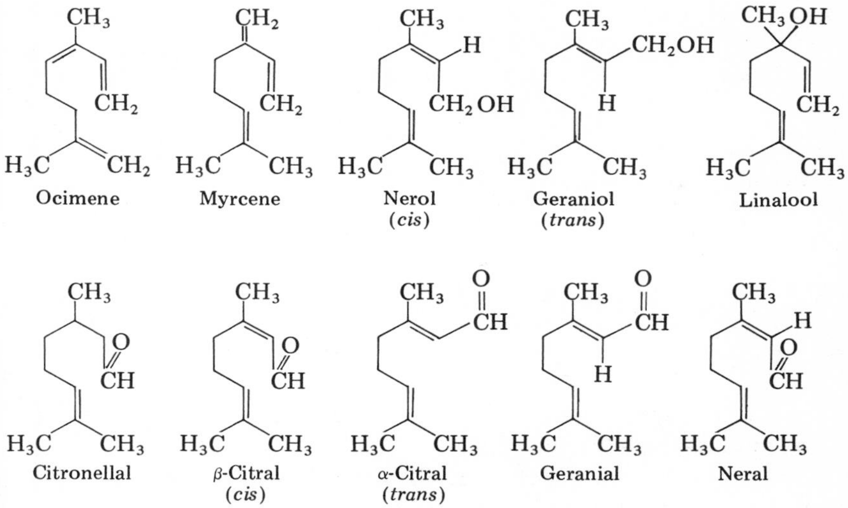

FIG. 15.1. STRUCTURES OF ACYCLIC MONOTERPENES

and *cis* configurations of the same alcohol, undergo closure on acid treatment to yield, 1,8 terpine hydrate.

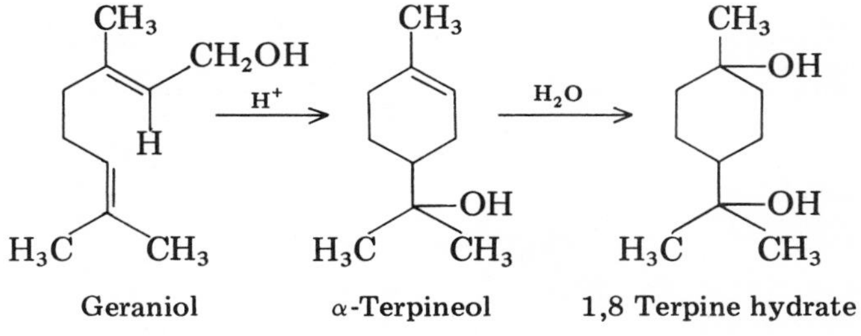

Biosynthesis of Acyclic Monoterpenes.—*In vivo*, the acyclic terpenes arise from the isoprenoid pathway. The starting material for the formation of the isoprene unit is acetyl-SCoA. Mevalonic acid is the key substance for the synthesis of isoprenoids. See carotene and steroid synthesis in Chap. 8.

Geranyl pyrophosphate and farnesyl pyrophosphate serve as the parent compounds for terpenes and sesquiterpenes, respectively. An example of the conversion of geranyl pyrophosphate to an acyclic monoterpene is as follows:

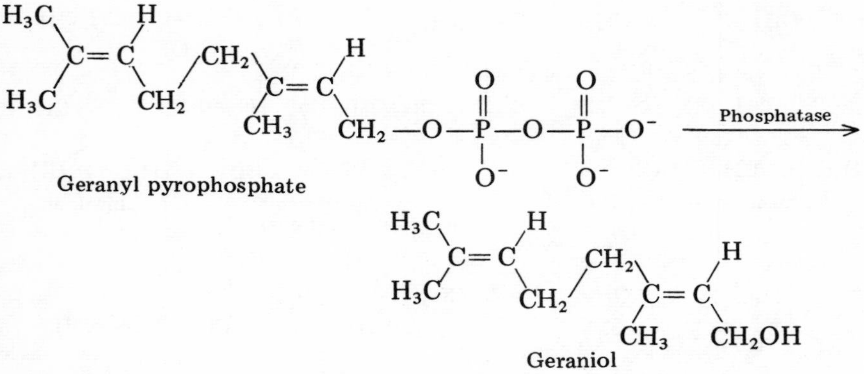

Geranyl pyrophosphate

Geraniol

The loss of pyrophosphate from geranyl pyrophosphate by the action of a phosphatase yields geraniol.

Biosynthesis of Monocyclic and Bicyclic Monoterpenes.—The exact pathways of the biosynthetic reactions have been clarified in only a few cases. However, an outline for the conversion of geranyl pyrophosphate to monocyclic and bicyclic monoterpenes is shown in Fig. 15.2. Ring closure is indicated as taking place through carbonium

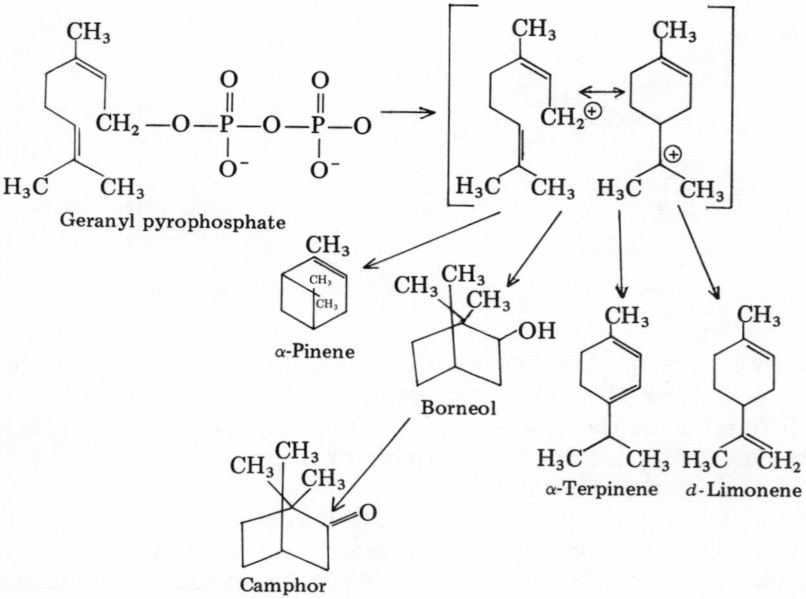

FIG. 15.2. CONVERSION OF GERANYL PYROPHOSPHATE TO MONOCYCLIC AND BICYCLIC MONOTERPENES

ion intermediates although radical mechanisms are a possibility. The loss of pyrophosphate yields a carbonium ion, which in turn may cyclize to form a cyclized carbonium ion. The latter intermediate may lose a proton to yield limonene or it may undergo a hydride ion shift with loss of a proton to yield α-terpinene. If the cyclized carbonium ion were to react with the pi electrons of the ethylenic bond, bicyclic monoterpenes would be formed.

Oxidation and Reduction Reactions of Monoterpenes.—The monoterpenes undergo many oxidation and reduction reactions. The introduction of a hydroxyl group can be accomplished through reduction of a carbonyl group, through hydration of an ethylenic bond, and direct oxidation. For example, citral is reduced to geraniol, terpineol is formed by hydration of limonene, or the hydroxyl group can be introduced directly into the terpene compound, e.g., borneol.

Methyl group oxidation plays an important role in biochemical oxidation of monoterpenes. The methyl group oxidation of α-pinene is presented below:

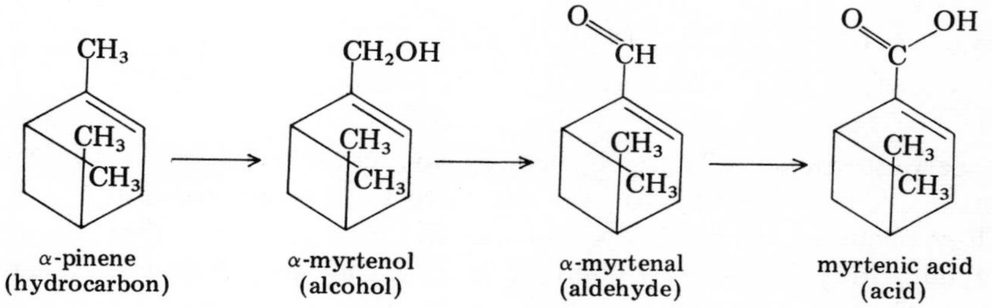

| α-pinene (hydrocarbon) | α-myrtenol (alcohol) | α-myrtenal (aldehyde) | myrtenic acid (acid) |

Examples of other substances that undergo similar functional group oxidations are:

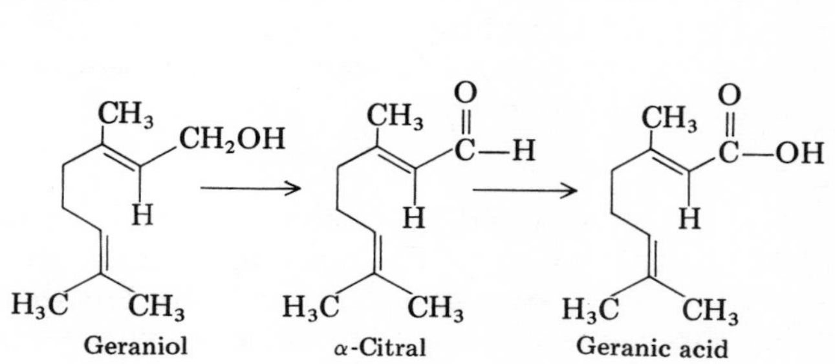

| Geraniol | α-Citral | Geranic acid |

Dehydrogenation of the monoterpene limonene gives rise to *p*-cymene.

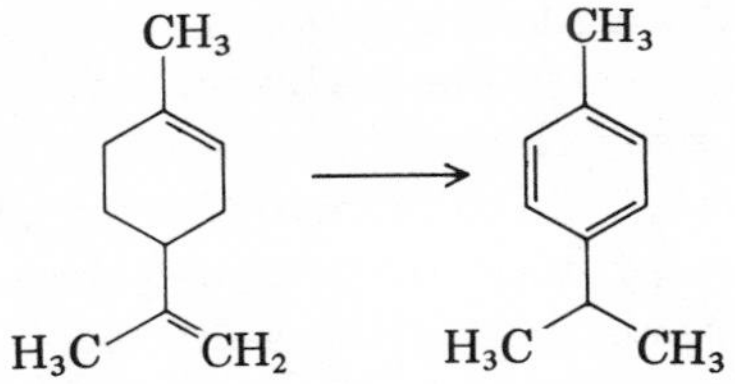

Limonene   p-cymene

Hydrogenation as well as dehydrogenation plays an important part in the biogenesis of many compounds. Thus, citronellol could be formed by hydrogenation of citral by way of citronellal or from geraniol.

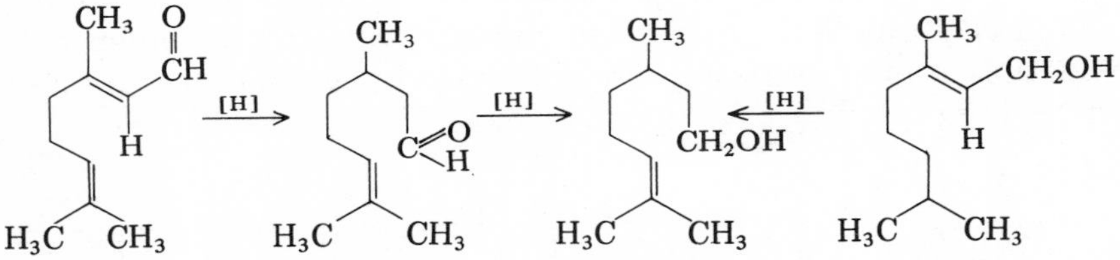

α-Citral   Citronellal   Citronellol   Geraniol

Sesquiterpenes.—These hydrocarbons consist of three isoprene units, connected head to tail, and have the general formula $C_{15}H_{24}$. They occur in essential oils and like the monoterpenes they exist in acyclic, bicyclic, and tricyclic forms. The sesquiterpenes have a relatively high boiling point, 250–280°C at atmospheric pressure, and as a consequence they have very little odor.

The direct precursor of the sesquiterpenes is farnesyl pyrophosphate which is a product of the condensation of isopentenyl pyrophosphate and geranyl pyrophosphate (cf Fig. 8.7). Farnesyl pyrophosphate serves as a precursor of a wide variety of sesquiterpenes in a manner similar to the monoterpenes.

Oleoresins

An oleoresin is manufactured by extracting a suitable ground spice with a volatile organic solvent. The nonvolatile components of the spice determine whether one solvent is more efficient than another for extracting the oleoresin. Ethanol, hexane, benzene, petroleum ether, and methyl chloroform have been used as solvents. The extract is concentrated by vacuum distillation, leaving the oleoresin. The resulting product is similar to the spice from which it was derived but not identical.

Prepared oleoresins are viscous and highly colored substances. Many on cooling, harden to a resinous mass which can be dissolved only with difficulty. Wetting agents are added to produce a water-soluble material.

Oleoresins are extracted from some spices primarily for their color characteristics rather than for their flavor. Tumeric oleoresin is widely used as a food color.

Other Flavor Materials

Fruits and Fruit Juices.—This group of natural flavorings is used either directly as a juice or concentrate. Included in this group are apple, apricot, blackberry, cherry, grape, loganberry, peach, pineapple, raspberry, and strawberry. Concentration is accomplished by freezing or vacuum distillation. In general fruit extracts can be used only where low temperature processing is involved and large quantities of the extract can be tolerated.

Synthetic Flavorings.—This group of flavorings makes up the largest and most diversified group. Included are aliphatic, aromatic and terpene alcohols, organic acids, esters, ethers, lactones, phenols, phenol ethers, and organic derivatives of sulfur. More than one of the above types of compounds may be contained in a single synthetic flavoring agent. Some of the synthetic compounds may contain more than one functional group as in vanillin with an alcohol, aldehyde, and ether group. An infinite number of combinations of materials for compounding flavorings is possible. In many instances combinations of natural and synthetic flavoring agents may be used to produce a flavoring for a specific use.

BIBLIOGRAPHY

ARTHUR D. LITTLE, INC. 1958. Flavor Research and Food Acceptance. Van Nostrand Reinhold Co., New York.
BONNER, J. 1965. The isoprenoids. In Plant Biochemistry. J. Bonner, and J. E. Varner (Editors). Academic Press, New York.
BUCH, A. J., and SMITH, H. 1959. Biosynthesis of Terpenes and Sterols. Ciba Foundation Symposium, Churchhill, London.
COCHRANE, V. W. 1958. Physiology of Fungi. John Wiley & Sons, New York.
GOODWIN, T. W. (Editor). 1970. Natural Substances Formed Biologically from Mevalonic Acid. Academic Press, New York.
GUENTHER, E. 1948–1952. The Essential Oils, Vols. 1–6. Van Nostrand Reinhold Co., New York.
GUENTHER, E. 1966. Flavors and spices. In Encylopedia of Chemical Technology, Vol. 9, 2nd Edition. John Wiley & Sons, New York.
HENDRICKSON, J. B. 1965. The Molecules of Nature. W. A. Benjamin, New York.
IKAN, R. 1969. Natural Products. Academic Press, New York.
MERORY, J. 1968. Food Flavorings, 2nd Edition. Avi Publishing Co., Westport, Conn.

National Formulary XIII. 1965. American Pharmaceutical Association, Washington, D.C.

RICHARDS, J. H., and HENRICKSON, J. B. 1964. The Biosynthesis of Steroids, Terpenes and Acetogenins. W. A. Benjamin, New York.

SWAINE, R. L. 1968. Natural and synthetic flavorings. *In* Handbook of Food Additives, T. E. Furia (Editor). Chemical Rubber Co., Cleveland Ohio.

U.S. Pharmacopeia XVII. 1965. Mack Publishing Co., Easton, Pa.

Index

NOTES

NOTES

NOTES

NOTES

NOTES

NOTES

NOTES

NOTES

NOTES

NOTES

NOTES

NOTES